Reconstructing the Old Country

Reconstructing the Old Country

AMERICAN JEWRY IN THE POST-HOLOCAUST DECADES

Edited by Eliyana R. Adler and Sheila E. Jelen

Wayne State University Press | Detroit

© 2017 by Wayne State University Press, Detroit, Michigan 48201. All rights reserved. No part of this book may be reproduced without formal permission. Manufactured in the United States of America.

ISBN 978-0-8143-4437-8 (hardcover) | ISBN 978-0-8143-4166-7 (paper)
ISBN 978-0-8143-4167-4 (e-book)
Library of Congress Control Number: 2017950995

∞

Wayne State University Press
Leonard N. Simons Building
4809 Woodward Avenue
Detroit, Michigan 48201-1309

Visit us online at wsupress.wayne.edu

גר הייתי בארץ נכריה

I have been a stranger in a strange land
(Exodus 2:22)

To refugees and those who shelter them.

Contents

Acknowledgments ix

HASIA DINER Preface: Encountering the Holocaust: Postwar American Jewry and the Catastrophe xi

ELIYANA R. ADLER AND SHEILA E. JELEN Introduction: On Account of a Suit: American-Jewish Encounters with Eastern European Jewish Life in Fantasy and Reality 1

Part I
Refugees: Commemorating the Past

ELI LEDERHENDLER The Eastern European Jewish Past and Its Historians: Cultural Interventions in Postwar America 23

DAVID SLUCKI "One of the Greatest Martyrologies": *The Black Book of Polish Jewry* and the Beginnings of Holocaust Memory in the United States 44

ELIYANA R. ADLER Mapping a Lost World: Postwar Jews and (Re)creating the Past in Memorial Books 68

MARKUS KRAH Partisan Reviews and Commentaries on Eastern European Judaism: Postwar American-Jewish Intellectual Journals and the Reconstruction of the Eastern European Past 87

GENNADY ESTRAIKH A Mid-Twentieth-Century Quest for Jewish Authenticity: The Yiddish Daily *Forverts*' Warming to Religion 111

Part II
Literature: Inventing a Legacy

SHEILA E. JELEN A Treasury of Yiddish Stories: Salvage Montage and the Anti-Shtetl 137

CONTENTS

GIL RIBAK "The *Shkotsim* Were Even Worse Than the Dogs": Yiddish Memoirists and the Reimagining of the Eastern European Jewish Experience in Postwar America 152

ELLEN KELLMAN Constructing the Eastern European Jewish Past in Post-Holocaust Children's Literature (1950–1975) 173

HOLLI LEVITSKY "You Have Known Them with Your Eyes": *Dusk in the Catskills* as Postwar Literary Legacy 199

SAMANTHA BASKIND Leon Uris's *Mila 18*, Muscular Judaism, and the Warsaw Ghetto Uprising in American Culture 215

Part III
Politics: Mobilizing for the Future

RACHEL DEBLINGER Purim, Passover, and Pilgrims: Symbols of Survival and Sacrifice in American Postwar Holocaust Survivor Narratives 247

ANN KOMAROMI Canadian Communist J. B. Salsberg and the Response to Soviet Jewry in the Wake of the Holocaust 273

DAVID JÜNGER In the Presence of the Past: Rabbi Joachim Prinz, Holocaust Memory, and the Fight for Jewish Survival in Postwar America 297

RACHEL ROTHSTEIN Haunted by History, Fueled by the Present: American-Jewish Efforts to Halt Poland's Anti-Zionist Campaign 319

Contributors 345
Index 351

Acknowledgments

THIS VOLUME was conceived as a showcase for the wonderful discussions and presentations that took place in March 2014 at the University of Maryland, College Park, at a conference entitled "Absorbing Encounters: American Jewry in the Post-Holocaust Decades." Scholars from across the United States, Canada, the Middle East, and Europe came together in order to discuss the reception of Holocaust refugees, the political organizations that consolidated their efforts on behalf of Jews the world over, and the ways in which Eastern European pre-Holocaust Jewish life was imagined (and reimagined) with the help of literature, journals, anthologies, and the like.

We would like to thank all those participants in the original conference who inspired this volume but did not contribute to it, including Jeffrey Shandler of Rutgers University and Henry Sapoznik of the University of Wisconsin, our two keynote speakers; as well as Bernard Cooperman and Marsha Rozenblit of the University of Maryland, College Park; Lara Trubowitz, an independent scholar; Marc Caplan of Yale University; and Constance Paris de Bollardier of L'ecole Hautes Études en Sciences Sociales, Paris. We are grateful as well for all the hard work and persistence of those participants in the conference who did contribute to this volume, as the labor of writing and editing over and over again can be arduous. This volume would not exist without their good humor, cooperation, intelligence, and commitment.

We would also like to thank the following institutions at the University of Maryland for their funding of the original conference, without which this volume would never have developed: The College of Arts and Humanities, The Center for the History of the New America, The Lewis L. Kaplan Chair of Jewish History, The Center for Literary and Comparative Studies, and The Joseph and Rebecca Meyerhoff Center for Jewish Studies. The following individuals at the University of Maryland helped

ACKNOWLEDGMENTS

with various aspects of the conference: Michelle Cerullo, of the Program in Comparative Literature; Debra Kirsch, of the Joseph and Rebecca Meyerhoff Center for Jewish Studies; and Ira Berlin and Bernard Cooperman, of the History Department. Professor Chip Manekin, then Director of the Meyerhoff Center, supported this project from its inception. The Jewish Studies Program of the Pennsylvania State University contributed a much-appreciated subvention to help with publishing costs.

In addition to the hard work of the authors, this volume benefitted greatly from the feedback given by anonymous readers as well as from the press' excellent professional staff. Finally, our sincerest thanks go to Kathryn Wildfong, the Editor-in-Chief at Wayne State University Press, for believing in this project and ushering it competently and compassionately through every stage of its development.

Engagement with these essays, and issues over the past several years has heightened our awareness of the plight of refugees: those we have known, those we write about herein, and those wandering the planet today. We dedicate this volume to refugees everywhere, and to those who, however imperfectly, seek to help them.

Preface

ENCOUNTERING THE HOLOCAUST:
POSTWAR AMERICAN JEWRY
AND THE CATASTROPHE

Hasia Diner

THE JEWS of the United States, about five million in number, entered the postwar era as a very different group of people than those who in 1939 witnessed from afar the outbreak of hostilities in Europe. By the war's end, after a military conflict in which so many of their young men, and some of their young women, had participated, they constituted the largest Jewish community in the world. The great Jewish population centers of Europe, of Poland in particular, had been dramatically reduced in number and in vitality due to the murderous actions of the German Nazis and their allies, who had been bent on the destruction of the Jewish people.

While the number of Jews who lived in the Soviet Union may have been approximately the same size as the number in the United States, only those who lived in America had the freedom to create whatever kinds of Jewish institutions and practices they wanted. Only they had the financial means to build, and rebuild, Jewish life, and in particular to assist the remnants of European Jewry, whether in the displaced persons camps on the continent, in transit to Palestine, or bound for America. Furthermore, the Jews of the United States in the aftermath of the Holocaust lived in the political epicenter of the "free world." As *American* Jews they played a role in the politics and culture of the west's unmatched superpower, the one locked in a cold—and at times not so cold—battle with the Soviet Union. They could, and they did, attempt to use their clout as American citizens, as a visible voting bloc, to address the trauma of the Holocaust and to remake the world to prevent future such slaughters. While not always successful, they persevered in trying to teach America about what had happened to the Jews of Europe.

The history of the Jews of the United States in the postwar period, from 1945 through the latter part of the 1960s, involved in part their encounter with the Holocaust, its victims, its survivors, and its perpetrators. Those encounters did not constitute the sum total of what they did in this period, nor did the legacy of the war against the Jews constitute the sole motivation for their actions, whether political, cultural, or social. They also faced a multitude of circumstances, both positive and negative, that shaped the ways in which they reacted to the issues of the day.

They had to contend with the implications of their increased affluence, the beginning of their almost wholesale move to new suburban neighborhoods, and the greater acceptance offered to them by their non-Jewish neighbors. How, the Jews asked themselves through their communal bodies and organs of public opinion, would such new realities change the kinds of communities in which they had lived? They had for the most part before the war lived in relatively dense urban neighborhoods, in which they had tended to cluster near each other, partly out of choice and partly out of a sense of discomfort. How, their rabbis, educators, writers, and community leaders pondered, would Jews and Jewish communal institutions respond to living in an American world where barriers in institutions of higher education and workplaces began to crumble? How would the decline in ethnic and religious tensions in America and the emergence of powerful engines of mass culture like television alter the nature of the Jews' relationships with the vastly larger American world? What would the religious revival of the postwar years mean for the Jews? While not all American Jews answered such questions the same way, they collectively faced these matters that had little or nothing to do with the Holocaust.

The history of postwar American Jewry depended on forces that had no real connection to the Holocaust. Less than ten years after the end of the war, in 1954, Jews celebrated the 300th anniversary of life in America. The anniversary would have taken place had there been no Holocaust, and Jews would have marked it with public programs, conferences, meetings, and pageants, designed to both honor America and contemplate their presence in it, just as they had done in 1904 for the 250th anniversary.

But the Holocaust had happened and loomed large in their planning and participation in Tercentenary events. As they created programs, whether for adults or children, whether for Jews alone or designed for broader audiences, the Holocaust entered into the 1954 programs. American Jews had absorbed the facts of the Holocaust, as they knew them at the time, and they used the anniversary celebration to, in part, reflect on it.

They understood that they, through their communities, had been charged with picking up the pieces of the shattered Jewish world. Most American Jews, the children or grandchildren of immigrants who came from eastern Europe to America during the great migration of the late nineteenth and early twentieth centuries, understood that but for an accident of history, they might have experienced a very different fate. If their immediate ancestors had not gotten on one of those boats sailing from Antwerp, Hamburg, or Rotterdam, they themselves might in fact have ended up as ashes in Auschwitz, as skeletons under the soil of the killing fields of Ukraine, or huddled in displaced persons camps in Germany, awaiting a move to some permanent home, rather than as denizens of new ranch style homes in the suburbs of Chicago or Detroit or as comfortable apartment dwellers in Brooklyn and the Bronx. As such, when they marked the 300th in their synagogues, religious schools, and Jewish summer camps in 1954, they did so as a way to absorb their confrontation with recent history and also in spite of it.

The history of the American Jewish encounter with the Holocaust involves a rich, varied, and complicated narrative, one that has only recently begun to be told by historians with accuracy, objectivity, and nuance. The essays in this book offer a kind of panoramic view of the confrontation of American Jews with the Holocaust, and they explore the multiple ways in which the horrors of Europe shaped the world of postwar American Jewry. These essays stand as fine pieces of scholarship that together tell a story about a moment in time, when the Holocaust made its way into American Jewish life and American Jews embarked on the long process of absorbing it.

While this preface does not seem to be the appropriate place to tout my own scholarship, it does offer me a chance to reflect upon my book of 2009, *We Remember with Reverence and Love: American Jews and the Myth of Silence after the Holocaust* (New York University Press), in conjunction with the articles that appear in this volume. The title of my book came from a document that I had known basically my entire life, a Passover text for use at the seder tables, in both English and Hebrew, which in my home accompanied the opening of the door for the imaginary entrance of Elijah the prophet, who in legend would herald the beginning of the messianic age. After my father chanted in his beautiful Hebrew the call upon God to "cast down your wrath" upon the peoples who "did not know you," and who had persecuted the Jewish people, he shifted to this next document, printed on a piece of paper and not formally included in the Haggadah, the booklet with the sacred evening's script. I had no way of knowing as a child that the words (which we heard only in Hebrew) beginning with the invocation, "on this seder night we remember with reverence and love the six million of our brothers who died at the hands of a tyrant more wicked than the Pharaoh who enslaved our ancestors in the land of Egypt," had been written in 1952 by a committee called together by the American Jewish Congress. I only knew it as an awesome, terrifying, and difficult part of the night's ritual, because my stepmother, a Holocaust survivor, went into paroxysms of weeping and keening as she heard these words.

That reading, known as the Seder Ritual of Remembrance, which eventually gave me the title for my book, I learned had a life beyond my home. Every year in my community of Milwaukee, Wisconsin, a Warsaw ghetto memorial program took place, and I got recruited as a child orator to read this text in English and Hebrew to what seemed like a large gathering of people. Every year the mayor of Milwaukee, Frank Zeidler and then Henry Maier, sat on the dais, as did our two congressional representatives, Henry Reuss and Clement Zablocki. I had no idea that similar memorial events, using this same text, took place in Chicago, Kansas City, Pittsburgh, Cincinnati and elsewhere, in which other youngsters participated, as did public officials, survivors of the catastrophe, rabbis, and other community leaders. I would discover that only when I went to the archives in search of material to answer a scholarly question.

How, I wanted to know, did American Jews of the postwar period absorb the Holocaust into their public culture? How did they argue among themselves as to what constituted a fitting way to encounter it, and how did they go about the process of weaving the Holocaust into their communal fabric, text by text, act by act, and artifact by artifact? I wanted to know

PREFACE

how the circumstances of their lives, including their growing affluence and suburbanization, the crumbling of exclusionary barriers, the burgeoning of the African-American civil rights struggle, and the conflict with the Soviet Union, among other forces, shaped the way they made the Holocaust theirs.

I asked this question for a particular reason and am so pleased not only that I got a chance to write my book, but that *Reconstructing the Old Country* is moving the scholarly project even further than I did. The question intrigued, if not obsessed me, because I found myself so discomforted by the prevailing paradigm, heard as early as the late 1960s, that postwar American Jews closed off their minds and memories to the gravity of what had happened to Europe's Jews in the years from Hitler's accession to power until the war's end. The brutal deaths of the six million, according to the dominant mode of thinking, meant little, or even nothing, to them as they went along their way to the suburbs and to the social acceptance of the postwar era. Nearly all commentators who remarked upon this matter asserted that American Jews, for a range of reasons, would not, could not, and did not incorporate the Holocaust into their public culture and their communal lives.

While their explanations varied and their political stances diverged, they converged around this truth, claiming that silence about the Holocaust prevailed among the American Jewish public. I found this statement puzzling. After all, I remembered the Seder Ritual of Remembrance. I recalled the Warsaw Ghetto memorial program where I did my stint as a little girl on a stage, listening to the greetings offered to the local Jews by the mayor and congressmen. I remembered, in fact, so many other bits and pieces of Holocaust commentary, printed in Jewish magazines I read (particularly a publication for children called *The World Over*), and discussed at the summer camp I went to.

As a scholar I had to ask myself two questions, and these two questions drove me to the sources. First, I wondered if I misremembered. Perhaps with the passage of time I just had gotten it wrong and the jumble of facts and impressions from my childhood that I believed to be accurate maybe were not. Or, per the second question, maybe my experiences were just that: mine. Perhaps only in Milwaukee did a Warsaw Ghetto memorial program take place; perhaps only in my home did we recite those words, "We remember with reverence and love." Maybe only at my summer camp did we perform Holocaust plays and sit around on the grass and discuss what had happened in recent history.

In addition it seemed to me that if it really were the case that American Jews in the years after the Holocaust had created nothing in the way of a memorial culture to their kin, literal and figurative, who had been so brutally killed, they would have been remarkably unlike nearly all people in all times. I knew as a historian that human societies engage in memorial undertakings. After enduring wars, famines, slaughters, earthquakes, and other disasters whether natural or not, people have in the main felt the need to mark their tragedies. Having absorbed the facts of these devastations, survivors and their descendants throughout history have sought to reflect upon them. They did not all do it the same way, but they did do so, in ways that reflected their circumstances. No single model of how to memorialize others exists.

Had American Jews truly been able to consign the Holocaust to some kind of taboo, subterranean place, had they actually not spoken about it and incorporated it into their communal culture, they would have been absolutely unique in human history. Could that, I asked myself, have been the case?

I had no way of solving these two problems, and so many more, without doing what a historian is supposed to do. Namely, I knew that I had to go to the primary materials, to libraries and archives. I realized that no single repository could tell me much about what went on in postwar American Jewish life vis-à-vis the Holocaust.

I went into the project with no intention of writing a book on the subject. I thought that the question of how Jews incorporated the Holocaust into their own American lives in the postwar period might make an article. It seemed that a reasonable chronology would be to look at the years from the immediate end of the war until the early 1960s. I chose the closing date based on one fairly widely accepted idea among the scholars. They nearly all said that the Eichmann trial of 1961 and his execution in Israel in 1962 brought the issue of the Holocaust out of the closet and into general consciousness. These writers asserted that at this point, essentially, American Jews could no longer hide the Holocaust, and hide from it, because it constituted the daily fare of world news.

Having chosen a time period to study, I set out to work, assuming that a short piece I might write on the subject ought to be just enough to stimulate others to go out and wade more deeply into the archives. I had in mind my doctoral students in American Jewish history and others embarking on their scholarly careers. I gave myself initially a summer to collect material, not at all sure what I would find.

I decided to look, for this short project, only at published primary sources, particularly the always informative *American Jewish Yearbook* and the *Jewish Book Annual,* for the full run of these years. What, I wanted to know in this phase of my project, did these two annual reference volumes tell about the Holocaust in American and American Jewish life? What books and articles that dealt with the Holocaust did they reference? How did they explain American Jewish political, cultural, religious, and social life in the context of the Holocaust and its aftereffects? What metaphors stemming from the Holocaust years pervaded these "official" American Jewish sources? In what ways did American Jews, their organizations, communal bodies, and institutions discuss the Holocaust with the larger American society?

Clearly I did not stop with that summer's research, nor did those two sources, however rich, constitute the totality of what I looked at. Those few months brought me so many pieces of paper—handwritten and typed notes I took on the material I found—that I had to invest in a four-drawer file cabinet, which quickly overflowed, and the drawers would not close. Having found so much in so short a time and in such a limited set of sources convinced me that I had stumbled onto something worth researching.

This, I said to myself, offers me a chance to tell a dramatic story of how a relatively small group of people, American Jews, decided on their own to construct a memorial culture, to enshrine the memory of their kin who had perished at the hands of the German Nazis and their collaborators. Without any real partners to work with them, with few precedents from the past to guide them, and with no central authority to tell them what to do and how to do it, they commenced on their own in creating a mass, grassroots, experimental enterprise they believed paid homage to the recent tragic past and would help them understand a very new present, as well as their American and Jewish futures. Behind every example in the book lay dozens in my file folders, unused and never cited, which made the same point. Across

PREFACE

America and across the spectrum of divides that splintered American Jewry by class, geography, language, ideology, age, and gender, I found an absorption with the Holocaust, and a profound encounter with it.

In no community, in no genre of text, in no language, in no political corner, did American Jews refrain from mentioning something about the Holocaust in these years, whether designed for internal Jewish consumption or for the bigger, outside world. *Reconstructing the Old Country* takes *We Remember with Reverence and Love* further in terms of depth and specificity. It provides even more illustrations, offers even more example of the multiple ways in which American Jewry dealt with the Holocaust in the decades after it came to a close. It demonstrates the complexity of that history. It should not only broaden what we know about this crucial historical subject, but should inspire yet more scholars to consider it.

Introduction

ON ACCOUNT OF A SUIT:
AMERICAN-JEWISH ENCOUNTERS
WITH EASTERN EUROPEAN JEWISH
LIFE IN FANTASY AND REALITY

Eliyana R. Adler and Sheila E. Jelen

PHILIP ROTH's "Eli, the Fanatic," first published in *Commentary* in 1958, addresses the place of European refugees and Jewish Orthodoxy in the American suburbs, newly populated by Jews in the decades after the Holocaust. In the story, Eli Peck, a young lawyer about to become a first-time father, is tasked with finding the legal basis for evicting a boys' yeshiva whose student body is comprised of a group of refugee boys and their two caregivers, a Mr. Tzuref and his silent assistant, known in town as "the greenie." The yeshiva population does not look the way the Jewish community of the small fictional town of Woodenton, somewhere on the Eastern Seaboard, wants them to look. Mr. Tzuref, the greenie, and their eighteen boys look Orthodox, impoverished, unrefined.

But Eli Peck has a conscience. Mr. Tzuref, the greenie, and the children have just survived the hell of Hitler's war. So for the bulk of the story, Eli attempts to be a peacemaker, offering solutions to Mr. Tzuref that might appease Eli's neighbors and peers, and delaying the onset of legal proceedings for as long as he can.

The year is 1948, the month is May, as specified in a letter written by Tzuref, and presented to one of the retailers in town by the greenie when he attempts to buy eighteen pairs of boys' shoes. A Jewish homeland in Palestine is being established exactly at the moment that the Jews of Woodenton are trying to kick their co-religionists out of their newfound home. The implications of this contrast are simply too obvious to be coincidental; the "real" Jews—the refugees, the Orthodox, the Yiddish-speaking, European-born survivors of Hitler's war—belong in Israel, not in America. But is this the best reading we can provide of this complex and fascinating story? On so many different levels, "Eli, the Fanatic" provides an engaging starting point for our discussion of this exploration of the encounter between American Jews and European Jews in the decades following World War II.

To deepen our understanding of the story, a bit more plot summary is in order. Eli Peck decides that his friends and peers will leave well enough alone if only the greenie looks less like a "greenie," if only he will change out of his European suit, tuck his ear-locks behind his ears and his ritual fringes into his pants, and wear a proper tie. But Mr. Tzuref, in response to an epistolary proposition from Peck, replies,

> Mr. Peck:
> The suit the gentleman wears is all he's got.
> Sincerely,
> Leo Tzuref, Headmaster[1]

Eli Peck crushes several suits from his own wardrobe into a Bonwit box and drops them off on the doorstep of the Yeshiva of Woodenton. In return, the greenie drops off his suit, the suit he presumably wore all the way from Europe, on Eli's doorstep.

The greenie need only wear Eli's suit to fit into Woodenton, but what happens when Eli wears the greenie's suit? Like the character in Sholem Aleichem's story "On Account of a Hat," Eli does not just come to resemble the greenie, he becomes the greenie, even to himself. Eli wears the suit all over town as his wife gives birth to their son. In the hospital, where he goes to visit his wife and his son, he is understood to be having a nervous breakdown, and he is restrained and sedated. He will soon, with some medical help, and time away from home, be back to his usual Jewish American self: modern, fashionable, and secular.

What has transpired in Woodenton on the day that Eli becomes the greenie? Is it an act of compassion, a bout of mental illness, a moment of identification? The exchange of suits in both directions, and not just one,

INTRODUCTION

wherein the greenie takes Eli's generous donation but only on the condition that Eli takes his, undoes the usual balance between the United States and Eastern Europe in the years immediately following the war. The greenie feels that in spite of the alarm of the community, in spite of his lack of fluency in English, and in the absence of any form of communication with Eli or anyone else of Eli's ilk, he has something distinct to offer. And what happens in that moment of offering is unpredictable.

How, in 1948, could an American Jewish community, even a fictional one, be so oblivious to the needs of a community of Holocaust survivors? The word "Holocaust" does not appear in "Eli, the Fanatic" because of course it had not yet come into use as the accepted shorthand term for the genocide perpetrated against the Jews in Europe. More than that, however, the recent horrific past is purposely left unnamed in the story. The only references to it are oblique.

The reader first hears of the "mysterious babble" of the children.[2] Then, in a broad reference to what they have been through, we learn from Tzuref that, "We are tired. The headmaster is tired. The students are tired."[3] Several pages later, when another character asks whether Tzuref is American, Eli replies, "No. A DP. German."[4] Further hints appear in the story. The children, orphans, are easily spooked. The man in the black suit has lost everything. Yet while the Holocaust clearly provides the historical background to the story, its absence is conspicuous.

Indeed, the Jews who oppose the yeshiva make it clear that they do not want to hear about what happened in Europe. In the dismissive words of one of them, Ted, "Making a big thing out of suffering, so you're going oy-oy-oy all your life, that's common sense?"[5] The middle-class, assimilated Jews of Woodenton seek to shield themselves, and especially their children, from the taint of the Jewish past.

Nor are the survivors prepared to tell their stories. The children, with their "mysterious babble" and shy ways, provide no access to information. The greenie is socially mute. While he can and does communicate with Tzuref, in the streets of Woodenton he uses only notes and gestures. Tzuref himself, although portrayed as both intelligent and insightful, expresses himself by implication and innuendo. He appears to find the English language lacking the capacity to truly capture the meanings of words like "nothing" and "suffer."[6]

And just as the Holocaust remains behind the scenes in the story, so too it goes mostly unacknowledged as a factor motivating the tension between the refugee yeshiva and the Americanized Jews of Woodenton. The committee of local Jews opposed to the yeshiva express their outrage in terms of the incursion of an old-style, old-fashioned type of Judaism into their hard-won suburban idyll. "Eli, in Woodenton, a yeshiva! If I want to live in Brownsville, Eli, I'll live in Brownsville."[7] They complain of a "guy dressed like 1000 B.C." and "hocus-pocus abracadabra stuff."[8] Yet the specter of the Holocaust haunts Eli's and Ted's anxieties.

As Ted tries desperately to articulate his disdain, he eventually narrows in on the fear at its core: "Look, Eli—pal, there's a good healthy relationship in this town because it's modern Jews and Protestants. That's the point, isn't it, Eli? Let's not kid each other, I'm not Harry. The way things are now are fine—like human beings. There's going to be no pogroms in Woodenton. Right? 'Cause there's no fanatics, no crazy people . . . just people who respect each other, and leave each other be."[9]

Ultimately for Ted, and presumably for the remainder of the chorus representing mid-century American Jewry, the peace and security of suburban life are predicated upon Jews remaining invisible, and thus inoffensive. The danger in the old world Jews with their outdated languages and practices is that they might precipitate another holocaust.

This conflation between Orthodoxy, immigrants, and genocide lies at the heart of "Eli, the Fanatic." The yeshiva, with its staff and students, represents everything that the suburban American Jews fear. At the same time, much within the story is left open to interpretation, especially in its frightening yet enigmatic ending.

We would suggest that what we witness in the story as it unfolds is, interestingly, more a case of excessive identification than alienation, more a case of intense projection than cruelty. Indeed, in the course of the story, the process of Eli Peck's evolution into a "fanatic" through the donning of the greenie's European suit, his ritual fringes, his black hat, and even his socks and shoes, speaks to a community's experience of traumatizing identification.

Alluding to Shoshana Felman's description of the effect on her class at Yale of her screening of Holocaust testimonies, an effect that she calls "extreme traumatization," Dominick LaCapra in *Writing History, Writing*

INTRODUCTION

Trauma suggests an alternative to excessive, traumatizing identification with the victims of a trauma: "empathic unsettlement."[10] "Empathic unsettlement" is effected when the historian, or the reader, or the viewer of a testimony becomes aware of his or her own empathic position vis-à-vis the testimony and is able to recognize the implications of over-identification, both positive and negative. In LaCapra's discussion, extreme identification leads to an excess of empathy, and an inability to distinguish between the self and the traumatized victim whose testimony one is witness to.

While in Roth's fictional Woodenton there seems to be no excess of empathy for the newly arrived survivors of the Holocaust, there is an over-identification with them. Eli Peck, in particular, spokesman for the collective Jewish population of Woodenton, empathizes with the voicelessness of the greenie. Eli empathizes with the greenie's singularity, even among the collective that is the yeshiva for which he works. A lawyer among businessmen, a sensitive soul among rather insensitive men, Eli Peck has suddenly found a kindred spirit among the strange Jews who have arrived at his doorstep. He exchanges his identity with the greenie by giving him his own green suit and donning the greenie's black one. Eli wholly identifies with, merges with, indeed becomes the greenie at the climax of the story. But his empathy, his identification, is only the other side of his peers' apathy and cruelty.

Traumatizing identification takes different forms, of course. In the case of the Jews of Woodenton, their over-identification with the Jewish refugees has a traumatizing effect, not only on the refugees themselves, as they are forced to fight for their right to stay in town, but on Eli, who feels that he is being pushed into an unethical position as a lawyer finding legal ways to render the refugees homeless once again.

In 1958 when this story first appeared in *Commentary*, Philip Roth was among the first American authors to have published on the sordid elements of human experience as focalized through the prism of Jewish characters and Jewish communities. The public furor aroused by the stories in his first book, *Goodbye, Columbus*, in which "Eli, the Fanatic" was republished in 1959, and then by *Portnoy's Complaint*, published a decade later in 1969, was based on the premise that in the decades after the Holocaust, any unfavorable representation of Jewish individuals or Jewish communities would be an act of disrespect towards the recent victims of European antisemitism, and fodder for antisemitism in America. In an essay called "Writing About Jews," Philip Roth defends himself from accusations of being "self-hating" and "tasteless." He accuses his accusers not only of being "timid" and "paranoid," but of being literary Luddites who do not understand that "the test of any literary work is not how broad its range of representation—for all that breadth may be characteristic of a kind of narrative—but the depth with which the writer reveals whatever he has chosen to represent." Roth asserts, "The concerns of fiction are not those of a statistician, or of a public relations firm. The novelist asks himself, 'What do people think?' The PR man asks, 'What will people think?' But I believe this is actually troubling the rabbi when he calls for his 'balanced portrayal of Jews': What will people think? Or, to be exact: What will the goyim think?"[11]

Is it fear over what the non-Jewish population will think of the Jews in their midst that motivates Roth's critics to call him a "self-hating Jew" in response to stories such as "Eli, the Fanatic"? And is it fear over what the non-Jewish population will think of the Jews in their midst that motivates the characters of Woodenton to treat their fellow Jews badly? When Eli becomes the greenie, and the greenie becomes Eli, through a simple exchange of suits and hats and underclothes, what are we to understand? That we are what we wear? That the distance between an Eastern European-born, ultra-Orthodox Holocaust survivor and an American-born Jewish professional in 1948 can be minimized through the simple act of getting dressed or undressed?

We have to keep in mind that Eli Peck has clearly had a nervous breakdown, regardless of whether or not our sympathies lie with him. He has only become the greenie in his own addled mind, just as his Jewish friends asking him to sue the yeshiva of Woodenton on their behalf feel the pressure to do such a thing only in their own addled minds. Both Eli's and their behavior, according to Dominick LaCapra, can only be remedied by taking a step back and learning to be empathic. Is Eli's donation of his suit to the cause of the greenie an act of empathy? If one accepts the proposition that the only reason the greenie is being run out of town is because he is wearing a weird suit, it is. But if one considers the fact that such a proposition is shortsighted and intolerant in the extreme, just the placing of a Band-Aid over a gaping wound comprised of paranoia and intolerance, then it is not.

INTRODUCTION

The nameless blackness at the close of the story, as well as the satirical and sympathetic treatment of the two sides in the conflict, have captivated readers and critics for many years. For Sol Gittleman, "Eli, the Fanatic" may be Philip Roth's "finest work of short fiction."[12] Gittleman sees the story as a meditation on American Jewish marginality consciously juxtaposed with the birth of the State of Israel. The impending births of Eli's son and of the Jewish state stand in direct contrast to the old world Orthodoxy of the survivors. "From that very first thought, Roth would assure his audience that the future of the Jews in America would be anchored by both the past and the future: the one a memory which would not die; the other a nation just born."[13] James Duban also notes Roth's deliberate choice to tie the story temporally to Israel's foundation, but for him the tension in the story revolves chiefly around survivor's guilt.[14] Elliott Simon represents the confrontation within the story as taking place within the character of Eli. Like the Biblical prophet Balaam, he is charged with cursing the camp of Israel but ends up embracing it.[15]

All of these approaches read "Eli, the Fanatic" in a strictly American context. In a fascinating reversal, Hana Wirth-Nesher describes the transformation of her reading of the story as she moved from teaching in the United States to doing so in Israel. The secular Israelis who populated her classes refused to accept the conflation of Orthodoxy and survival central to the story. In fact their negative views toward the religious community made them far less sympathetic to Tzuref and his assistant. Wirth-Nesher describes how this influenced her own interpretation of the story:

> Reading "Eli, the Fanatic" now, in this time and in this place, compels me to take a more historical approach to Roth's work than I had previously done, to see that it is of another time and another place. It is a tale of America in the 1950s, a brilliant satire about a community torn between the promise held out by America for self-fulfillment at the price of communal attenuation and its *own* pledge, in the shadow of the Holocaust, for collective responsibility and continuity.[16]

Roth wrote "Eli, the Fanatic" over fifty years ago, and all of the critics, to one degree or another, recognize that it is, in Wirth-Nesher's words, "of another time and another place." Yet, at the same time, many seem to read it as an accurate, if exaggerated, depiction of the tensions of that era. This assumption fails to note the significance of the fact that Roth set the story ten years in the past. Only twenty-seven years old at the time of its publication, he was thus describing a period when he was just barely an adult. Even more importantly, it turns out that Roth based his story on an actual occurrence but changed it in crucial ways.

Steven Fink has convincingly demonstrated that Roth based "Eli the Fanatic" on a controversy profiled in *Commentary* magazine in 1949. There was in fact an attempt by Holocaust survivors to found a yeshiva in an upscale suburb after the war, and the non-Jewish inhabitants of that suburb vehemently opposed it. It is unlikely that Roth knew (in one of those cases where truth really is stranger than fiction) that Rabbi Michael Dov Weissmandl, the director of the yeshiva, had already gained considerable notoriety for his attempts to rescue Jews during the Holocaust. But of course Roth was far less interested in the Holocaust than in its repercussions for American Jews. Fiction has its revenge on truth in Roth's replacement of the non-Jewish leaders of the yeshiva's opposition with Jews.

Fink shows that while Roth incorporated many aspects of the Weissmandl incident into his story, he made it an entirely intra-Jewish conflict. Whereas the historical yeshiva in Westchester received funding from Jewish sources and faced legal challenges from local gentiles, "Roth makes only passing references to the gentiles of Woodenton, and they seem either oblivious or indifferent to the presence of the yeshiva Jews."[17] American Jews, on the other hand, while marginal to Herrymon Maurer's 1949 article, are at the heart of Roth's story. "Roth finds in Maurer's passing reference to the 'embarrassed' acculturated Jews of Westchester County another opportunity to expose the shallow, neurotic, materialistic, and self-absorbed world of suburbanized Jews, morally desensitized by their eagerness to belong."[18]

Roth, of course, is a writer of fiction. His métier is to make life into stories. There is nothing wrong with writing a short story based loosely on an event described in a magazine article. What is significant is how Roth has reshaped the event for his own purposes. Fink concludes that basing "Eli, the Fanatic" on a real occurrence led Roth to offer an uncharacteristically positive portrayal of Orthodox Judaism. Because his own issue was class, but the conflict required a religious organization, Roth was forced to portray that institution, and its leader, in a favorable light. Yet Roth's abiding ambivalence about traditional Judaism is evident in the ending, lending itself to no clear interpretation.

Roth's main concern, however, was not religious but cultural. In transforming a real occurrence involving American Jews—refugees and native born, working together to stand up for their rights against non-Jewish opposition—into a story in which refugee and native born Jews are at odds with one another, Roth helped to create the myth of silence and alienation that this volume seeks to address. Already in 1958 he was rewriting a relatively cooperative and collaborative early relationship between American Jews and post-Holocaust immigrants as a satire on the emptiness of American Jewish culture. Roth's story illustrates a profound tension in immediate postwar American Jewry, in which American Jews both over-identified and under-identified with their Eastern European brethren. While many American Jews sought to lend a helping hand to the incoming refugees as well as to survivors abroad, as we will explore in depth throughout the volume, there were also those that chose to stay away from the messy reality of European antisemitism and its implications for American Jews and American antisemitism. What Roth's story opens up for our volume is the fascinating and productive tension between different elements of American Jewish culture during the immediate post-Holocaust years: between those who cared and those who did not, those who became engaged and those who remained on the sidelines. Roth's story, according to one of our astute reviewers, "is valuable precisely because it represents two sides of the same coin, silence and engagement alike." [19]

Postwar America

The 1950s and early 1960s have traditionally been viewed, in both popular and academic circles, as a time when American Jews shook off the vestiges of their immigrant, old world past and fully entered the American mainstream. American Jews left the crowded, urban, ethnic neighborhoods of their youth for the middle-class melting pot of the suburbs. They put aside the languages, accents, and customs of their parents for everything that American education and culture could offer; they replaced the radicalism of Socialism and Orthodoxy for the more temperate and conciliatory promises of liberalism and Conservative Judaism. Only in the wake of the 1967 Six Day War in Israel did American Jews actively and publically return to Jewish politics, culture, and religion, and begin to engage with their Eastern European past and the Holocaust, according to this view.

Recent scholarship, however, has demonstrated that previous assumptions about the early silence and shame of American Jews with regard to the Holocaust and life in the old country were exaggerated. And while historians have been expanding their borders and definitions to encompass the postwar decades, scholars from other disciplines have been paying increasing attention to the unique literary, photographic, artistic, dramatic, political, and other cultural creations of this period and the ways in which they hearken back not only to the Holocaust itself, but also to images of pre-war Eastern Europe.

This volume brings together scholars of literature, history, ethnography, art, cultural studies, and related fields to examine how the American Jewish community in the post-Holocaust era was shaped by its encounter with literary relics, living refugees, and other cultural productions that grew out of an encounter with Eastern European Jewish life from the pre-Holocaust era. In particular, we are interested in three different narratives and their occasional intersections. First, we consider the real, hands-on interactions between American Jews and European Jewish refugees, and the ways in which the two groups influenced one another. Second, we examine how the imaginative reconstructions of a wartime or pre-war Jewish world met the needs of a postwar American Jewish audience. Finally, we explore the ways in which the Holocaust was mobilized to justify postwar political and philanthropic activism. The photograph on the cover of the book encapsulates these three ideas. The two refugee girls, dressed in American clothes and with new dolls, are pointing back toward Europe and their origins, while facing the United States, their new home. The photo was created in 1949 as part of a fund-raising campaign to help new immigrants.

Historical Narratives

Holocaust memoirs published in the United States often close with the shock of arrival in America shortly after the war; the wonder of survival and the excitement surrounding beginning to build a new life are tempered by an incomprehensible lack of interest and sympathy from family already living in America, and from community members. Similarly, survivors interviewed by the Shoah Foundation in the 1990s frequently end their testimonies by thanking Steven Spielberg and the volunteers for recording their stories at last. They say that they never shared their experiences before because no one wanted to listen.

This trope of American Jewry refusing to engage with its past informs scholarship about the era as well. In the words of Peter Novick, "Between the end of the war and the 1960s, as anyone who has lived through those years can testify, the Holocaust made scarcely any appearance in American public discourse, and hardly more in Jewish public discourse—especially discourse directed to gentiles."[20] Alan Mintz devotes a chapter of his book, *Popular Culture and the Shaping of Holocaust Memory in America*, to the topic of "From Silence to Salience." As he explains:

> Jews were too deeply engaged in the energetic enterprise of entering American society and seizing the opportunities offered to them to be available to the subversive sadness provoked by the Holocaust. It was not until this process was complete and Jews felt more at ease in America as Americans and, moreover, the luster of America itself dimmed, that American Jews were ready for this dark encounter.[21]

In her 2009 book, Hasia Diner seeks to disrupt this narrative.[22] She shows that within the Jewish community, youth groups, summer camps, synagogues, sisterhoods, rabbis, lay leaders, and many others were engaged in an ongoing struggle to understand and commemorate the tragic events in Europe throughout the postwar period:

> Spontaneous and disorganized, lacking a single icon to symbolize the catastrophe or a central address to coordinate programs and publications about it, American Jews, through their local and national bodies, religious, educational, associational, and political, incorporated into their many endeavors the details of the *hurban*, the great destruction of European Jewry. Not always appearing

under the rubric "Holocaust" or "the six million," the European catastrophe wound its way into their culture organically, yoked to Jewish texts on nearly every cultural and political issue, to Jewish history, civil rights, the observance of Jewish ritual, and a host of other concerns.[23]

Nor is Diner the only scholar to challenge the so-called "myth of silence." An entire volume dedicated to this project appeared in 2012. The introduction by David Cesarani offers an excellent synopsis and analysis of the historiography, albeit from a wider perspective. Indeed, examining the involvement of American Jews in transnational Holocaust commemoration, often in languages other than English, points to one of the reasons that some of this activism remained invisible. Scholars producing high-level Holocaust scholarship in Yiddish, for example, may have had a tangible impact on the development of the field, but their impact on American Jewish culture was negligible.[24]

It is also worth underlining Diner's point in the quote above about the "spontaneous and disorganized" nature of the early attempts to incorporate the Holocaust into American Jewish life. Not only was a single, all-encompassing term not yet in use, but even the scope of the event had yet to be conceptualized. American Jews were still finding the words and rituals to work through what had occurred. It is hardly surprising then that much diverse, local, education and commemoration went under the radar of historians.

Similar points can be made about other spheres of Jewish American life and culture. While the reception of the book and play *The Diary of Anne Frank*, as well as the musical and film *Fiddler on the Roof*, have received wide attention in academic writing[25], these particular works have often been presented as unique in terms of their genre and subject matter. On the contrary, they were in fact published alongside other diaries and memoirs of the Holocaust, and imaginative reconstructions of life in the old country, in both English and Yiddish. And although Jewish political engagement may have reached new heights in the late 1960s, this does not mean that Jews did not advocate on behalf of issues close to their hearts in the postwar decades.

INTRODUCTION

What all scholars of the era might well agree upon is that times have really changed. The ways in which American Jews engage with their past have undergone fundamental shifts in the decades since the Second World War. The language, the images, and the salience, to return to Mintz's term, have indeed been transformed. Yet there is still a great deal that we do not know about these shifts, and about how American Jews in the postwar era acted out their conflicted feelings toward the Eastern European Jewish past and its tragic end.

Volume Themes

Given recent scholarship on Jewish American engagement with the events of World War II, not only in the 1960s and beyond, but in the decades contemporaneous with and immediately following the war, *Reconstructing the Old Country: American Jewry in the Post-Holocaust Decades* strives to flesh out some of the institutional, cultural, literary, and religious encounters between American Jewry and their European co-religionists, both actual and imagined, from the 1940s through the 1960s. In this interdisciplinary collection of essays and analyses, historians, literary scholars, linguists, and cultural critics explore questions that bring their disciplines into fruitful dialogue on a wide range of issues. The volume has been divided into three sections: "Refugees: Commemorating the Past," "Literature: Inventing a Legacy," and "Politics: Mobilizing for the Future." The dominant organizing principle for the volume has been the past, present, and future, as the volume's contributors discuss the ways in which American responses to the Holocaust and to their own largely Eastern European Jewish heritage affected the production of a distinct American Jewish literary, political, and memorial culture in the postwar years.

In "Refugees: Commemorating the Past," Eli Lederhendler provides a historiography of postwar trends in American historical scholarship of Eastern European Jewish life, as it compares to English-language histories written before the war, as well as to Israeli historical approaches to Eastern European Jewry after the establishment of the State. David Slucki and Eliyana Adler consider the historical value of texts such as *The Black Book of Polish Jewry* and *yizker-bikher*, or memorial books compiled by native sons and daughters of particular towns in Eastern Europe, published during the war years and afterward, with non-scholarly goals and incomplete knowledge of the scope of the Holocaust. Both authors conclude that efforts at memorialization of Eastern European Jewish culture during and after the war years is an important aspect of the stories American Jews tell about themselves. Markus Krah and Gennady Estraikh explore the changing definitions of Jewish identity in both the Yiddish and English popular Jewish presses, as they trace the religious rhetoric and concerns of publications such as the *Forward*, *Commentary*, *Partisan Review*, and *Judaism*. All of the essays explore ways in which the absorption of European refugees before, during, and after the war influenced the development of American Jewish culture.

In "Literature: Inventing a Legacy," Sheila Jelen, Gil Ribak, Ellen Kellman, Holli Levitsky, and Samantha Baskind address American Jewry's literary construction of sites of memory. In literary works authored or edited by Leon Uris, I.L Peretz, Reuben Wallenrod, Irving Howe, Eliezer Greenberg, and others, these contributors consider the ways American Jewry in the postwar era utilized literary texts and images in order to better understand the people and the places that were destroyed. They also probe the degree to which literary and artistic reconstructions reflected the historical reality and the needs of the time in which they were produced.

"Politics: Mobilizing for the Future" features essays by Ann Komaromi, Rachel Deblinger, and Rachel Rothstein, who consider the responses of American institutions such as the American Jewish Congress, the Joint Distribution Committee, B'nai Brith, Hadassah, the National Council of Jewish Women, ORT, the United Jewish Appeal in the United States, and the Communist United Jewish People's Order in Canada, to the plight of Jewish refugees as well as to their fellow Jews who remained in the Soviet Union and Poland during the Cold War. Also in this section, through the lens of Joachim Prinz's leadership of the American Jewish Congress, David Jünger examines tensions among American Jewish agencies over the role Jews should take in the nascent Civil Rights Movement during the years of Martin Luther King Jr.'s leadership. Attention to the ways in which memories and "lessons" from the Holocaust are used by political activists and community organizers animates these essays.

INTRODUCTION

Throughout the essays included here, questions arise about continuity and rupture between pre-Holocaust and post-Holocaust perceptions of Eastern European Jewish life. Several of our authors, including Eli Lederhendler, in his overview of the historical scholarship on Eastern European Jewish life, as well as Gil Ribak, Markus Krah, and Sheila Jelen, allude to the ever popular iconic works that have done so much to flavor American perceptions of Eastern European Jewish life during the second half of the twentieth century: Maurice Samuel's *The World of Sholem Aleichem*, *Fiddler on the Roof*; Mark Zborowski's and Elizabeth Herzog's *Life Is with People*; and Abraham Joshua Heschel's *The Earth Is the Lord's*, to name just a few. In their introduction of texts such as Yiddish memoirs written before the war, scholarship that captured more than just the contours of fictionalized *shtetlakh*, and fictional anthologies that suggest more than the idealized view of the monolithic Eastern European Jewish world popular in the 1950s, each of these authors acknowledges the realities of American-Jewish myopia. All of the essays in this volume consider the important osmosis between the American Jewish sense of itself and its sense of its European cohort, still in Europe and/or newly arrived in America.

In addition to contributing directly to the scholarly conversation about the postwar period in the American Jewish community, this volume also joins the emerging subfield of Aftermath Studies. The growing realization—by scholars in diverse fields—that not only did the war and the Holocaust end at different moments in different areas, but also that its shadows, scars, and consequences continue on into the present, has led to an increased focus on the immediate postwar period in recent years. Books on the displaced persons themselves, as well as their literature, historical scholarship, judicial proceedings, and testimonial collection projects have all appeared within the past few years.[26] The essays by David Slucki and Eliyana Adler contribute to this conversation. By focusing on the survivors, who were largely in motion, these works are perforce transnational. While our volume looks primarily at the United States, focus on the postwar period demonstrates the relevance of following migrants to all of their destinations.

The centrality of communication across international borders is also evident in the essays contributed by Ann Komaromi and Rachel Rothstein. The plight of Jews in the Soviet Union, as well as in the People's

Republic of Poland, animated the concern of North American Jews not only because of their shared origins, but also due to the enormous losses of the Holocaust. Western Jewish reactions were, in Rothstein's words, "haunted by history." Komaromi's work illuminates similarities between the Canadian and American Jewish communities, as well as ways in which they differed.

Although this volume does not seek to systematically cover the breadth and depth of American Jewish experiences, various essays hint at the diversity of individuals and groups grappling in the postwar years with their own responses to recent history and representing their divergent approaches to a shared past. Ellen Kellman, for example, highlights the "collaboration" between authors and illustrators of different generations, such as Isaac Bashevis Singer and Maurice Sendak, or Y.L Peretz and Uri Shulevitz, in popular children's publications. In so doing she emphasizes the multivalent constructions of a single work spanning the creative energies of different moments in time, both pre- and post-Holocaust. And while David Jünger and Gennady Estraikh focus on responses of left-leaning individuals and institutions, Samantha Baskind describes a more right-wing reading of the lessons of the war. Rachel Deblinger also highlights the variety of discourses that came together at a formative moment in American Jewish identity and communal life—the traditional Jewish and the contemporary American—in her exploration of the rhetoric and symbols of sacrifice and salvation from ancient Jewish and modern American traditions in order to mobilize American Jewish funds for the support of displaced persons in Europe.

Indeed, the different disciplinary threads but common intellectual interests underlying the conception of the March 2014 conference at the University of Maryland, College Park, out of which this volume grew, has been a long and productive one between its editors: Eliyana Adler, being a historian of Eastern European Jewish life, and Sheila Jelen, a scholar of modern Jewish literature. Having shared many interests over the years, but from different disciplinary perspectives, we have affirmed our belief, through teaching in each other's classrooms, co-organizing several conferences, and co-editing several volumes, that the synergy created through interdisciplinary discourse can significantly enhance our understanding of modern Jewish culture. We hope that the proliferation of perspectives evident within many of the individual essays, as well as across the many essays collected for this volume, will serve as a model for future directions in the study of the postwar period in Jewish experience.

The essays in this volume build on Hasia Diner's important insights, and take them into new fields of inquiry, but in no way exhaust the subject matter. Indeed there are many important aspects of the postwar North American Jewish community that receive little to no attention in this volume. We thus hope that it will serve to encourage other scholars to engage with the materials and questions from this period of time in the modern history of the Jewish people. To return to the point with which this volume began, Philip Roth's dramatic commentary on American Jewish experience in the immediate postwar years has as much to tell us about what was spoken and understood as what was unspoken and incomprehensible at that moment in time. How much did Jewish Americans know about what happened to their fellow Jews in Eastern Europe, and what effect did their knowledge, or lack thereof, have on their reception of European Jewish refugees, modern literary texts newly adapted from their original European contexts for an American audience, and political and communal organizations that aimed to redress the distress of Jewish communities in Europe and the United States after the end of World War II? All of these questions underlie the collaboration that inspired this volume; the conference that preceded it; and the many conversations that have taken place during the rewarding experience of compiling, editing, and publishing it.

Notes

We would like to thank the anonymous reviewers of the manuscript and Professor Eli Lederhendler for useful comments on this essay.

1. Philip Roth, "Eli, the Fanatic," *Goodbye, Columbus and Five Short Stories*, thirteenth edition (Boston: Houghton Mifflin Company, 1989), 263.
2. Ibid., 250.
3. Ibid., 252.
4. Ibid., 257.
5. Ibid., 278.
6. Ibid., 264–265.
7. Ibid., 255.
8. Ibid., 275, 277.

9. Ibid., 277–278.

10. Dominick La Capra, *Writing History, Writing Trauma* (Baltimore: Johns Hopkins, 2001), 102–103.

11. Philip Roth, "Writing About Jews," in *Reading Myself and Others* (New York: Farrar, Strauss & Giroux, 1975), 200.

12. Sol Gittleman, "The Pecks of Woodenton, Long Island, Thirty Years Later: Another Look at 'Eli, the Fanatic'," *Studies in American Jewish Literature* 8:2 (1989): 139.

13. Gittleman, 142.

14. James Duban, "Arthur Koestler and Meyer Levin: The Trivial, the Tragic, and Rationalization *Post Factum* in Roth's 'Eli, the Fanatic,'" *Philip Roth Studies* 7:2 (Fall 2011): 171–186.

15. Elliott M. Simon, "Philip Roth's 'Eli, the Fanatic': the Color of Blackness," *Modern Jewish Studies Annual* 7 (1990): 39–48.

16. Hana Wirth-Nesher, "Resisting Allegory, or Reading 'Eli, the Fanatic' in Tel Aviv," *Prooftexts* 21:1 (2001): 110.

17. Steven Fink, "Fact, Fiction, and History in Philip Roth's 'Eli, the Fanatic,'" *MELUS* 29:3 (Fall 2014), 95.

18. Ibid., 104.

19. From a Reader's Report for Wayne State University Press, dated October 31, 2016.

20. Peter Novick, *The Holocaust in American Life* (Boston: Houghton Mifflin Company, 1999), 103.

21. Alan Mintz, *Popular Culture and the Shaping of Holocaust Memory in America* (Seattle: University of Washington Press, 2001), 7.

22. Diner was not the first scholar to engage critically with this narrative. On the contrary, it is challenged in Jeffrey Shandler, *While America Watches: Televising the Holocaust* (New York: Oxford University Press, 1999); Eli Lederhendler, *New York Jews and the Decline of Urban Ethnicity, 1950–1970* (Syracuse, New York: Syracuse University Press, 2001); and Michael E. Staub, *Torn at the Roots: The Crisis of Jewish Liberalism in Postwar America* (New York: Columbia University Press, 2002), among other works. Diner was, however, the first to devote a full-length monograph to the topic and thus to raise it to prominence.

23. Hasia R. Diner, *We Remember with Reverence and Love: American Jews and the Myth of Silence after the Holocaust, 1945–1962* (New York University Press, 2009), 366.

24. For more on this phenomenon, see Mark L. Smith, "No Silence in Yiddish: Popular and Scholarly Writing about the Holocaust in the Early Postwar Years," in *After the Holocaust: Challenging the Myth of Silence*, ed. David Cesarani and Eric J. Sundquist (London: Routledge, 2012): 55–66.

25. On Anne Frank's *Diary*, see Cynthia Ozick, "Who Owns Anne Frank?" in *Quarrel and Quandary: Essays* (New York: Vintage International, 2000); Laurence Graver, *An Obsession with Anne Frank* (Berkeley: University of California, 1995); and Ralph Melnick, *The Stolen Legacy of Anne Frank* (New Haven: Yale University Press, 1997). On *Fiddler on the Roof*, see Alisa Solomon, *Wonder of Wonders: A Cultural History of Fiddler on the Roof* (New York: Metropolitan Books, 2013); Barbara Eisenberg, *Tradition! The Highly Improbably, Ultimately Triumphant Broadway to Hollywood Story of Fiddler on the Roof, the World's Most Beloved Musical* (New York: St. Martins Press, 2014); and Jeremy Dauber, *The Worlds of Sholem Aleichem: The Remarkable Life and Afterlife of the Man Who Created Tevye* (New York: NextBook, Shocken, 2013).

INTRODUCTION

26. See for example Laura Jockusch, *Collect and Record! Jewish Holocaust Documentation in Early Postwar Europe* (Oxford: Oxford University Press, 2012); Alan Rosen, *The Wonder of their Voices: the 1946 Holocaust Interviews of David Boder* (Oxford: Oxford University Press, 2010); Zoe Vania Waxman, *Writing the Holocaust: Identity, Testimony, Representation* (Oxford: Oxford University Press, 2006); Atina Grossmann, *Jews, Germans, and Allies: Close Encounters in Occupied Germany* (Princeton: Princeton University Press, 2007); Avinoam J. Patt, *Finding Home and Homeland: Jewish Youth and Zionism in the Aftermath of the Holocaust* (Detroit: Wayne State University Press, 2009); Avinoam J. Patt, ed., *"We are Here": New Approaches to Jewish Displaced Persons in Postwar Germany* (Detroit: Wayne State University Press, 2010); Margarete Myers Feinstein, *Holocaust Survivors in Postwar Germany, 1945–1957* (Cambridge: Cambridge University Press, 2010); Jan Schwarz, *Survivors and Exiles: Yiddish Culture after the Holocaust* (Detroit: Wayne State University Press, 2015); and Laura Jockusch and Gabriel N. Finder, eds., *Jewish Honor Courts: Revenge, Retribution, and Reconciliation in Europe and Israel after the Holocaust* (Detroit: Wayne State University Press, 2015). This is only a selection and does not include the many articles on related topics.

Part I: Refugees
COMMEMORATING THE PAST

The Eastern European Jewish Past and Its Historians

CULTURAL INTERVENTIONS
IN POSTWAR AMERICA

Eli Lederhendler

FROM THE 1940s to the late 1960s, English-language publications related to Eastern European Jewish life appeared in growing numbers and in increasingly rapid succession. They appeared in various genres: belles-lettres, historiography, ethnography, works of popular culture, and religious texts. Together, this bookshelf of publications furnished an interpretive framework, giving readers an overall sense of a social, historical, and cultural space to which many of them were related directly or indirectly, but that now lay beyond reach.

As I will discuss, a great deal of this activity was, in the first instance, facilitated by the transfer to the United States of a crucial human resource: a small but qualitatively significant Eastern European-based Jewish intelligentsia, some of whom arrived as refugees, and some who were born or came of age in America but were raised in refugee families. Without them, the revived American Jewish interest in the Eastern European Jewish heritage might still have taken place, but it would undoubtedly have taken a different form. With them, the United States emerged in the postwar era as a major center of Eastern European Jewish heritage activity.

Primarily, of course, the eclipse of Eastern European Jewish life on its native soil was due to the deportations and annihilations under the Nazi occupation. Secondarily, Stalinism in Soviet Russia, of which the full ramifications were only then beginning to be understood, added to the sense of closure vis-à-vis the culture of earlier generations. During the postwar years, this was compounded in the communist satellite regimes in Eastern Europe, where a remnant of prewar Jewry was rebuilding a new life under uncertain and even volatile circumstances.

English-language works published in America cast Eastern Europe mainly as the scene of lost Jewish authenticity, spirituality, and a coherent past. In an inversion of an older pattern, in which Europe had actively seeded the language, religion, political attitudes, and folk culture of immigrants who went to America, thus affording immigrant Jews an ethnicity that could "make it" in America, the postwar cultural products generated in America worked the other way around: they afforded a representational afterlife to the Jews of Eastern Europe. Thus, during the early twentieth century, cultural products of Eastern Europe were directly transplanted to American shores. After the Holocaust, these transplanted and remembered cultural features took on quite a different role. No longer a link to a living Jewry in the old country, they became a vestige and a remembrance: at least as much an evocation of an earlier generation of Jewish immigrants in America as they were a symbolic homage to the old Europe. American Jewish life—in its evolving second-and third-generational phase—provided the context and the desire for a postwar image of parental and grandparental origins. This "demand," as we will see, was answered by a supply that, initially, depended on a select milieu of recent immigrants.

There are several points to consider here, beginning with the language that served, for the most part, as the primary cultural medium in postwar American Jewry. Although Yiddish was undoubtedly the central cultural artifact of Jewish Eastern Europe, in the postwar context it functioned less and less as the primary vehicle for cultural reproduction. Alongside an extant Yiddish literature—still published after the war, albeit by fewer writers and aimed at a smaller public—most postwar publications *about* Yiddish-speaking Jewry were in English. For most Jews in America, Yiddish-language material tended to be supplanted by English-inflected representations of Jewish Eastern Europe, which in turn became the basis for later cultural representations and for future academic teaching.[1]

By no means did American Jews write all of this English-language material. Quite a lot of it was produced in Israel and Europe and translated into English. Some was written by sojourner figures who lived for a while in the United States before moving elsewhere—mainly to Israel.

We are, therefore, dealing here with a form of cultural transnationalism as much as the advent of homegrown American Jewish writing; but, I argue, translation for the large-scale US-Jewish market is itself testimony to a new cultural moment.

Once English became established as the main linguistic vehicle, it followed that American concerns and modes of thought would affect how these writings were presented and received. American discursive dimensions are reflected in the gesture toward a former homeland, now abandoned for the sake of a better life: a gesture that reinforced the finality of the Jewish migratory trek to America. America, as readers would infer, was the ultimate destination of Jewish life, and Eastern Europe could represent its prelude.

This effectively framed the Jews' cultural heritage as an aspect of American integration (in the sense of being a component part of the Jews' new host culture). Margaret Mead, the foremost American anthropologist of her day, struck this integrative note when she summarized the significance of Eastern European Jewish folklore research (in her foreword to *Life is With People*, 1952): "[T]his book has further implications for Americans of all kinds, all beliefs, every origin, from Africa, China or Europe, who as they have learned ways in which diverse peoples may live together, also have as their cultural birthright a share in the traditions of each."[2]

But the representation of Eastern Europe as the background culture of American Jewry could also be used to epitomize and to recommend Jewish group survival. Lucy Dawidowicz, writing in the introduction to her venerable Eastern European cultural anthology, *The Golden Tradition* (1967, 1996), said, "Eastern European Jews searched for ways to harmonize tradition and modernity, to preserve their Jewish identity and retain their community. . . . Eastern European Jewry was cruelly cut down. But vital elements of its culture survive. Perhaps we, heirs of that culture, can continue its tradition of conserving Jewish identity by fusing the old and the new."[3]

Cold War issues, as seen from the West and presented to the English-reading audience, were another factor that influenced postwar representations of Jewish Eastern Europe. The premier Jewish historian of his day in the American academy, Salo W. Baron, noted that postwar Russia's surviving Jewish population was "deeply grateful to the Red Army" for its role in defeating the Nazis, but he also averred that "it meekly submitted to the Stalinist terror of 1948–52, which shattered whatever expectations it may have cherished for its postwar reconstruction."[4] Several years later, in a volume of essays entitled *The Jews in Soviet Russia since 1917*, the London-based political scientist Leonard Schapiro affirmed that "the only form of society which can cater to [a] variety of aspirations," as manifested with regard to a minority group such as the Jews, "is one in which the liberal tolerance of opinions, faiths and mores prevails within the framework of equality under the law." Such liberality of personal choice and equality of status, he concluded, was "quite inconsistent with the 'totalitarian' society into which the Soviet state has evolved."[5]

Third, English-language American discourse about history, culture, religion, and politics in general was naturally formulated according to American-based agendas. Given the prevailing academic concerns at the time, those agendas included a quest for an updated American ideology. Against that background, writing in English on Eastern Europe could be represented as a contribution to contemporary humane discourse, to a better understanding of American society in particular, and to a theory of convergence among originally disparate strands of the national heritage. In that spirit, the Harvard-trained historian Moses Rischin registered the following note that revised older American melting pot ideas: "This migration, made up of Jews seeking a homeland, was to help shape New York into a unique metropolis."[6] It was time for America (or at least New York) to be represented as a product—not just as a shaper—of immigrant destinies.

For reasons of space, I will focus here mainly on the production of scholarly works on Jewish history in Eastern Europe, albeit with the understanding that they represent only a fraction of a much larger and more varied body of literature. I do so because, in terms of abiding influence, such scholarly activity has become a principal hallmark of the American Jewish contribution to world Jewish culture in the postwar era. Jews in various countries, from Argentina to Australia, have produced reverential, elegiac, memoiristic, or generally nostalgic material related to the Eastern European Jewish heritage. However, a substantial and institutionally sustained academic engagement with these topics has remained limited to just a few of these postwar venues. North America is one of them (both the United States and Canada), closely paralleling Israeli academic discourse.

In more recent years, we can say the same of Britain and Germany, and there is now a reputable body of post-communist scholarship among young academics in (or from) Poland and Russia.[7]

It would be fair to say that American Jewish scholars' contributions constitute a core component of contemporary academic work in this field. Indeed, the Historical Society of Israel, as well as other prestigious Israeli publishers, have seen fit to render accessible to Hebrew readers key works by American scholars written in English, via translated editions.[8] Intellectual and academic endeavor, though not widely exposed to public view, furnish resources that eventually reinforce other cultural products in a particularly authoritative way. Moreover, the effort to document and reinterpret the Eastern European Jewish experience is both a replication and a direct continuation of efforts that had been undertaken in prewar Eastern Europe itself, and, therefore, it does what commemoration alone cannot do. These are perhaps the best instances of a critical and secular approach to the heritage of Jewish Eastern Europe, if we compare them to sacralizing and iconic approaches.

To acknowledge the importance of the North American academic milieu for the ongoing cultural reconstruction of Eastern European Jewry is to point out an event of some historical significance in cultural affairs: namely, the appearance of a new geographic center of gravity in Eastern European Jewish scholarship. The historiography of Eastern European Jewry had formerly been nearly completely European and had been conducted in European languages (including Yiddish, German, Russian, and Polish), with a Hebrew offshoot in Palestine. In the field of Eastern Europe and its Jewish heritage, America before 1940 was no powerhouse.[9]

To be sure, Eastern Europe's cultural imprint within American Jewry was vibrant and almost self-evident during the first few decades of the twentieth century—beginning at the grassroots level in people's homes and working its way through organizations, institutions, and cultural life. There was a well-endowed corpus of literary, journalistic, musical, theatrical, and film production, primarily in Yiddish, that was solidly based in the ethno-religious heritage of the immigrant Jewish community. But the conditions needed for reconstituting the European Jewish intellectual enterprise for American publishers, American readers, and American academic institutions—in English—were barely available between the wars, and this is precisely what changed afterwards. The more popular forms of Yiddish-and European-inflected cultural consumption between the wars were by-products of the mass immigration and, hence, were entirely dependent upon the already fading impressions, desires, and tastes of people in one stage or another of cultural transition. The power to generate new cultural content in an idiom adapted for the post-migration generations was limited, unless someone played a facilitating role—by which I mean people equipped to re-stock the dwindling supply of firsthand information and make it accessible.

The few outstanding English-language works published on Eastern European Jewish history and culture extant before World War II can be counted on two hands. These include standard works, like Simon Dubnow's *History of the Jews in Russia and Poland*—a Jewish Publication Society project commissioned specifically for American readers, which dated back to the First World War. Similarly, one can cite Jacob Raisin's *The Haskalah Movement in Russia* (1913), as well as Leo Weiner's Yiddish literary anthology, *Songs from the Ghetto* (1898), and his historical study, *The History of Yiddish Literature in the 19th Century* (1899). There was an important comprehensive work by Myer Waxman, *A History of Jewish Literature*, published in 1936, in which four chapters dealt at length with Eastern Europe. Shorter but significant interventions by European-born scholars who transferred to America include Solomon Schechter's chapter on Hasidism in his *Studies in Judaism* (1920), as well as the book-length essay on Lithuanian rabbinic lore and learning penned by Louis Ginzberg, *Students, Scholars, and Saints* (1928). The migration studies scholar Samuel Joseph produced an early statistical study on Jewish immigration to the United States between the 1880s and 1910, which appeared in print in 1914.[10]

There had also been a few early discussions of the "Jewish Question" in Russia, dating back to the 1880s (some of it in translation), and other items of this genre were updated after the First World War.[11] Arthur Goodhart, an American Jew attached to the Morgenthau Commission, the US fact-finding mission in postwar Poland, published a political survey, *Poland and the Minority Races*, in 1920. Horace Kallen, the prominent philosopher and social thinker, produced a detailed field report on post-World War I Jewish life in Palestine, Poland, and Russia, published as *Frontiers of Hope* (1929). Similar works by Henry Morgenthau and Oscar Janowsky, concerning Poland's Jews in the context of the political and legal status of the minority nationalities, were published in the 1920s and '30s.[12] Little is known about the reception these works received, but the paucity of this literature does speak to the point, at least indirectly. English-language works were a trickle, compared with the stream produced in other countries, and were therefore not apt to constitute a core part of Jewish discourse on the subject.

In that light, it was a significant moment when Louis Greenberg (1894–1946), a Ukrainian-born American Conservative rabbi who immigrated to the United States at age nineteen, and served a congregational pulpit in New Haven, CT, wrote a doctoral thesis at Yale on the Jews in Imperial Russia from 1772 to 1880, which he completed in 1940 and published in 1944. At that time, the only previously published English-language title in the field that he could recommend to his readers was Dubnow's 1916-vintage *History*, in Israel Friedlaender's translation.[13] Twenty years later, the Galician-born and European-educated Salo W. Baron published his own survey of Russian Jewish history (quoted above), and here, again, English-language citations in his references to secondary literature were extremely sparse.[14]

It is also noteworthy in this regard that Louis Finkelstein's widely circulated omnibus survey, *The Jews: Their History, Culture, and Religion*, initially planned in 1943 and first published in 1949, included relatively little material on Eastern European Jewish history. It contained an essay by Yudel Mark on modern Yiddish literature; a survey of the Jews' fate during the Second World War, by Arieh Tartakower, which bore the chillingly understated title, "The Problem of European Jewry, 1939–1945"; and an essay on modern Jewish migration up to 1946, by Jacob Lestchinsky, that dealt with historical conditions in Eastern Europe. In the preface to that first edition, Finkelstein regretted the absence of several other essays that had been commissioned for the volume, including one on modern Jewish culture in Eastern Europe (by Abraham Menes), which had not been prepared in time.[15]

Finkelstein's anthology affords us some initial insight into the question of reception and audience, insofar as it contained the results of a modest survey that was conducted (as described in the Appendix) among "scholars and educators." The survey (conducted in 1947) asked respondents to indicate which questions about Judaism they were most eager to see answered. The survey produced a list of twenty-eight questions deemed to be of significant current interest. The results were cross-indexed with material actually published in the book, so that interested readers could easily find the relevant chapter with information on a given subject.

Topics of primary interest that emerged from the survey in the first edition (1949) included "What is a Jew?"; "What are the ceremonials and rituals of Judaism?"; "What is the Jewish attitude toward members of other religions, and what is the Jewish attitude to marriage with members of other faiths?"; "What was the Jewish participation in the wars fought by the USA?"; "What is the relation of the Jews throughout the world to Palestine?"; and "What are the contributions of Jews to the cultural development of civilization?" It seems apparent that what these people expected from a basic sourcebook about Jews and Judaism, past and present, included an "authoritative" summary of beliefs and practices that could be used to educate Jews and non-Jews alike; some account of the Jews' political and civic posture; and some information related to current events. The minor place of Eastern European topics and concerns, as gauged by this roughly sketched agenda, may reflect a 1940s-era localism on the part of the respondents. At the very least, the turn toward images of Eastern Europe still awaited the intervention of authoritative cultural transmitters, working independently from the mainstream American milieu.

The same survey procedure was repeated in 1957 and circulated among a wider group of respondents. A few new questions appeared, indicating the sensitivity of contemporary political issues, such as "What is the relation in Judaism between culture, nationality and religion?"; "How did World War II and the preceding events affect the Jews?"; "What is the situation of Jews behind the Iron Curtain?"; and "What are the bases of anti-Semitism?"[16] Apart from the brief interest expressed in the status of Jews behind the Iron Curtain—pregnant with meaning during the Cold War of the mid-1950s—the sole geographical spaces that rated frequent mention in the survey were the United States and the Land of Israel.

Later editions of Finkelstein's oft-reprinted *The Jews* were significantly reinforced with new chapters on Eastern Europe: one on pre-partition Poland-Lithuania by the Israeli historian Israel Halperin; one by Bernard Weinryb (who was then at Dropsie College and Columbia) on Eastern

European Jewry since the Polish partitions; and one by Abraham Menes on Judaic religious scholarship in Eastern Europe. Arieh Tartakower's essay on the Holocaust and its aftermath had updated material on the survivors' lives in contemporary Europe, and the essay now bore a new title that communicated closure if not catastrophic finality: "The Decline of European Jewry."

Weinryb's essay on Eastern European Jewry since the end of the eighteenth century sounded a general note that, in many ways, was emblematic of the range of writing at the time: "Between times of deepening crisis—or parallel with them—there were years or decades of heightening hopes for political or social freedom and elevation, for renaissance of national cultures, for improving prospects for human brotherhood, equality, and co-operation."[17] Not only did Weinryb harken back to pre-Hitler days when Jewish communities and cultures in Eastern Europe could be depicted as thriving, but he also used language that postwar American Jewry was used to hearing ("freedom," "brotherhood," and "equality").

Finkelstein's survey of Judaism is a benchmark, perhaps, of what became a trend. Despite the marginality of American-produced literature on Jewish Eastern Europe up to 1940, in the years that followed, scholarship and publishing about Jewish Eastern Europe began to achieve increased numerical and qualitative significance. At Columbia, Isaac Levitats finished his dissertation on nineteenth-century Jewish communal life in Russia, which was published in 1943.[18] Louis Greenberg's volume on Russian Jewish history (1944), already mentioned, was followed by the posthumous publication of a sequel volume that covered the final decades of Romanov rule, which first appeared in 1951. (In the 1970s the two volumes became available in a popular, one-volume, paperback edition.)

The library of works in English devoted to the Eastern European heritage was beginning to expand, and it was not limited to the academic or textbook genre. Maurice Samuel published his *World of Sholom Aleichem* in 1943—a quasi-literary evocation of the Old World before its destruction. (On December 14, 1959, a television film with the same title was released, featuring an array of television and film stars and stories drawn from the works of I. L. Peretz and Sholem Aleichem.) In 1946, Bella Chagall published *Burning Lights*, containing thirty-six drawings by her husband, the celebrated artist. The year 1952 saw the publication of *Life Is with People*, by

Elizabeth Herzog and Mark Zborowski, in the wake of the famous Columbia University study, long considered a landmark ethnographic achievement (although more recent skepticism has reduced its near-canonical status).

In the following table, I present a select bibliography arranged in order of appearance, from 1947 to 1969. It includes belles-lettres and semi-popular works, as well as histories and other scholarly works. If we add the early to mid-1940s-era publications already mentioned, including the first edition of the Finkelstein anthology, then the 1940s show twelve titles, the 1950s are represented here by thirteen published works, and the 1960s by twenty-two. This is a preliminary list and is not an exhaustive catalogue by any means. I have not listed separately the invaluable scholarly material published in English in the *YIVO Annual of Jewish Social Science*, beginning with its first volume in 1946. Similarly, the table does not include thumbnail descriptions of Eastern European Jewish life that were integrated either as chapters or as brief discussions in books dealing primarily with the history and social background of American Jewry.[19]

> I. J. Singer, *The Brothers Ashkenazi* (1945)
> Georgii Lukomskii, *Jewish Art in European Synagogues: From the Middle Ages to the 18th Century* (1947)
> Roman Vishniac, *Polish Jews: A Pictorial Record* (1947)
> Martin Buber, *Tales of the Hasidim* (1947)
> Martin Buber, *Hasidism* (1948)
> Mark Wischnitzer, *To Dwell in Safety: The Story of Jewish Migration Since 1800* (1948)
> Abraham J. Heschel, *The Earth Is the Lord's* (1949)
> Simon Halkin, *Modern Hebrew Literature, from the Enlightenment to the Birth of the State of Israel: Trends and Values* (1950)
> Isaac Bashevis Singer, *The Family Moskat* (1950)
> Solomon Schwartz, *The Jews in the Soviet Union* (1951)
> Mark Zborowski and Elizabeth Herzog, *Life Is with People* (1952)
> Irving Howe and Eliezer Greenberg, eds., *A Treasury of Yiddish Stories* (1953)
> Peter Meyer, *The Jews in the Soviet Satellites* (1953)
> Isaac Bashevis Singer, *Gimpel the Fool* (1954)

Martin Buber, *The Legend of the Baal Shem* (1955)
Martin Buber, *The Tales of Rabbi Nachman* (1956)
Martin Buber, *Hasidism and Modern Man*, ed. and trans. Maurice Friedman (1958)
Isaac Bashevis Singer, *Satan in Goray* (1958)
Simon Dubnow, *Nationalism and History: Letters on Old and New Judaism*, ed. Kopel S. Pinson (1958)
Max Weinreich, *History of the Yiddish Language* (1959)
Marc Chagall, *My Life* (1960)
Samuel Dresner, *The Zaddik: The Doctrine of the Zaddik According to the Writings of Rabbi Yaakov Yosef of Polnoye* (1960)
Martin Buber, *The Origin and Meaning of Hasidism* (1960)
Leon Uris, *Mila 18* (1961)
Sholem Asch, *Salvation* (1962)
B. Z. Goldberg, *The Jewish Problem in the Soviet Union* (1961)
Jacob Katz, *Tradition and Crisis* (1961)
Marvin Herzog, *The Yiddish Language in Northern Poland: Its Geography and History* (1965)
Harry Rabinowicz, *The Legacy of Polish Jewry: A History of Polish Jews in the Inter-war Years, 1919–1939* (1965)
Alon Schoener, ed., *The Lower East Side: Portal to American Life (1870–1924)* [Jewish Museum catalogue] (1966)
Maurice Samuel, *Blood Accusation: The Strange History of the Beilliss Case* (1966)
Jacob Frumkin, et al., *Russian Jewry 1860–1917* (1966)
William Glicksman, *In the Mirror of Literature: The Economic Life of the Jews in Poland as Reflected in Yiddish Literature, 1914–1939* (1966)
Shmarya Levin, *Forward from Exile*, trans. Maurice Samuel (1967)
Lucy S. Dawidowicz, *The Golden Tradition* (1967)
Bernard K. Johnpoll, *The Politics of Futility* (1967)
Janusz Korczak (Henryk Goldszmit), *Selected Works of Janusz Korczak* (1967)
Charles Madison, *Yiddish Literature—Its Scope and Major Writers* (1968)
Jacob Glatstein, Israel Knox, Samuel Margoshes, et al., eds. *Anthology of Holocaust Literature* (1968)

Abraham Cahan, *The Education of Abraham Cahan*, trans. Leon Stein, et al. (1969)

Gregor Aronson, et al., *Russian Jewry 1917–1967* (1969)

In 1986, a detailed and comprehensive world bibliography of published materials related to Polish Jewish history listed over 2,700 separate items in a variety of languages, including English.[20] Checking the publication dates of the English-language materials, we can say the following: the relevant articles, essays, books, pamphlets, memorabilia, literary works, and reference materials published in English over the century between 1869 and 1969 totaled 154 items. Starting with a sluggish and sporadic publication rate, by 1940 there was at least one such publication every year. The average annual rate of publication quadrupled from 1940 to 1969, and grew once again in subsequent years. Thus, in the fifteen-year period from 1970 to 1985 alone there were 106 new publications, or about seven per year.

International intellectual importation was crucial for the field of Eastern European Jewish studies, without which a successor generation, trained in America, would likely have emerged much later than it did. Immigrant scholars took up posts mainly in Jewish-sponsored institutions, and special mention in this regard must be made of the YIVO Institute (*Yidisher vissenshaftlekher institut*)—itself a transplant from European soil (Vilna)—whose annual journal has already been mentioned. YIVO's director, Max Weinreich, and his colleagues painstakingly reconstituted core resources for scholarship through a library, archives, and a bilingual Yiddish-English publishing program. Likewise, they created study programs to attract students to the Yiddish language and culture and afforded a berth for professional Eastern European Jewish research during the interim years before universities became a major venue for the field.[21]

The indispensable input of European-born scholars in general and Holocaust-era refugees in particular was not felt in historiography alone. Indeed, throughout the postwar era and extending into and beyond the 1960s, American Jewish scholarship was led by the most recent immigrants and their children, active across a variety of disciplines and areas of study. Child-immigrants or children born to refugee families cannot be counted as cultural immigrants in quite the same way as academics and scholars who were trained abroad before the war; yet, their firsthand exposure to

European-derived and Yiddish culture in their parental homes must be reckoned as imported cultural capital and a crucial factor that enabled them to constitute a second generation. Typically, their intellectual and emotional baggage became part of their later reflections upon their career choices.[22]

Individual instances of this phenomenon among post-Holocaust scholars are many, as evidenced by first-person accounts. Anita Norich, for one (born 1952), an important figure in Yiddish literary history and criticism and a long-time professor at the University of Michigan at Ann Arbor, has reflected on the trajectory of her life and scholarship in light of her parents' experiences "in the Lodz ghetto . . . Auschwitz, Bergen-Belsen and Dachau," and her birth "in a Displaced Persons camp in Germany [and] growing up as a child of these survivors." Norich observes, "When my dead spoke to me, they always spoke Yiddish. They never spoke of how they had been murdered but always of Lodz and Zakopane and family and cooking and the fur trade and, sometimes, of the subversive power of books."[23]

Similarly, Samuel Kassow (born 1946), another postwar baby born at a displaced persons camp, became a professor at Trinity College, Hartford, and a key figure in writing the history of Russian, Lithuanian, and Polish Jewish history. I myself (born in New York City) would probably never have gone into the field of Eastern European Jewish history had I not had a postwar immigrant father, born in Poland, and had I not grown up in a family milieu in which Yiddish and Hebrew secular culture was strongly present.

Canvassing such fields as Yiddish language and literary studies, European Jewish history, Holocaust research, philosophy, theology, and the study of religion, we would find over thirty key figures who derive from this small migration stream in the first or second generation. Some of them left Germany or Poland in the 1930s and early '40s, either as mature adults or as children, and came to the United States directly or via a third country (England, Canada, Israel, and Cuba). The youngest among them, as noted, were born to postwar refugee parents. They did much to put American Jewish scholarship in the front ranks of Jewish intellectual endeavor, and helped re-establish post-Biblical Jewish history and culture as part of the humanistic tradition of the American academy.[24]

Thus, the stage afforded by the United States to scholars specializing in Eastern Europe was not coincidental, but rather formed one wing of a postwar transplantation of Jewish studies to North American venues. By roughly 1990, Jewish studies had become nominally integrated within the American academy,[25] but for the first postwar decades, as mentioned at the outset, we are dealing with a transitional and transnational cultural moment. Some European-born historians who worked and published in the United States between the wars and in the early postwar years later moved to Israel, such as Raphael Mahler, Bernard Dov Weinryb, Jacob Lestchinsky, and Arieh Tartakower. The fact that American Jewish cultural and academic institutions, as well as American publishers, turned to these people as translators and primary communicators of the Eastern European heritage made all the difference in the long run. Their lectures, courses, personal libraries and archives, publishing output, and roles as public intellectuals made crucial resources available to the wider American Jewish public. Those resources, in turn, could be gathered in at a later stage—beginning roughly in the 1970s—in what would prove to be a rich harvest.

The first to undertake a rudimentary survey of Eastern European historiography in America was Mark Friedman. Friedman identified what he called three "generations." In the first generation he listed men like Abraham Duker, Isaac Levitats, and Louis Greenberg—who came to America before 1920 and were born and partly educated in Eastern Europe—including their own direct encounters with some of the leading Polish Jewish historians of the day. A second cohort included European-born scholars who immigrated during the 1920s, '30s, and early '40s, such as Jacob Shatzky, Salo Baron, Raphael Mahler, Arieh Tartakower, Eliyahu Tcherikower, Jacob Lestchinsky, Zosa Szajkowski, Bernard Weinryb, Max Weinreich, and Alfred (Avraham) Greenbaum.[26] In Friedman's third "generation," or, perhaps more accurately, cohort, postwar survivor immigrants like Isaiah Trunk and, after 1968, Lucjan Dobroszycki were joined by American-born, second-generation scholars, such as Marvin Herzog, Zvi Gitelman, and Ezra Mendelsohn.[27]

To Friedman's third generation, which focused mainly on historians, we might add scholars in other fields, who were contemporaries or students of those already mentioned. Those would include Uriel Weinreich, Mordkhe Schaechter, and (the American-born) Joshua A. Fishman in Yiddish linguistics and socio-linguistics; European-born Ruth Wisse and her Canadian-born brother David G. Roskies in literature; and the

American-born historian Lucy Dawidowicz and Barbara Kirshenblatt-Gimblett in anthropology. Uriel Weinreich and Mordkhe Schaechter arrived in the United States as adults (at the beginning of the war and just afterward, respectively), while the others either arrived as children or were born in North America.[28]

The image of Eastern European Jewry, as it was cultivated in the American scholarly orbit, closely followed upon the intellectual endeavor of the prewar, secular Eastern European intelligentsia. Indeed, it built directly on that foundation, via the intervention of immigrant and refugee savants. There was, therefore, an initial family resemblance between American-based postwar reconstructions and the ones performed, simultaneously, in Israel, where much effort was likewise made to build upon prewar work in Europe. Indeed, some of the English-language corpus of Eastern European Jewish subject matter was imported from Israel (or from Europe via Israel, as in the case of Martin Buber's works on Hasidism). The resemblance was exhibited, for example, in the way that both American-based and Israeli-based historians seemed most impressed by the communal, national character of Jewish life in Eastern Europe. American and Israeli students of Eastern Europe alike devoted significant parts of their work to such non-Zionist aspects as Yiddish culture and Bundism. Both groups of historians, once again, were heavily engaged in historicizing the political, social, and economic relations of Jews in their Eastern European habitat. In a recent essay, Scott Ury suggests other parallels, such as a common quest for "order" and an implicit commemoration of the dead.[29]

However, I would tentatively argue that, over time and across the gamut of all that was published in the field, as American-based scholars began to predominate, some daylight was bound to open up between them and their Israeli cultural partners. I make no hard and fast distinctions here, but I suggest that the Israeli scholarly tradition is filtered or nuanced differently. The "daylight" I refer to has less to do with methodologies and research aims, or even ideology—if defined in terms of supposed Diasporic vs. unreconstructed Zionistic commitments—than with language, generation, and venue, all of which have influenced scholarly purpose and emphasis.

Presentation in English presupposes the filter of translation. That is one kind of *mimesis*. Metaphorically speaking, presentation in Hebrew is of another sort. In Hebrew, there is the air—perhaps the presumption—of transliteration, not translation: a closer segue from the Yiddish that, at the very least, may still be read from right to left and in the same alphabet.

Frequently, Israeli academics are still second-generation natives in a society that is composed to a significant degree of first-generation immigrants and their second-generation offspring, and is still very much engaged with the anxieties of a new society.[30] Russia, Poland, and their history and heritage bulk large in the public sphere of Israeli life, and so does the black-clad Orthodoxy of both Hasidic and non-Hasidic varieties. There is nothing quaint or already distilled into memory about either of them. This is but one aspect of what the Israeli venue implies—and the result, I think, has been a sobering effect on scholarly writing. Israeli historiography on Eastern Europe is largely shorn of exuberance.

American Jewish scholarship, written in English, manages a feat of a different sort. Its practitioners seem to say—if I may generalize—that the more intricate and varied the tapestry of Eastern European Jewish history, the better and the more estimable it is as a template for cultural diversity and the persistence of Judaism. These two values (diversity and persistence) underlie the American Jewish academic endeavor, as we already saw adumbrated in Lucy Dawidowicz's 1960s-vintage anthology. They constitute the desiderata at the ethical level that can motivate Jewish research as an avocation. Gershon D. Hundert, for example, writing not long ago in his history, *Jews in Poland-Lithuania in the Eighteenth Century* (2004), reaffirmed his belief that, despite the vicissitudes, changes, dissonance, inner frictions, and outright danger experienced by Eastern European Jews, the majority retained a subjective sense of continuity that was "irreducible," and a "sometimes painful, but invincible, prerational, and positive feeling about their Jewishness."[31] Reading between these lines, it is not at all far-fetched to see Hundert's assertion of "positive feeling" about Jewishness not just as a feature of eighteenth-century Polish Jewry, but as an essential attribute and an abiding, perennial concern, perhaps especially so wherever Jews persist as a minority culture. There is something of a parable, an ethical prescription for the present, in this representation of Eastern European Jewry in its finest hour.

Similarly in texture and in message, Kenneth Moss concluded his 2009 study, *Jewish Renaissance in the Russian Revolution*, with the suggestion that despite the crisis that overtook them, Jewish cultural activists in revolutionary Russia—in the brief moment allotted to them in history—"sought to lay the groundwork for a different kind of Jewish future—one in which Jews as individuals, liberated from inner crisis and outer siege, might engage the full range of creative possibilities, questions, and freedoms that modernity offers."[32] That is, memory and cultural memory have some relation to the status of Jewish distinctiveness in the past, present, and future, but choosing affinities (as the Jewish cultural revolutionists had done) takes place on an individual basis.

A subtle contrast might be found in the rhetoric deployed by their Israeli counterparts. Fractious Jews in their Eastern European guise augured less a plethora of open-ended, individual possibilities than a reading back of the deep divisions and internal conflicts in contemporary Israel. In his recent brief survey of Eastern European Jewish history, and again in a collection of essays on Jewish enlightenment, nationalism, and socialism, Israel Bartal assessed the Eastern European Jewish narrative as essentially fractured, fluctuating between dissent, controversy, and partial (limited) attempts at synthesis:

> The tension between tradition and innovation, insularity and openness, construction and demolition has continued to operate in Jewish society ever since the beginnings of the Jewish enlightenment.... The inner ambivalence, the Janus-faced turning both toward radical change and toward cultural self-preservation, found its way from Eastern Europe to the Land of Israel and is indelibly fixed at the heart of today's Israeli culture.[33]

The upshot here, as we see, is another parable, formulated with the fractious and fissured Israeli cultural and political scene in mind, and viewed as a natural continuation of the unmitigated divisiveness of Eastern European Jewish life.

In both the Israeli and the American versions, recapitulations of the Eastern European experience are seen as enabling, but they enable different things. In Israel, they enable the framing of critical questions, prompted by the politics of Jewish nationhood: questions that ask just what a modern Jewish collective might be, what a Jewish democracy entails, and in what sense (if at all) a Jewish social order might be greater than the sum of its parts.[34] For North American Jews, the Eastern European recapitulation enables a balancing act between minority self-esteem and individual autonomy. Israeli representations of Eastern European Jewish life can be viewed as a continuation of political discourse about legitimacy; American Jewish representations of Eastern European Jewry can be viewed as discourse concerning identity.

Notes

1. See Steven Zipperstein, "Underground Man: The Curious Case of Mark Zborowski and the Writing of a Modern Jewish Classic," *Jewish Review of Books* (Summer 2010); http://jewishreviewofbooks.com/articles/275/underground-man-the-curious-case-of-mark-zborowski-and-the-writing-of-a-modern-jewish-classic. See also Jan Schwarz, *Survivors and Exiles: Yiddish Culture after the Holocaust* (Detroit: Wayne State University Press, 2015).

2. Margaret Mead, foreword to *Life Is with People: The Jewish Little-Town of Eastern Europe*, by Mark Zborowski and Elizabeth Herzog (New York: International Universities Press, 1952), 19.

3. Lucy Dawidowicz, *The Golden Tradition: Jewish Life and Thought in Eastern Europe* (Syracuse: Syracuse University Press, 1996; originally published by Henry Holt and Co., 1967), 5–6.

4. Salo W. Baron, *The Russian Jew under Tsars and Soviets* (New York: Macmillan, 1964), xiv.

5. Leonard Schapiro, "Introduction," in *The Jews in Soviet Russia since 1917*, ed. Lionel Kochan (New York: Published for the Institute of Jewish Affairs by Oxford University Press, 1972), 4.

6. Moses Rischin, *The Promised City: New York's Jews 1870–1914* (New York: Harper and Row, 1970), 20.

7. On Jewish studies in post-Communist Eastern Europe see Zvi Gitelman, "The Phoenix? Jewish Studies in Post-Communist Europe," *Journal of Modern Jewish Studies* 10, no. 1 (March 2011): 65–69.

8. Steven Zipperstein, *Elusive Prophet: Ahad-Ha'am and the Sources of Zionism* (Hebrew) (Tel-Aviv: Am Oved, 1998); Gershon Hundert, *A Minor Redemption and a Little Bit of Honor: Jewish Society in Poland-Lithuania in the Eighteenth Century* (Hebrew) (Jerusalem: Merkaz Zalman Shazar, 2008); Michael Stanislawski, *A Murder in Lemberg: Politics, Religion, and Violence in Modern Jewish History* (Hebrew) (Jerusalem: Merkaz Zalman Shazar, 2010); Benjamin Nathans, *Beyond the Pale: The Jewish Encounter with Late Imperial Russia* (Hebrew) (Jerusalem: Merkaz Zalman Shazar, 2013); ChaeRan Freeze, *Marriage and Divorce in Jewish Society in the Russian Empire* (Hebrew) (Jerusalem: Merkaz Zalman Shazar, 2014).

9. On the relative dearth of published historical scholarship in the interwar years, especially publications that were accessible to Western readers, see the comment by Steven Zipperstein, *Imagining Russian Jewry: Memory, History, Identity* (Seattle: University of Washington Press, 1999), 93.

10. Samuel Joseph, *Jewish Immigration to the United States from 1881 to 1910* (New York: Columbia University Press, 1914).

11. Prince Demidoff San-Donato, *The Jewish Question in Russia*, trans. J. Michell (London: 1884).

12. Henry Morgenthau, *All in a Lifetime* (New York: 1922), 348–384 ("My Mission to Poland") and Appendix, 405–437 ("Report of the Mission of the United States to Poland"); Oscar I. Janowsky, *The Jews and Minority Rights 1898–1919* (New York: Columbia University Press, 1933); and *People At Bay: The Jewish Problem in East-Central Europe* (New York: Oxford University Press, 1938).

13. Louis Greenberg's first volume was his PhD dissertation at Yale, written under the supervision of the Russian (and Russian-trained) historian George Vernadsky, a research associate at Yale until his appointment as full professor in 1946. Greenberg was an ordained JTS rabbi, class of '26. Born in Russia in 1894 (Novy Konstantinov in Ukraine), he had a traditional education before immigrating to the United States in 1913. He earned his PhD in 1940 while serving as rabbi in New Haven's B'nai Jacob congregation (1928–46). He died in 1946. See *American Jewish Year Book* 48 (1946–7), 490; and Pamela S. Nadel with Marc Lee Raphael, *Conservative Judaism in America: A Biographical Dictionary and Sourcebook* (Westport, CT: Greenwood Press, 1988), 118–19.

14. Baron, *Russian Jew*.

15. "Prefatory Letter," July 1949, in *The Jews: Their History, Culture, and Religion*, ed. Louis Finkelstein (Philadelphia: Jewish Publication Society of America, third edition, 1966), vol. 1, xvi.

16. Finkelstein, ibid., third ed., vol. 2, 1803–1811.

17. Bernard D. Weinryb, "East European Jewry since the Polish Partitions," in Finkelstein, ed., *The Jews*, 3rd ed., vol. 1, 322.

18. Isaac Levitats, *The Jewish Community in Russia, 1772–1844* (New York: Columbia University Press, 1943).

19. See, e.g., Bernard D. Weinryb, "Jewish Immigration and Accommodation to America," in *The Jews: Social Patterns of an American Social Group*, ed. Marshall Sklare (New York: The Free Press and Collier-Macmillan, 1958), 15–16; Nathan Glazer, *American Judaism* (Chicago: University of Chicago Press, 1957, 1968), 60–65; Rischin, *Promised City*, 19–47.

20. George J. Lerski and Halina T. Lerski (comp.), *Jewish-Polish Coexistence, 1772–1939: A Topical Bibliography*, with a foreword by Lucjan Dobroszycki (New York: Greenwood Press, 1986).

21. Cecile Esther Kunitz, *YIVO and the Making of Modern Jewish Culture: Scholarship for the Yiddish Nation* (New York: Cambridge University Press, 2014), esp. 181–95.

22. See Anita Norich, "On the Yiddish Question," in *Mapping Jewish Identities*, ed. Laurence J. Silberstein (New York: New York University Press, 2000), 147–58; David G. Roskies, "A Hebrew-Yiddish Utopia in Montreal: Ideology in Bilingual Education," first published in *Bilingual Education: Focusschrift in Honor of Joshua A. Fishman on the Occasion of His 65th Birthday*, vol. 1, ed. Ofelia Garcia (Amsterdam: John Benjamins, 1991), 151–62; see also Ruth R. Wisse, "A Golus Education," *Moment*, vol. 2, no. 4 (1977): 26–28, 62.

23. Anita Norich, "On the Yiddish Question," in *Mapping Jewish Identities*, ed. Laurence J. Silberstein (New York: New York University Press, 2000), 147–48.

24. Apart from Yiddish and Eastern European studies, the gallery of such scholars in the refugee generation (or those born to refugee parents) would include the historians

George Mosse, Peter Gay, Selma Stern, Ismar Schorsch, Michael A. Meyer, Henry L. Feingold, Jehuda Reinharz, Marion Kaplan, Michael Stanislawski, David Engel, Samuel Kassow, Jack Wertheimer, Steven Lowenstein, Marsha Rozenblit, and Robert Lieberles; in religion, philosophy, and theology: Nachum N. Glatzer, Abraham Joshua and Susannah Heschel (father and daughter, although the younger Heschel's interests span feminist and Christian theological issues as well as Jewish ones per se), Jakob Petuchowski, Michael Wyschogrod, and David Weiss-Halivni; the pioneers of Holocaust research in America: Philip Friedman, Isaiah Trunk, Jacob Robinson, and Raul Hilberg; in Jewish economic history, Arcadius Kahan; and in librarianship, the near-legendary Dina Abramowicz, librarian of the YIVO Institute for Jewish Research. From 1945 to 1965, the number of American universities (not including Jewish theological colleges) that offered Jewish Studies courses at either undergraduate or graduate levels expanded sevenfold. Arnold J. Band, "Jewish Studies in American Liberal-Arts Colleges and Universities," *American Jewish Year Book,* vol. 67 (1966): 3–30.

25. Shaye J. D. Cohen and Edward L. Greenstein, eds., *The State of Jewish Studies* (Detroit: Wayne State University Press, published for the Jewish Theological Seminary of America, 1990), 13.

26. Avraham (Alfred Abraham) Greenbaum was born in Germany and emigrated with his family to the United States during World War II, where they settled in the Boston area. He graduated Harvard University and received a PhD from Brandeis University in Judaic Studies. In 1960, Greenbaum moved with his family to Detroit, Michigan, where he worked as an academic librarian at Wayne State University. In 1968, the family immigrated to Israel, and Greenbaum taught for over twenty years at the University of Haifa. Greenbaum wrote or edited about twelve books and many articles. Most of his research centered on various aspects of the history of Soviet Jewry.

27. Mark Friedman, "American Scholarship on East European Jewry" (*Response,* no. 37: Summer 1979), 41–49.

28. As of the late 1970s, we could add a fourth cohort. Indeed, most of the contributors to the present volume, the present author included, are younger products of the immigrant milieu peopled by veterans of Eastern European Jewish scholarship: the historians David Engel, David Fishman (third-generation), Gershon Hundert, Samuel Kassow, Moshe (Murray) Rosman, Marsha Rozenblit (whose work includes research on the eastern reaches of the Habsburg Empire), Nancy Sinkoff, Michael Stanislawski, and Steven Zipperstein; and among literary scholars, Anita Norich.

29. Scott Ury, "Lost and Found? Jewish Historians, Jewish History, and Narrativization of Order in East European Cities," *AJS Review,* 41: 1 (2017), 9–36.

30. As of 2012 data, 73.5% of Israeli Jews are native-born, but 41% have non-native parents. Israel Central Bureau of Statistics, 2013 *Annual Report,* Table 2.6 (http://www.cbs.gov.il/shnaton64/st02_06x.pdf).

31. Gershon David Hundert, *Jews in Poland-Lithuania in the Eighteenth Century: A Genealogy of Modernity* (Berkeley and Los Angeles: University of California Press, 2004), 234.

32. Kenneth B. Moss, *Jewish Renaissance in the Russian Revolution* (Cambridge: Harvard University Press, 2009), 296.

33. Israel Bartal, *Letaken 'am: neorut uleumiyut bemizrach eiropah* (Jerusalem: Carmel, 2013), 7, 19; cf.; and *The Jews of Eastern Europe, 1772–1881* (Philadelphia: University of Pennsylvania Press, 2005), 12.

34. See, e.g., Israel Bartal, "The Lost Community: Jewish Identity and Social Anchor," (Hebrew) in *Who Is a Jew in Our Day?* (Hebrew), ed. Maya Leibovitch, David Ariel-Joel, and Motti Inbari (Tel-Aviv: Miskal-Yedioth Ahronoth Books, 2006), 131, 138; Mordechai Zalkin, "Tradition, Enlightenment and Democracy in East European Jewish Society, the 19th Century" (Hebrew), in *In the Democratic Way: On the Historical Sources of the Israeli Democracy* (Hebrew), ed. Allon Gal, Gershon Bacon, Moshe Lissak, Pnina Morag-Talmon (Sede Boqer: The Ben-Gurion Research Institute for the Study of Israel and Zionism, Ben-Gurion University of the Negev, 2012), 141; and Gershon Bacon, "Nalewki Street in Tel-Aviv? On the Political Heritage of East European Jewry in the Yishuv and the State of Israel" (Hebrew), in *In the Democratic Way*, 153–68.

"One of the Greatest Martyrologies"
THE BLACK BOOK OF POLISH JEWRY AND THE BEGINNINGS OF HOLOCAUST MEMORY IN THE UNITED STATES

David Slucki

WHEN *The Black Book of Polish Jewry* was published by the American Federation of Polish Jews in December 1943, the vast majority of Polish Jews had already been murdered. With the killings continuing for over another year, including the deportation and murder of around half a million Hungarian Jews, the book was necessarily limited as a source of information on the Nazi extermination of European Jewry. Moreover, its weaknesses—its strict focus on Polish Jewry, and lack of detail about the death camps and the *Einsatzgruppen*—meant that even when it was released it did not reflect the most up-to-date information on the situation in Europe. It was among the many publications that came out during the hectic war years, when information traveled mainly through underground smugglers, and when sources were difficult to verify in a continent that was largely closed to the western world. For historians, it is of limited value as a way to shed light on the destruction of Europe's Jews, particularly in light of the mountains of literature and research produced in the decades since.

Still, the *Black Book* provides chilling accounts of conditions in the ghettos, operations at the death camp at Treblinka, and atrocities committed by mobile killing squads in Eastern Poland and the Soviet Union. It offers an overall picture of Jewish suffering that is shockingly graphic. Moreover, its appearance in December 1943 represents perhaps the earliest attempt to synthesize the experiences of Polish Jews under Nazi occupation into a single volume with a cohesive narrative. In this biography of the

Black Book project, I trace its development and the reaction to it, arguing that despite its methodological problems and its lack of immediate political impact, the *Black Book* is a forerunner to American Jewish remembrances of the events that would come to be known as the Holocaust. It is perhaps the earliest comprehensive published account of Nazi atrocities against Jews in Poland, and in its approach and format, it foreshadowed later developments in Jewish Holocaust memorialization. In particular, it prefigures the more widely known *Black Book of Soviet Jewry* as well as the hundreds of *yizker-bikher* (memorial books) that share aspects of the *Black Book*'s form and content. Its memorial function distinguished it in its era, as an early indication that Polish Jews, at least those outside Europe, understood as early as 1942 that their world had been utterly crushed, and would no longer be the dominant force in global Jewish culture.

Thus far, the book has been of little interest to historians. It has rarely been cited, and until recently has not even been analyzed for its historiographical value.[1] I argue that *The Black Book of Polish Jewry* is important not only because it was, at that time, the most extensive single volume documenting Nazi atrocities, but also because it serves as an early example of Holocaust memorialization from survivors in the United States and abroad, with the printed word a central component of the emerging memorial culture. Holocaust memory in the United States can partly find its roots in this text, which imagines the victims of Nazi persecution as martyrs, and carves out a special place for those who took to armed struggle against their oppressors.

Further, by focusing specifically on one national group of Jews, the *Black Book* foreshadowed central aspects of the postwar discourse among Jewish refugees and migrants about the Holocaust, casting it as a particularly Polish Jewish tragedy. The book is an early meditation on the question of whether the Jewish persecution during World War II was a singular, connected event, or whether Jews from different places experienced Nazi persecution in substantively different ways. As a single volume, it does what the many pamphlets and newspaper reports could not, formulating an overarching narrative for what would, decades later, come to be known as the Holocaust. As part of this process, the *Black Book* explicitly crafts the first metanarrative of the Holocaust, one that privileges the local over the universal suffering of Europe's Jews. On the one hand, it suggests complexity—the Holocaust experience depended to a large extent on geography. On the other hand, it offers an interpretation that is totalizing and that suggests the suffering of Polish Jews supersedes in importance the targeting of other European Jews. It is a prelude to the kinds of hierarchies of victimhood that emerged among survivors—in this case, the experiences of Polish Jews and the destruction of Polish Jewish civilization serves as the most significant part of the story. By focusing on this particular story, the book reflects later developments among survivors in the United States and abroad. Just as the Holocaust did not constitute a singular experience, so were survivors divided along many different lines, including country and city of origin, wartime experience, ideology, and resettlement location.

Compiling the Black Book

The *Black Book* began its life as an initiative of the American Friends of Polish Jews, an organization established in 1941 and led by Zelig Tygel. Tygel, a native of Warsaw, had been in the United States since 1920, where he developed a profile in the American Jewish press (in Yiddish and English), as well as gaining prominence among Polish-Jewish organizations in the United States, including the American Council for Warsaw Jews and the American Federation for Polish Jews.[2] The New York-based American Friends was not a representative body, registering only five hundred members in two branches, nor was its purpose to foster Polish-Jewish cultural life in the United States. Rather, the organization saw itself as playing a political role, negotiating with the American administration and Polish government-in-exile on behalf of the Jews in Poland and Polish-Jewish refugees.[3] Among many other Jewish organizations, it lobbied the Roosevelt administration, particularly the War Refugee Board, established in 1944, to rescue the remaining Jews of Poland.[4] One of its early tasks was to publish an English-language volume that would shed light on Nazi atrocities in Eastern Europe, and put pressure on the American administration to intervene against German aggression on behalf of Polish Jewry. In correspondence from January 1942, Zelig Tygel, Executive Vice President of the American Friends of Polish Jews, had already indicated that his organization would be publishing a six hundred-page account of Nazi atrocities against the Jews in Poland.[5] When the organization publically announced they would be putting the book together, their prospectus promised that it would cover 450 cities, towns, and villages, drawing on a range of different source materials, and providing graphic details of the slaughter and expulsion of Poland's Jews. The aim of the book was "to bring to the attention of the world the black record of Jewish martyrdom in Poland in all its stark and naked horror."[6] Its advisory board was made up of the central leaders among Polish Jewish organizations, including Tygel and Joseph Tenenbaum, who was also President of the American Federation of Polish Jews; it included Jewish cultural and intellectual figures Julian Tuwim, Jacob Glatstein, Maurice Samuel, and Arthur Szyk. Among its sponsors were significant figures in the American literary and journalistic world, such as Thomas Mann, Herbert Agar, and Louis Adamic.

In April 1942, the Jewish Telegraphic Agency confirmed publically for the first time that the *Black Book*, carrying "documentary material on the atrocities perpetrated by the Nazis upon the Jews in occupied Poland," would "soon" be published by the American Friends.[7] Even though Operation Reinhard was still in its early months, and the killing machines were not yet operating at the intensity they would adopt later in 1942, the leadership of Polish Jewish émigré organizations like the American Friends of Polish Jews recognized the existential danger facing their *landsleit*. They possessed information on the ghettoization of Polish Jews and the mobile killing squads in the east that they understood needed to be publicized to a broader American audience.

The urgency of this task was clear. At that stage, information about the Jews' plight was not yet widely publicized, nor had there been any concrete details disseminated about the Nazi Final Solution. By the middle of 1942, after the American Friends of Polish Jews had signaled their intent to publish a chronicle of the Jews' victimization, news of the Nazi slaughter of Jews was well established within the Jewish world.[8] At the same time, the mainstream American press was carrying reports of anti-Jewish violence. The *New York Times* reported in mid-June on the massacre of sixty thousand Jews in Vilna, and by the end of June, it carried reports passed on from an underground courier of the Jewish Labor Bund revealing that Polish Jews were being murdered on a large scale in mobile gas vans. The reports estimated that up to seven hundred thousand Polish Jews were among the one million European Jews who had been murdered.[9] By

August 1942, Rabbi Stephen Wise, president of the World Jewish Congress, had received information that the Nazi leadership was planning the extermination of Europe's Jews using prussic acid.[10] This news was confirmed by the State Department within months.[11] It was without question that by late 1942 the Jews were slated for extermination and the process was well underway. When the American Friends identified the urgency of publishing the information they had received, though, there was little public attention being paid to the Jews' suffering.

Ultimately, the American Friends of Polish Jews would not publish the *Black Book*, instead producing an English-language volume in 1944 on the destruction of Warsaw Jewry: the translation of a diary from a Polish official working in the Warsaw ghetto.[12] It is not clear when or why the task of publishing the book fell to the American Federation of Polish Jews, but there does seem to be some overlap between the leadership of the two organizations, including Tygel. It may be these ties that led to Tygel handing over the reins of the project to the Federation's leadership. There may also have been a distinction between the aims of the two organizations. The Federation was larger, with ties to the scores of hundreds of *landsmanshaftn* in the United States. The Friends, by contrast, was a much smaller organization, with only several hundred members, and its aims were to assist with the settlement of Polish Jews in the United States and to provide relief activities

As early as March 1942, the Federation had established its own Black Book committee at the insistence of Jacob Apenszlak, a former editor of the Polish-Jewish newspaper *Nasz Przegląd*.[13] Apenszlak had by then distinguished himself as a leading Polish-language journalist and editor in Poland. After his migration to the United States in 1939, he established the Polish-language Jewish bi-weekly *Nasza Trybuna*. Before he died in 1950, Apenszlak had served the Federation, as well as the Institute for Jewish Affairs of the World Jewish Congress and the Jewish Agency for Palestine, and he also worked as part of the Israeli delegation to the United Nations.[14] The Federation was very different from American Friends, established in the first decade of the century to coordinate the activities of the many *landsmanshaftn*. It was by no means a major and influential organization like the JDC, the Jewish Labor Committee, or the American Jewish Committee—but it did, as Polish sociologist Andrzej Kapiszewski argued, play an important role in publicizing Nazi atrocities to a broader American audience, partly through its publications.[15] Although it claimed a membership of around 65,000 in 1943, the likelihood is that it was much smaller and did not play as authoritative a role among the *landsmanshaftn* as it claimed.[16] Still, in the middle years of the war, its central focus became raising awareness about the plight of Polish Jewry, and then later it shifted attention to relief and rehabilitation.

Once the Federation took responsibility for the book, the editors revised its aims, acknowledging that it was arriving as the momentum had shifted in favor of the Allies, and recognizing the fact that the majority of Polish Jews had already been killed. The book would no longer be a means to pressure Western governments to act against Germany, but would provide evidence against Germany once the war had concluded. A report on the Federation's activities stated that the book would serve as "a basis for the charge against Germany to be presented at the Peace Conference," and would also fulfill a memorial function, commemorating the destruction of the Jewish civilization that had been dismantled by Nazi Germany.[17] This signaled a major and necessary shift from the initial goal of alerting the world to the destruction of Polish Jews, which by then was a fact well known among western governments. These shifting goals—with the focus now on the importance of the volume for the postwar period—conceded the reality that Polish Jewry had no hope for survival. This explains the inclusion of a historical overview of the world that was lost, not part of the initial prospectus of the project released by the American Friends of Polish Jews, but perhaps the most critically important aspect of the volume for present-day readers to understand.

Publishing the Black Book

For contemporary readers, the book might seem unremarkable in light of the subsequent body of literature on the Nazi extermination of European Jews. The *Black Book* describes, in a systematic way, the isolation, starvation, deportation, and ultimate extermination of the Jewish communities of Poland. It covers smaller towns like Wieruszów (near Łódz), and Włocławek (near Warsaw), as well as the major centers of Jewish life, with a special emphasis on Warsaw, Łódz, Kraków, Lublin, and Vilna. It also devotes special chapters to the killing operations at Treblinka, and to the Warsaw Ghetto Uprising, with several chapters focused on various aspects of the Nazi extermination of the Jews, including legal and economic discrimination, the undermining of communities and religion, and the various ways in which Jews were targeted for physical extermination. The editors' approach shifts between a chronological, geographic, and thematic account of the Nazi persecution of Polish Jewry. In some ways the book is surprisingly comprehensive—it details living conditions in dozens of ghettos, small and large, throughout Poland. In other ways it is terribly inadequate. For example, the murderous rampage of the *Einsatzgruppen* is outlined in only a few pages. Auschwitz, although mentioned by its Polish name, Oświęcim, is not clearly shown to be a factory of death.

The Black Book of Polish Jewry is written in English, with all the documentation and eye-witness accounts translated from German, Polish, and Yiddish. It is divided into two main sections: one that gives an account of Nazi atrocities against Polish Jews and another, much shorter, section that documents different aspects of the Polish-Jewish world that was destroyed. The first section begins chronologically, documenting the Nazi invasion of Poland before shifting to an account of a number of the major ghettos that were established. A chapter is devoted to the killing operations at Treblinka. It then takes a thematic turn, looking at a number of different aspects of the destruction process in turn, before finishing with the reprinting of documents, principally from the Warsaw Ghetto. The second section consists of descriptions of Jewish economic and cultural life, as well as profiles of Jewish leaders and personalities. A section in the middle is devoted to images, particularly ones depicting ghetto life in Warsaw. A number of Nazi decrees are reproduced, and the book contains a map of Poland, indicating both the political boundaries of the country on the eve of the war and its present state under Nazi occupation. The book's sponsors included prominent figures in American and Jewish public life, such as Eleanor Roosevelt, Fiorello La Guardia, Albert Einstein, and Salo Baron.

The volume draws on a wide array of sources, including reports from the Polish underground, eyewitness accounts and affidavits from those that managed to escape, press reports from within Nazi-occupied Poland, and Nazi decrees smuggled out of the Warsaw Ghetto and reproduced in the book. The portrait that the editors manage to paint, then, is comprehensive and devastating. In a time when details of the Nazis' genocidal program were not freely available, and could only be ascertained through reports and information smuggled out by members of the underground, the level of detail contained in the *Black Book*'s account is an impressive feat, especially considering the relative speed of its compilation, translation, and publication.

The book highlights for contemporary readers what the world did know at the time. For example, there is a very strong focus on the early months of occupation and on ghettoization. With the exception of a chapter on Treblinka, though, very little is written on the topic of the death camps. As historian Michael Fleming has observed, although the *Black Book* refers to a camp at Oświęcim ten times, it fails to construct a cohesive narrative of what was taking place there and to give a strong indication that it was, in fact, a death factory.[18] The text focuses particularly on conditions and events in the Warsaw Ghetto, understandably, given the sheer number of Jews concentrated there. The authors barely cover the atrocities in the East, devoting only a couple of pages to the topic. Nor is there a huge focus on Jewish armed resistance, which may surprise contemporary readers, given the degree to which those who participated in such activities were lionized during the war. The book's compilers either did not know enough about other aspects of the situation in Europe to commit them to paper, or they were prioritizing certain experiences. One factor here might have concerned the strength of what they could and could not corroborate. As the editors were committed to verifying the accuracy of the information presented, they may not have wanted to include materials for which they could not provide sufficient evidence.

The book's tone is matter-of-fact and analytical. Aside from the foreword, the editors clearly made the decision to present the information without embellishment. In the main chapters, those that detail Nazi attempts to exterminate Polish Jews, there is little editorializing. The editors simply lay out the evidence that they have compiled, including tables full of statistics, photographs smuggled out of Europe, and maps of the ghettos that they could reconstruct. The materials needed to be presented in a scientific manner, using the tools available to scientists and demographers to assess the number of deaths and their causes. Even in describing the Warsaw Ghetto Uprising, which in later accounts would take on mythic and heroic qualities, the summation reads like a newspaper report: "A Jewish fighting organization led the defense in the Ghetto. Their forces were small, they did not have much ammunition. Nevertheless they fought for four weeks in this tragic struggle."[19] This was in marked contrast to later descriptions of Jewish armed resistance, with their rhetorical flourishes and heroic symbolism.

The sense of urgency is there, if only in how shocking and incomprehensible the narrated events are. The report on the Treblinka death camp not only details the physical layout of the camp, but also the hierarchical structure within and the logistics of the killing process. A passage describing the herding of prisoners into the gas chambers shows the authors' despair, but maintains a restrained tone:

> Now comes the last act of the Treblinka tragedy. The terrorized mass of men, women and children starts on its last road to death.... The cries and laments of the women together with the shouts and curses of the Germans interrupt the silence of the forest. The people finally realize that they are going to their death. At the entrance of death-house No. 1 the chief himself stands, a whip in hand; beating them in cold blood, he drives the women into the chambers.... When the execution chambers are filled the doors are hermetically closed and the slow suffocation of the living people begins, brought about by the steam issuing from the numerous vents in the pipes. At the beginning, stifled cries penetrate to the outside; gradually they quiet down and 15 minutes later the execution is complete.[20]

This passage highlights the attempt to present an unvarnished truth. The approach to describing the Nazi crimes had to be objective and scientific. To this end, there is a big emphasis on statistics and facts, as a way to present the case as unassailable, and to prove that the book's editors had considered the issue from all angles. Some examples of the kinds of statistics the editors focused on include the amount of rations Jews received, the numbers of people killed in particular towns, and mortality rates in the period prior to the Holocaust. By systematically describing the process of destruction, the authors mirror and highlight the Nazis' methodical approach, foreshadowing future trials in which prosecutors forged a legal path toward proving the truth of Nazi atrocities against Jews.[21]

Reviews of the book were, for the most part, favorable. Most reviewers agreed it was an important historical document that would be valuable for publicizing what had happened in Europe, and for serving as a basis for postwar trials of the Nazi perpetrators. In June 1944, the sociologist and historian Aryeh Tartakower, writing in the journal *The Reconstructionist*, argued that the *Black Book* filled a vacuum in writing about the destruction of the Jews of Poland and its meaning for world Jewry. "It is a great and tragic document," he wrote. "Let us hope that this book will reach not only libraries and research institutions, but also all those for whom justice and humanity are more than words and who may understand their duties as human beings at the present moment."[22] Tartakower was a communal leader in the Polish-Jewish intellectual world, serving as director of the World Jewish Congress Department of Relief and Rehabilitation during this period.[23] In his role with the World Jewish Congress, and with his experience and understanding of Polish-Jewish issues, he especially recognized the emergency facing Polish Jewry.

In the *Contemporary Jewish Record*, Alfred Werner wrote that the book was of great historical value, and he was particularly moved by the stories out of the Warsaw Ghetto. Its *Judenrat* leaders, he wrote, made "superhuman efforts" on behalf of the ghetto inhabitants, and the memory of the Warsaw Ghetto Uprising would "never die". He lamented, though, that the section documenting the history and richness of Polish Jewry was far too short, as no comprehensive account existed in English. This was certainly recognition that a civilization had been destroyed and needed to be documented.[24]

Beyond the Jewish press, Walter Bara wrote in the *New York Times* that "long after the end of active hostilities this book will serve as a perennial testimonial of barbarity."[25] He wrote particularly of the significance that the destruction of Europe's Jews held for Americans, claiming that the *Black Book* would help to counteract any spread of antisemitism in the United States. Perhaps even more significant and far-reaching than a favorable review in the *New York Times* was the reaction of Eleanor Roosevelt, who was clearly moved by its contents. In her nationally-syndicated newspaper column "My Day," in June 1944—a full six months after the book first appeared—she wrote that she hoped many people would see the book and share in her feelings of shame that people could treat others which such brutality.[26] The first lady had already publicly expressed her concern about the persecution of the Jews. This was especially noteworthy as her husband's response to news of Nazi brutality was more muted. She had written about the Jews' plight a number of times in her column, including on April 14, after attending a performance in Washington of the pageant *We Will Never Die*, written by screenwriter and journalist Ben Hecht, highlighting the Nazi persecution of European Jews.[27] Several months later, on August 13, 1943, she devoted her whole column to expressing her dismay at the situation Jews faced in Europe.[28] Having written previously about the matter, and with her name attached to the project as a sponsor, the use of her daily column to publicize the *Black Book* must certainly have given it wider exposure.[29]

As well as gaining prominence within the United States, the *Black Book* was also transported to an international audience, although it is difficult to measure its reach. *The Palestine Post*, for example, announced the *Black Book*'s publication in February 1944, and a review appeared toward the end of the year. The reviewer wrote, "Whoever has any doubts about the Nazi policy of extermination and the method applied to this end must read this book and will be convinced."[30] Even as far away as Australia, the *Sydney Morning Herald* selected the *Black Book* as its book of the week, arguing that it was the "story of a human tragedy that has probably never been exceeded since the days of Genghiz [sic.] Khan or Timur the Lame." The reviewer espoused the volume's importance as a "powerful and unassailable accusation against the Nazi-fascist ruling gangsters of Europe and their hirelings."[31] In another international endorsement of the book's power, the Russian Marxist émigré Victor Serge described the details outlined in the *Black Book* as "horrifying." "It is beyond imagination," he wrote, "lucidity falters. Hard to think straight."[32] It is not clear whether or not there was any international reaction to the book beyond a few lone reviewers. Nonetheless, the fact that the *Black Book* was reviewed in the major English-language newspaper in Palestine, and particularly that it reached the major daily broadsheet newspaper in a relatively remote location like Sydney, suggests that by the middle of 1944, news out of

Nazi-occupied Europe had reached the world, in some part thanks to the publications and activities of organizations like the American Federation of Polish Jews.

In contrast to those commendations, prominent Jewish historian Raphael Mahler wrote a scathing critique in *Jewish Social Studies*. His complaints were manifold. First, he argued, the *Black Book*'s narrow focus on only one section of European Jewry was extremely problematic, and it undermined the editors' aims to serve as a source of information to the world about Nazi crimes. "The council of nations," Mahler wrote, "is far more likely to pay attention to a single cumulative indictment than to a multiplicity of local reports."[33] Moreover, the methodology and analysis were "careless and slipshod," with the editors relying on underground reports and failing to incorporate the mass of materials that had been compiled in the Soviet Union. In his view, the volume paid far too little attention to the atrocities on the eastern front.[34] Mahler also highlighted a series of inaccuracies and contradictions within the text, and finally dismissed the section on the history of Polish Jewry, claiming that the authors idealized and misrepresented that history. Such a project, he concluded, was "far too serious a task to be discharged in this utterly inadequate fashion."[35] Mahler was a distinguished professional historian, which may help explain why he, unique among most other reviewers, was concerned specifically with the book's methodology. His understanding of the craft of writing and communicating historical and sociological research most likely led to his skepticism. It was of paramount importance to get the facts right.

It is difficult to argue with Mahler's critique that the book was hastily compiled, left huge gaps, and therefore proved problematic as a de facto legal charge against Nazi Germany. The inadequacy of the book as a historical record is even more apparent in light of what followed the book's publication—particularly the deportation and mass murder of Hungarian Jews—and in light of the enormous volume of research that has been carried out on that period since. As an authoritative source, the *Black Book* was rapidly succeeded by other published accounts, not to mention the frighteningly large record of atrocities compiled across Europe in the years following the war. These accounts included other black books, notably *The Black Book: The Nazi Crime against the Jewish People*, an account published in the United States in 1946 by the Jewish Black Book Committee and based on materials collected by Russian-Jewish journalists Ilya Ehrenburg and Vassily Grossman.[36] There were memoirs, particularly in Yiddish, documenting life under Nazi occupation, with special emphasis on Jewish military resistance.[37] There were also the accounts collected by Jewish Historical Commissions throughout Europe, staffed mainly by amateur survivor historians, who worked to compile a comprehensive record of Nazi atrocities.[38] The Nuremberg Tribunals and other postwar trials also made a major contribution to the historical record of German crimes against Jews.[39]

The *Black Book* was certainly not a complete or definitive account, nor was it entirely accurate, a fact acknowledged by Apenszlak in his introduction, where he states that, at the time the book was compiled, the truth could only be partially known.

At the time though, Mahler's disparagement seems to have been an isolated voice of criticism. The positive response shows that despite its deficits, the *Black Book* was considered to make a resoundingly effective case against Nazi Germany, organizing scattered pieces of information into a coherent narrative for the first time. Readers reacting to the book typically expressed their shock at the materials presented, and encouraged others to absorb the almost unbelievable story within its pages. It is unlikely that the book had any concrete impact on lawmakers, the US administration, or the international community. Still, it marks an earnest attempt to provide the basis for international action, postwar justice, and a memorial culture that would keep the legacy of the Jewish victims alive into the future.

The Black Book as a Memorial Site

In general, the response to the book focused on its importance as evidence against Nazi Germany, particularly as a support for the prosecution in postwar trials. The reviews mostly didn't mention its other, ultimately more enduring function: to serve as a memorial for a society that had been destroyed, for the millions of Jews who embodied the creativity, energy, and complexities of that one-thousand-year old civilization. Perhaps those reviewers could not yet appreciate this aspect of the book, with the war still raging and Jews still dying in the hundreds of thousands. Still, the *Black Book* marks the earliest manifestation of two genres in postwar Jewish writing and publishing: general histories of the Holocaust and *yizker-bikher*. It constitutes the first attempt to provide a general history of what, decades later, would popularly come to be known as the Holocaust. It takes a scholarly approach and crafts an overarching narrative. It is a precursor to some of the earliest English-language literature that seeks to document the Holocaust, including the much more well-known *Black Book of Russian Jewry*, published in 1946, and other black books that followed.[40]

Perhaps more significantly, the *Black Book* also echoed the now-canonical *yizker-bikher* (memorial books) recording the history of Eastern European Jewish communities that were destroyed, as well as telling the story of their destruction. These *yizker-bikher*, published in the hundreds by *landsmanshaftn* in the decades after the war, gave a snapshot of Jewish life in the cities and towns throughout Eastern Europe and provided an account of Jewish life under Nazi occupation. Published predominantly in Israel, the United States, and Argentina, the *yizker-bikher* themselves became sites of mourning—places where survivors could, through histories, vignettes, drawings, and images, revisit the world that was lost to them, as is discussed in the essay in this volume by Eliyana Adler. They could also, through these books, learn about the fate of their families and loved ones. Ethnographers Jonathan Boyarin and Jack Kugelmass described *yizker-bikher* as "the single most important act of commemorating the dead on the part of Jewish survivors."[41]

The *yizker-bikher* were different in many ways from the enormous body of general histories that would later appear, not least because they were predominantly written in Yiddish and Hebrew, and were more likely to be published in Tel Aviv than in New York. Moreover, given their place and language of publication, the *yizker-bikher* were designed for a very specific audience—Jewish, Eastern European, and with ties to a specific town. The audience for a particular *yizker-bukh*, especially one from a small town, was not very large. *Yizker-bikher* were also a "grassroots enterprise," as Rosemary Horowitz has shown, with a single volume including up to one hundred participants, perhaps more. They tended to be intimate and personal, commemorating the lives of individuals that lived in certain towns, as well as the communities that were lost.[42] The *Black Book of Polish*

Jewry, on the other hand, was designed primarily for a broader, non-Jewish audience, with the aim of pressuring Allied governments to save European Jews. At the time it was written, it was not yet even clear if there would still be a Polish-Jewish constituency to read such a text at the war's finish. Moreover, unlike the grassroots approach of the *yizker-bikher*, the volume was very much prepared by the leadership (at least, the self-proclaimed leadership) of Polish Jewry in the United States.

Still, there are strong parallels that we can draw in terms of form and intent. For example, just as the writers of *yizker-bikher* idealize their hometowns, depicting them as a kind of "paradise," so too does the *Black Book* paint a somewhat romanticized picture of Polish Jewry.[43] As Raphael Mahler complained, the editors of the *Black Book* went to great lengths to idealize the political and economic situation in which Polish Jews lived. More importantly, though, if we read the *Black Book* as one prototype for the *yizker-bikher* (although it is not the only one), we begin to appreciate much more closely the function it served as a memorial site to mourn the loss of Polish Jewish civilization.[44] The *Black Book* is perhaps the earliest work of Holocaust literature that accounts for both the richness of Polish-Jewish civilization and its ultimate demise.[45]

The *Black Book* should not, though, be read only as a precursor to the *yizker-bikher* that would come later. It must also be read as part of a much longer tradition of memorializing Jewish suffering through the written word. This book was just the latest in the genre of writing Jewish history and memory that dates back long before World War Two. This context seems not to have been lost on the book's editor, Jacob Apenszlak. In his foreword, Apenszlak describes the Jews' plight as "one of the greatest martyrologies of modern times."[46] The idea that the *Black Book* is a martyrology is crucial to understanding both the book's purpose and the extent to which the editors and compilers imagined its significance and sanctity. By describing it in this way, Apenszlak was indicating to the reader that this book fits into a history of Jewish martyrdom that stretches all the way back to the Second Temple period and the martyrdom recorded in 2 Maccabees, a book celebrated by both Jews and early Christians.[47] Even more than simply suggesting that the victims of Nazism were martyrs, Apenszlak may have been placing the book in a long written tradition in which Jews chronicled and lamented their own suffering since medieval times, when Jewish victims of the Crusades chronicled the anti-Jewish violence that they endured as the Crusaders swept across Europe towards the Middle East.[48]

This martyrological framework indicates to the reader immediately that this book serves multiple purposes for different audiences. For the world, it is a record that proves, beyond doubt, the guilt of the Nazis in their attempts to exterminate the Jews. For Jewish audiences, though, particularly American Jewish audiences, for whom English was by now the mother tongue, this book was itself a memorial site, a place for American Jews to project their grief for the families and communities they had left only a generation or two earlier. Further, by placing the book within this tradition, Apenszlak signals that the annihilation of Polish Jewry is the modern manifestation of the broader history of Jewish persecution that was by then burned into Jewish memory. Indeed, the Federation's leadership believed that "as a memorial of the greatest martyrdom in Jewish history," the *Black Book* "ought to be distributed in every Jewish house to take its place with the traditional lamentations over the Destruction of the Temple and the persecutions and massacres throughout Jewish history."[49] In this way, the book also constructed the European Jewish experience as the latest episode in a long history of Jewish persecution—another destruction of the Temple, a more recent Crusade, the culmination of centuries of anti-Jewish hatred. This reflected the view of the traditional community that the Holocaust was not necessarily unique in Jewish history, but part of the Jews' historical plight dating back thousands of years.

Within the context of this memorial function, the *Black Book* aimed to construct a specific narrative, with Polish Jews at the center of the Nazi extermination program. In his review of the book, Raphael Mahler highlighted this as particularly problematic. He argued that by focusing on Polish Jews, the book was not as useful as it might have been had it conceived of the Holocaust more broadly. This focus was most likely a conscious decision on the part of the compilers. Although the book appeared before the liquidation of Hungarian Jewry in 1944, it was compiled with detailed knowledge of how extensively European Jewry was targeted. Still, rather than putting together a Black Book of European Jews, the American Federation and its leadership chose to limit it to Polish Jewry.

As editor, Apenszlak was making a clear claim for the particularity of the Polish-Jewish experience during the war, and also for the historic centrality of that civilization in the Jewish world. This was consistent with his vision of a Jewish Polishness, characterized by a strong attachment to Polish soil that informed the Jews' sense of identity and self-worth. For Apenszlak, Polish Jewry was a distinct national grouping that was culturally, historically, and linguistically different from Jews in other European countries.[50] Indeed, the text supports this vision. In his foreword, Apenszlak suggests that he restricted the book to the area of Poland because it was chosen by the Nazis as the "central slaughter-house for all Jews".[51] Yet what is more revealing is that in introducing the history of Polish Jews, the authors emphasized the Jews' connection to Polish soil and to the Polish people. In their collective narrative, Polish Jewry formed a distinct entity, a symbiosis of Polish and Jewish cultures and traditions. Although many nations had risen and fallen since Jews first settled in Poland, Polish Jews "remained a distinct people, true to their faith and their adopted home".[52] Here, Apenszlak suggests not only that Polish Jewry was a distinct entity, separate from other Jewish populations, but that Jews in Poland shared a deep, organic connection to their country that Jews in other countries did not have.

It is tempting to say that in the wake of the Holocaust, the national distinctions of Jews were no longer relevant. All Jews were victims, no matter what their citizenship, and in light of this, it would seem natural that the things that bound Jews across political borders were stronger than the things that separated them. In the territories they conquered, Nazis did not, on the whole, distinguish Jews by nationality. Polish, Czech, French, Hungarian, Greek, Russian, Italian, Dutch, and German Jews all ended up together at Auschwitz. Even if they did not speak the same language or share the same history when they arrived in the cattle cars, by the time they were killed or liberated, victims and survivors shared a common language of suffering. On the other hand, it was at this very moment, when the world of Polish Jewry had been shattered, that survivors—and their de facto representatives in the United States—needed to cling to the idea that the civilization of which they had been a part had not been destroyed. The *Black Book* suggests that the need for differentiation was strong even through the process of migration to the United States, and in light of the general slaughter of European Jews.

The effect of this narrative is to create tiers of suffering among survivors, particularly in the process of resettlement. By focusing mainly on Polish Jews, the *Black Book* suggests that the Holocaust experience was, at its heart, a Polish-Jewish experience. This idea, that Polish Jews experienced the worst excesses of Nazism, is implicit in the text of the *Black Book*. On one level, this claim has some factual basis. Although a number of other European Jewish communities, such as those of Czechoslovakia, Lithuania, and Latvia, suffered proportionally similar losses, none could match the sheer number of Polish Jews that fell victim to the Nazi onslaught. Nor could they compete with the role Polish Jews played in shaping contemporary Jewish life in Europe and abroad. At the precipice of the German invasion, Jewish Poland was among the liveliest and most creative of Jewish civilizations in history. The destruction of Polish Jews, therefore, carried special significance. Additionally, the most mechanized centers of the killing, the gas chambers of Auschwitz-Birkenau, Treblinka, Majdanek, Chelmno, and Sobibor, were situated in Poland, adjacent to the cities and towns of what had been, arguably, the most lively manifestation of this Jewish civilization in that period. Poland was the site not only of the demise of Polish Jewry, but of the destruction of millions of Jews from around Europe. That the *Einzatsgruppen* swept through Jewish communities in the Ukraine, Lithuania, Belarus, and Latvia, murdering over a million Jews at close range, only confirmed the centrality of Polish Jewish victimhood, in that much of this territory was tied up in the long and rich history of Jewish life in Poland. The Polish lands in which Hasidism flourished and in which *shtetlach* abounded may no longer have been within the political borders of the Second Polish Republic, but they continued to loom large in Jewish history and memory.[53]

This all flags an issue that would become contentious in the decades after World War II: by which boundaries would we define the experience of the Nazi persecution of the Jews? What narratives would be privileged in Jewish remembrance of the war? Were there editorial decisions in this and other volumes that would determine what information was presented and in which ways, what experiences would be excluded and what would be privileged? Debates over these boundaries would sharpen in later years, particularly with the controversy over German reparations in the 1950s, when a legal definition for the victims of Nazi persecution was sought. A hierarchy of suffering would emerge in response to these questions, with certain experiences—resistance, survival in death camps, for instance—becoming privileged as the defining narratives of the Holocaust. As early as 1943, though, the *Black Book* certainly staked a claim for what its editors believed to be the greatest tragedy of World War II—the annihilation of Polish Jewry and its civilization. The *Black Book* was an early site in which these questions were raised, over a year before the liberation of the remaining surviving remnant of European Jews.

Conclusion

In his introduction to the 1995 re-release of the *Black Book*, the historian and survivor Arno Lustiger wrote that the *Black Book* serves as a "gravestone and memorial for the once-largest national group of the Jewish people."[54] Published while the events of the Holocaust were still going on, it does not stand the test of historical accuracy, nor does it provide a comprehensive picture of Jewish suffering during World War II. Its importance lies not so much in the specific details it provides but in its self-conscious mission to memorialize the Jewish victims of Nazism as the tragedy was unfolding. *The Black Book of Polish Jews* was a forerunner to the enormous body of Holocaust literature and memory that has by now become so well known. Published at a time when only scraps of disconnected information were available to the public, the *Black Book* marks the first attempt to construct an overarching narrative of Jewish persecution in Europe for a broad audience. For this reason alone, *The Black Book of Polish Jewry* is an underappreciated text. It is at once a record of charges against the Nazi state and an overarching account, however flawed, of Jewish experiences during World War Two.

More important though, is its role as a memorial site into which the editors, on behalf of Polish Jews in the United States, channeled their grief. The text became a portable site of memory, a place for Jews to reformulate their national narrative, to communicate this past to future generations so that the memories would not disappear, a symbolic site and testament to a lost civilization.[55]

In this way, the *Black Book* foreshadowed the Holocaust memorial culture that emerged as early as the 1940s and would continue to evolve through the second half of the twentieth century.[56] It was a memorial culture without an accepted, overarching narrative, with individual memorials dedicated to specific experiences, locations, and populations. The nationalistic character of Jews' suffering was emphasized in this initial phase. Unlike much later, when Holocaust survivors would downplay the national, cultural, political, and religious differences among survivors of Nazi terror, the *Black Book* indicates that these differences were integral to the way in which memories of Jewish suffering were being constructed as early as late 1943, and would continue to be a part of the landscape of Holocaust memorialization for decades to come.

Moreover, the *Black Book* anticipated the conversation that would take place within survivor communities and among Jews more broadly, namely, how should we come to terms with what happened to European Jewry during World War II? How were we to understand the multitude of experiences that victims and survivors endured? Was the suffering of Polish Jews fundamentally different from that of French, Hungarian, and Italian Jews? This raises yet broader questions connected to how we memorialize the past: who should be considered a survivor? Could survivors relate to other Jews, in places like the United States, who lived comfortably through the war? Were survivors of Auschwitz joined in a community of suffering with those who survived in the forests, in hiding, in labor camps? What about with those who escaped in the early months of the war and survived life in the Soviet Union? Was their suffering and starvation in the Soviet gulags, or in Kazakhstan or in Uzbekistan, part of the same experience endured by concentration camp inmates? These questions, of course, have no fixed or simple answers, and the history that the *Black Book* recorded is insufficient and incomplete. Yet the book reveals one of the earliest attempts to begin to come to terms with such questions, and provides a picture of how refugees and survivors in the United States, from even before the end of the war, embarked on a project to memorialize the victims of Nazi terror. Over the next few decades, the legacy of the Holocaust would come to occupy a central place in American life.

Notes

1. See Jacob Apenszlak, Claire Darmon, and Willy Coutin, *Le livre noir des Juifs de Pologne* (Paris: Calmann-Lévy, 2013).

2. "Zelig Tygel, Noted as Yiddish Author; Aide of American Federation for Polish Jews, dies at 56—also had been editor," *New York Times*, March 15, 1947, 13.

3. Harry Schneiderman, *American Jewish Yearbook*, vol. 44 (Philadelphia: Jewish Publication Society of America, 1943), 363.

4. See Letter from Zelig Tygel to J.W. Pehle, 10 March 1944, Archives of the Franklin D. Roosevelt Library, Records of the War Refugee Board, 1944–1945, Box 1, American Friends of Polish Jews Folder.

5. Letter from Zelig Tygel to Mr. Irwin Smith, 27 January 1942, Zelig Tygel Papers, YIVO Institute for Jewish Research, RG253, Folder: correspondences.

6. Prospectus for Black Book (undated), Jacob Apenszlak Papers, YIVO Institute for Jewish Research, RG732, Box 7, Folder 73.

7. "'Black Book' of Polish Jewry Will Be Published in U.S.A.," *Jewish Telegraphic Agency*, April 14, 1942, accessed February 6, 2015, www.jta.org/1942/04/15/archive/black-book-of-polish-jewry-will-be-published-in-u-s-a.

8. See, for example, the report from a national *landsmanshaft* conference on 8 February 1942, describing how "entire Jewish communities have been wiped out," and "tens of thousands of children have been killed by the Nazi sword." YIVO Institute for Jewish Research, RG1015, Box 3, Folder 6.

9. See, for example, "Article 6—No Title," June 27, 1942, 5; "1,000,000 Jews Slain By Nazis, Report Says," *New York Times*, June 29 ,1942, 2; "Allies Are Urged To Execute Nazis," *New York Times*, July 2, 1942, 6. The literature on what was known is extensive, and the debate over the US reaction to the news of Jewish suffering hotly contested. See, among others, Richard Breitman and Allan J. Lichtman, *FDR and the Jews* (Cambridge, MA: Belknap Press, 2014); Rafael Medoff, *FDR and the Holocaust: a Breach of Faith.* (Washington D.C.: David S. Wyman Institute for Holocaust Studies, 2013); Robert N. Rosen, *Saving the Jews: Franklin D. Roosevelt and the Holocaust* (New York: Thunder's Mouth Press, 2006); David S. Wyman, *The Abandonment of the Jews: America and the Holocaust, 1941–1945* (New York: The New Press, 2007).

10. Breitman and Lichtman, *FDR and the Jews*, 199.

11. Ibid., 205.

12. The diary describes the large-scale deportations that took place in the spring and summer of 1942, and was released in early 1944, shortly after the *Black Book* came out. See American Council for Warsaw Jews and American Friends of Polish Jews, *The Extermination of 500,000 Jews in the Warsaw Ghetto* (New York: American Council of Warsaw Jews and American Friends of Polish Jews, 1944).

13. Minutes of Office Committee, 16 March 1942, Papers of the American Federation for Polish Jews, YIVO Institute for Jewish Research, RG1015, Box 1, Folder 1.

14. "Jacob Apenszlak, 55, Israeli U.N. Official," *New York Times*, March 30, 1950, 29; "Member of Israel U.N. Staff Dead," *The Palestine Post*, April 20, 1950, 2; "Polish Language Newspaper Started Here," *Jewish Telegraphic Agency*, November 17, 1940, accessed March 14, 2015, www.jta.org/1940/11/17/archive/polish-language-jewish-paper-started-here.

15. Andrzej Kapiszewski, "The Federation of Polish Jews in America in Polish-Jewish Relations during the Interwar Years (1924–1939)," *Polish-American Studies* 56, no. 2 (1999): 67.

16. The claim of 65,000 was published in the 1943 *American Jewish Yearbook*. See Schneiderman, *American Jewish Yearbook*, vol. 44, 362. One indication that the Federation's reach among Polish Jews was not as strong as its claim is that in 1944, when the JDC called a meeting with leaders of *landsmanshaftn* and national federations to clarify their relationships vis-à-vis relief funds to Europe, the Federation was not among those represented. While the federations of Jews from Hungary, Romania, Yugoslavia, and Bulgaria were among the invitees, only the bodies representing Warsaw Jews and Galician Jews were present on behalf of Polish Jewry. See JDC NY Archives, Records of the New York Office of the American Jewish Joint Distribution Committee, 1945–1954, Folder AR194554/2/4/30, "Minutes from Meeting of Landsmanshaftn and Federations with the Joint Distribution Committee, 3 August 1944." Kapiszewski also indicates that despite claims to represent all Polish Jews in America and all *landsmanshaftn*, their membership numbers remained much lower than they publicly reported, and the *landsmanshaftn* only participated sporadically. See Kapiszewski, "The Federation of Polish Jews," 48.

17. Outline of Program activities, American Federation of Polish Jews, YIVO Institute for Jewish Research, RG1015, Box 1, folder 1.

18. Michael Fleming, *Auschwitz, the Allies and Censorship of the Holocaust* (Cambridge: Cambridge University Press, 2014), 190–94.

19. Jacob Apenszlak, ed., *The Black Book of Polish Jewry: an Account of the Martyrdom of Polish Jewry under the Nazi Occupation* (New York: American Federation for Polish Jews with the Association of Jewish Refugees and Immigrants from Poland, 1943), 151.

20. Ibid., 145.

21. The most notable of these is Holocaust denier David Irving's libel case against historian Deborah Lipstadt. See Deborah E. Lipstadt, *History on Trial: My Day in Court with David Irving* (New York: Ecco, 2005).

22. Arieh Tartakower, "De Profundis," *The Reconstructionist*, no. 4 (1944): 16.

23. Although he would later immigrate to Palestine in 1946, where he served as the chairman of the Israel Executive of the World Jewish Congress and chair of the Department of Sociology at the Hebrew University of Jerusalem. See "Aryeh Tartakower Dead at 85," *Jewish Telegraphic Agency*, November 30, 1982, accessed March 30, 2015, www.jta.org/1982/11/30/archive/aryeh-tartakower-dead-at-85.

24. Alfred Werner, "Twilight of Terror," *Contemporary Jewish Record*, vol. 7, no. 5 (1944): 549.

25. Walter Bara, "Chapter and Verse on the Nazi Pogrom," *New York Times*, January 30, 1944, BR21.

26. Eleanor Roosevelt, "My Day," June 8, 1944, *The Eleanor Roosevelt Papers Project*, accessed March 20, 2015, www.gwu.edu/~erpapers/myday/displaydoc.cfm?_y=1944&_f=md056817.

27. Eleanor Roosevelt, "My Day," April 14, 1943, *The Eleanor Roosevelt Papers Project*, accessed March 30, 2015, www.gwu.edu/~erpapers/myday/displaydoc.cfm?_y=1943&_f=md056470.

28. Eleanor Roosevelt, "My Day," August 13, 1943, *The Eleanor Roosevelt Papers Project*, accessed March 30, 2015, www.gwu.edu/~erpapers/myday/displaydoc.cfm?_y=1943&_f=md056569.

29. For more on Eleanor Roosevelt, the Holocaust, and the Establishment of Israel, see Monty N. Penkower, "Eleanor Roosevelt and the Plight of World Jewry," *Jewish Social Studies* 49, no. 2 (1987): 125–136; and Michelle Mart, "Eleanor Roosevelt, Liberalism, and Israel," *Shofar: an Interdisciplinary Journal of Jewish Studies* 24, no. 3 (2006): 59–89.

30. Ploni, "What About Their Conscience? Black Record," *The Palestine Post*, December 12, 1944, 7; "'Black Book' of Jewry Published in U.S," *The Palestine Post*, February 7, 1944, 1.

31. A.R., "Books of the Week: Hitler's Massacre of the Jews," *Sydney Morning Herald*, July 22, 1944, 6.

32. Victor Serge, "Mexican Notebooks, 1940–1947," *New Left Review* 82 (2013), 53.

33. Raphael Mahler, Review of *The Black Book of Polish Jewry*, ed. Jacob Apenszlak, *Jewish Social Studies*, 6, no. 4 (1944): 402–403.

34. Indeed, it is not until page 100 that the editors refer to the mobile killing squads accompanying the German push into the Soviet Union. This may reflect a relative lack of information compared to the reports being smuggled out of the ghettoes in the general government.

35. Ibid., 403–405.

36. See Jewish Black Book Committee, *The Black Book: the Nazi Crime against the Jewish People* (New York: Duell, Sloan and Pearce, 1946). The original Russian manuscript was blocked from publication in the Soviet Union and did not appear until the 1980s, when it was published in Israel. See Ihrina Ehrenburg, "Preface to the 1993 Russian Edition of *The Black Book*," in Ilya Ehrenburg and Vassily Grossman, *The Complete Black Book of Russian Jewry* (New Brunswick, NJ: Transaction Publishers, 2009), xviii.

37. For a detailed account of the publication of Yiddish language memoirs on the Holocaust in the immediate aftermath of the war, see Margaret Taft, *From Victim to Survivor: The Emergence and Development of the Holocaust Witness, 1941–1949* (Edgware, UK; Portland, OR: Vallentine Mitchell, 2013).

38. On the historical commissions, see Laura Jockush, *Collect and Record! Jewish Holocaust Documentation in Early Postwar Europe*, New York: Oxford University Press, 2012.

39. See especially Donald Bloxham, *Genocide on Trial: War Crimes Trials and the Formation of Holocaust History and Memory* (Oxford: Oxford University Press, 2001).

40. For example, Jewish Black Book Committee, *The Black Book*; Jenő Lévai, *Black Book on the Martyrdom of Hungarian Jewry* (Zurich: Central European Times Publishing Company, 1948). Black Books were not necessarily a Jewish phenomenon—*The Black Book of Polish Jewry* must have been partly inspired by the appearance of the *Black Book of Poland*, published in 1942. Other black books in the second half of the twentieth century have focused, among other crimes, on those committed by Nazis against Europeans more broadly, and on crimes committed by Communist China, by Communist Czechoslovakia, by the United States in Chile, and by Serb militias against Bosnians during the breakup of Yugoslavia.

41. Jonathan Boyarin and Jack Kugelmass, *From a Ruined Garden: The Memorial Books of Polish Jewry* (Bloomington, IN: Indiana University Press, 1998), 1.

42. Rosemary Horowitz, "A History of Yizker Books," in *Memorial Books of Eastern European Jewry: Essays on the History and Meaning of Yizker Books*, ed. Rosemary Horowitz (Jefferson, NC and London: McFarland & Company, Inc. Publishers, 2011), 7.

43. On *yizker-bikher* and idealizing their towns, see Horowitz, "A History of Yizker Books," 15.

44. Horowitz traces the history of *yizker-bikher* back to the practice of memorializing ordinary people in the aftermath of the First Crusade. She also identifies influences from the Bible on this genre. Ibid., 8–9.

45. We might also, in this context, consider the *Black Book* as a precursor to the *Poylisher Yidntum* series published in Buenos Aires between the 1940s and 1970s, which saw 175 Yiddish volumes published that memorialized Polish Jewry in a variety of ways. Jan Schwarz, *Survivors and Exiles: Yiddish Culture after the Holocaust* (Detroit: Wayne State University Press, 2015), 92–117.

46. Apenszlak, *The Black Book of Polish Jewry*, viii.

47. See Shira Lander, "Martyrdom in Jewish Tradition," paper presented at The Catholic-Jewish Consultation Committee Meeting of the U.S. Conference of Catholic Bishops Committee on Ecumenical and Interreligious Affairs and the National Council of Synagogues, St. Mary's Seminary, Baltimore, MD, December 11, 2003, www.bc.edu/content/dam/files/research_sites/cjl/texts/cjrelations/resources/articles/Lander_martyrdom/index.html#_ftn7. On martyrdom and Rabbinic Judaism, see Daniel Boyarin, *Dying for God: Martyrdom and the Making of Christianity and Judaism* (Stanford, CA: Stanford University Press, 1999).

48. There is some evidence to suggest that Jewish martyrologies may date back as far as the Second Temple period. On this issue, see particularly Shlomo Eidelberg, *The Jews and the Crusaders: The Hebrew Chronicles of the First and Second Crusades* (Madison: University of Wisconsin Press, 1977); and Robert Chazan, *European Jewry and the First Crusade* (Berkeley: University of California Press, 1987).

49. Outline of Program activities, American Federation of Polish Jews, YIVO Institute for Jewish Research, RG1015, Box 1, folder 1.

50. On Apenszlak's ideas about Jewish Polishness, see Katrin Steffen, "'Jewish Polishness'—Tragic Delusion or Workable Design? Jakób Appenszlak and the Polish-Jewish Press in the Interwar Period and its Aftermath," Conference Paper presented at Between Coexistence and Divorce: 25 Years of Research on the History and Culture of Polish Jewry and Polish-Jewish Relations, Jerusalem, March 2009. I thank the author for her permission to cite this paper.

51. Apenszlak, *Black Book*, viii.

52. Ibid., 249.

53. Much of Lithuania, Belarus, and western Ukraine were part of the Second Polish Republic.

54. Arno Lustiger and Jacob Apenszlak, eds., *The Black Book of Polish Jewry: An Account of the Martyrdom of Polish Jewry Under the Nazi Occupation* (Bodenheim: Syndikat Buchgesellschaft, 1995), x.

55. See Pierre Nora, "Between Memory and History: les lieux des memoires," *Representations* 26 (1989): 7–24.

56. Hasia Diner's pioneering work has shattered what she describes as a "myth of silence," the belief that American Jews in the immediate post-Holocaust period deliberately did not discuss the Holocaust publicly. See Hasia Diner, *We Remember with Reverence and Love: American Jews and the Myth of Silence after the Holocaust, 1945–1962* (New York: New York University Press, 2009); see also David Cesarani and Eric J. Sundquist, eds. *After the Holocaust: Challenging the Myth of Silence* (London: Routledge, 2012).

Mapping a Lost World
POSTWAR JEWS AND (RE)CREATING
THE PAST IN MEMORIAL BOOKS

Eliyana R. Adler

We had hardly gotten settled in America when we went to a "Landsmenshaft" meeting, a gathering of people from Tarnow who now lived in America. We met people who had arrived years ago, and some others who had survived the Holocaust like ourselves. Both oldtimers and newcomers formed circles around us. The oldtimers asked about their relatives: "Did you know such and such? Did they survive or what happened to them?" All marveled that we survived, but many walked away disappointed that their relatives had not. The newcomers hugged and embraced us and asked where and how we survived and what our plans were here in the United States."[1]

WHILE THERE are certainly memoirs and testimonies of Jewish refugees arriving in the United States after the war only to be greeted with indifference by their fellow Jews, there are also stories like William Kornbluth's, quoted above. For Kornbluth, like so many others, the natural place to go for companionship and help was his *landsmanshaft*. As émigrés from the same city, the people there all had a shared past, even if they had not known one another in the old country. And just as the *landsmanshaft* could provide aid to new arrivals like Kornbluth, he brought them crucial firsthand information about their families and their hometown. Over time, the *landsmanshaftn* became sites for both absorption and memorialization.

This essay will explore the ways in which models of memorialization spread transnationally, just as Jewish refugees moved across the globe in search of new homes. It will suggest that the emergence and development of the particular genre of memorial books, or *yizker-bikher*, that came out of the Holocaust, while certainly owing a debt to previous methods of memorialization in the Ashkenazi Jewish world, are also the unique product of the engagement between Holocaust survivors and the *landsmanshaftn* that took them in.² To put it in broader terms, as human beings were integrated into new societies, so too was their knowledge of the war and ideas about how to commemorate shared losses incorporated into their adopted homelands.

The story of the *yizker-bikher* cannot be told from a single location. It is a transnational story wherein Holocaust survivors and more settled Jewish communities pooled their intellectual and financial resources and worked toward a common goal. But while it is not solely an American story, there is no question that the concerns of American Jews, the organizing power of the *landsmanshaftn*, and the funds these better-off Jews could offer, profoundly shaped the developing memorial culture.

In order to illustrate that point, this paper will focus on the use of maps. The very first memorial books, produced in the late 1940s, either did not contain maps at all or, when they did, the photocopied pages were used to show changes wrought by the Nazi occupation. There was no need to include a map of the relevant location in a book produced entirely for and by recent residents of that very location. Yet later *yizker-bikher* conspicuously displayed intricate and embellished maps. This essay will demonstrate that the creation and inclusion of the maps represent a synthesis of the nostalgia performed in the *landsmanshaftn* in the United States and other centers of Jewish immigrant life with the early types of memorial culture developed by the Displaced Persons in Europe. While it is not possible to show definitively that the inclusion of maps was entirely at the behest of the American participants in the collaborative process, using *yizker-bikher* produced by international committees in the 1950s and 60s, I will demonstrate that the types of maps created reflect the concerns and culture of American Jews and their *landsmanshaftn*. Moreover, in addition to offering a physical image of the former place of residence before it was destroyed, the maps provided readers with a virtual mode of return.

Mapping the Genre

Nearly all of the hundreds of memorial books created in the wake of the Holocaust use the symbol of a gravestone at some point to communicate their primary purpose. Gravestones appear frequently in the subtitles of the books, in the introductions, dedications, poetry, and imagery. Coming from a religious tradition in which respectful burial and marking of graves of the deceased are of paramount importance, and having witnessed a period of such enormous death and desecration, the symbol is painfully apt. In the introduction to his book on Holocaust memorials, James Young states:

> In keeping with the bookish, iconoclastic side of Jewish tradition, the first "memorials" to the Holocaust period came not in stone, glass, or steel—but in narrative. The Yizkor Bikher—memorial books—remembered both the lives and destruction of European Jewish communities according to the most ancient of Jewish memorial media: words on paper. For a murdered people without graves, without even corpses to inter, these memorial books often came to serve as symbolic tombstones.[3]

It would appear that the first such paper memorials developed out of memorial events held in the Displaced Persons camps.

As survivors from across Europe converged in the DP camps, they gathered together with others from their own regions and towns to share information and provide assistance. Historian Gabriel Finder notes that the mutual aid societies created were based on the model of such organizations in the United States, although they served different needs. "Now in the DP camps *landsmanshaftn* evolved into kinship groups, substitute families for survivors deprived for the most part of their own families."[4] The groups held formal commemorative events, often on the anniversary of the day on which the Jewish communities of their hometowns were completely destroyed.

As Finder has pointed out, photographs from these events typically show a group of survivors surrounding a memorial plaque, which is often designed to look like a gravestone.[5] According to written accounts of the assemblies, published in the DP newspapers, speeches were also a regular feature. Leaders of the *landsmanshaft* organizing the particular event would talk about the legacies of the towns, as well as their sad ends.[6] All of this, then, came to form the basis for the first memorial books.

Es shtarbt a shtetl: megiles Skalat [The Village Dies: The Scroll of Skalat], published in Germany in 1948, provides a useful illustration. It opens with an introduction and some brief historical information, including several prewar photographs. This comprises the first fifteen pages of the book, which contains just under two hundred pages in all. The bulk of the book is taken up with describing various experiences of the Holocaust in roughly chronological order. Two small maps are provided, one of the ghetto and the other of the region, including train lines. The final section of the book includes photos depicting the genocide, as well as portraits of the survivors; a chart with approximate numbers of victims; and a sort of prose poem.[7]

Also produced in Germany in 1948, *Khurbn Otvotsk, Falenits, Kartshev* [The Destruction of Otwock, Falenica, and Karczew], a memorial book for three Polish Jewish communities, is about the same length, and similarly focused on the trauma and losses of the war years. In this case the two maps show the German camp established in Karczew and the ghetto in Otwock. The book closes with decorated funerary plates purchased and dedicated by particular families.[8] These and the other early *yizker-bikher* I was able to examine conform to a fairly narrow definition of a memorial book. They exist to memorialize the dead, to provide a collective tombstone, albeit one that is portable, and on paper.

In title, as well as in their primary function, these modern memorial books harken back to certain Medieval precedents.[9] Additionally, the First World War and interwar period saw the production of some works lamenting the loss and destruction of Jewish communities in Eastern Europe.[10] As David Slucki demonstrates in this volume, *The Black Book of Polish Jews* is certainly a related phenomenon.[11] Indeed, in the words of Jack Kugelmass and Jonathan Boyarin, "if there were no precedent for them in Jewish history and culture, they would never have appeared as a distinct genre so soon after the war nor taken hold in such a massive way."[12] Yet in order to reach their full potential, and full audience, the memorial books produced by European refugees needed the input and resources of American Jewry.

From Mutual Aid to Memorialization

Daniel Soyer's work on *landsmanshaftn* in the United States shows how as the immigrant generation aged and became more prosperous, the *landsmanshaftn* moved from providing mutual aid to offering a forum for engaging in nostalgia for the old country. After the passage of restrictive immigration laws following the First World War, there were few new arrivals to assist. Having successfully established themselves in America, many of the aging immigrants were contemplating their origins and the paths their lives had taken. Anniversaries and annual dinners, and the ad books created for them, increasingly centered around speeches and essays idealizing people's shared hometowns. As Soyer notes, "For many immigrants, then, their image of their hometown was, at least in part, a product of their own desires, longings, and memories."[13]

Hannah Kliger's in-depth study of New York *landsmanshaftn* provides further detail. Her chapter on the souvenir journals produced by such societies for their annual or anniversary banquets highlights thirty-two separate items that these booklets typically held. The contents ranged from jokes and songs to obituaries and honors, but also included photographs and reminiscences of former homes. Nostalgic descriptions often accompanied the photographs, which could be of street scenes and landmarks or of political clubs, schools, or other institutions that the *landsmanshaft* was supporting financially from afar.[14] Kliger goes so far as to suggest, albeit in a footnote, that "the souvenir journals may be seen as a predecessor of the memorial books which would be predominantly published after World War II, offering a forum for the expression of feelings and longing for the hometown."[15]

Following the Second World War, members of the *landsmanshaftn* threw themselves into collecting donations, writing affidavits, and trying to help the Sh'erit ha-Pletah in any way they could. This was an immediate need, allowing American Jews to aid those still in Europe in a way they had not been able to during the war. And in addition to meeting the physical needs of the survivors, it responded to the emotional needs of American Jews to connect to the communities they had left behind but still longed for. Once the refugees were settled in new homes, the *landsmanshaftn* turned to engagement with the memorial books, which was also to be their own last chapter. As Daniel Soyer explains, they had outlived not only their original purpose, but also several additional ones. "The landsmanshaftn's final important function was to memorialize their obliterated hometowns and their landslayt who had fallen victim to the Nazis."[16]

Expanding the Genre

What began as a form of textual gravestone in Europe after the war soon spread around the world and came to encompass a diversity of forms. For example, the *yizker-bukh* devoted to Falenica, just one of the three towns memorialized in the aforementioned volume and published in Tel Aviv in 1967, is close to five hundred pages long. It opens with a lovingly hand-drawn map of the town on the book's inner binding (figure 1). The bulk of the book is in Yiddish, and includes a lengthy history, followed by sections on prewar political parties and organizations as well as individuals from the town. Only after almost two hundred pages of such personal reminiscences and photographs of youth groups, rabbis, and sites in the town, does the treatment of the Holocaust begin. A brief section of reports on the *landsmanshaftn* in various parts of the world precedes the Hebrew portion of the book, which is roughly one hundred pages and includes essays on similar topics to the Yiddish language text. The book ends with a somber listing of names of the deceased and some full pages dedicated to particular individuals or families, purchased and illustrated by their survivors—comprising about thirty pages in all.[17]

It is not entirely clear how the ideas for new sections and inclusions in the *yizker-bikher* spread and evolved, but clearly editors of new books had access to some selection of previously published ones and felt free to take ideas from them. In some cases, *landsmanshaftn* chose to hire professional writers or editors to produce their volumes. Several individuals appear on the title page of more than one memorial book. On the whole, however, the volumes were produced by committees, which explains the repetition and the uneven quality of the text that can sometimes be found in them, as well as, perhaps, the creativity and innovation.

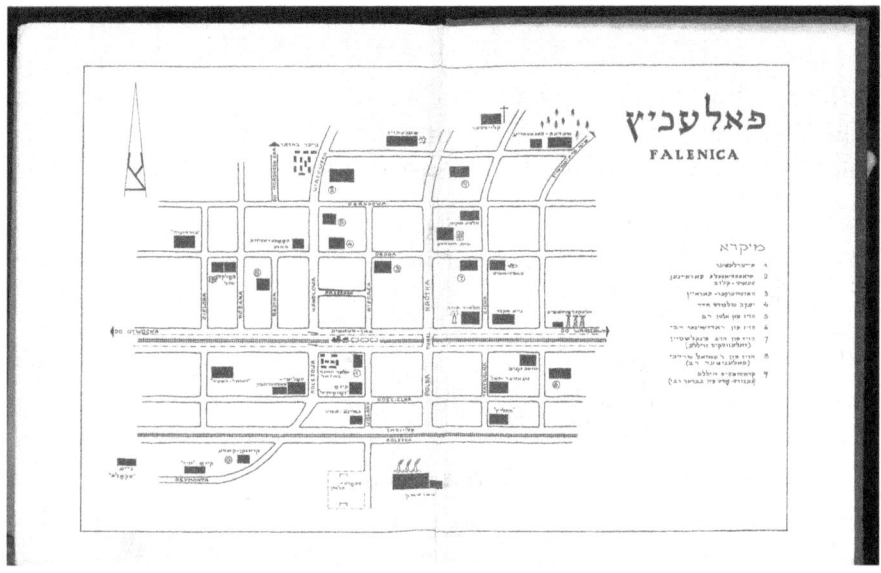

Figure 1. *Sefer Falenits* (inner binding of front from Hebrew direction)

The international composition of some of the editorial committees, and of the people who donated both funds and submissions to the volumes, also helps to account for their inclusiveness. While the very first *yizker-bikher* were published in Germany, entirely by people who had survived the war in Poland or in the Soviet Union, most of the hundreds of others published in subsequent years came out in either the United States or the State of Israel. A small number appeared in France, Argentina, or other countries, but as Michlean Amir has demonstrated, the majority were published in Israel.[18] Regardless of their place of publication, the books all refer to the active participation of members of their *landsmanshaftn* in other countries. While the centrality of *landsmanshaftn* to the production of memorial books has been duly noted by scholars, the degree to which the groups influenced the development of the volumes has yet to be fully explored.

Whatever their place of publication, the memorial books always thank editorial board members, contributors, and donors from other countries. Often the individual articles list not only the authors' names, but also their location. Many of the volumes also include a section of photographs of their town's *landsmanshaft* groups in various countries. Other books include memorial plaques purchased by subscription to help pay for publication costs, in addition to the somber listing of the names of the dead. In all of these ways, it is easy to see the involvement of American and Canadian Jews, who were often in the best position to finance the books. While the exact ways in which their involvement influenced the books is less obvious, there can be no question that the expansion of the pool of participants also expanded the nature of the books.

In addition to the maps, for example, the memorial books from the 1950s and afterward typically include an extensive collection of photographs. Like the *landsmanshaftn* souvenir journals, the images show an idyllic prewar Jewish existence with portraits of rabbis, youth groups, and families, and Jewish institutional buildings. William Glicksman notes that these photographs, which could only have been saved and donated by American Jews, provide crucial information for scholars of prewar Jewish life.[19] Refugees were fortunate to have survived with their lives and were unlikely to have been able to hold onto their most important documents, let alone photographs from home. Relatives in the Jewish communities outside of Europe, however, of which the United States was the largest, had been receiving family photos from the old country for decades. This important method of maintaining family connections would prove a boon for the memorial books.[20]

There is, of course, no single formula for a *yizker-bukh*. They range from *Toldot kehilat Pinsk Karlin* [Chronicles of the Community of Pinsk Karlin]—published in Hebrew in the 1970s, and comprising two volumes, each over five hundred pages in length and written by professional historians—to the far more modest *Dubrowa: A Memorial to a Shtetl*, at thirty-eight pages.[21] Yet despite the diversity, certain sections appear in almost all of the volumes. Chief among these is the necrology, the ideological core of the book. Interestingly, however, the listing of the names of the dead usually appears at the very end. The majority of each book is filled with poetry, artwork, photographs, maps, depictions of life in the town, and descriptions of death and survival during the war. All of these areas, are worthy of further study. There has been some exploration of the *yizker-bikher* art and, of course, the testimonies, but little has been written about the maps, despite their prevalence and prominence in the volumes.

Theorizing the Map

As discussed above, the earliest *yizker-bikher* use maps mainly to illustrate the changed conditions during the war. The assumption was that all of the readers were intimately familiar with the town itself, but that the exact contours of the ghetto or the variety of transports out of it might not be known to all. Soon, however, a map of the town itself came to be a regular feature of the volumes. Often these maps serve as the interior binding of the books. In other cases they appear in the introductory sections. Sometimes they require unfolding to reach their full size. The maps are thus prominently placed. But to what end? If all of the people reading these books knew the towns backwards and forwards, why include a map at all?

Maps serve many purposes, ranging from the purely informational to more political and ideological aims. In the Eastern European Jewish context, Israel Bartal has demonstrated how late nineteenth- and early twentieth-century Hebrew and Yiddish writers used their fiction to creatively map an ahistorical *shtetl* that represented their critical evaluations and literary imaginings far more than the reality of Jewish life in small towns during the previous century. In particular the presence of non-Jews was virtually erased and the chaotic nature of the layout was emphasized. This was significant for the ways in which it helped to shape popular conceptions of Jewish life decontextualized from the geography and history of Eastern Europe.[22] In a different context, James Linville draws a distinction between locative and "utopian" maps. The latter, he insists, are unfettered from actual territory, instead mapping ideology.[23] These literary portrayals of the *shtetl*, and the plays and films based upon them, have been particularly influential in shaping the American Jewish view of the Old World, as discussed in essays by Gil Ribak, Sheila Jelen, and others in this volume.

The maps produced for the memorial books share some of these fictionalizing qualities. While many of the volumes include a copy of a page from an atlas to show the town's general location, the maps of the towns themselves are hand-drawn and either lack scale entirely or are rendered in relatively large scale. Thus the folksy, artistic, and subjective maps of the *shtetl* are juxtaposed with more official, scientific, and objective maps of

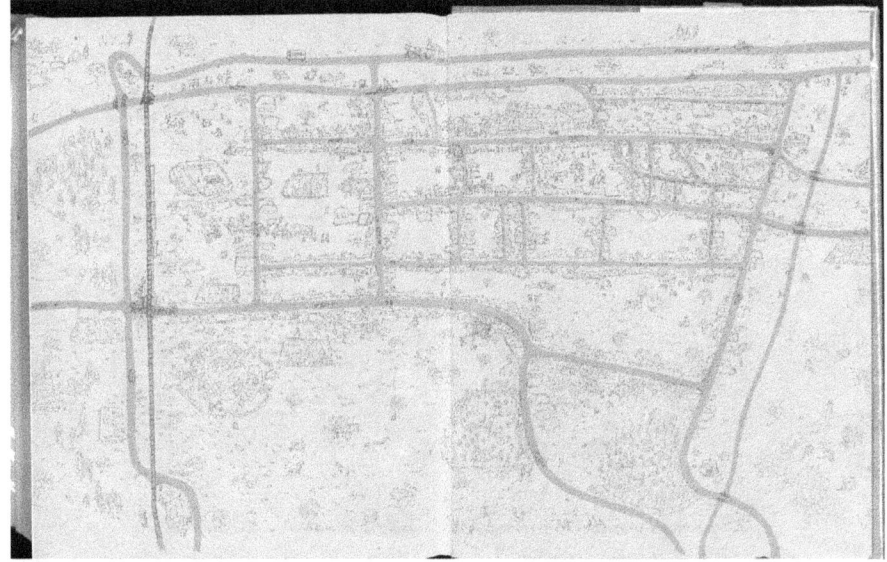

Figure 2. *Sefer Yanovah* (unnumbered pages preceding title page in Hebrew).

the larger territory. This is particularly evident in the Janowa *yizker-bukh*, in which the town map includes not only streets and houses, but also trees, bushes, people, and animals (figure 2).[24] In addition, many of the maps, like the one from Chmielnik (figure 3), specifically note that they are drawn from memory.[25] The map of Antopol (figure 4) includes the moment in time it represents—1914.[26]

The maps thus seemingly signal their constructed or reconstructed nature. Their purpose, however, remains obscure. Why include a map in a volume created entirely by and for former residents of a single town? The idea that the map would allow the next generation to envision their parents' hometowns is not a sufficient explanation in that, like the rest of the books, the maps were often produced in Yiddish. While the Yiddish language united the survivors across borders, even at the time the books were published, it was already clear that it would not be the lingua franca of their children. How then can we account for the inclusion of these so often beautifully rendered and prominently placed maps?

Jeffrey Shandler, in his study of the construction of the idea of the *shtetl*, suggests that the ubiquitous hand-drawn maps serve a re-orienting

מפת העיר — מאפע פון כמיעלניק. געצייכנט לויטן זכרון פון מ. קליינהענדלער

Figure 3. *Pinkes Khmyelnik* (p. 55). Caption in original reads "Map of the city" (in Hebrew). "Map of Chmielnik, rendered from memory by M. Kleynhendler" (in Yiddish).

purpose for the former town residents. "Local geography orients discrete memories, proffered in a *yizker-bukh* to one another, situating various individuals, social institutions, and events as recalled by different writers, within an integral space. Beyond memory mapping, *yizker-bikher* reconstitute textually what was displaced or eradicated from its original, indigenous physical place."[27] Thus, in a certain sense, they serve as the hearts of the volumes, allowing the other pieces to function and circulate meaning around them.

Kugelmass and Boyarin, always sensitive to the nuances of the *yizker-bikher*, refer to this phenomenon as the "architecture of memory." For them it holds both mnemonic and practical significance. Providing detailed maps of their former homes thwarted the erasure of Jewish memory on the ground in those same towns. As Jewish homes, streets, and institutions were repurposed and renamed in Eastern Europe, the books held the key to an earlier reality.[28] Indeed it was not only the Holocaust that laid waste the Jewish presence in the towns of Eastern Europe. Subsequent policies, especially in the newly Sovietized states, eradicated even the memory of Jewish life there.

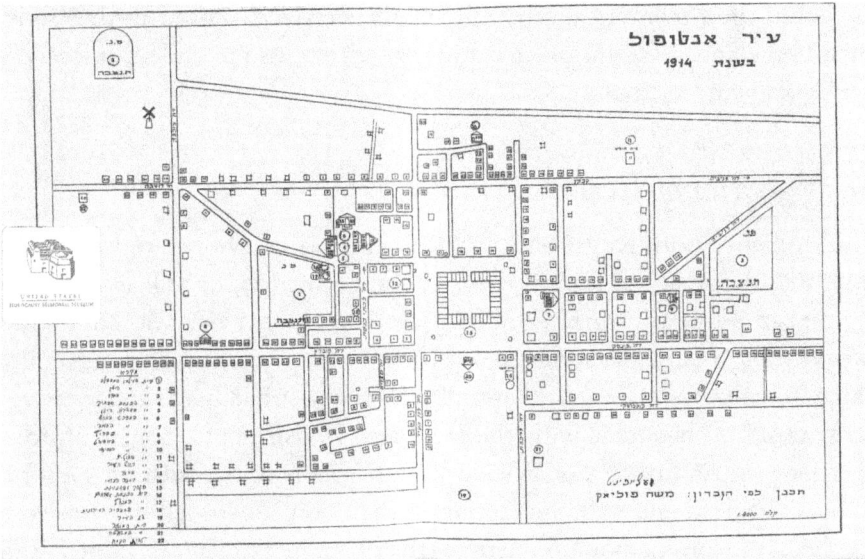

Figure 4. *Antopol* (inside front covers).

This tension between the past and the present of the towns—their simultaneous disappearance and continued existence—is also discussed by Annette Wierviorka and Itzhok Niborski. In a discussion on "The Geography of Memory," they point to the inclusion, in so many of the *yizker-bikher*, of an excursus on nomenclature. By stating explicitly that the town once had two or three names, for example, one Yiddish, one Polish, and one Ukrainian, the authors can justify their claim that the town has been utterly destroyed, even with an awareness that it still stands. The Yiddish town is no more, while in fact a Polish or Ukrainian one may still exist in its former location.[29] Even though Wierviorka and Niborski do not discuss maps directly, their insight into the geography of memory helps to explain why an idiosyncratic map could serve as an important souvenir of what was lost.

It is worthwhile to point out that the effects of the Holocaust were geographic as well as physical and emotional. In the words of the editors of an innovative new work seeking to integrate the methods of Geography into Holocaust Studies, "The Holocaust transformed the meaning as well as the materiality of every place and space it touched."[30] For the survivors, this meant that everything they knew was gone or distorted. The maps anchored their memories, especially as the survivors moved farther from their homelands in terms of time and space. They also provided, at least on paper, a way to return.

Geographies of Return

The studies of both Kugelmass and Boyarin and Wieviorka and Niborski note that many of the *yizker-bikher* contain a section, or at least one testimony, of postwar return. For many survivors such a visit was an important turning point. "In returning to their hometowns, survivors generally came to realize how total the rupture with the past had been, and even the most positive encounter with the local non-Jewish population reinforced that sense of rupture."[31] For Wieviorka and Niborski, the frustrated efforts to bury the dead and build memorials in their hometowns led the survivors to the only commemoration left to them: "a monument in paper. The *yizker-bukh*."[32]

While depictions of immediate postwar return appear in nearly all of the volumes, prior and later returns also appear, albeit with less frequency. Only a few *yizker-bikher* contain testimonies of emigrants returning to visit their former homes. Yet, as Shandler has shown, this was a relatively popular activity for American Jews during the inter-war years. Whether to seek authenticity, enjoy a family reunion, pursue a philanthropic endeavor, or engage in other business or entertainment purposes, American Jews traveled to Eastern Europe and documented their trips. "Travel writing," according to Shandler, "regularly recounts the disparities between the actuality of *shtetl* life and how authors had remembered or imagined it, thereby measuring both personal transformation and the growing divergence between *shtetl* Jews and immigrants as well as their perceptions of one another."[33]

Quite a few of the volumes, especially those published in recent years as travel to Eastern Europe has become easier, contain depictions of heritage travel. Former residents of a town, now firmly established in some faraway location, return, sometimes with their families, to see what remains of their place of birth. In other cases the return is specifically for the purposes of memorialization. In 1990 the Organization of Former Residents of Hrubieszów in Israel, for example, published a supplement to their 1962 *yizker-bukh*, including additional photographs and testimonies, as well as a detailed chronicle of their efforts to erect a memorial in Hrubieszów, Poland.[34]

In all of these texts, those from immediately after the war as well as those from decades before or after, a sense of alienation—of the impossibility of return—is present. Of course it is all the more painful after the Holocaust, when the murder of so many people, as well as the destruction of infrastructure wrought by war, meant that many locales were truly transformed. In Shandler's words, "The loss of the remembered *shtetl* leaves its postmemory bereft of its defining referent."[35] After the war there could be no return to what had existed previously. The map thus offered a sort of posthumous, pictorial return.

The maps in the *yizker-bikher* are an attempt to reconstruct from memory a place that no one can ever return to, and yet that means so much, especially in retrospect. The level of detail and attention, the prominent placement, and other aspects of the individual maps demonstrate that they provide far more than a straightforward, geographic layout. Figure 1, for example, from Falenica, might at first appear bereft of noteworthy design elements, but in fact it encodes a highly particular sense of space. The street names throughout the town are written in Polish. At each end of the town an arrow points, again in Polish, to the nearest city. This is a Polish town in a Polish country. And yet, within the town, the sites are all marked in Yiddish, as they were experienced by the Jewish residents. Not only the synagogue and Jewish school, but also the post office and church are marked in Yiddish. Without explicit explanation, the labels provide a cultural key to the shared space of a multi-ethnic town.

Figure 2, the colorful and elaborate map of Janowa, almost requires no explication as a return trip. This is not merely a schematic rendering of an urban landscape but a virtual Pompeii. With the individual bushes, the horse and cart meandering on a byway, the farmers in their fields and the shoppers in the square, it is as if a vibrant village suddenly froze in time. With the map spread over two pages and containing such a high level of detail, the viewer can almost get lost, at least in memories, while visiting.

Other maps, while perhaps less homey in their aesthetic, also use intricate detail to draw in the viewer. Figure 4, of Antopol, initially presents as a series of meaningless boxes, but in fact the boxes are numbered and the lengthy key, on the next page (figure 5), shows the former inhabitants of

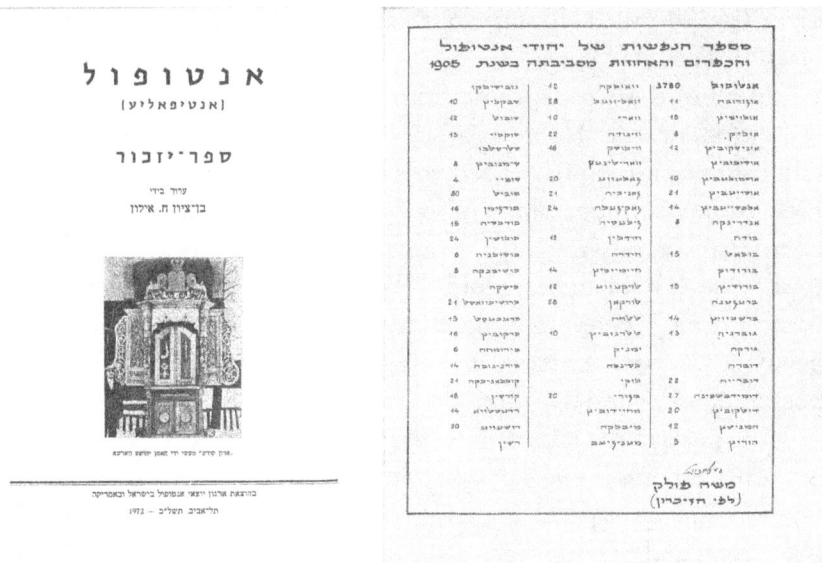

Figure 5. *Antopol* (facing front page). Title: "Number of Jewish people in Antopol and the surrounding villages in 1905." Attribution: Moshe Polak (from memory).

each of the dwellings. The largely blank space becomes a canvas for the imagination. Anyone who lived in Antopol would recognize many of the names. Was the X's house really so close to the Y's? Was there not a barn behind Z's? While the map, with its small, hand-written key to major sites, is dated 1914, the printed house-by-house key on the next page claims to represent the year 1905 in the Jewish community of Antopol.

The map of Chmielnik (figure 3), while not as detailed as that of Antopol and not as vibrant as that of Janowa, features various buildings and sites, both Jewish and general, rendered with a great deal of character and individuality. Anyone who had spent time in the town would be able to visualize and revisit the ritual bath or local theater based on the miniature versions on the map. Indeed the map has a friendly, even cartoon-like feel, that immediately engages the viewer. It is only on close reading, after following many of the curving roads and noting the names and locations of many local sites, that one notices what can only be barbed wire surrounding a small area labeled as the Last Ghetto. Thus the map, which seems at first to portray a welcoming and innocuous prewar town, turns out to contain the end of the Jewish community that once lived there.

Of course not all of the maps in the *yizker-bikher* are as evocative as those discussed here. Some are quite simple. Yet for the former residents of the towns, each and every one of the maps encoded a wealth of information and provided a physical model, however small and schematic, for an imaginary return trip. While the many autobiographical pieces and photographs in the volumes might also provoke memories from the distant past, only the map offered a geography for return.

Collected Memory

In his important work *The Texture of Memory*, James Young attempts to supersede the popular concept of "collective memory" with that of "collected memory." No two individuals can ever share a memory, but they can decide upon and share a sense of meaning, and this can be built into memorial sites and cultures.[36] The *yizker-bikher* would then appear to be the quintessential site of collected memory, stitched together from the individual memories of a transnational community of mourners. They include essays, memoirs, histories, biographies, photographs, necrologies, and maps in their quest to represent what the towns they commemorate once felt like. The lovingly collected materials aim toward a quixotic goal of recreating, in two dimensions, a vibrant place that once existed.

This re-creation came to rely, among other factors, on the use of maps. Carefully rendered maps, at the hearts of the volumes, allow for a form of return, especially in conjunction with the accompanying photographs and memoirs. But this hybrid genre could only develop as the survivors of the Holocaust moved farther from their actual hometowns and closer to other communities of Jews around the world. Survivors who established themselves in new homes, and still harbored hopes of memorializing their towns in book form, found that previous generations of refugees from those same towns wanted to be part of the effort, but that their visions for the memorial books were more expansive. In particular, American Jews, in their *landsmanshaftn*, had developed written and oral traditions of commemoration that they wanted the Holocaust survivors to incorporate.

Whether as a result of practical concerns (as the Jews of the previous Eastern European Jewish diaspora had the funds to underwrite the books), out of a genuine acceptance of the validity of their contributions, or some combination of both, the survivors brought the wider group into their projects. The memorial books expanded into vast scrapbooks containing elements of the original *yizker-bikher* from the DP camps, as well as elements from the *landsmanshaftn* souvenir journals and other components created to meet the needs of this wider constituency, including maps.

The highly detailed and painstakingly keyed map of Antopol by Moshe Poliak (figure 4) is dated 1914. Poliak thus left the town before the First World War. The image he created from memory was produced approximately fifty years after his departure and represented the town twenty-five years before its destruction. This is not to suggest that all of the maps were produced by those who left before the Holocaust, but that the desire to include a map may have been felt particularly strongly by those who had left earlier and felt farther away from their origins.

It is somewhat difficult to differentiate between the life histories of the many contributors to the memorial books. The collecting process brought them together. In the words of Jeffrey Shandler, "The art of documenting these destroyed communities created, if temporarily, new virtual communities, by establishing a network of former Jews from each town, now living scattered throughout the Americas, Europe, Africa, Oceana, and Israel."[37] The volumes they created are truly collected memories, as they present a myriad of narratives and images of their shared hometowns. The *yizker-bikher* offered the many contributors a process for respectfully honoring their past, but also for rebuilding some semblance of their home communities and revisiting their hometowns. They offer scholars a unique genre combining history, literature, and memorial, and an entre into understanding the memorial culture that brought together long-established immigrants to America and other states with newly arrived refugees, in an expansive effort to chronicle the towns they could now only visit in the pages of books.

This is not solely an American story, not could it be. Even if I had chosen to look only at *yizker-bikher* published in the United States, they would reflect the international "virtual communities" discussed above. Indeed my research thus far does not reveal important differences in the memorial books based on place of publication, beyond language preference. The creation of the *yizker-bikher* demonstrates the close and intense interaction between Jews in the United States, Canada, Israel, Europe, Australia, South Africa, and South America, as they worked collaboratively to commemorate their loved ones and their homes. It also highlights the ways in which the more established American Jewish community came to terms with the Holocaust and welcomed the Surviving Remnant. Moreover, the expansion and development of the memorial books over time, with the input of funds and nostalgia from North American Jews, exposes the ways in which the collaboration between Holocaust survivors and more established Jews in the United States and elsewhere literally changed the map of the *yizker-bikher*.

Notes

1. William Kornbluth, *Sentenced to Remember: My Legacy of Life in Pre-1939 Poland and Sixty-Eight Months of Nazi Occupation*, ed. Carl Calendar (Bethlehem, Pennsylvania: Lehigh University Press, 1994), 169.

2. For more on the genre, see the introductions to Jack Kugelmass and Jonathan Boyarin, eds., *From a Ruined Garden: The Memorial Books of Polish Jewry*, second edition (Bloomington: Indiana University Press, 1998) and Rosemary Horowitz, ed., *Memorial Books of Eastern European Jewry: Essays on the History and Meanings of Yizker Volumes* (Jefferson, North Carolina: McFarland & Company, 2011).

3. James E. Young, *The Texture of Memory: Holocaust Memorials and Meanings* (New Haven: Yale University Press, 1993), 7.

4. Gabriel N. Finder, "Yizkor! Commemoration of the Dead by Jewish Displaced Persons in Postwar Germany," ed. Alon Confino, Paul Betts and Dirk Schumann, *Between Mass Death and Individual Loss: The Place of the Dead in Twentieth-Century Germany* (New York: Berghahn Books, 2008): 240.

5. Finder, 242.

6. *Ibid.*

7. Abraham Weissbrod and Israel Kaplan, eds., *Es shtarbt a shtetl: megiles Skalat* (Munich, 1948).

8. Benjamin Orenstein, ed., *Khurbn Otvotsk, Falenits, Kartshev* (Germany, 1948).

9. Yosef Hayim Yerushalmi, *Zakhor: Jewish History and Jewish Memory* (New York: Schocken Books, 1989), 46.

10. Kugelmass and Boyarin, eds., "Introduction," 18–20; Rosemary Horowitz, "A History of Yizker Books," 8–11.

11. David Slucki, "'One of the Greatest Martyrologies': *The Black Book of Polish Jewry* and the Beginnings of Holocaust Remembrance in the United States," ed. Eliyana R. Adler and Sheila E. Jelen, *Absorbing Encounters: Constructing American Jewry in the Post-Holocaust Decades* (Detroit: Wayne State University Press, 2017), 14–15.

12. Kugelmass and Boyarin, "Introduction," 17.

13. Daniel Soyer, *Jewish Immigrant Associations and American Identity in New York, 1880–1939* (Cambridge, Massachusetts: Harvard University Press, 1997), 195.

14. Hannah Kliger, ed., *Jewish Hometown Associations and Family Circles in New York: The WPA Yiddish Writers' Group Study* (Bloomington: Indiana University Press, 1992), 67–68.

15. Kliger, 151–52.
16. Soyer, 202.
17. David Shtokfish, ed., *Sefer Falenits* (Tel Aviv: Irgun yots'e Falenits be-Yisra'el, 1967).
18. Michlean Amir, "Israel as the Cradle of Yizker Books," *Memorial Books of Eastern European Jewry*, 31.
19. William M. Glicksman, *Jewish Social Welfare Institutions in Poland: As Described in the Memorial (Yizkor) Books* (Philadelphia: M. E. Kalish Folkshul, 1976), xiv.
20. For more on the importance of family photographs in far-flung Jewish families, see David Shneer, *Through Soviet Jewish Eyes: Photography, War, and the Holocaust* (New Brunswick, NJ: Rutgers University Press, 2011), 15.
21. Mordechai Nadav, *Toldot kehilat Pinsk Karlin, 1506–1880* (Jerusalem, 1973); Azriel Shohet, *Toldot kehilat Pinsk Karlin: 1881–1941* (Jerusalem: 1977); Mark Mirsky and Murray Jay Rosman, eds., *The Jews of Pinsk, 1506–1881*, trans. Faigie Tropper and Moshe Rosman (Stanford, California: Stanford University Press, 2008); Mark Mirsky and Murray Jay Rosman, eds., *The Jews of Pinsk, 1881–1941*, trans. Faigie Tropper and Moshe Rosman (Stanford, California: Stanford University Press, 2012). Michael A. Nevins, *Dubrowa (Dabrowa Bialostocka): Memorial to a Shtetl*, second edition (self-published, 2000).
22. Israel Bartal, "Imagined Geography: The Shtetl, Myth, and Reality," in *The Shtetl: New Evaluations*, ed. Steven T. Katz (New York: New York University Press, 2007).
23. James R. Linville, "Playing with Maps of Exile: Displacement, Utopia, and Disjunction," in *The Concept of Exile in Ancient Israel and its Historical Context*, ed. Ehud Ben Zvi and Christoph Levin (Berlin: De Gruyter, 2010), 288.
24. Shimon Noi, ed., *Sefer Yanovah: le-hantsahat zikhram shel Yehude ha-'ayarah sheneherevah ba-Sho'ah* (Tel Aviv: Irgun yots'e Yanovah be-Yisra'el, 1972), unnumbered pages preceding title page in Hebrew.
25. Efrayim Shedletski, *Pinkes Khmyelnik: yizker-bukh nokh der horev-gevorener Yidisher kehile* (Tel Aviv: Irgun yots'e Hmyelnik be-Yisra'el, 1960), 55.
26. Ben-Tsiyon H. Ayalon, *Antopol: Antipolye sefer-yizkor* (Tel Aviv: Irgun yots'e Antopol be-Yisra'el uve-Amerikah, 1972), inside front cover.
27. Jeffrey Shandler, *Shtetl: A Vernacular Intellectual History* (New Brunswick, New Jersey: Rutgers University Press, 2014), 75.
28. Kugelmass and Boyarin, "Introduction," *From a Ruined Garden*, 12–15.
29. Annette Wieviorka and Itzhok Niborski, *Les Livres du Souvenir: Memoriaux juifs de Pologne* (Paris: Collection Archives, 1983), 53–54.
30. Alberto Giordano, Anne Kelly Knowles, and Tim Cole, eds., *Geographies of the Holocaust* (Bloomington: Indiana University Press, 2014), 4.
31. Kugelmass and Boyarin, "Introduction," 29.
32. Wieviorka and Niborski, 47.
33. Shandler, 40.
34. *Our Roots Shorashim Shelanu: In Memory to the Jewish Victims of the Holocaust, 1939–1945* (Tel Aviv: Organization of Former Jewish Inhabitants of Hrubieszow in Israel, 1990).
35. Shandler, 44–45.
36. Young, xi.
37. Shandler, 75.

Partisan Reviews and Commentaries on Eastern European Judaism

POSTWAR AMERICAN-JEWISH INTELLECTUAL
JOURNALS AND THE RECONSTRUCTION
OF THE EASTERN EUROPEAN PAST

Markus Krah

IN 1950, Arthur Hertzberg, then a young Conservative rabbi, made a proposal that in retrospect reads like a program for a crucial development in postwar American Jewish cultural life. Writing in the important journal *Commentary*, he argued that, "One of the dominant spiritual necessities of the present moment is to come to terms with the last several centuries of Eastern European creativity, which recently ended so tragically before our eyes. That world must be assimilated into the canon of the tradition and into the stream of Jewish history."[1] In fact, Hertzberg described a process already under way since the 1940s: an outpouring of texts by mid-century American Jewish thinkers and writers, engaging and reconstructing the Eastern European Jewish past as a way to grapple with the challenges and opportunities of the American Jewish present and future.

A few examples may illustrate this assertion. Since its relocation from Vilna to New York in 1940, YIVO presented a specific Eastern European past to American Jews as a model of a broad, positive Jewish identity. In 1943, Maurice Samuel published *The World of Sholom Aleichem*, popularizing a different image of Eastern European Jewry. In 1944, YIVO presented the first exhibition of Roman Vishniac's photographs of Jewish life in Eastern Europe, which visually defined Eastern European Jewry for many viewers. One year later, Abraham Joshua Heschel delivered, in Yiddish, his famed eulogy of Ashkenazic Jewry. In 1950, his speech became the bestselling book *The Earth Is the Lord's*. The late 1940s and 1950s marked a high point in the reception of Martin Buber's writings on Hasidism. In 1952, the popular study *Life Is with People: The Jewish Little-Town of Eastern Europe* brought the anthropological perspective of the sympathetic outside observer to the rich cultural heritage of the *shtetl*, which it presented as a *pars pro toto* of Eastern European Jewish civilization. One year later, Isaac Bashevis Singer's story "Gimpel the Fool" presented a very different image of the *shtetl*. In 1954, the year when the Tercentenary let American Jewry take stock of their state, many American Jews became acquainted with Yiddish stories through an anthology edited by Irving Howe and Eliezer Greenberg. In 1959, Philip Roth published his short story "Eli the Fanatic," in which the recent Eastern European past faces American Jewry in the figure of a Holocaust survivor. Almost simultaneously, Leon Uris presented the Zionist perspective on the Jewish past in *Exodus*. The lessons it drew differed fundamentally from another highly popular depiction of Eastern European Jewry: *Fiddler on the Roof*, the 1964 Broadway musical, based on stories by Sholem Aleichem.[2]

Through such cultural products—in works of fiction and scholarship, in countless journal articles (in both the English-language and Yiddish press), and in sermons and pamphlets, lectures and exhibitions—American Jews encountered and absorbed a wide variety of images, themes, narratives, and lessons, all drawn from the Eastern European experience. Its archetypical place could be the *shtetl* as much as Warsaw, a yeshiva, or the market square. Its archetypical figure could be a pious Hasid, a revolutionary Socialist, the victim of a pogrom, a dairy man, the *Vilna Gaon*, or the town fool.

The wide range of images suggests that in the postwar decades there was a competition going on to define the Eastern European past. In some cases, this competition was quite overt. In 1952, another Conservative rabbi, Herbert Parzen, also writing in *Commentary*, launched a broadside against influential thinkers by attacking their reconstruction of the Eastern European past. "A legend has been created by the spiritual leaders of what is the largest section of American Jewry. [. . .] Unhappy over the nature and prospects of Jewish life in America, [they] have projected the wishful picture of a holy, integral life, untainted by modernism, that is supposed to have been lived by our fathers in Eastern Europe. Against this, they point up what they claim is the disintegration and emptiness of present-day American Jewish life."[3] One unnamed target of Parzen's attack was Heschel, who used his idealized image of the lost world of Ashkenaz to criticize American Jewry, whereas Parzen defended America and de-mythologized Eastern Europe.

This exchange makes explicit what is otherwise an unacknowledged force driving many of the texts: Heschel, Parzen, Hertzberg, and other intellectuals used their diverging re-constructions of the Eastern European past to define the American Jewish present. The diversity of these images reflected not just the complexity of Eastern European life over several centuries, but also different visions for American Jewish life. Writers from a wide ideological spectrum claimed authenticity and legitimacy for their respective ideas for American Jewry by presenting them as continuities (more often than as discontinuities) with the Jewish past; in other words, they were creating a usable past.[4]

In these efforts to make the Eastern European Jewish past usable for the American Jewish present and future, journals played a crucial role. As has been the case in the development of ethnic or national consciousness (within Jewish and other histories), journals constituted a crucial element of the cultural infrastructure by which a group expressed itself and reflected on its identity, past and present.[5] This function was particularly relevant for mid-century American Jewry, which had advanced economically, educationally, and socially. A new middle class could afford (and valued) higher levels of education and spawned an elite of academics, rabbis, writers, and intellectuals, as well as the associated institutions—journals among them—for communal self-reflection. A potent combination of world historical and domestic developments, sketched in the following section, made such self-reflection an important communal need.

The community's new cultural elite intellectually engaged with the Eastern European heritage in journals that revealed an ideological reformation of postwar American Jewry and a desire for greater grounding in a legitimizing, authenticating, identity-supporting past. This article analyzes imagery of the Eastern European Jewish past as it was transmitted in three journals that were particularly influential in this process: the highbrow *Partisan Review,* which harnessed this past to its modernist cultural agenda; the religious journal *Judaism,* which sought to conceptualize a religion-based Jewishness; and *Commentary,* which in many ways occupied the crucial middle ground between the other two. These journals represent different ideological positions, as a new ideological landscape of postwar American Jewry gradually crystallized over the span of a generation, from World War II to the mid-60s. The analysis presents the journals' competing images of the Eastern European past as expressions of various ideologies and identities that were advocated for in a community asking fundamental questions about its role in the Jewish past and the Jewish and American present and future.

Social Inclusion vs. Distinctiveness: A Need to Redefine Jewishness

As American Jewry gradually came to play a profoundly transformed role in postwar America and in the post-Holocaust Jewish world, journals became important venues for discussion of different concepts of Jewishness. Unalloyed traditionalism, ethnic particularism, ideological secularism, and radical leftism were all presented and challenged in journals, as cultural modernization, social integration, a new appreciation of religion, and Cold War liberalism shaped American society's expectations of postwar Judaism.

Domestically, the divisive role that religion had played in the interwar years and the exclusion of Jews that made for an "anxious subculture" gave way to greater social and cultural inclusion in the 1940s and 50s.[6] The price to be paid for this inclusion was the continuing reduction of Judaism to the narrow definition of "religion," the flip side of which was the contemporaneous disdain for other categories of difference and particularisms, such as ethnic identities that would have made for a broader sense of distinctiveness. Concretely, the nature and role of Jewishness had to be consciously redefined as Jews moved in droves to suburbia, Jewishly uncharted territory where the balance of integration and distinctiveness had to be renegotiated in the context of the postwar "religious revival." Suburban synagogues became the most important locus for expressing Jewishness. As "ethnic churches" they served as venues for social activities and thus spoke to widespread needs for other, less fragmented concepts of Jewishness that transcended the narrow definition of religion.[7]

At the same time, American Jewry had to define itself within the Jewish world, particularly when it emerged as the largest and most potent Jewish community after the Holocaust. Engaging the Eastern European Jewish past was also a way to mourn the vanished world of its victims. Last but not least, the near-obsessive occupation of many American Jewish writers with this past can also be seen as a response to the founding of the State of Israel, with American Jews constructing an Eastern European heritage that would authenticate them against Zionist attacks on their legitimacy. Like the developments in American society, the changes in the Jewish world presented American Jews with challenges, but also new opportunities.

Taken together, all these factors made for much greater ambivalence, restlessness, and ferment among American Jews than what is suggested by the common narrative of a postwar period of relative consensus among American Jews on fundamental questions of Jewishness in America. This article aims to add another perspective to the ongoing revision of this perception. Symptomatic of the popular narrative has been Arthur Goren's optimistic description of the years from 1945 to 1955 as "a golden decade for American Jews."[8] Other historians have extended this "golden era" until the mid-1960s.[9] While still popular, this narrative no longer dominates the scholarly discourse on the postwar era.[10] In her history of the American Jewish experience, Hasia Diner added an illuminating question mark to the phrase "golden era," indicating an ongoing revision of the earlier narrative of a largely static, consensual, and harmonious period.[11] Historians have related new perspectives on American society to the formation of new types of Jewishness that emerged amidst severe birth pangs.[12] Riv-Ellen Prell argues that, "[How] Jews emerged from the devastations of World War II in the 1940s to enter a utopian moment in 1967, which led to a reshaping of American Jewish life, is a more complex story than most scholars have assumed."[13] Prell sees these decades as a period of broad and deep transformation, characterized by questions, tensions, and mixed feelings, particularly about the issue of Jewishness. "The postwar period, then, is best understood as a dynamic moment when the fundamental definitions of what it meant to be an American Jew were worked out in the new synagogues, living rooms, organizations, and political debates of the time."[14]

The intense American Jewish engagement with the Eastern European past analyzed here adds another indicator that beneath the surface of communal consensus and conformity, the very meaning of Jewishness in this period was unstable and contested.

Secular and Religious Intellectuals Probe New Forms of Jewishness

As the need arose to invoke, or even invent, a past that could endow Jewishness with meaning, writers in *Commentary*, *Partisan Review*, and *Judaism* rose to the challenge and presented a broad range of images and understandings of the Jewish past, in the service of different concepts of postwar American Jewishness. These journals provided cultural space—in the form of ink and paper—for the exploration of new concepts of Judaism and Jewishness, as part of the assimilation of a common narrative of the past and present into the collective imagination and memory. Even though they did not have a defined agenda (let alone a mandate), the intellectuals editing and writing for the journals took on a special responsibility for their community—partly as they themselves found the need to redefine their role vis-à-vis the community and their Jewish heritage.

In light of the importance of secularism for second-generation thinkers on the one hand, and of the outsized role of religion in postwar America on the other, the competition of secular and religious thinkers was crucial to the community's transformation. Juxtaposing the perspectives of secularists and religious thinkers through an analysis of their most important outlets will bring into clearer relief the different positions on competing concepts of Jewishness, an issue around which much of the debate about the nature of Judaism in modern times has pivoted.

The secular intellectuals running *Commentary* and *Partisan Review* were at some point quite fascinated with certain aspects of the Eastern European past, which was part of their family histories. *Commentary* founding editor Elliot Cohen's parents were immigrants; his father had attended the famous Volozhin yeshivah. The parents of *P.R.* editor William

Phillips hailed from Ukraine; his co-editor Philip Rahv was even born there, under the name Feivel Greenberg. These thinkers tapped into their Old World heritage after they discovered it behind the disliked immigrant culture of their parents' generation. Literary critic Irving Howe (né Horenstein) was a case in point. He was born in 1920 to parents who had come to the United States from Bessarabia. He grew up in the East Bronx, which formed a "thick tangle of streets crammed with Jewish immigrants from Eastern Europe, almost all of them poor." More than half a lifetime later, he created a loving monument to these immigrants in his 1976 *magnum opus*, *World of Our Fathers*.[15] Like Howe, many other second-generation thinkers (re-) discovered this world in the course of personal and generational transformations in the postwar decades. Young *Commentary* editor Norman Podhoretz, son of immigrants from Galicia, wrote that in the 1950s, "at least half of them had become enthusiasts of Martin Buber, while the whole of the New York literary world was ringing with praise of the Yiddish storytellers [and] the Hasidim."[16] In the eighteenth-century movement of religious renewal, and in other aspects of the Eastern European past, they found and reconstructed aspects of traditional Judaism that appealed to their own spiritual and intellectual needs. For some, this was a way to re-appropriate their Jewishness, after they had overcome their famed "alienation," a key notion by which second-generation intellectuals articulated the sense of unease felt by many American Jews vis-à-vis both parts of their hyphenated identity. In his eponymous essay of 1946, Howe portrayed "the lost young intellectual [as] a marginal man, twice alienated," both from America, which he perceived as hostile to Jewish difference, and from Jewishness, which he therefore tried, unsuccessfully, to suppress. For this figure, his Jewishness is a mere sociological fact, lacking any positive meaning: "it is, in the circumstances, unavoidable, [but] Jewishness is no longer a vital part of his life."[17]

Therefore, in the 1940s and 50s, this important segment of the group of second-generation Jewish intellectuals publicly explored new ways to find relevance in their Jewishness, through writing in an array of journals. At the same time, many of them noted that the social and intellectual climate of the time presented them with an unprecedented opportunity to move out of their relative cultural isolation and inscribe themselves in an emerging mainstream of sophisticated American culture. For some, the solution lay in integrating the two newly appreciated aspects of their identity as American Jews into a unified whole.[18] In the ironic description of Podhoretz, this was the "Grand Design" of Elliot Cohen, the head of the "family" of New York intellectuals: "to lead the family out of the desert of alienation in which it had been wandering for so long and into the promised land of democratic, pluralistic, prosperous America where it would live as blessedly in its Jewishness as in its Americanness, safe and sound and forevermore, amen."[19]

These intellectuals differed starkly, however, in how they would balance the cultural universalism they brought to the table with any Jewish particularism, about which many were highly ambivalent. The journals in which they published—*Partisan Review, Judaism,* and *Commentary*—thus represented distinct points on a wide ideological spectrum.

Commentary and *P.R.* shared a background in political radicalism and literary modernism, as well as topics, a cultural sensibility, and a group of writers, many of whom were Jewish. "The main difference between *Commentary* and *Partisan Review*," Elliot Cohen is quoted as saying, "is that we admit to being a Jewish magazine and they don't."[20] This quip both masks and reveals a key difference between the two journals, when it came to the role of Jewishness and the shared project of contributing to a sophisticated, progressive, modern American culture.[21]

Partisan Review: *Alienated Intellectuals and Incidental Jewishness*

Partisan Review, which grew out of a leftist intellectual milieu, and its Jewish writers, addressed their cultural modernism, political leftism, and ethnic (rather than religious) Jewish identities in complex ways. These factors intersected in their embrace of "cosmpolitan values," which to them represented the cultural sophistication and political progressivism to which they aspired (in themselves and for their audience). This notion could also accommodate a sense of Jewishness that related more to the aesthetic aspects of Jewishness (as expressed in literary texts) than to any ethnic or religion-based forms of belonging as a dominant factor shaping their identities.[22] Like other New York intellectuals, some *P.R.* writers over time moved closer to a conscious appreciation of their Jewishness. In the words of cultural historian Stephen Whitfield, "Some made gestures of ethnic return, and some had never really left."[23] Jewishness unquestionably was part of the magazine's *milieu* and was reflected in its texts; not coincidentally, Isaac Bashevis Singer's "Gimpel the Fool" was first published in *P.R.* in 1953. In their literary criticism, however, these writers refused to subordinate the aesthetic evaluation of a cultural product to external standards, such as the Jewishness of its author, a merely incidental attribute that would not and should not determine the cultural production of individuals or a group.

Two examples can illustrate how the journal subordinated Jewishness and Judaism to cosmopolitan cultural and political commitments. Susan Sontag praised Singer's novel *The Slave* for taking the ingredients of a specific historical and cultural environment—seventeenth-century Polish Jewry—and transforming them in ways that spoke to modern sensitivities: "On the face of this highly local and historically dense environment, Singer inscribes the universal conflicts of reason versus the flesh, and of creedal and ritual religion versus a free spirituality. Entirely absent from his work is any merely historical motive, the impulse to evoke this world and thereby to preserve it simply because it is both past and mercilessly destroyed." Historical Jewish distinctiveness is not a value in itself, Sontag seems to be arguing, but a means to a higher end, such as getting to the core of universal issues.[24] In a similar vein, Isaac Rosenfeld, in a text about Peretz, reinterpreted Hasidism as a means to an end, here artistic creativity and cultural progress. "The Chassidic ecstasies to [Peretz] were appearances in real historical time, but they are seen under a holy light," Rosenfeld wrote in a review of Maurice Samuel's book, *Prince of the Ghetto*. "It is the holy light of progress, enlightenment, brotherhood, the revelation of that face of the Godhead in which liberalism seeks its own image."[25]

Partisan Review reconstructed Eastern European Jewishness as a resource for spiritual sensitivity, which begat aesthetic creativity. Eastern Europe provided the venue and the cultural matrix for this creativity. Editor Phillip Rahv was so thoroughly influenced by Russian literature that he was jokingly referred to as "Phillip Slav"; the importance of Eastern Europe as a point of reference also shone through the journal's nickname, "Partisansky Review."[26] But whatever was specifically Jewish about this Eastern European past and culture, including traditional religion, was assimilated into a modern concept of literature. The Jewishness of a writer was incidental to his or her larger perspective. Jewishness meant a shared sensitivity, in aesthetic and political terms. If it had a contribution to make, it would be to the modern American culture to which *Partisan Review* was committed. The revitalization of Jewishness or of organized Jewish life, as values in themselves, was not part of the magazine's mission.

Expanding the Concept of Judaism—Retaining the Primacy of Religion

In this regard, the magazine *Judaism* can be seen as *Partisan Review*'s opposite. Founded in 1952 by the American Jewish Congress with an explicit commitment to Judaism as a religion and a value in itself, its purpose was to "foster the affirmation of Jewish religious, cultural, and historic identity."[27] Its writers and readers, many of them rabbis, but also academics and other religious thinkers and professionals, formed a new religious-intellectual elite within American Jewry, and the journal served as a forum for a modern religious discourse within American Judaism. Its authors were dedicated to revitalizing Judaism under new circumstances and in the face of low levels of observance and ambivalence about Jewishness. It publicly probed new ways to balance a commitment to the Jewish tradition and organized religious life with the recognition that American Jewry, like Judaism as an intellectual edifice, was largely post-traditional, yet in search of a meaningful Jewishness. Toward this end, *Judaism* was created to serve as a forum for "the creative discussion and exposition of the moral, religious, and philosophical concepts of Judaism and their relevance to the problems of modern society."[28]

The journal was committed to a distinctly religious concept of Judaism and Jewishness, but one that was in line with the spiritual universalism of the regnant zeitgeist. Founding editor Robert Gordis spelled out the constitutive belief that Judaism as a religion could offer meaning to Jewishness, while also speaking to spiritual needs beyond the Jewish group: "The revival of interest in Judaism, rather than in Jewish political action or organizational problems, derives [. . .] from one far-reaching factor which is broadly human rather than specifically Jewish—the spiritual unease of modern man," he wrote in a programmatic article in the first issue of the journal.[29]

In developing their vision for a vital American Judaism, the religious intellectuals writing in the journal committed themselves to a particular view of Judaism in relation to competing ideologies. Their most obvious target was secularism. Critiquing it both as an ideology and as a social reality, the religious thinkers also rethought the Eastern European Jewish past, which for many of them, as much as for their secular antagonists, was family history. Gordis, born in 1908 in New York to Yiddish-speaking parents, looked back at a long line of scholarly ancestors, among them a dean of the Mir yeshiva.[30] Ben-Zion Bokser, a Polish-born, unusually learned Conservative pulpit rabbi, pointed out that the saintly leaders of Eastern European Jewry, in their helpless passivity, allowed secularism to undermine traditional life. Lest American Jews repeat this mistake, he urged that "[religion] will also have to enter more boldly into the war of ideas, [. . .] to undertake with vigor the intellectual defense of religion against secularism."[31] Herbert Parzen positioned Jewish secularism as a phenomenon specific to the constellation of circumstances that had been present at its birth in Eastern Europe. As a reaction to traditional Judaism's rejection of modernity, it was thus out of place in America, where religious Judaism was modernized.[32] Hebrew literary critic Baruch Kurzweil found the most pernicious response to the secularizing forces in a cultural Judaism, à la Ahad Ha'am, that relegated religion to an inferior role. "The Judaism of Ahad Ha'am is a Judaism without the authority of Torah, and a Judaism without God." The error was all the greater, since this descendant of a Hasidic family born near Kiev should know better: "As a Russian Jew, steeped in Jewish tradition, Ahad Ha'am knew that religion occupies a position so dominant in Jewish culture as to make the latter inconceivable without it."[33]

Kurzweil's last sentence offers a hint at a second major theme on the journal's agenda for the revitalization of American Judaism: his use of the phrase "Jewish culture" illustrates many religious intellectuals' recognition that the modern concept of "religion," particularly in its postwar American expression, was problematically reductive and deprived Judaism of its full meaning-making potential. Gordis warned that "in the past, protagonists of Judaism as a 'religion' have all too often been advocates of a minimal, scarcely identifiable Jewish content in their lives." They erred by "giving to religion a narrow and thoroughly un-Jewish connotation." Therefore, the understanding of "religion" should be expanded to create conceptual space for Judaism conceived more broadly in distinctly Jewish terms: "Torah embraces the law, the lore, and the learning of Israel, the world-view of Judaism, and the Jewish way of life through which it is expressed."[34] Similarly, Orthodox rabbi Eliezer Berkovits urged that "Judaism, representing a comprehensive philosophy of life and living," be revitalized in its traditional, broad scope of "Jewish living"—to the degree this was possible under modern, American conditions.[35]

Thus, in order to expand the concept of "Judaism," the eponymous journal served as a forum for a wide range of ideas to revitalize Judaism in America, a mission for which many thinkers invoked the Eastern European past. Many authors, Gordis among them, expounded on what may be the most important trope in postwar American Jewish accounts of the past: Eastern European Jewish life, with its spirituality and human warmth, could infuse American Jewry with its dignity and distinctiveness. American Jews, Gordis wrote, "have retained much of [Eastern European Jewry's] warm sense of Jewish identification."[36]

Other authors of the journal pushed the conception of Jewish spirituality toward a broader aesthetic of Jewishness. Art critic Stephen Kayser, a friend of Heschel's, used an essay on Jewish art to highlight his vision of the rich, holistic Jewishness that shaped the creativity of Jewish artists in Eastern Europe or of Eastern European extraction: "Their Jewishness was but a natural part of their lives."[37] Art historian Maurice Schmitt presented Eastern European Jewish art, such as Marc Chagall's, as inspired by a sense of beauty that was distinct from Western standards, like Buber's dialogical philosophy and Sholem Aleichem's stories, all of which bespoke a spiritual depth that impressed Western Jews with its alien grandeur.[38] A glowing tribute to Yiddishist critic Shmuel Niger suggests an even bolder move toward an ethno-cultural understanding of Judaism. The journal appreciated Niger's notion of *Yiddishkayt*, derived, as it was, from the Eastern European experience, including the transformation of a religious conception of Jewishness into a cultural one.[39] These and other invocations of the Eastern European heritage pointed to the ideal that Kurzweil, as mentioned, had presented in his critique of Ahad Ha'am: a "Jewish culture" dominated by religion.[40]

Yet Gordis and his stable of writers insisted on keeping "religion" and "culture" apart conceptually, often walking a linguistic and conceptual tightrope. The impetus as well as the problems of this approach crystallized in the strenuous rejection of "cultural pluralism," which many writers dismissed as insufficient in practice to stem the mighty tide of assimilation to the American mainstream.

> [C]ultural pluralism is little more than a retarding factor, useful in making the process of assimilation more gradual and thus reducing the tension between immigrant and native generations. It does not constitute a permanent ideal for American democracy, for whether we lament or applaud it, the basic drive in American society is toward uniformity in language, culture, and mores. The only enduring type of pluralism which the structure of American life envisages lies in the field of religion.[41]

This distinction marks the crucial difference between the perspectives of *Judaism* and *Commentary*. In order to expand the scope of "religion," Gordis and other writers associated with *Judaism* contracted the scope of culture and ordered the two in a hierarchy: "to stimulate Jewish creativity in the fields of literature, music, and art alone, while neglecting the areas of religion, philosophy, and ethics, would mean presenting Hamlet without the Prince of Denmark," Gordis wrote. The deeper reason why these writers went to such great lengths to dismiss the cultural pluralism they found in *Partisan Review* and in *Commentary* relates to *Judaism* contributor Richard Fein's warning that the "subjective 'aestheticizing' of religion [as] the personal literary-cultural imagination replaces the communal religious one."[42] These thinkers sought to strengthen Judaism as a religion by defining it more expansively to encompass forms of Jewish expression and identification.

Commentary: *Appreciating an Emerging American Jewish Culture*

Commentary, founded in 1945 and sponsored by the American Jewish Committee, occupied the middle ground between *Judaism* and *Partisan Review* on two important and related counts. Like *Judaism*, but unlike *P. R.*, it took Jewishness as a value in itself that was worth exploring; like *P.R.*, it saw Judaism as a cultural phenomenon. Secondly, it struck a distinct balance of "culture" and "religion" as categories out of which an American Jewishness could be fashioned. *Commentary* was all the more influential as it bridged the divide between younger Jewish intellectuals and the elites of the religious community from which they had distanced themselves. As an upper middle-brow publication, it helped to span the gap between intellectuals in search of identification and a community in search of guidance, and provided the vehicle by which intellectuals could take responsibility in leading the community.[43] To do so, the intellectuals had to re-embrace the sociological fact of their Jewishness as something potentially meaningful. In Podhoretz's words, the magazine "arrange[d] for certain members of the family to shake hands in public with their own Jewishness for the first time in their lives."[44]

To arrive at this re-affirmation, *Commentary* thinkers turned to the Jewish past as a resource for the present. In the process, the magazine became the most important intellectual forum in which to probe new ways to conceive and express Jewishness. It was far from coincidental that Hertzberg's quasi-agenda for the absorption of the Eastern European past and its competing reconstructions by Heschel and Parzen were published in *Commentary*. The journal looked critically at *Life Is with People*, *Fiddler on the Roof,* and writings by Bundist leader Vladimir Medem and by the Vilna Gaon, as well as at fiction by Sholem Aleichem, Isaac Babel, and Isaac Bashevis Singer. Reflecting the intellectuals' fascination with Hasidism, *Commentary* presented Buber's "Hasidic Tales" and Norman Mailer's six-part reaction to them, and an essay by Leslie Fiedler that traced back to Hasidic origins American Jews' nostalgia for pastrami and *gefilte fish* as well as certain attitudes to sex.[45]

Exploring the Eastern European Jewish past in greater breadth than *Partisan Review* and *Judaism,* the journal went beyond the extant conceptualizations of Jewish identity. It broadened it beyond the narrow concept of religious Judaism, hovered above its institutional confines, and elevated ethnic Jewishness to something more meaningful. In this process the thinkers set parameters that shaped much of the larger debate about postwar Jewishness in America, as they redefined the concept of Jewishness by turning to cultural matters. At a 1948 *Commentary* symposium on American Jewry, Cohen articulated a notion of Jewish culture as integrating the quotidian and the profound in a time-tested whole:

> [T]he Jews, uniquely among all people, developed a cultural tradition in which religion, ethics, and intellectual values are felt as inseparably bound up with [and] expressed through the march of issues and events on this every-day-earth. This gave, some say, their religion and ethics their salty, realistic, this-worldly flavor. And, at the same time, some think it served to lend to their every-day pre-occupations the deeper human meanings that come from a sense of long historic perspective.[46]

In order to tap into the meaning-making potential of Judaism under modern conditions, these thinkers redefined the tradition in cultural terms rather than in strictly religious or ethnic terms—an idea that shaped their individual trajectories as well as their common intellectual project.

Critic Shmuel Niger argued that culture would be the best way to give positive direction to the increased but unguided identification with Jewishness that he saw among American Jews in general: "The emotional 'Jewishness' in America has increased, but our consciousness of Jewish cultural values has not become sufficiently profound."[47] Along similar lines, Cohen articulated a mission statement for the great project of the intellectuals: to lead American Jews toward a broader, richer, integral sense of Jewishness that would draw on the untapped cultural potential of a community in search of an identity:

> American Jews hunger for some kind of culture. Only consider how much our conversation in our homes is about the problems of Jewish education and the ideology of Jewish living and the relative truth of various Jewish ideas.

And yet so little happens. The Jewish community officially still tends to classify culture as a seductive but forbidden luxury—like that second mink coat.[48]

Therefore, much as some American Jews made room in their closets for that second mink coat, *Commentary* made room for cultural reconstructions of Jewishness, by presenting the Eastern European past as a rich and highly diversified Jewish culture that drew on and translated traditional concepts of Judaism into an American-Jewish idiom. This pluralism was implicit in the spectrum of time periods, persons, places, and ideas that were represented in the magazine's pages. Heschel's account of poverty as part and parcel of the spiritual nature of Ashkenazic Jewry appeared only six issues away from the memories of *Bund* leader Medem, son of an assimilated family, who fought poverty as a product of the capitalist order; both articles appeared as alternative ways to express Jewishness as an inspiring commitment. In another example, their inclusion in the column "Cedars of Lebanon" suggested that thinkers as different as Franz Rosenzweig and Hayyim of Volozhin could equally inform American Jews' identification with Judaism.

Pluralism was explicitly presented as a value that contributed to making the Jewish heritage rich and meaningful. Numerous texts specifically called for a pluralism that would liberate the Jews from the monopoly of religion as the only legitimate expression of Jewishness. Reviewing Heschel's *The Earth Is the Lord's*, Irving Kristol argued that missing from the idealized picture were "our harassed and disbelieving ancestors, who fled to America, not only from the pogroms, but—very many of them—also from the rebbe, the Hasid, the ghetto."[49] Ezra Spicehandler extolled the secular humanism of Ahad Ha'am as relevant for American Jews. Hertzberg called on American Jews to add the *"veltliche yid"* (secular Jew) to their reservoir of images of Eastern Europe, on which they drew for inspiration and guidance in their own time.[50]

Similarly, Yiddish educator Saul Goodman urged a "revaluation" of the ideas of Simon Dubnow, which "have either been forgotten or ignored, perhaps because the exponents of a religious point of view have come to dominate the discussion of Jewishness." Goodman's essay is a model for how an intellectual might translate the Eastern European past to make it speak to his contemporary American goals. He concludes his essay on Dubnow with this question:

> what can we learn from him for today? First of all, in secularizing the idea of Jewishness, and in giving meaning to Jewish history without benefit of theology, he provided a rationale [...] for the free-thinking Jew's impulse to remain Jewish and to transmit the heritage of Jewishness to future generations. Those who assert that a creative Jewish culture is impossible without a firm religious commitment might reflect on Dubnow's analysis of how the Jews maintained their spiritual character in various periods of history. [...] Is it, however, at all likely that American Jews will remain committed to Jewishness in a broad cultural sense? My own feeling is that the signs point in this direction. Surely the much heralded religious revival of recent years has less to do with religion (as many observers agree) than with cultural identification. If we adapt Dubnow's conception of the three national types to the American Jewish community, we might say that it has passed through the first two stages of Americanization and integration and is now entering into the third stage—the search for its ancestral roots and its authentic 'self.'[51]

According to most of the intellectuals, the "authentic self'" that Goodman foresaw would not derive its distinctiveness and authenticity from Jewish cultural separateness. Rather, the new type of Jewishness that most intellectuals envisioned would be distinctive in its openness to engagement with other cultures and sensitive to various complexities and tensions.

The broad and open concept of culture that informed *Commentary's* selection of topics bespeaks the journal's overall approach: to embrace America on Jewish terms and Jewishness on American terms.[52] The Eastern European past provided a storehouse of topics and models that could bestow on these reconstructions the cachet of history and the legitimacy of tradition. It proved that the offshoot of American Jewishness à la *Commentary* had roots in the Eastern European soil of authentic Jewishness. This link could give legitimacy to even mundane expressions of the evolving American Jewish culture. Editor Cohen created a section called "From the

American Scene," which covered decidedly popular topics, including a survey of ritual objects on sale at Macy's and an appreciation of the Jewish delicatessen as "an important Jewish cultural institution in the American scene."[53] American Jewry could look toward a legitimate Jewish culture of its own, if the concept of culture was defined broadly and if relating the present to the immigrant and pre-immigrant Eastern European past could make for authenticating continuities within the stream of Jewish history.

Culture and Memory—A New Paradigm of Jewishness

While the elevation of the corner shop where pastrami was sold with a Yiddish accent was certainly too middlebrow for *Partisan Review*, it was also too much ethnic Jewishness and not enough religion for the taste of the journal *Judaism*. These differences, indicative as they were, should not occlude the commonalities among the journals. *Commentary* and *P.R.* shared a fundamental interest in culture as an alternative source of meaning to religion. The thinkers involved with *Commentary* and *Judaism* agreed on the need to create a new, American sense of Jewishness. The Eastern European past could be an inspiration, but not the yardstick to measure its authenticity. *Commentary's* Cohen was adamant that American Jewry could not merely perpetuate an Eastern European type of Jewishness, or *Yiddishkayt*, or live off the memories of it—on principle and in light of the situation of post-Holocaust Jewry. As early as January 1945, in the editorial statement announcing *Commentary's* mission, he had passionately laid claim to the new responsibility devolving on American Jewry. "With Europe devastated, there falls upon us here in the United States a far greater share of the responsibility for carrying forward, in a creative way, our common Jewish cultural and spiritual heritage." Cohen took this responsibility as another reason to fashion a Jewish culture on its own American terms, whose legitimacy would not be measured by its adherence or fidelity to a past Eastern European culture that supposedly enshrined the essence of Jewishness. He continued in the statement: "And, indeed, we have faith that, out of the opportunities of our experience here, there will evolve new patterns of living, new modes of thought, which will harmonize heritage and country into a true sense of at-homeness in the modern world."[54] Similarly, Gordis, in several programmatic texts, presented the emerging American Jewish culture as a synthesis of Eastern and Western European Jewish experiences: "a 'mutation,' an amalgamation of both types of community," drawing its spiritual vitality from the Eastern European heritage. "American Jewry is a *novum*," not an attempt to replicate previous patterns of Jewish life.[55]

In this sense, the missions of the religious and the secular intellectuals were quite similar. The writers in *Judaism* strove to shape a new, expanded, and distinctly American concept of Judaism, which, like the Eastern European Jewish life on which it was patterned, would touch American Jews more deeply and more broadly than did the contemporaneous shallow, compartmentalized, and despiritualized sense of Jewishness. For the same purpose, *Commentary* encouraged the formation of a cultural definition of "Jewishness" informed by the traditional heritage, which would help to renew American Jewry as a "community of memory".[56] From this perspective, *Commentary* and *Judaism*, more than *Partisan Review*, expanded the parameters of the discourse that explored new paradigms of Jewishness. Culture—broadly defined—was the common denominator for these intellectuals as well as for other actors who submitted their own reconstructions of the Eastern European Jewish experience. The postwar decades were a period during which the discourse about this experience was in flux, with the imagery, lessons, and aesthetics of this past particularly contested, reflecting an American Jewish community in the process of refashioning its past for the sake of its present and future. The success of *Fiddler on the Roof* in 1964 suggests that the parameters of this discourse narrowed again sometime in the 1960s, as American Jews reviewed the past from a different perspective. Nevertheless, the postwar process of reconstructing the Eastern European past was influential beyond its time. The thinkers involved in this process created a repertoire of images, narratives, and aesthetics that has served as a resource for the continuing refashioning of Jewishness in a changing society.

Notes

1. Arthur Hertzberg, "The Worldly Jew" [Review of M. Ravitch, *Einems Yidishe Machshovos*; Y. Opatoshu, *Yidish un Yidishkeit*; and Y. Efroykin, *Kedushah un Gevurah bei Yidn*], *Commentary* 10, July 1950: 87.

2. Maurice Samuel, *The World of Sholom Aleichem* (New York: Knopf, 1943), and *Prince of the Ghetto: The Stories of Y. L. Peretz* (New York: Knopf, 1948); Abraham Joshua Heschel, "The Eastern European Era in Jewish History," *YIVO Annual of Jewish Social Science* 1, 1946: 86–105 (Yiddish original *YIVO Bleter* 25, no. 2 (1945): 163–83), and *The Earth Is the Lord's: The Inner World of the Jew in Eastern Europe* (New York: H. Schuman, 1950); Martin Buber, "Tales of the Hasidim," *Commentary* 3 (January 1947): 73–78; Mark Zborowski and Elisabeth Herzog, *Life Is with People: The Jewish Little-Town of Eastern Europe* (New York: International Universities Press, 1952); Isaac Bashevis Singer, "Gimpel the Fool," *Partisan Review* 20 (May 1953): 300–313; Irving Howe and Eliezer Greenberg, eds., *A Treasury of Yiddish Stories* (New York: Viking, 1954); Philip Roth, "Eli, the Fanatic," *Commentary* 27 (April 1959): 292–309; Leon Uris, *Exodus* (Garden City, NY: Doubleday, 1958).

3. Herbert Parzen, "When Secularism Came to Russian Jewry," *Commentary* 13 (April 1952): 355.

4. See David G. Roskies, *The Jewish Search for a Usable Past* (Bloomington: Indiana University Press, 1999) and Arnold M. Eisen, "Constructing the Usable Past: The Idea of 'Tradition' in Twentieth-Century American Judaism," in *The Uses of Tradition: Jewish Continuity in the Modern Era*, ed. Jack Wertheimer (New York: Jewish Theological Seminary, 1992), 429–61.

5. For the role of periodicals in the development of a modern Jewish/Yiddish culture in nineteenth-and twentieth-century Eastern Europe, see David E. Fishman, *The Rise of Modern Yiddish Culture* (Pittsburgh: University of Pittsburgh Press, 2005): 6–8, and passim.

6. Jonathan D. Sarna, *American Judaism: A History* (New Haven: Yale University Press, 2004), 208–27.

7. Marshall Sklare, *Conservative Judaism: An American Religious Movement* (Glencoe, Ill.: Free Press, 1955), 35; also see chapter 2.

8. Arthur Goren, "A Golden Decade for American Jews: 1945–1955," in *A New Jewry? America Since the Second World War [Studies in Contemporary Jewry, VIII]*, ed. Peter Y. Medding (New York: Oxford University Press, 1997), 3–20. According to Goren's analysis, American Jewry enjoyed a broad consensus based on the "doctrinal core" identification of Jewishness as a religious category: the supposed congruence of Jewishness and Judaism made for a stable communal identity. (8) Albert Gordon, in *Jews in Suburbia* (Boston: Beacon, 1959), particularly the concluding chapter 10, also presented a largely positive and optimistic picture of Jewish life in the suburbs, which contributed to the overall narrative that, for American Jews, the positive developments in their postwar lives by far outweighed any negative ones.

For an example of the narrative that emphasizes the positive dimensions of choice and success, see Pamela S. Nadell, "Jews and Judaism in the United States," in *The Cambridge Guide to Jewish History, Religion, and Culture*, ed. Judith R. Baskin and Kenneth Seeskin (Cambridge: Cambridge University Press, 2010), 208–32.

9. Cf. Leonard Dinnerstein, *Antisemitism in America* (New York: Oxford University Press, 1994), 178.

10. This revision of the narrative of the Jewish experience in mid-century America corresponds to a tendency toward a more nuanced view of American society at large during this period; cf. Mary Caputi, *A Kinder, Gentler America: Melancholia and the Mythical 1950s* (Minneapolis: University of Minnesota Press, 2005) and Grace Elizabeth Hale, *A Nation of Outsiders: How the White Middle Class Fell in Love with Rebellion in Postwar America* (New York: Oxford University Press, 2011).

11. Hasia Diner, *The Jews of the United States, 1654 to 2000* (Berkeley: University of California Press, 2004), 259. This revision includes recognition of a greater role of the Holocaust in more American Jewish discourses before 1967; Also see Diner, *We Remember with Reverence and Love: American Jews and the Myth of Silence after the Holocaust, 1945–1962* (New York: New York University Press, 2009).

12. Placing the Jewish experience in the larger perspective of the "politics of consensus," literary historian Wendy Wall points out that the broad agreement on values associated with the "American way" was actually created as a political project that responded to the ethnic and other tensions characterizing the interwar years. *Inventing the "American Way:" The Politics of Consensus from the New Deal to the Civil Rights Movement* (Oxford: Oxford University Press, 2008).

13. Riv-Ellen Prell, "Triumph, Accommodation, and Resistance: American Jewish Life from the End of World War II to the Six-Day War," in *The Columbia History of Jews and Judaism in America*, ed. Marc Lee Raphael (New York: Columbia University Press, 2008), 114–42.; see also her "Community and the Discourse of Elegy: The Postwar Suburban Debate," in *Imagining the American Jewish Community*, ed. Jack Wertheimer (Hanover, NH: Brandeis University Press, 2007), 67–90. For another revisionist study, see Lila Corwin Berman, "American Jews and the Ambivalence of Middle-Classness," *American Jewish History* 93, no. 4 (December 2007): 409–34.

14. Prell, "Triumph, Accommodation, and Resistance": 115. Historian Michael Staub has undermined the idea that postwar American Jewry rested stably on a liberal political consensus. *Torn at the Roots: The Crisis of Jewish Liberalism in Postwar America* (New York: Columbia University Press, 2002). More broadly, Susan Glenn replaces the "golden era" image with the notion of a "Jewish Cold War" that was waged in the postwar years. Its eponymous global counterpart impacted Jewish life much more disruptively than previously acknowledged, as it "triggered a complex debate about postwar pressures for Jewish group loyalty and conformity." Susan A. Glenn, "The Jewish Cold War: Anxiety and Identity in the Aftermath of the Holocaust" (David W. Belin Lecture, Frankel Center for Judaic Studies, University of Michigan, 2015). Glenn hints at the distinct function of the reconstructed Eastern European experience as a positive foil by pointing out that the fear of assimilation was often expressed by the negative example of prewar German Jewry.

15. Irving Howe, *A Margin of Hope: An Intellectual Autobiography* (San Diego: Harcourt Brace Jovanovich, 1982), 1; and *World of Our Fathers: The Journey of the East European Jews to America and the Life They Found and Made* (New York: Harcourt Brace Jovanovich, 1976).

16. Norman Podhoretz, "Introduction-Jewishness and the Younger Intellectuals: A Symposium," *Commentary* 31 (April 1961): 307–8.

17. Irving Howe, "The Lost Young Intellectual: A Marginal Man, Twice Alienated," *Commentary* 2 (October 1946): 362. Writing two years later, fellow *Commentary* contributor David Bernstein extended the assessment to American Jews in general, stating that "of all the insecure people in America (except for Negroes), Jews are the most unhappily insecure." "Jewish Insecurity and American Realities: A Prescription Against Mental Escapism," *Commentary* 5 (February 1948): 119

18. Nathan Abrams, "'America Is Home:' *Commentary* Magazine and the Refocusing of the Community of Memory, 1945–1960," and Ruth R. Wisse, "The Jewishness of *Commentary*," in *Commentary in American Life*, ed. Murray Friedman (Philadelphia: Temple University Press, 2005), 9–37, 52–73.

19. Norman Podhoretz, *Making It* (New York: Random House, 1967), 135, and "Jewish Culture and the Intellectuals: The Process of Rediscovery," *Commentary* 13 (May 1955): 451–57.

20. Quoted in Benjamin Balint, *Running Commentary: The Contentious Magazine That Transformed the Jewish Left into the Neoconservative Right* (New York: Public Affairs, 2010), 18.

21. See Nathan Glazer, "Commentary: The Early Years," in *Commentary in American Life*, ed. Friedman; Eugene Goodheart, "The Abandoned Legacy of the New York Intellectuals," *American Jewish History* 80, no. 3 (Spring 1991): 361–76; Alexander Bloom, "Partisan Review," in *Encyclopedia of the American Left*, ed. Mari Jo Buhle, Paul Buhle, and Dan Georgakas (New York: Oxford University Press, 1998), 583–84.

22. Terry A. Cooney, "New York Intellectuals and the Question of Jewish Identity," *American Jewish History* 80, no. 3 (spring 1991): 344–360. On the interaction of Jewish and non-Jewish writers at P.R., see S. A. Longstaff, "Ivy League Gentiles and Inner-City Jews: Class and Ethnicity Around *Partisan Review* in the Thirties and Forties," *American Jewish History* 80 (spring 1991): 325–43.

23. Stephen J. Whitfield, "The Ethnicity of the New York Jewish Intellectuals," *Revue LISA/LISA e-journal* 1, no. 1 (2003), 13.

24. Susan Sontag, "Demons and Dreams" [Review of I. B. Singer, *The Slave*], *Partisan Review* 29, no. 3 (1962): 461.

25. Isaac Rosenfeld, "The Ghetto and the World" [Review of Maurice Samuel, *Prince of the Ghetto*]," *Partisan Review* 16, no. 2 (1948): 210. In another example, literary critic Elizabeth Hardwick reviewed Isaac Babel's collection of stories, *Benya Krik, the Gangster*. She offered the highest praise for Babel as "a magical Russian writer." But she concluded the review by scolding the publisher, Schocken, for the decision "to present him so meekly and meagerly by isolating the Jewish stories." "Fiction Chronicle [Review of Babel, Benya Krik et al.," *Partisan Review* 15, no. 12 (1948): 1352.

26. Whitfield, "The Ethnicity of the New York Intellectuals": 11; Wisse, "The Jewishness of *Commentary*": 194f.; Alfred Kazin, *New York Jew* (New York: Knopf, 1978), 44.

27. American Jewish Congress, "Statement of Sponsorship," *Judaism* 1, no. 1 (January 1952): 2.

28. *Ibid.* For its editorial agenda, see also Robert Gordis, "Toward a Renascence of Judaism," *Judaism* 1, no. 1 (January 1952): 4–5; "The Task Before Us: A Preface to Our Journal," *Conservative Judaism* 1, no. 1 (January 1945): 1; and "The Genesis of *Judaism:* A Chapter in Jewish Cultural History," *Judaism* 30, no. 4 (fall 1981): 390–95.

29. Gordis, "Toward a Renascence": 4, 5.

30. Harvey E. Goldberg, "Becoming History: Perspectives on the Seminary Faculty at Mid-Century," in *Tradition Renewed: A History of the Jewish Theological Seminary of America [vol. 1]: The Making of an Institution of Jewish Higher Learning*, ed. Jack Wertheimer (New York: JTS Press, 1997), 389.

31. Ben Zion Bokser, "Religion and Secularism," *Judaism* 1, no. 2 (April 1952): 156–57.

32. Herbert Parzen, "The Passing of Jewish Secularism in the United States," *Judaism* 8, no. 3 (summer 1959): 197.

33. Baruch Kurzweil, "Judaism-The Group Will-to-Survive? A Critique of Ahad Ha'Amism," *Judaism* 4, no. 3 (summer 1955): 211, 215. See also Saul Goodman, "Jewish Secularism in America—Permanence and Change," *Judaism* 9, no. 4 (fall 1960): 319–30; Harold M. Schulweis, Review of H. Kallen, *Secularism Is the Will of God*, *Judaism* 4, no. 4 (fall

1955): 367–371; C. Bezalel Sherman, "Nationalism, Secularism and Religion in the Jewish Labor Movement," *Judaism* 3, no. 4 (1954; Tercentenary issue): 354–65.

34. Gordis, "Toward a Renascence": 7, 8.

35. Eliezer Berkovits, "Jewish Living in America," *Judaism* 2, no. 1 (January 1953):72. Berkovits qualified his hopes for such a development in America by stating that ultimately "Jewish living" was possible only by living in one civilization in the State of Israel, "the natural home of Judaism.... Jewish living in America is not fully realizable" (73–4).

36. Robert Gordis, "American Jewry Faces Its Fourth Century," *Judaism* 3, no. 4 (fall 1954; Tercentenary issue): 300.

37. Stephen S. Kayser, "Visual Arts in American Jewish Life," *Judaism* 3, no. 4 (1954; Tercentenary issue): 444.

38. Maurice Schmidt, "Marc Chagall—The Jewish Painter," *Judaism* 13, no. 3 (summer 1964): 328–34; See also Alfred Werner, "Max Weber: Hasidic Painter," *Judaism* 9, no. 3 (summer 1960): 260–68; Ernest M. Wolf, "Martin Buber and German Jewry," *Judaism* 1, no. 4 (October 1952): 346–52.

39. Samuel Kreiter, "Sh. Niger: Yiddish Humanist," *Judaism* 6, no. 4 (fall 1957): 334–39.

40. Kurzweil, "The Group Will-to-Survive," 215.

41. Gordis's polemic ("Toward a Renascence of Judaism": 7) appeared some twenty pages away from a text by Horace Kallen, which re-affirmed the concept that Kallen created, albeit without using the term. ("What Price 'Jewish Living'?" *Judaism* 1, no. 1 (January 1952): 27–35.) See also Parzen, "Passing of Jewish Secularism," 195; Schulweis, Review of Kallen, 367; Will Herberg, "Religious Trends in American Jewry," *Judaism* 3, no. 3 (summer 1954): 229–240.; Melvin M. Tumin, "Conservative Trends in American Jewish Life," *Judaism* 13, no. 2 (spring 1964): 135–36.

42. Richard J. Fein, "Jewishness—The Felt Ambiguity," *Judaism* 16, no. 2 (spring 1967): 140.

43. Wisse, "The Jewishness of *Commentary*," 69.

44. Podhoretz, *Making It*, 133.

45. A selection: Moshe Decter, "The 'Old Country' Way of Life: The Rediscovery of the Shtetl" [Review of Zborowski and Herzog, *Life Is with People*], *Commentary* 13 (June 1952): 600–604; Irving Howe, "Tevye on Broadway" [Review of *Fiddler on the Roof*], *Commentary* 38 (November 1964): 73–75; Vladimir Medem, "Youth of a Bundist: A Jewish Labor Leader Recalls His Beginnings," *Commentary* 10 (November 1950): 477–82; "The Tanya and the Gaon: A Dispute," *Commentary* 21 (January 1956): 67–68; Sholem Aleichem, "Journalism in the New Kasrilevke: Liveliness Above All," *Commentary* 22 (July 1956): 62–65; Isaac Babel, "The Awakening," *Commentary* 3 (February 1947): 132–35; Isaac Bashevis Singer, "Taibele and Hurmizah," *Commentary* 35 (February 1963): 132–38; Norman Mailer, "Responses & Reactions," *Commentary* 34 (December 1962):504–506; Leslie A. Fiedler, "Hasidism and the Modern Jew" [Review of Martin Buber, *Tales of the Hasidim, Hasidism*, et al.] *Commentary* 7 (January 1949): 195–98.

46. Elliot Cohen, in "Report on a Conference on the Jewish Experience in America" [sponsored by *Commentary*], typescript May 1948: 63–64. (YIVO Archives, Max Weinreich Collection, RG 584, folder 225A): 5.

47. S. Niger, "The Amalgam Which Is Jewish Life" [Address at National Conference for Jewish Education, January 1951], *Workmen's Circle Call* 19, no. 2 (March 1951): 4.

48. Elliot E. Cohen, "Jewish Culture in America: Some Speculations by an Editor," *Commentary* 3 (May 1947): 413, emphasis in the original.

49. Irving Kristol, "Elegy for a Lost World" [Review of Heschel, The Earth Is the Lord's] *Commentary* 9 (May 1950): 490–91.

50. Ezra Spicehandler, "A Jewish Humanist" [Review of L. Simon, Ahad Ha-Am-Asher Ginzberg], *Commentary* 32 (September 1961): 266–68; Hertzberg, "The Worldly Jew," 88.

51. Saul Goodman, "Simon Dubnow: A Revaluation," *Commentary* 30 (December 1960): 511, 515.

52. See Podhoretz, "Jewish Culture and the Intellectuals," *Commentary* 13 (May 1955): 451–57.

53. Morris Freedman, "The Real Molly Goldberg: Baalebosteh of the Air Waves," *Commentary* 21 (April 1956): 359–64; Ruth Glazer, "The Jewish Object: A Shopper's Report," *Commentary* 12 (July 1951): 63–67; and "The Jewish Delicatessen: The Evolution of an Institution," *Commentary* 1 (March 1946): 58–63.

54. Cohen, "Act of Affirmation," 2. Abrams quotes Cohen registering his "contemptuous disdain" toward "European-Yiddish values," as an indication of *Commentary*'s conscious rejection of mere nostalgic engagement with the Eastern European past ("America is Home," 34).

55. Gordis, "American Jewry Faces Its Fourth Century," 298–99.

56. Abrams, "America is Home."

A Mid-Twentieth-Century Quest for Jewish Authenticity
THE YIDDISH DAILY *FORVERTS'*
WARMING TO RELIGION

Gennady Estraikh

Catering to the Observant

American Jews of the 1940s and 1950s, especially first-generation Yiddish-speaking immigrants and to some extent their offspring, tended to validate Jewish authenticity using Eastern and Central European traditional religious values and attitudes. This study analyzes the attitude towards religious Judaism as articulated by writers and readers of the New York Yiddish Daily *Forverts* (Forward), which had the biggest share of American Yiddish readers, even when its circulation declined from over a quarter of a million in the 1920s to 80,000 in 1951 and 44,000 in 1970.[1] The material used in this study offers insights into two areas: first, articles and readers' letters reflect attitudes toward religion among journalists and their readers; and second, most central to this study, the work published in the *Forverts* reveals the editorial policy during the same period.

Although secularism was one of the pillars of the socialist program of the *Forverts*, its editor, Abraham Cahan (1860–1951), advocated respectful treatment of religious people and their traditions and observance. For instance, in 1908, an editorial comment in the advice column *"Bintl Briv"* (Bunch of Letters) that may reveal the hand of Cahan, instructed readers: "Every man has the right to his religion as the freethinker to his atheism. To parade one's acts that insult the religious feeling of the pious, especially on *Yom Kippur*, the day they hold most holy, is simply inhuman."[2] Joel Entin

(1875–1959), a pioneer of Yiddish secular education in the United States, wrote that, "active anti-religiosity was, by 1910, an outworn relic among American Jews."[3]

Characteristically, in his 1909 essay "The Poetic Rebirth of the Jewish Religion," Chaim Zhitlovsky (1865–1943), the leading light among American Yiddishists, advanced the neo-romantic argument that secular Jewish activists should revamp Jewish holidays and employ their deep national meaning.[4] On Rosh Hashanah eve 1913, a *Forverts* editorial encouraged its freethinking readers to restrain themselves from acting as fanatical atheists.[5] According to Annie Polland, "the development of the *Forverts* . . . reflects the shared world of 'religious' and 'secular' Jews, and the way in which religious sentiments and practices had to be honored, or at least not offended, as avowedly socialist institutions moved beyond their rank-and-file base to court immigrant masses."[6]

In 1942, the newspaper advised a reader, a convinced freethinker, to find a compromise between his personal convictions and traditional family obligations, such as attending bar mitzvah celebrations:

> Act according to your conscience, as your principles dictate. If you don't want to participate in the [grandson's bar mitzvah] ceremony in the synagogue at all, no one should force you to participate. . . . There are freethinkers who aren't scared of a synagogue and do attend the bar mitzvahs of very close relatives. They merely stipulate that they should not receive an *aliyah*. . . .[7] If you don't want to be at the synagogue for the ceremony at all, you can still heartily celebrate at the party together with your family and the invited guests.[8]

It seems that by the end of the 1930s, the policy of respecting the spiritual feelings of readers who fell somewhere in between observant and secular changed into a policy of catering to the observant. Meanwhile, the *Forverts* had altered its political stance, becoming more Rooseveltian than socialist, and, as a result, religion was considered to be one of the "institutions indispensable to Americans."[9] Still, the newspaper did not begin printing openly pro-religion articles, nor did it drop its Saturday or Jewish holiday issues out of religious observance. Rather, the choice of material increasingly took into account the interests and sensitivities of the traditional reader. The *Forverts* ferociously attacked its celebrity author Sholem Asch (1880–1957) for writing the novel *The Nazarene*. After reading the novel's first chapters in March 1938, Cahan strongly advised Asch to destroy his "Christian" work. When Asch, much to Cahan's fury, did not follow this instruction and the novel, translated into English, became a bestseller in 1939, his prose pieces and essays entirely disappeared from the pages of the newspaper.

The *Forverts*' journalistic community had excommunicated their star colleague for crossing what they considered to be uncrossable lines of separation between their proper Jewish world and the Jewish world that already behaved in a *goyish* manner. These were the lines between Americanization-without-assimilation, which the *Forverts* professed, and rabid assimilation or even apostasy, all signs of which Cahan and his ilk found distasteful. As the storm gathered, Cahan and several other *Forverts* staff writers, most notably Chaim Lieberman (1890–1963), repeatedly decried Asch as a profound embarrassment, accusing him of betraying the national interests of the Jewish people.[10] To all appearances, Asch, who lived predominantly in Europe, either failed, or, in his larger-than-life manner, was unwilling to detect the metamorphosis in the outlook of the *Forverts*' editorial staff and to understand that his desire to explore common roots in Christianity and Judaism could not resonate with a considerable portion of the readers.

Jacob (Yakov) Lestschinsky (1876–1966), a leading Jewish social scientist in the first half of the twentieth century, also lived in Europe, though it did not stop him from becoming one of the most attentive observers of American Jewish life. From December 1921, Lestschinsky headed the Berlin bureau of the *Forverts*, but his arrest in March 1933, following Hitler's rise to power (he was released by the police several days later under the pressure of the American State Department), led him and his family to wander the continent—Czechoslovakia, Poland, Switzerland, and France—until November 1938, when the Lestschinskys, with the help of the *Forverts* staff, eventually arrived in New York.[11] Lestschinsky's very first impression of America was favorable, even euphoric. However, soon he began to see American Jewish life as an unstable, makeshift construction. Ten weeks after disembarking in New York, he penned an article, entitled

"American Jews," that appeared in the Warsaw daily *Haynt* (Today). Lestschinsky acknowledged that it was too early for him, a "greenhorn," to come to any far-reaching conclusions about the peculiarities of the American setting. Still, he argued, his hunch might be valuable because it was fresh. Lestschinsky was pleasantly surprised by Jewish storekeepers' readiness to speak Yiddish, and he observed that generally New York Jews happily employed this language in public spaces, whereas in Warsaw, Jews preferred to speak Polish. However, he soon understood that this did not mean Yiddish was in better shape in New York. The same Jews who had no problems with publicly speaking Yiddish (often a broken one) usually preferred to converse in English at home, whereas in Warsaw, Yiddish more often continued to function as the language of family communication. In all, Lestschinsky came to the conclusion that "the air of freedom was dangerous for Jewish culture" and that the Jewish façade of New York was misleading. Even the impressive ten-story *Forverts* building, which towered over its environs as the skyscraper of the Lower East Side, seemed to him a shaky construction. On the one hand, he could see clear similarities with the urban landscape of the old country: synagogues, stores selling religious paraphernalia, etc. Yet, after a while, he realized that it was not an organic part of local life but some kind of well-performed theater, as religion had been marginalized and children grew up without knowing Jewish traditions. As a result, Jewish culture was losing its foundation.

> Every honest Jewish intellectual has to admit that modern Jewish culture has benefited a lot from Jewish [O]rthodoxy—from its conservatism, its stubbornness, and its desperate clinging to each minor constituent of Jewish traditions. Jewish [O]rthodoxy has provided consumers for the culture and continues to provide the vast majority of its producers, both in Yiddish and Hebrew.[12]

According to Lestschinsky's article published in the New York Labor Zionist journal *Der yidisher kemfer* (Jewish Fighter), he realized that processes of what he called "denationalization rather than assimilation" were going on in New York and other cities. In other words, Jews were losing their Jewish traits and acquiring a new, American touch, but nevertheless they remained visible as Jews, and "stuck in gentiles' throats like a bone."

Therefore, he maintained (certainly applying to America his European, notably German and Polish, experience) that one day Americans might try to get rid of this visible minority. Lestschinsky also noticed the cultural abyss that had opened wide between the first and second generations of Jewish immigrants. He called it the "abyss between the present and the future." Seeing how little in common the young generation had with their parents, he began to understand why so many people were attracted to moving back to the "religious ghetto."[13]

Cahan, too, admitted that a very significant number of American Jews remained religious, or, "to be precise, more or less religious." He maintained that in many cases national tradition rather than piety determined their behavior. Either way, the majority of American Jews kept kosher and almost universally circumcised their sons.[14] Although Cahan claimed to deeply respect Marx and highly value the great man's economic theories, he saw Marx as a fallible human being, albeit a genius. For instance, as early as 1915, or even earlier, Cahan disagreed with Marx's views on Jews and argued that, in general, he was not ready to "hock his brain" to anyone, even Marx. He also questioned the validity of socialist internationalism, maintaining that people would always persist in their loyalties to their ethnic group.[15] Recognizing the importance of religion in Jewish life, he disavowed Marx's definition of religion as "the opium of the people." In his 1941 anti-Asch pamphlet, he formulated his understanding of Jewishness: "A Jew remains a Jew even if he is an atheist. Nonetheless, he ceases being Jewish if he converts to any other creed."[16] Interestingly, a version of this definition would appear in the 1970 Israeli Law of Return.[17]

The Sixth Lubavitch Rebbe

In 1940, the *Forverts* paid a lot of attention to the arrival in New York of the sixth Lubavitch Rebbe, Yosef Yitzchok (or Joseph Isaac) Schneersohn. On March 20, 1940, the day after his arrival, the newspaper reported about it in a front-page feature, with a photo of the spiritual leader. The editorial article was entitled "Masses of Hasidim and Rabbis Came to Welcome the Lubavitch Rebbe on His Arrival."[18] Coincidentally, the same voyage of the S.S. Drottningholm brought to New York the head of the Vilna-based YIVO institute Max Weinreich (1894–1969), who had been a regular contributor to the *Forverts* since 1920. Though one would expect more attention to be paid to one of the leading figures in Jewish secular circles, his arrival was less prominently reported.[19]

The *Forverts* described various details of the ceremonial welcoming of the rebbe, which included the recitation of the blessing "*Mechaye Hametim*" (Revival of the Dead) by the popular cantor Samuel Kantoroff, and the singing of Chabad melodies by the Hasidim who came to New York Harbor, while younger Hasidim expressed their exaltation with a celebratory dance called a *rikudl*.[20] According to the newspaper's estimate, about 1,600 people stood at the pier. In addition, some other people were waiting at the Greystone Hotel, at the corner of Broadway and 91st Street, where the rebbe would stay during the first six months following his immigration. An article with the headline "The Hotel on Broadway, Where the Lubavitch Rebbe is Staying" was penned by William Reswick (1890–1954), a Ukrainian-born journalist who had graduated from the New York University Law School. He later spent several years as head of the Associated Press bureau in Moscow (his 1952 book *I Dreamt Revolution* is still referred to in Soviet-related writings) and worked as a *Forverts* staff writer beginning in 1934. Reswick began his narrative on a nostalgic note:

> The atmosphere created following the recent arrival of the worldwide-known Lubavitch Rebbe is a rare phenomenon in the life of American Jews.
>
> It is something that recalls images of our Jewish environment of the past, full of things that were so beautiful and honorable in those unforgettable years—all these had revived virtually overnight on a street corner in the very heart of New York.
>
> Are there people among us, immigrants in America, who cannot recall scenes of commotion in a shtetl visited by the Zinkever, Lubavitcher or Chenobyl rebbe?
>
> Excitement would overwhelm every resident. People were building tents for communal repasts. Klezmorim welcomed the rebbe who was being paraded through the streets of the shtetl. The residents would rush to him to ask his blessing and to get their problems off their chests. Both the poor and the rich used to do

it. Sometimes, but not exceptionally rarely, even landlords from surrounding estates would come in their elegant carriages to intimate to the rebbe their own aristocratic worries, asking him to give them his advice and blessing.

Something of this kind is taking place at the New York Greystone Hotel.

Reswick's two-minute-long audience with the rebbe made a very strong impression on the seasoned journalist. He was so mesmerized by the rebbe's "exceptionally pretty eyes," which were looking at the visitor "with such tender goodness (*tsertlekher gutskayt*)" that Reswick almost lost his facility to speak and left the rebbe's temporary residence in a state of enchantment.[21] This was in stark contrast to the tone of the feature article "Hasidic Rabbis in New York and Their *Shtiblekh*," published in the *Forverts* twelve years earlier, in which the author, B. Salant (no information about him is known), wrote with irony that at the time when Jews were involved in building skyscrapers—modern towers of Babel—some other Jews were moving the clock of history backward to the middle ages. He lamented the appearance in New York of women with shaved heads and men with "wild forests" of hair on their faces.[22]

It seems that in the 1920s and increasingly in the 1930s, the attitude to Hasidim had changed, with American Jews becoming more favorable toward them. This change could be a result of increased feelings of nostalgic affinity with the *alte heym*, old home, and with the arrival of larger numbers of immigrants from traditional Hasidic areas, as well as of several *real* Hasidic rebbes or their *eyniklekh* (offspring). In addition, a milder attitude to Hasidim could be a reaction to the process described by Lestschinsky as "denationalization rather than assimilation." As a result, many Jews did not want to be part of this "pointless" transformation. In 1934 the *Forverts* wrote that Hasidic *shtiblekh* increasingly attracted American Jews who found the atmosphere of mainstream synagogues unsatisfying, lacking in authenticity. The "geographical affiliation" of Hasidic dynasties often did not play an important role in America. One could see Lithuanian, Ukrainian, Polish, Romanian, and Galician Jews praying and socializing in the same *shtibl*.[23] Apparently, it was important for them that Hasidim tried to avoid any "Americanization" of the traditions. Thus, the Passover seder looked exactly as it did in the old country, "*vi got hot gebotn*" (as God had ordained).[24]

In the beginning of 1941, the Lubavitch yeshiva Tomchei Temimim was established at 770 Eastern Parkway in Brooklyn. It carried, and still carries, the same name, meaning "supporters of the pure ones," as the yeshiva founded in 1897 (the same year when the *Forverts* was born) in the shtetl of Lubavitch by the fifth Rebbe Sholem Dovber Schneersohn. Under this same name, the yeshiva then reestablished itself in Warsaw and later in Otwock, Poland. The *Forverts* journalist Haim Abraham Hurvitz (1893–1952), or H. Vital, as he signed his articles, visited the yeshiva in May 1941. By that time, New York was home to eighteen yeshivas with about seven thousand students. Five of these yeshivas had been established in the previous four years. Hurvitz, himself a former yeshiva student in *Lite*—the historic area where the shtetl of Lubavitch was situated and the Lithuanian dialect of Yiddish was spoken—explained that American yeshivas usually differed significantly from their Eastern European prototypes. Most importantly, traditional yeshivas functioned as full-time institutions of higher religious training, aimed at preparing new cadres of rabbis, whereas students who attended American yeshivas usually did so part-time, because they also studied at regular American schools. (A decade later, the *Forverts* praised the Yeshiva Rabbi Solomon Kluger, then situated on Manhattan's Houston Street, for teaching students in Yiddish, using, in particular, Yehoash's Yiddish translation of the Bible. This yeshiva, established in 1902, taught both secular and religious subjects.)[25]

The Tomchei Temimim Yeshiva appeared to Hurvitz as an authentic recreation of traditional Eastern European yeshivas. Moreover, the students looked even "less modern" than their counterparts at such yeshivas as Slobodka and Telz in the *Lite* of Hurvitz's youth. Thus, in Slobodka and Telz, it was considered acceptable to shave faces, but it was forbidden to do the same at 770 Eastern Parkway. At the time of Hurvitz's visit, the yeshiva had fifty students. Initially, there were only twenty students: the Americans who studied at the Tomchei Temimim in Otwock; thanks to their American citizenship, they were allowed to leave Poland following the beginning of World War II. The other students managed to join them later, while fifty-five students were stuck in Japan, waiting for travel documents, and thirty-eight students were on their way to Japan.[26] (In the

1930s, young Americans, including graduates from Harvard, Columbia, New York and other universities, studied at several yeshivas in Poland. For instance, in 1932, according to the *Forverts*, forty-eight Americans studied at the renowned yeshiva of Mir.)[27]

Dual Identity

In the new climate, the *Forverts* assumed a dual identity. On the one hand, its editors and journalists and many of its readers belonged to the cohort of lifelong socialists, or at least leaned toward socialism, deeming religion to be a retrograde form of Jewish allegiance. On the other hand, the newspaper strove to dominate America's Yiddish readership, which increasingly turned or warmed to the tradition. The editorial response to readers' letters revealed this stance. Thus, as mentioned above, the newspaper advocated tolerance toward bar mitzvah ceremonies, even if the boys' grandparents, readers of the *Forverts*, belonged to overtly secular circles and therefore felt uncomfortable or humiliated participating in the rituals. In 1944, Ben Zion Hofman (1874–1954), aka Tsivion, wrote about the bar mitzvah as an increasingly popular fashion, which, he argued, usually reflected an attraction to essentially superficial forms of religiosity, similar to what he recently observed when he visited a journalist on a Saturday and found him sitting at his desk, smoking a cigarette, and writing an article about the necessity of keeping the Sabbath as a holy day. In general, Tsivion saw around himself numerous Jewish intellectuals who turned to religion in some way or another. As a sign of this turn, in March 1944, Rabbi Joseph Dov Soloveitchik, a major authority in American Jewish Orthodox circles, appeared as an invited speaker at the YIVO, introduced by its director Max Weinreich, whose relocation to New York in 1940 effectively meant also the relocation of the institute.[28] Berl Botwinik (1885–1945), a veteran *Forverts* writer, hailed the lecture as a historic event symbolizing a peace established between traditional *Yiddishkayt* and secular socialist Jewry.[29]

Boris Smolar (1897–1986), editor-in-chief of the Jewish Telegraphic Agency and a regular *Forverts* contributor, was in the audience of three hundred people when Rabbi Soloveitchik delivered his YIVO lecture entitled "Secular Jewishness and Modern Jewish Religious Ideologies: How an Orthodox Jew (*Gemoreh Yid*) Sees It?" According to Smolar, the speaker focused on the question of what American-born Jews—who at that time, under the influence of the tragic events in Europe, turned to their national roots—found appealing in the Jewish tradition. Soloveitchik's conclusion was that secular Jewish culture, notably as articulated in the writings of Sholem Aleichem, I. L. Peretz, Hayim Nahman Bialik, and Saul Tchernichowsky, usually did not resonate with young Jews (though some of them could relate to Sholem Aleichem's writings), whereas many of them, including university students, were increasingly drawn to religion.[30]

Meanwhile, Isaac Bashevis Singer (1902–91) ridiculed the new form of religiosity that he noticed among Jewish intellectuals—a religiosity of word rather than of deed, which, he believed, made their Jewishness similar to Christianity. Singer had no problem with cultural Jews, but he caricatured those who were religious only in words but ate pork and did not go to synagogue.[31] In his *Forverts* articles, published under the pseudonyms of Yitshok Varshavski and D. Segal, Singer returned many times to the issue of changes in American Jews' religiosity. By 1950, he noticed among some young people the tendency to become pious, even if their parents were completely secular. Moreover, he argued that such young Jews caught his sight more often in America than in Poland, which he left in 1935. According to Singer, four main reasons caused young people to find spiritual refuge in religion: (1) some people had "religious souls" and were unable to live without a belief; (2) the Holocaust brought disillusion about the ability of society to save humanity, and therefore many people turned to individual quests, to self-improvement, which ultimately led them to religion; (3) some people believed that Hitlerism was a punishment for modernization, and, in addition, the small percentage of Jews used by the Nazis as collaborators were as a rule not religious, and it left an impression of the steadfastness and moral righteousness of religious people; and (4) the association of secularism with communism made religion attractive in contrast.

Singer's writings on religious issues often mentioned Sholem Asch and the latter's "Christian novels." Thus, in Singer's 1944 article, Asch appeared as one of the "caricature Jews," while in 1950 Singer wrote that he would have preferred Asch to become a religious person than to watch him turning to "idolatry" (*avoyde-zore*).[32] The breach between the *Forverts* and Asch remained unhealed. The 1943 publication of Asch's novel *The Apostle*, featuring the life of Paul (the same year *The Nazarene* appeared in Yiddish under the imprint of the New York communist daily *Morgn-Frayhayt*), and of his 1945 essay *One Destiny: An Epistle to the Christians* provided new ammunition for criticism by his former colleagues. Chaim Lieberman applied to Asch the language of the apostle Paul's detractors: Thomas Jefferson's definition of Paul as "first corruptor of the doctrines of Jesus" and Ernest Renan's "ugly Jew" (*dos paskudne yidl*).[33]

From People to People

In the fall of 1944, several readers' letters discussed the issue of selecting the right kind of burial for a secular Jew. Summing up the debate about the place of freethinkers in this world and in the afterworld, the newspaper praised the good-natured tone of the letters. The editorial comment was full of self-admiration, hailing the *Forverts*, its editor, and other members of the staff for creating a stable climate of tolerance among its readers, whereas three decades previously a civilized debate between freethinkers and their opponents would have been impossible. The commentary explained that in those days, before the *Forverts* began to play an influential role in shaping the views of the public, both sides remained fanatical, full of hatred for one another. Nonetheless, the *Forverts* had succeeded in uprooting fanaticism among secular readers and, thanks to its respectful attitude toward "honestly pious Jews," attracted religious readers to the newspaper.[34]

To a certain degree, it was the editors' wishful thinking. Letters published in the newspaper reveal a lack of ideological harmony among its readership and, in particular, the older core readers' frustration at seeing the *Forverts* increasingly targeting the religious segment of its constituency. Thus, D. Gitis, a member of the Workmen's Circle and a one-time card-carrying socialist, who began to read the *Forverts* in 1911, wrote from Los Angeles (his letter, entitled "An old *Forverts* reader reveals his heart," appeared under the rubric "Fun folk tsum folk," or "From people to people") that his secularity did not stop him from respecting "honestly pious Jews" and even "dissident rabbis." The *Forverts* was, in Gitis's words, his Decalogue; he fully agreed with the newspaper's attitude toward communism and Israel. Yet he could not say the same about some articles on religious themes, most notably by Rabbi Aaron Ben-Zion Shurin (1914–2012) and the journalist Chaim Lieberman.[35] N. Chait, a reader from the Bronx whose letter appeared under the rubric "From people to people," contended that any Saturday or Sunday issue of the *Forverts* carried more *yidishkayt*, or Eastern European Jewishness, than a synagogue could deliver during an entire year.[36]

Rabbi Shurin, who had been working for the *Forverts* since November 1944, maintained that his "hiring reflected the feeling of the founding editor, Abraham Cahan, that the newspaper needed to speak to the religious Jews who flooded the United States in the 30's and 40's."[37] In his articles, some of them signed with the pseudonym A. B. Rutzon, Shurin put Jewish religious traditions into the context of contemporary events. Thus, in his September 1945 article, entitled "Yom Kippur—the Gentile World Should Have Such a Day," he wrote that real peace could not come without Germany's public repentance.[38]

It seems that Lieberman, previously a Labor Zionist secular activist, turned to religion after a tragedy in his family. When asked by a colleague how he, an educated person, could take seriously such things as the *Shulchan Aruch*, Leiberman replied that, according to the Talmud, there was no difference in principle between believing and striving to believe. Cahan liked Lieberman, but restrained his desire to publish pro-religion articles. Such articles, which pleased the religious reader and irritated the secular one, found a place in the newspaper after the old editor's demise in 1951.[39]

To counterbalance Gitis's criticism, the *Forverts* carried another letter in the same issue and under the same "From people to people" rubric: "The *Forverts* and religious Jewry," by Yakov Ross of Bradley Beach, New Jersey, who had been reading the newspaper for almost fifty years. Ross introduced himself as an old Bundist and a follower of the *Forverts* columnist Tsivion. He periodized the *Forverts*'s attitude to religion into three phases: negative, neutral, and (recently) positive. In his understanding, the murder of six million Jews and the establishment of Israel contributed to the rise of religiosity, and the *Forverts*, a "people's newspaper," had no choice but to reflect this change.[40] The Holocaust appeared to be a major factor driving American Jews to turn to religion by joining synagogues.[41]

Even the ideologues of the communist camp began to reassess the content of their cultural products. Some aspects of Jewish tradition, discarded in the iconoclastic climate that dominated the communist circles of the 1920s and 1930s, were gradually reinstalled in the 1940s and onwards. Itche Goldberg (1904–2006), the leading American Yiddish leftist educator and editor, played a central role in this cultural retrieval, mirrored, for instance, in his edited children's journal *Yungvarg* (Young People). In March 1938, the journal, then printed in the Soviet-style de-Hebraized orthography, published a letter from Chicago by a ten-year-old girl. The girl, named Sheila Goldblat, wrote that on one day when she did not feel well and could not go to school, her mother entertained her with a story of how shtetl dwellers used to celebrate Passover. The girl previously knew virtually nothing about the holiday and traditions associated with it. Brought up as a committed internationalist, Sheila was appalled to learn that only the Jews had been liberated thanks to Moses's endeavors. In April 1947, however, the same journal published a Passover poem by the poet Martin Birnbaum (1904–86), describing Exodus as an important historical event. Significantly, from 1943 on, *Yungvarg* introduced the traditional spelling of Hebraisms.[42] It is known that the secular Jewish identity of those who studied at American Yiddish non-religious schools often transformed itself into a religious identity with relative ease as the former students matured in the 1940s and 1950s.[43]

In the *Forverts*, Max Weinreich, writing under the pseudonym of P. Berman, reacted to two publications in the journal *Commentary*.[44] These articles described and analyzed the recent developments in Jewish society, particularly following the increase in the suburban Jewish population. As a result, hundreds of new synagogues had been opened, and thousands of Jews had become members of Jewish centers, which combined educational, religious, and leisure time functions. In fact, migration to affluent neighborhoods also invigorated the migrants' desire to be "more Jewish" than in the areas of compact settlement of Eastern European Jewish immigrants, where they "were Jewish" with or without any particular manifestation of their ethnic-cum-religious affiliation. Riv-Ellen Prell has characterized Jewish life in the suburbs as a "paradox" of "doing more but feeling less Jewish."[45] Joseph Blau, the Columbia University scholar of Jewish history and religion, has surmised that American Jews' affiliation with synagogues at that time was not so much a sign of their desire to identify themselves as Jews as it was a phase of their American affiliation.[46]

Sarcastic about the religiosity of the Jewish centers' members, Weinreich argued that a half-hearted revival of Judaism was taking place.[47] He punned on the Yiddish word *tsenter*, meaning both "center" and "tenth," arguing that at such centers it was often difficult to find the tenth person for a *minyan*. (Albert I. Gordon, who studied Jewish life in the suburbs of the 1950s, came to the conclusion that, without mourners saying Kaddish for a blood relative, "most suburban synagogues would find it difficult to maintain the traditional daily prayer service," and surveys in the late 1950s revealed that the majority of American Jews attended synagogues on High Holidays only.)[48] Weinreich hoped that some Jews would ultimately switch their interest from playing cards at a Jewish center to reading Sholem Aleichem. He admitted, however, that secular Yiddishists were failing in competition with those who advocated for a "return to Jewishness" via religion. One of the main roots of this failure he saw in the respectability of religion in American society.[49] The journalist Yitshak Shmulevitsh (1911–?), who began to work at the *Forverts* in 1954, soon after his arrival from Europe, also emphasized that religious organizations trumped secular ones, for instance at the housing cooperative on the Lower East Side of Manhattan built by the International Ladies' Garment Workers' Union, whose members used to be known as staunch socialists and freethinkers.[50]

In April 1963, the *Forverts* printed another letter from Ross, under the title used in 1956 for Gitlis's letter. Indeed, this time Ross was in Gitlis's camp, criticizing the newspaper's "intolerant attitude to [politically] conscientious workers (*bavustzinike arbeter*), who had set the *Forverts* on its feet and continue to form the basis of its existence." Ross was ready to countenance the careful and respectful selection of materials for "honestly pious Jews," because he understood that otherwise they would stop reading the newspaper. However, he also felt that the newspaper did not show enough sensitivity to their old readers and essentially "pulled them to the synagogue" by propagating religion in its pages. Ross argued that following the death of Tsivion, who for many years wrote on current issues in Jewish life, the *Forverts* lost the balance between secularity and religiosity. As a result, Lieberman's apology for Orthodoxy began to dominate the newspaper. For a while, Borekh Shefner (1896–1977) became a secular voice in the newspaper, but Abraham Menes (1897–1969), who later stepped in, "saw beauty only in the past and praised Jewish [O]rthodoxy."⁵¹

The alte heym

In November 1942, Yakov Sklar, a Brooklyn-based reader, wrote in a letter to the *Forverts*:

> Grandfathers who immigrated here thirty or forty years ago and threw their prayer shawls and phylacteries in the ocean thinking that that would free them from Judaism, now suddenly realize that their American-born grandchildren don't know of any such tricks for evading their heritage. The grandchildren see their Christian classmates go to church on Sunday and wonder why they shouldn't go to synagogue on Saturday. And if the grandchildren go to synagogue they must also know how to pray, so they end up going for religious instruction after school or on the weekends. Once they go for religious instruction, when they become thirteen years old the teachers tell them they must have a bar mitzvah. . . .
>
> I will tell you from my own life experience. I am also a grandfather, and my son, a physician, is far from being religious. My grandson, an American-born . . . became bar mitzvah three years ago. I felt that being in the synagogue together for the bar mitzvah helped bring the three generations closer, the synagogue brought us together. No birthday party or graduation party was able to accomplish what the synagogue during the bar mitzvah was able to accomplish.⁵²

In 1949, the Yiddish poet and journalist Naftali Gross (1896 or 1897–1956) praised the Passover seder as a unifying occasion for religious and non-religious families.⁵³ Around the same time, a Chicago-based reader's suggestion to make the rituals and melodies of the Rosh Hashanah celebration "merrier" in order to compete better with Christmas decorations and carols, was met with revulsion by other readers.⁵⁴ The turn to *yidishkayt* found a reflection in the textbook *College Yiddish*, written by Max

Weireich's son Uriel and first published in 1949 under the imprint of YIVO (in 1959, Uriel Weinreich inaugurated the position of Professor of Yiddish language, literature, and culture at Columbia University). In one of the lessons, he included the following text constructed as sentences in an exercise for translating into Yiddish:

> 1. My grandfather said that he learned to pray when he was going to *kheyder*. 2. When he came to the United States he noticed that not all Jews were pious. 3. He could not understand why. 4. For some time he himself prayed only on Saturdays. 5. Now he again prays three times a day. 6. On *Yonkiper* [Yom Kippur] I went with my grandfather to the synagogue. 7. I understood the prayers because I know a little Hebrew. 8. I wasn't sure how to conduct myself in a synagogue, but I did what everybody did. 9. I liked the old rabbi with the long white beard. . . . 13. Since he spoke in Yiddish, it was easy to understand almost everything. . . . 19. I am glad that I went to the synagogue and I am preparing to go again.[55]

Clearly, the author wanted to emphasize the affinity of the American synagogue with the synagogue of the grandfather's *alte heym*. Indeed, the same secular Eastern European Jewish immigrants who were unhappy with the revival of religious life were also irritated by the innovations imposed on religious rituals. Paradoxically, radicals on the scale of secular ideology, they remained conservative in their attitude to Jewish traditions. Thus, David Shub (1887–1973), a veteran socialist and a leading journalist of the *Forverts*, wrote that at the funeral of the historian Saul Ginsburg (1866–1940), a *Forverts* contributor, he could not stand the modern *nigun* (tune) of *El male rachamim* (prayer for the dead) recited by a cantor with a shaved face.[56] In 1945, Haim Abraham Hurvitz, aka Vital, stressed that young Orthodox Jews preferred traditional-style cantors to those who "sang like opera singers" and became a staple at retreats in the Catskills. During his research for the article on American cantors (who, in his evaluation, numbered about 1,500 nationwide, including over a thousand in New York City), Hurvitz found out that their status had risen of late, because their service began to be better paid and many of them received contracts with synagogues on an annual basis rather than only for the duration of holidays. He attributed this to the general increase in synagogue-goers and their soaring contributions to synagogue funds. At the same time, he emphasized that a cantor could expect to be remunerated at a higher level by Orthodox synagogues than by (usually wealthier) Reform and Conservative congregations.[57] Shmuel Horetz, a reader residing in Brooklyn, agreed with Hurvitz that a yeshiva student turned into an amateur cantor could deliver a more authentic cantorial performance than an "opera-style" professional cantor could.[58]

Americanization and commercialization of Jewish holidays galled *Forverts* writers and readers. Boris Smolar grumbled that, whereas the majority of the Jews remain ignorant about Shavuot and Sukkot, ubiquitous advertising of such merchandise as wine and matzoth made Passover the most popular Jewish holiday in America, even among the sixty percent of the Jews who were not synagogue affiliated.[59] Commercialization of Jewish and non-Jewish holidays began in the 1920s or even earlier. Berl Botwinik wrote sardonically in 1930 that Americans tended to seek pleasure rather than to seek God, and only advertisements reminded them that the holidays were coming up.[60] The poet and essayist David Eynhorn (1886–1973), a one-time Bundist, felt lonely in the suburb where he'd moved after a decade spent in Manhattan's East Side. Sitting at the locked doors of a local Reform synagogue, he paraphrased Abraham Goldfaden's lines from the play *Shulamith*. In Eynhorn's version it read:

Shabes, yontev un rosh-khoydesh
davn ikh far zikh aleyn;
mayn harts iz der orn-koydesh,
un der khazn—mayn geveyn.[61]

On the Sabbath, holiday, and beginning of a Jewish month
I pray on my own;
my heart is my Holy Ark,
my lament is my cantor.

According to Shifra Kuperman, a student of Eynhorn's life and oeuvre, "Eynhorn did not believe that Jewry could exist without the synagogue; accordingly, he fought against assimilation and called for preservation of

Jewish traditions."[62] For Eynhorn, Asch embodied a treacherous trend in contemporary Jewish life; the poet feared that American Jews would replace "Moses's Passover" with "Sholem Asch's Passover."[63] At the same time, he found signs of degradation in the image and behavior of the contemporary Jewish ultra-Orthodoxy, particularly in the thousands of men shouting in front of Israel's consulate in New York in February 1954, when they protested against the conscription of Israeli women into military service. This kind of religiosity was as alien to him as Reform Judaism, if not more. He felt nostalgic for the pious old Jews of the bygone days in his native Belorussia, whose beards were similar to the beards of old Frenchmen or Americans of the Civil War era.[64]

The *Forverts* staff writer Isidor (Isser) Ginsburg (1872–1947), who studied at the Volozhin Yeshiva and later at Cornell University's medical school, ridiculed Reform Judaism, which in the eyes of Ginsburg and his like embodied rabid assimilation behind the façade of observance. He saw the Reform constituency as a hypocritical group of people with only one annual Yom Kippur commitment: to enjoy a satisfying breakfast and then drive to a synagogue in order to spend some time there, usually at least thirty minutes, but certainly not longer than an hour. According to Ginsburg, they also had two articles of belief, both negative ones: first, Jews should be considered as a religious group, not a nation; second, Jews could not be successful in establishing their own country.[65]

Lestschinsky found it ridiculous, even denigrating, to see or hear anecdotes about American modifications of Jewish rituals. To him, and many people with his background, religion, if practiced, had to be part and parcel of *normal* Jewish life. In other words, he was one of those freethinking "old-timers" who treasured the religion for its national cultural significance, but only in the form they understood to be an authentic expression of Jewish piety. He also was of the opinion that in America, religion should play a more important ethno-consolidating role than in Eastern Europe, where other factors kept Jews united, most notably social and economic discrimination, and a common language—Yiddish.[66] He abhorred such modifications as a lunch break during Yom Kippur, when some people would leave synagogue to go home or to a restaurant, and he was unhappy to see an increasing number of Jewish homes decorated both for Chanukah and Christmas. At the same time, he believed that the establishment of

Israel and the revival of Hebrew protected Chanukah from being fully replaced by Christmas. In addition, he diagnosed a radical change in American Jews' perception of identity: while it was almost a non-issue for the first, "organically Jewish" immigrant generation, the second and third generations tended "to make an effort in order to be Jewish." [67]

This does not mean that the first generation, at least part of it, did not "make an effort." As Eli Lederhendler asserts in his study of the changes that occurred in American Jewish life in the post-World War II period, it was the first, not the second, generation of Eastern European Jewish immigrants who "were primarily responsible for establishing the guiding parameters of Jewish ethnicity" in the United States.[68] Baruch Charney Vladeck (1886–1938), manager of the *Forverts* and a prominent figure in socialist circles, spoke in 1934 about American Jews' attempts "to assimilate themselves by going back on their tradition, on their culture, and on their very religion."[69] As a Marxist, he characterized this behavior as occurring exclusively among upper and middle class Jews. In reality, Jewish workers tended to act similarly, with many of them ultimately joining the middle class. Reclaiming tradition or what was considered to be authentically Jewish became one of the principal parameters of Yiddish-speaking immigrants' behavior, and the shrinking world of the *Forverts* increasingly participated in this process, which continued and intensified in the following years, though the newspaper never became a religious forum.

In 1956, Hillel Rogoff (1883–1971), a veteran journalist of the *Forverts* and its editor in 1951–1962, stressed that Cahan's and other *Forverts* writers' "tolerance" towards religion in most cases did not reflect a decline in the strength of their freethinking. Rather, it related to the streak of nationalism in their ideological makeup.[70] Still, Rogoff admitted that the position of religion had become much stronger than it had been at the turn of the twentieth century. He listed three contributing factors: (1) many more children attended Jewish day schools; (2) introduction of a five-day week made keeping Shabbat much easier; (3) kosher food could be bought at numerous stores. Rogoff's article was a reply to the letter of Joseph Breslaw, a leading figure in the International Ladies' Garment Workers' Union. Breslaw wrote that socialists used to see religion as an effective instrument in the hands of capitalists and wanted to know why the *Forverts* changed its stance. Rogoff explained the position of the newspaper:

The *Forverts* has no special attitude to religion. It is not its task to preach religion or anti-religion. As a newspaper, the *Forverts* mirrors the life, events, and political currents in the Jewish street. Therefore religion also finds a place in our newspaper. . . .

Some of the *Forverts* writers are religiously inclined, whereas the others are anti-religiously inclined. Some of them are entirely freethinkers, but with sympathies to religious institutions. This is a sentiment, a kind of nostalgia, which they are unable to surrender to the past.[71]

Many thousands of freethinkers healed their nostalgia by reading the *Forverts* and being members of its related organizations, notably the socialist-rooted Workmen's Circle. For some of their children, this family tradition gave them the answer, or part of the answer, to their quest for Jewishness. However, much more often, the second and third generations became one way or another involved in the process of becoming religious. In 1990, when the author of this study took part (as a Soviet guest) in a Workmen's Circle convention, one of its activists—a lifelong reader of the *Forverts*—described the paradigm of generational change as it affected his own family: "My father was a socialist and freethinker, I am a liberal and belong to a Reform congregation, and my son is an Orthodox." I could hear irony in his words, but no bitterness.

Notes

1. Hillel Halkin and Gennady Estraikh, "Jewish Daily Forward," *Encyclopedia Judaica*, 2nd edition, vol. 11 (Detroit, MI: Macmillan Reference USA, 2007), 290.
2. Isaac Metzker, ed., *A Bintel Brief: Sixty Years of Letters from the Lower East Side to the Jewish Daily Forward* (Ballantine Books, New York 1971), 98–99.
3. Joel Entin, *Gezamlte shriftn*, vol. 1 (New York: Pinhas Gingold Farlag, 1960), 80.
4. Joshua M. Karlip, *The Tragedy of a Generation: The Rise and Fall of Jewish Nationalism in Eastern Europe* (Cambridge, Mass.: Harvard University Press, 2013), 57, 320.
5. "Rosheshone un apikoyres," *Forverts*, October 3, 1913, 4.
6. Annie Polland, "'May a Freethinker Help a Pious Man?': The Shared World of the 'Religious' and the 'Secular' Among Eastern European Jewish Immigrants to America," *American Jewish History* 93.4 (2007): 379.
7. *aliyah*—an honor of reading from the Torah or reciting a blessing over the reading.
8. Gennady Estraikh and Zalman Newfield, "Grandfathers against Bar Mitzvahs: Secular Immigrant Jews Confront Religion in 1940s America," *Zutot* 9 (2012): 77–78.

9. F. D. Roosevelt and C. Hutchins, *State of the Union Addresses* (Kessinger Publishing, New York 2004), 92.

10. Hannah Berliner Fischthal, "Abraham Cahan and Sholem Asch," *Yiddish* 11.1–2 (1998): 1–17.

11. Gennady Estraikh, "Jacob Lestschinsky: A Yiddish Dreamer and Social Scientist," *Science in Context* 20.1 (2007): 227–231.

12. Jacob Lestschinsky, "Amerikaner yidn," *Haynt*, April 7, 1939, 5. Similar motifs were central in Lestschinsky's book *Vuhin geyen mir?* (New York: Yidisher natsyonaler arbeterfarband, 1944).

13. Jacob Lestschinsky, "Ershte ayndrukn fun amerikaner yidntum," *Der yidisher kemfer*, June 16, 1939, 8–9.

14. Abraham Cahan, *Sholem Ashs nayer veg* (New York: n.p., 1941), 4.

15. Abraham Cahan, "Der internatsyonal," *Forverts*, December 27, 1915, 5; and "Far vos ken nokh nit zayn keyn emeser internatsyonal?," *Forverts*, December 29, 1915, 5.

16. Cahan, *Sholem Ashs nayer veg*, 4.

17. See, e.g., Izhak Englard, "Law and Religion in Israel," *The American Journal of Comparative Law* 35.1 (1987): 195; Nahshon Perez, "Israel's Law of Return: A Qualified Justification," *Modern Judaism* 31.1 (2011): 61.

18. "Masn khsidim un rabonim bagegenen lyubavitsher rebe bam onkumen," *Forverts*, March 20, 1940, 1.

19. For the history of the YIVO and the role of Max Weinreich in its establishment and operation, see Cecile E. Kuznitz, *YIVO and the Making of Modern Jewish Culture: Scholarship for the Yiddish Nation* (New York: Cambridge University Press, 2014).

20. For details of the rebbe's arrival, see Bryan Mark Rigg, *Rescued from the Reich: How One of Hitler's Soldiers Rescued the Lubavitcher Rebbe* (New Haven: Yale University Press, 2004), 152–54.

21. William Reswick, "Hotel af Brodvey, vu der Libavitsher Rebe shteyt ayn," *Forverts*, April 4, 1940, 6. See also "William Reswick, News Writer, 64: Former Reporter in Moscow Had Worked with Hoover, Baruch and Otto Kahn," *New York Times*, June 3, 1954, 27.

22. B. Salant, "Khsidishe rabeim in Nyu-york un zeyere khsidim-shtiblekh," *Forverts*, June 10, 1928, section 2, 1.

23. Charles Rodek, "Emes vegn di khsidishe rabeim un khsidishe 'shtiblekh' in Amerike," *Forverts*, January 29, 1934, 3.

24. Charles Rodek, "Der hayntiker peysekh in Amerike iz ful mit tifshte gefiln un di raykhste kolirn," *Forverts*, April 18, 1935, 3, 4.

25. S. Regensberg (Shmuel-Arye Regenbogen), "'Galitsyaner yeshive' oyf ist-sayd vu me lernt toyre oyf yidish," *Forverts*, March 14, 1952, 4, 7.

26. H. Vital, "Der Lyubavitsher Rebe firt a groyse yeshive in Bruklin," *Forverts*, June 15, 1941, section 2, 3–4.

27. L. Hoyzner, "Masn yidishe yungelayt fun Amerike, geendikte koledzsh, lernen itst in di barimte Poylishe yeshives," *Forverts*, January 29, 1933, 4.

28. Tsivion, "Yidishe interesn," *Forverts*, April 8, 1944, 6.

29. See David E. Fishman, introduction to Joseph Dov Soloveitchik, *Droshes un ksovim* (Jersey City, NJ: Ktav Publishing House, 2009), 22.

30. Boris Smolar, "Dem gantsn lebn hobn zey geveykht fun yidishkayt; itst zukhn zey tsu dergeyn dem 'sod' fun der eybiker yidisher ekzistents," *Forverts*, April 2, 1944, section 2, 2.

31. Itskhok Varshavski, "Zey rufn zikh religyeze yidn, ober zey zaynen nit frum," *Forverts*, April 3, 1944, 2.

32. D. Segal, "Tate-mame zaynen fraydenker un di kinder—frum," *Forverts*, September 11, 1950, 2.

33. Chaim Lieberman, "A briv tsu Sholem Ash," *Forverts*, October 10, 1945, 2; "Yidntum un kristntum," *Forverts*, October 11, 1945, 2; and "Dos paskudne yidl," *Forverts*, October 12, 1945, 2.

34. "A bintl briv," *Forverts*, November 23, 1944, 5.

35. D. Gitis, "Fun folk tsum folk: An alter lezer fun Forverts redt zikh arop fun hartsn," *Forverts*, February 9, 1954, 6.

36. N. Chait, "Religyeze yidishkayt un veltlekhe yidishkayt," *Forverts*, January 20, 1958, 5.

37. Alex Mindin, "A Religious Voice in a Secular Forest," *New York Times Magazine*, November 28, 2004, 12.

38. A. B. Rutzon, "Yonkiper—di goyishe velt volt aza tog gedarft," *Forverts*, September 9, 1942: 2.

39. Hillel Rogoff, *Der gayst fun Forverts: materyaln tsu der geshikhte fun der yidisher prese in Amerike* (New York: Forverts, 1954), 172; David Shub, *Fun di amolike yorn: bletlekh zikhroynes* (New York: CYCO, 1970), 914–915. As early as 1914, Lieberman advocated a place for religion in secular Jewish education—see Entin, *Gezamlte shriftn*, vol. 1, 209.

40. Yakov Ross, "Fun folk tsum folk: Der Forverts un dos religyese yidntum," *Forverts*, February 9, 1954, 5.

41. See Nathan Glazer, *American Judaism* (Chicago: University of Chicago Press, 1989), 115.

42. Gennady Estraikh, *Yiddish in the Cold War* (Oxford: Legenda, 2008), 11.

43. David E. Fishman, "From Yiddishism to American Judaism: The Impact of American Yiddish Schools on Their Students," in *Imaging the American Jewish Community*, ed. Jack Wertheimer (Lebanon, NH: Brandeis University Press, 2007), 280.

44. Morris Friedman, "New Jewish Community in Formation," *Commentary* 20 (1955): 36–47, and Nathan Glazer, "The Jewish Revival in America: Its Religious Side, *Commentary* 21 (1956): 17–24.

45. Riv-Elen Prell, "Community and the Discourse of Elegy: The Postwar Suburban Debate," in *Imaging*, ed. Wertheimer, 69.

46. Joseph Blau, "Some Historical Facets of Jewish Affiliation," *Jewish Social Studies* 31.3 (1969): 252.

47. See Jeffrey S. Gurock, "Twentieth-Century American Orthodoxy's Era of Non-Observance, 1900–1960," *The Torah U-Madda Journal* 9 (2000): 97.

48. Albert I. Gordon, *Jews in Suburbia* (Westport, CT: Greenwood Press Publishers, 1959), 148; Bernard Lazerwitz, "A Comparison of Major United States Religious Groups," *Journal of the American Statistical Association* 56 (1961): 572–573.

49. P. Berman, "Vi shtark iz der religyezer oyfbli ba amerikaner yidn," *Forverts*, February 4, 1956, 6.

50. Yitshak Shmulevitsh, "Vegn nayem yidishn 'shtetl' oyf der Ist Sayd," *Forverts*, February 1, 1956, 2.

51. Yakov Ross, "An alter Forverts leyener redt zikh arop fun hartsn," *Forverts*, April 27, 1963, 3, 6.

52. Estraikh and Newfield, "Grandfathers against Bar Mitzvahs," 82. There were also parents who themselves lost their faith during the Holocaust, but wanted their son to be part of a Jewish community. "So they sent him to synagogue alone. Even when he became bar mitzvah, when he was called to the Torah, they waited outside." See Susan Jacobowitz, "The Conflict and Challenges of Traditional Judaism in Second Generation Texts," *Studies in American Jewish Literature* 25 (2006): 41.

53. Naftali Gross, "Peysekh, der yontev fun frayhayt," *Forverts*, April 14, 1949, 2, 5.

54. Harry Block, "Di kristlekhe un yidishe yontoyvim," *Forverts*, January 20, 1949, 5; Abraham Tsizevsky and Anna Goldberg, "Yidishe un kristlekhe yontoyvim," *Forverts*, March 1, 1949, 3.

55. Uriel Weinreich, *College Yiddish* (New York: YIVO, 1949), 264–265.

56. Shub, *Fun di amolike yorn*, 671.

57. H. Vital, "Der bester erev yontev vos di khazonim hobn ven es iz," *Forverts*, August 27, 1945, 2. In fact, cantors' salaries in Orthodox synagogues were traditionally high, in most cases higher than the salaries of rabbis—see Kimmy Caplan, "In God We Trust: Salaries and Income of American Orthodox Rabbis, 1881–1924," *American Jewish History* 86.1 (1998): 89–93, 104.

58. Shmuel Horetz, "Fun folk tsum folk: Yeshive bokherim un khazonim," *Forverts*, September 25, 1945, 5.

59. Boris Smolar, "Peysekh in Amerike," *Forverts*, August 13, 1952, 4

60. Led Pensil [Berl Botwinik], "Fregt men nokh di fir kashes in Amerike?," *Forverts*, April 30, 1930, 4.

61. David Eynhorn, "Ba a farshlosener shul in a nayem gegnt: der krizis in der yidisher religye," *Forverts*, April 12, 1952, 3.

62. Shifra Kuperman, "Eynhorn, Dovid," *The YIVO Encyclopedia of Jews in Eastern Europe* (New Haven and London: Yale University Press, 2008), 488. Cf. Abraham Goldfaden, *Shulamis, oder bas-yerusholayim* (London: R. Mazin & Co., 1904), 23.

63. David Eynhorn, "Peysekh-tseremonyes—zeyer emese badaytung," *Forverts*, April 11, 1952, 4.

64. David Eynhorn, "Der geferlekher veg fun di ortodoksishe yidn," *Forverts*, February 28, 1954, 4. See also "3,000 at Consulate Here Scream Protests at Draft of Israeli Women," *New York Times*, February 9, 1954, 1; "3,000 Orthodox Jews Protest at Consulate Here," *New York Herald Tribune*, February 9, 1954, 1.

65. Isidor Ginsburg, "Kurtse bamerkungen," *Forverts*, September 22, 1945, 2. As late as the 1970s, foreign-born Eastern European Jews tended to affiliate with Orthodox synagogues—see Bernard Lazerwitz and Michael Harrison, "American Jewish Denominations: A Social and Religious Profile," *American Sociological Review* 44.4 (1979): 659–660.

66. Jacob Lestschinsky, "Eygnartikayt in amerikaner religyezn yidishn lebn," *Forverts*, December 18, 1949, section 2, 4.

67. Jacob Lestschinsky, "Yidishkayt—nusekh Amerike," *Forverts*, January 1, 1950, section 2, 1.

68. Eli Lederhendler, *New York Jews and the Decline of Urban Ethnicity, 1950–1970* (Syracuse: Syracuse University Press, 2001), 204.

69. Cited in Gerd Korman, " Ethnic Democracy and Its Ambiguities: The Case of Needle Trade Unions," *American Jewish History* 75.4 (1986): 415.

70. On the *Forverts*' turn to nationalism, see Gennady Estraikh, "American Yiddish Socialists at the Wartime Crossroads: Patriotism and Nationalism versus Proletarian Internationalism," in *World War I and the Jews: Conflict and Transformations in Europe, the Middle East, and America*, ed. Marsha L. Rozenblit and Jonathan Karp (New York and Oxford: Berghahn Press, 2017), 280–302.

71. Hillel Rogoff, "Religye oyf der yidisher gas," *Forverts*, November 24, 1956, 6.

Part II: Literature
INVENTING A LEGACY

A Treasury of Yiddish Stories
SALVAGE MONTAGE AND THE ANTI-SHTETL

Sheila E. Jelen

"Modern Yiddish literature focuses upon the shtetl during its last tremor of self-awareness, the historical moment when it is still coherent and self-contained but already under fierce assault from the outer world." Irving Howe and Eliezer Greenberg, *A Treasury of Yiddish Stories (1954)*

Modern Yiddish Literature

In their introduction to *A Treasury of Yiddish Stories*, Irving Howe and Eliezer Greenberg say of Avrom Reisen (1876–1953), "In the hundreds of stories he wrote—without dramatic accent or visible plot line, Reisen has provided one of the truest and fullest portraits that we have of Jewish life in Eastern Europe."[1] Elaborating on the origin of this attitude toward Reisen in his 1977 *World of Our Fathers*, Howe reports a conversation he had with the Yiddish-American poet Jacob Glatstein, in which Glatstein says, "If every record of Yiddish life were lost, a future archeologist could reconstruct it all from the stories of Reisen."[2] Howe, intrigued by Glatstein's claims for Reisen's work, asks, "could he learn from Reisen so elementary a fact as how the Jews had perpetuated themselves?" "For that," shot back Glatstein, "he would do better to go to the Bible."[3]

When Howe asks Glatstein whether or not the secret to Jewish continuity can be found in the pages of Avrom Reisen's fiction, Glatstein responds harshly with a reminder that the key to Jewish history is to be found in the Hebrew sacred texts, not in modern Yiddish literature. But what becomes clear in this intriguing exchange is the shifting valence of sacred texts within a single generation. If, for Glatstein, the Bible is the key to Jewish continuity in his generation, for Howe, Reisen plays that role. Although for Glatstein the possibility of an imaginative reconstruction of traditional Jewish life can take place through readings of Yiddish fiction, for Howe, it seems, Jewish values, Jewish knowledge, and Jewish identity itself can be reconstructed through readings of these same texts.

Just as the Bible holds the key to the vagaries of Jewish historical experience, so too, in Howe's and Greenberg's conception, can Yiddish literature for a postwar American Jewish readership represent the variegated experiences of Eastern European Jewry. Representations of pre-Holocaust Eastern European Jewish life in post-Holocaust America have been notoriously nostalgic. However, it is important to remember that literary representations of the shtetl, created in Yiddish before the war, are rarely idyllic or monochromatic. In Howe and Greenberg's anthology, these representations abound; because it is an anthology of translations that extends beyond the generally available works of Sholem Aleichem, Y.L. Peretz, and Mendele Mokher Sforim—the triumvirate of "classical" Yiddish writers—different visions of the shtetl prevail. *A Treasury of Yiddish Stories* provides an early precedent for a more measured, more realistic, and grimmer vision of the pre-Holocaust history of the Jews of East Europe than that which was made available through other works of ethnography, lexicography, and fiction written after the war.

For many years Yiddish literature was a vernacular medium for sacred Hebrew texts, allowing the Yiddish-proficient but Hebrew-illiterate hoi polloi ("for women and men who are like women") access to Hebrew religious texts through translations, adaptations, glosses, and mediations.[4] In post-Holocaust America, however, the sacred is no longer to be found exclusively in traditional Jewish religious texts, but rather, in literary texts that represent the Eastern European Jewish "world"; Yiddish stories become a type of sacred text in their own right. While Howe and Greenberg frame their introductory essay as an overview of the culture of the shtetl in order to better understand Yiddish literature, what I would argue here is that they provide, throughout the introduction and in the anthology itself, a presentation of Yiddish literature in English translation in order to better understand the culture of Eastern European Jews.

Indeed, in reviews of *World of Our Fathers*, several critics read Howe's work as a form of popular ethnography. Jacob Neusner, in a 1976 review of the book, calls Howe a literature scholar "turned anthropologist," while Robert Alter argues that Howe's book is essentially an auto-ethnography, "a book about the immigrant experience filled with oblique autobiographical vignettes."[5] Norman Podhoretz, in a 1955 review of Howe and Greenberg's *Treasury*, and in allusion to the extremely popular and influential 1952 ethnographic work, *Life is With People*, argues that "the publication of the Treasury is no isolated phenomenon. Within the last few years we have seen Mark Zborowsky turning the methods of cultural anthropology on the shtetl with striking results."[6]

Hybrid Texts

In what she calls "the popular arts of American Jewish ethnography," Barbara Kirshenblatt-Gimblett identifies a combination of literary and ethnographic discourses in post-Holocaust American popular culture.[7] Kirshenblatt-Gimblett points, in particular, to *The World of Sholem Aleichem*, by Maurice Samuel (1943), a gloss on the Eastern European Jewish origins of many American Jews at mid-twentieth century, based on the fiction of Sholem Aleichem. "In *The World of Sholem Aleichem*," she says, "Samuel fashioned a hybrid genre that mediates between literature and ethnography, between retelling the Tevye stories and providing an ethnographic gloss on them."[8] Aside from Samuel's book, in her discussion of "hybrid" texts, Kirshenblatt-Gimblett touches as well upon *The Earth Is the Lord's*, Abraham Joshua Heschel's 1945 elegy to Eastern European Jews, and *Life Is with People*, Mark Zborowski's and Elizabeth Herzog's 1952 ethnographic portrait of Eastern European Jewish life, written under the guidance of Margaret Mead.[9]

What makes these works "hybrid"? They are simultaneously documentary and imaginative; they aim to describe a culture even as they display an intensely literary self-consciousness. Heschel, for example, draws on Hassidic tales and Yiddidh literature as illustrative of Eastern European Jewish life.[10] For their part, Zborowski and Herzog's "native informants" were mostly people who came to the United States as young children and based their testimonies about the Eastern European Jewish experience on impressions gathered from reading modern Yiddish classics. As the authors themselves point out: "It would be impossible to list all the Yiddish and Hebrew literary and autobiographical works that have contributed as background to this study. Yet the works of such writers as Sholem Aleichem, Mendele Mokher Sforim, Peretz, Asch and others have probably contributed more than the academic discussions."[11]

This essay poses a new reading of the category of hybridity not explicitly named by Kirshenblatt-Gimblett in her discussion of popular American-Jewish ethnography during the post-Holocaust decades. Through a focus on Irving Howe and Eliezer Greenberg's wildly popular collection of Yiddish fiction, *A Treasury of Yiddish Stories* (1954), here I consider the hybrid features of the genre of the anthology within a post-Holocaust American popular ethnographic climate.

Salvage Montage

Salvage ethnography is the recording of the practices of cultures threatened with extinction, theorized by the American anthropologist Franz Boaz, who sought to record vanishing Native American cultures. The "salvage" attempted on Eastern European Jewry in the post-Holocaust era was, in fact, the continuation of salvage efforts begun even before the First World War. Traditional Jewry was threatened by modernity from the beginning of the period of the Jewish Enlightenment—in Western Europe, starting in the eighteenth century, and in Eastern Europe from the end of the nineteenth. Ethnographic expeditions and folklore projects dedicated to the world of Eastern European Jews were numerous throughout the late nineteenth and early twentieth centuries.[12] Best known of these was the ethnographic expedition in Volhynia and Podolia spearheaded and overseen by S. Ansky (1863–1920) from 1911–1914. He and his associates composed a 2000-question questionnaire to pose to native informants about their Jewish practices and traditions, and, using the most cutting-edge recording devices available, they also collected hundreds of folksongs, instrumental pieces, and other aural materials.[13] In the aftermath of the Holocaust, however, attempts to salvage the lost Eastern European world took on a less scientific cast, and was based on "found" literary and photographic materials that represented the culture before its destruction.

The term "salvage montage," coined for this essay, draws on the notion of montage introduced by Georges Didi-Huberman. In *Images in Spite of All*, he explores the outcry that occurred after he published an essay on the historical and philosophical value of four photographs taken in August 1944 by members of the Sonderkommando, a special team of prisoners at Auschwitz-Birkenau. These prisoners were selected by the Germans and "forced on pain of death to lead, often using deception, arriving Jews to the gas chambers, empty the gas chambers, shave the corpses and pull their teeth before they stacked the bodies on pyres in trenches for cremation, all the while knowing their own days were numbered."[14] The photographs were of members of the Sonderkommando incinerating hundreds of thousands of bodies in pits outside of the gas chambers and of naked women standing in line waiting to enter the gas chambers; they were taken at great personal risk with a smuggled camera and a snippet of film.

Critics of Didi-Huberman's analysis of these photographs accuse him of claiming to be able to capture the "truth" behind the Holocaust in these isolated images, of thinking that these photographs somehow transmit it "all." But Didi-Huberman, drawing on the concept of montage, argues that he presented these photographs "in spite of all," that they served as just a piece of the "all" that was the Holocaust. To repress them or silence them would be to negate the enormous risk undertaken by the Sonderkommando in secretly documenting their work on the eve of their own deaths. The photographs in question, he argues, function in tandem with the many written testimonies buried on the periphery of the gas chambers by members of the Sonderkommando. The notes and journals found after the war, taken alongside oral testimonies and the four Sonderkommando photographs, serve together, in Didi-Huberman's term, as a type of "montage."

While his critics call it impudent to try to "imagine" the war with the help of these isolated photographs, Didi-Huberman links the nature of imagination to the concept of montage: "imagination is a montage of various forms placed in correspondence with one another."[15] He further affirms that considering these materials as part of a montage "is a question of putting the multiple in motion, isolating nothing, showing the hiatuses and the analogies, the indeterminations and over-determinations."[16] Alluding to Walter Benjamin's *Arcades Project*, Didi-Huberman points to the kinds of "treasures" and "traps" to be found in works of montage.[17] "Montage," he insists, "is valuable only when it doesn't hasten to conclude or to close: it is valuable when it opens up our apprehension of history and makes it more complex, not when it falsely schematizes; when it gives us access to the singularities of time, and hence to its essential multiplicity."[18]

As is the case with these Sonderkommando images, it is necessarily impossible to reconstruct the "all" of the Eastern European Jewish life that was destroyed; its destruction mediates every attempt to comprehend what came before. I use the term "montage" in my formulation of "salvage montage" in order to try to characterize the dynamics underlying the efficacy of *A Treasury of Yiddish Stories* in a salvage context. Because anthologies collect works that were already published elsewhere, they serve to heighten our sense of their contents as a montage of various reception histories and publication contexts, in addition to being a collection of different stories written by different authors, or photographs taken by different photographers. Anthologies strive toward comprehensiveness, even while emphasizing their many lacunae, in subtle and sometimes not so subtle ways.

Literary Ethnography

How do contemporary literary critics read ethnography into classic Yiddish literature? Gabriella Safran's reading of Sholem Aleichem's well-known story "The Pot" (*Dos Tepl*) is punctuated by a rhetoric of the "ethnographic" value of fictional texts, when she argues that different translations of the same story have different ethnographic valences. Safran writes, "some critics stress the ethnographic quality of Sholem Aleichem's stories in general, suggesting that they offer a transcript of the speech of real people." She then characterizes several different translations on a scale of their ethnographic value. For example, Safran identifies two particular translations as "gently" ethnographic, and she argues that an ethnographic characterization of a literary text reflects the text's commitment to "preserving" a culture.[19]

Like Safran, Howe and Greenberg in an earlier generation articulate the ethnographic value of Yiddish literature by championing it as the guardian angel of a "twilight culture."[20] In their introduction, Howe and Greenberg explain,

> We recognize the danger of romanticizing the Jewish world, of assuming that it was all of one piece and forgetting that much of it was ignorant, provincial, superstitious, and sometimes even corrupt, as a good deal of Yiddish writing bears witness.... Indeed one of the immediate motive forces behind the appearance of the new Yiddish literature in the 19th century, especially behind the work of its founding father Mendele, was the desire to stir the blood of a society that had gone sluggish, to cleanse a people that had suffered too long from the effects of isolation, poverty, and violence. Once the foundations of this society began to crumble, an impulse arose among the Yiddish writers—most notably in the later stories of Peretz—to romanticize the very world that Mendele had so bitterly attacked. And once this world had been destroyed in the gas chambers, the romantic impulse became irresistible; it acquired a new and almost holy authenticity; for how could the Yiddish writers separate the sanctification of their martyrs from the celebration of the world that had given rise to them?[21]

This provides an astute synopsis of the dynamics of salvage poetics—they begin with the social forces of modernity, when a generation of writers wrote about the old world as part of their process of leaving it behind. One of the signs of modernity was the sense of self-scrutiny, of having one foot in and one foot out the door, the reflexivity, the laughter, and the parody. According to Howe and Greenberg, the literature was not just a sign of the times, but rather it participated in the revolutionary ethos of the moment and indeed helped to inspire it. After the Holocaust, the role that the literature itself played in a process of modernization and migration contributed to the fact of its being received and promoted in a salvage poetic sense—as a kind of elegy and a form of documentation. Modern Yiddish literature, they conclude, "focuses upon the shtetl during its last tremor of self awareness in the historical moment when it is still coherent and self contained, but already under fierce assault from the outer world.... Yiddish reaches its climax of expressive power as the world it portrays begins to come apart."[22]

The Shtetl and the Anti-Shtetl

Interestingly, in classic hybrid works on Eastern European Jewish life, the one thing that never "comes apart," to borrow Howe and Greenberg's terminology, is the shtetl. The image of the shtetl as a locus of Eastern European Jewish life has been well documented from a literary perspective.[23] When considering the origin of the shtetl trope in post-Holocaust America from an ethnographic perspective, however, we can better understand the revolutionary nature of Howe and Greenberg's anthology within the spectrum of hybrid works. In *Life Is with People*, according to Kirshenblatt-Gimblett, the shtetl is, for the first time, isolated and identified as a specific geographic site for the ethnographers writing the book to use as the locus for an in-situ ethnographic method. In order to write an ethnography of Eastern European Jews, the shtetl was appointed a locus for Eastern European Jewish life to create a pretense of participant observation.[24] This method, coupled with a salvage ethnographic method, in which a culture that has been destroyed or is undergoing destruction is "salvaged" through an investigation of its artifacts, customs, and life-ways, inspired the particular methodology of *Life Is with People*. In that work, the shtetl is designated a geographic container for the material lives of all Eastern European Jews—their customs, their foods, their schooling, their texts, their institutions, their religious observances, etc.—and becomes the singular, tangible, living protagonist of the 1952 ethnographic study. In fact, the shtetl even develops its own subjectivity and voice, cast by the authors of the study as having particular "needs," "wants," and "desires" of its own.

Despite having been published nearly simultaneously with the classic works that established the tone and tenor of the idealized shtetl within American Jewish popular ethnographies, the shtetlach depicted in Howe's and Greenberg's anthology are "anti-shtetlakh." Although I would not argue that their anti-shtetl quality is an explicit response and rejoinder to *Life Is with People*, the *World of Sholem Aleichem*, or *The Earth Is the Lord's*, it reflects an alternative trend in representations of Eastern European Jewry that may only have been possible immediately after the war. This was a relic of pre-Holocaust representations of that world, the voice of immigrants and their children who did not experience the unbridled destruction of the Holocaust and were therefore not invested in a hagiography of the locales and their victims lost to the Nazis.[25] While clearly World War One and the pogroms throughout the first decades of the twentieth century were also devastating, the move to idealize and simplify the world of Eastern European Jews only took place after the Holocaust. A more varied and realistic approach to the shtetl during the immediate post-Holocaust period, as can be observed in *A Treasury*, was short-lived. Indeed, it nearly vanished in subsequent decades.

Beginning with Maurice Samuel's *World of Sholem Aleichem*, the shtetl has been presented as a relatively monolithic, undifferentiated mass of piety and poverty.[26] In recent years, historians and literary scholars have both tried to understand the origins of that literary presentation as well as to mobilize primary sources and secondary sources to disprove it. Recent literary critiques of shtetl representations such as those published by Jeffrey Shandler and Yohanan Petrovsky-Shtern, as well as historical writings about specific shtetlach by Gershon Hundert and Yehuda Bauer, avoid hagiographic representations of the shtetl, but earlier attempts to depict it in realistic terms are few and far between.[27] *A Treasury of Yiddish Stories* alongside Lucy Dawidowicz's historical overview in *The Golden Tradition* serve as parallel precedents for such an effort in the 1950s and 1960s respectively, half a century before the most recent spate of historicized engagements.[28]

Thus, Howe and Greenberg's anthology represents a crucial salvage poetic voice in that it articulates a post-Holocaust response to the destruction of Eastern European Jewry that was a clear continuation of pre-Holocaust sentiments. This could be attributed to the fact that though Howe was a child of immigrants and more vulnerable to nostalgia and idealization of the shtetl, Greenberg was not. Howe was born to immigrant parents in 1920 in the East Bronx, while Greenberg was born in Russia in 1896 and immigrated to the United States in 1913. Intimately familiar with the immigrant experience, both first and second generation, Howe and Greenberg together published a book that played an important role in diversifying the types of hybrid texts attempted in the postwar years. In several stories in *A Treasury*, the shtetl—in its archetypical construction as a nuclear, autonomous, idyllic site—is subject to a deconstruction.

In Sholem Aleichem's "Dreyfus in Kasrilevke," the inhabitants of a fictional shtetl are yanked into the maelstrom of modern Jewish history during the Dreyfus affair by the uninvited appearance of a newspaper in town.[29] They rail not only against the news of the accusations levied against Dreyfus, but also against the very incursion of the news into their midst. They are beautifully, blissfully isolated until the paper destroys their peace. At the end of the story, they turn against the newspaper instead of turning against the perpetrators of the crimes reported there, asserting their lack of faith in the power of a piece of paper to wreak havoc on their world. The story deconstructs itself—written on paper, referring to real historic events, yet profoundly in denial of the efficacy of the former to transmit the latter. The fictional shtetl of Kasrilevke, which exists only on paper, has negated its own existence by challenging the very existence of paper as a medium for verbal and historical transmission.

The shtetl is more explicitly emptied out as a signifier in a story by Peretz called "The Dead Town," in which a town, unnamed, is invisible to the surrounding gentiles and even to the surrounding Jews.[30] The "dead town" is known only to its inhabitants. The homodiegetic narrator, trying to ascertain what kind of metaphorical meaning a dead town possesses, tries out different possible scenarios: A poor town? A small town? A town of ghosts? No, says his interlocutor, this is a "town like every other town" with living inhabitants, a synagogue, and even a hospital and a hotel (or at least there once was a hotel, and even if the hospital is small, it is still a place for sick people).[31] This dead town, it turns out, is a town where the inhabitants have lost their zest for life: "For even if a feather were placed under the nose of a living man, do you think he would bother to remove it? Or to brush aside a troublesome fly?"[32] And because there is no impulse toward life in that town, the dead return to live in it:

> And if sometimes it happens, as it did among us, that a corpse creeps out of his grave, he does not even begin to remember that he has already recited the last confession, gasped his final breath, and died. As soon as the potsherds fall from his eyes, he goes straight to the House of Study or to the ritual bath or home for the summer. And everything is again the way it was.[33]

As in many of his stories, this story by Peretz requires a suspension of the kind of reading norms that govern the reading of many of the other stories in the book. Instead of being charmed or galvanized or shocked, the reader is left simply confused. Is this a town of the dead or a town of the living? Does this town exist in this world or in the world to come?

The story that immediately follows "The Dead Town," called "Neilah in Gehennah," also by Peretz, takes us to the heavenly tribunal of a hated citizen of the town of LaHDaM, the acronym for "*lo hayu dvarim meolam*," meaning "these things never were."[34] The devil himself has never heard of this town because no citizens of this town are ever sent to hell. Why? Because there is a cantor in the town whose voice is so sweet, whose prayers are so poignant, particularly on Yom Kippur, the Day of Atonement, that the dead of LaHDaM are automatically admitted to heaven. In a Job-like gesture, the cantor's voice is taken away by Satan, and the cantor commits suicide and goes to hell (because suicide is forbidden), where he says the closing prayer for Yom Kippur, releasing all those imprisoned in cauldrons. Thus hell empties out. In time though, the story tells us in conclusion, hell fills up again, "and although additional suburbs were built, it still remains crowded."[35] Thus hell, in this story, has more of a real existence than does the shtetl.

"These things never were" is a Yiddish expression for the idea of a pure fiction. And in fact, these three stories at the heart of the anthology serve as a reminder that the portrait of the shtetl presented therein, carefully selected from the literary corpuses of some of the most well known Yiddish writers, is pure fiction. The shtetlach they represent exist only for their own inhabitants, in a historical vacuum, and they are invisible to the powers on high (and down low).

In Reisen's "The Poor Community," another shtetl is evacuated of everything with which shtetlach have become associated in the aftermath of the Holocaust.[36] Having spent all their communal money to pay a visiting cantor on a regular Sabbath, the town's inhabitants don't have the money to pay for a cantor and torah reader on the high holidays. They must leave their town and join a minyan in the neighboring town in order to pray: "On the morning of the first day of Rosh Hashonoh, when the townspeople on their way to Sosnovtchine, passed their old dilapidated synagogue, standing there with cloudy eyes, woebegone and orphaned, their hearts felt sore and tight, and silently, without words, only with their eyes, they begged its forgiveness."[37] The impossibility of prayer, of spiritual expression, in a town without money belies the common discourse, found in Heschel's *The Earth Is the Lord's* as well as in many other popularly read descriptions of Eastern European Jewish life. By the reckoning of many of these sources, prayer is the only thing Jews could do well in Eastern Europe without fiscal resources. But here, poverty leads to the emptying out of the symbolic locus of the Eastern European Jews. The shtetl without money is a shtetl with an empty synagogue, a shtetl without prayer.

This montage of empty, dead, evacuated shtetlach can be understood as a post-Holocaust phenomenon, a form, in Michael André Bernstein's formulation, of backshadowing, wherein Jewish experience in Europe before the Holocaust is viewed through a lens of inevitability.[38] In other words, these stories, one might argue, like Barthes' photographs, serve as a spectre of their own death.[39] But do they? I would assert that these images of shtetlach serve as a kind of photographic negative, but not necessarily a projection of death. They are reminders of the artifice underlying both the production of the stories and their insertion into the anthology. These evacuated shtetlach, these cities of the dead, emptied out of prayer, these cities named "*lo hoyu dvorim me-olam*" remind us that perhaps the singular, luminous shtetl identified in *Life Is with People*, in *The Earth Is the Lord's*, in *The World of Sholem Aleichem*, or even in *Fiddler on the Roof*, as the locus of Eastern European Jewish life, as the voice and face of Eastern European Jews, simply did not exist.[40]

Moshe Vorobeichic, in *The Ghetto Lane of Vilna* (1931), published a series of montage photographs in which pious Jews are set into strangely disembodied backgrounds, laid, like a palimpsest over scenes of Vilna. Carol Zemel argues that these images articulate a confrontation between tradition and modernity: "the picture's air of timelessness is interrupted not, however, by the photographer's intruding presence, but by the photograph's modernist montaged style, which shatters the cohesion of the image and flash forwards the Jewish elder into history as a small pale apparitional echo at the lower left."[41] This visual montage, while quite different from the type of montage presented in Howe and Greenberg's anthology, suggests a model for salvage montage. It is the future embedded in these images, the sense of transition and transformation always already to be found in them, that lays the foundation for their future application within a salvage poetic framework, or a popular ethnographic reinvention in a post-cataclysmic age. At the same time, the anthological format in which these stories appear allows for a kind of dialectic. The expected is presented, but the unexpected emerges as well because of the nature of the montage form. This synthesis of the unexpected and the expected, images of shtetlach interspersed with stories of the anti-shtetl, present opportunities to recognize and interpret both the strengths and the limitations of post-vernacular presentations and perceptions of pre-Holocaust Eastern European Jewish life in a post-Holocaust world.

Notes

1. Irving Howe and Eliezer Greenberg, *A Treasury of Yiddish Stories* (New York: Meridian Books, 1953), 43.
2. Irving Howe, *World of our Fathers* (New York: Harcourt, Brace Javonovich, 1976), 426.
3. Ibid.
4. Chava Weissler, *Voices of the Matriarchs: Listening to the Prayers of Early Modern Jewish Women* (Boston: Beacon Press, 1998).
5. Jacob Neusner, *National Review* 28 (May 14, 1976), 515; Robert Alter, *Commentary* 61 (April 1976), 83.
6. Norman Podhoretz, "Jewish Culture and the Intellectuals: The Process of Rediscovery," *Commentary* 19 (May 1955): 451–457.
7. Barbara Kirshenblatt-Gimblett, "Imagining Europe: The Popular Arts of American Jewish Ethnography," in *Divergent Jewish Cultures*, ed. Deborah Dash Moore and Ilan Troen (New Haven: Yale University Press, 2001), 155–91.
8. Ibid,168.
9. Ibid.
10. I.J. Heschel, *The Earth Is the Lord's and the Sabbath* (New York: Harper Torchbooks, 1966).
11. Mark Zborowski and Elizabeth Herzog, *Life Is with People: The Culture of the Shtetl* (New York: Shocken, 1952), 25.
12. Itzik Gottesman, *Defining the Yiddish Nation: The Jewish Folklorists of Poland* (Detroit: Wayne State University Press, 2003).
13. On An-sky's place within the field of modern Jewish ethnography, see Jack Kugelmass, "The Father of Jewish Ethnography?," in *The Worlds of S. An-sky: A Russian Jewish Intellectual at the Turn of the Century*, ed. Gabriella Safran and Steven J. Zipperstein (Stanford, Calif., 2006), 346–59.
14. I thank the anonymous reader from Wayne State University Press for providing this definition of the Sonderkommando in his review of this essay. The discussion of the iconic photographs appears in Georges Didi-Huberman, *Images in Spite of All: Four Photographs from Auschwitz* (Chicago: University of Chicago Press, 2008).
15. Ibid, 120.
16. Ibid.

17. In 1927 Walter Benjamin wrote to Gershom Scholem that he was undertaking a "collage" project of cultural criticism in which he would create a literary variation on the French "arcades," or distinctive street stalls in Paris. The Arcades project was written between 1927 and 1940 but was not completed, due to Benjamin's suicide on the French/Spanish border, in flight from the Nazis.

18. Didi-Huberman, 121.

19. Gabriella Safran, "Four English Pots and the Evolving Translatability of Sholem Aleichem," in *Translating Sholem Aleichem: History, Politics, and Art*, ed. Gennady Estraikh, Jordan Finkin, Kerstin Hoge, and Mikhail Krutikov (Great Britain: Legenda, 2012), 125.

20. Julian Levinson, "The Jewish Writer Flies at Twilight: Irving Howe and the Recovery of Yiddishkayt," in *Exiles on Main St: Jewish American Writers and American Literary Culture* (Bloomington: Indiana University Press, 2008), 178.

21. Howe and Greenberg, *Treasury*, 4.

22. Ibid, 28.

23. Dan Miron, *The Image of the Shtetl and Other Studies of Modern Jewish Literary Imagination* (Syracuse: Syracuse University Press, 2000); Steven Katz, *The Shtetl: New Evaluations* (New York: New York University Press, 2007); Jeffrey Shandler, *Shtetl: A Vernacular History* (New Brunswick: Rutgers University Press, 2014); Gennady Estraikh and Mikhael Krutikov, *The Shtetl: Image and Reality: Papers from the Second Mendel Friedman International Conference on Yiddish* (Oxford: Legenda, 2000).

24. Barbara Kirshenblatt-Gimblett, "Introduction" in *Life Is with People*.

25. On pre-Holocaust writings and their non-idealizing tendencies, see Gil Ribak's essay in this volume.

26. This juncture of terms, "piety and poverty," was first articulated by Lucy Dawidowicz in her critique of American representations of Eastern European Jewish experience. Lucy S. Dawidowicz, "Introduction," in *The Golden Tradition: Jewish Life and Thought in Eastern Europe*, ed. Lucy S. Dawidowicz (Boston: Beacon, 1967), 6.

27. Jeffrey Shandler, *Shtetl*; Yohanan Petrovsky-Shtern, *Golden Age Shtetl: A New History of Jewish Life in East Europe* (Princeton: Princeton University Press, 2014); Yehuda Bauer, *The Death of the Shtetl* (New Haven: Yale University Press, 2009); Gershon Hundert, *The Jews in a Polish Private Town: The Case of Opatow in the Eighteenth Century* (Baltimore: Johns Hopkins University Press, 1992).

28. Lucy Dawidowicz, *The Golden Tradition: Jewish Life and Thought in East Europe*.

29. Howe and Greenberg, *Treasury*, 187–92.

30. Ibid., 205–213.

31. Ibid, 206.

32. Ibid, 210–211.

33. Ibid, 211.

34. Ibid, 213–219.

35. Ibid, 219.

36. Ibid, 275–279.

37. Ibid, 279.

38. Michael André Bernstein, *Foregone Conclusions: Against Apocalyptic History* (Berkeley: University of California, 1994).

39. Roland Barthes, *Camera Lucida*, 96. "In front of the photograph of my mother as a child, I tell myself: she is going to die. I shudder, like Winnicott's psychotic patient over a

catastrophe, which has already occurred. Whether or not the subject is already dead, every photograph is this catastrophe."

40. Indeed, in a recent discussion of Mark Zborowski, Steven Zipperstein has re-read *Life Is with People* as similarly specious with regard to its presentation of the shtetl. Zborowski, he argues, a Soviet spy, was not the shtetl "insider" that Margaret Mead had imagined when she had hired him to write the book. Rather, he came from a large city and was profoundly suspicious of the shtetl as a backwater and religiously moribund place. In his citation of a transcript wherein Zborowski and Mead and their team were trying to find a unifying idea around which to organize their portrait of Eastern European Jewish life, he identifies the moment when Zborowski argues that traditional Jewish life is a spiritual and not a physical entity. The shtetl, therefore, as the organizing principle for the book, serves as just that: an organizing principle, not an accurate representation of a locale and its culture. Kirshenblatt-Gimblett points out Mead's role in the construction of the literary shtetl to compensate for Zborowski's claim about the lack of a physical locus for their study. See Steven J. Zipperstein, "Underground Man: The Curious Case of Mark Zborowski and the Writing of a Modern Jewish Classic," in *Jewish Review of Books* (Summer 2010). *http://jewishreviewofbooks .com/articles/275/underground-man-the-curious-case-of-mark-zborowski-and-the-writing-of -a-modern-jewish-classic/*. Also, see Kirschenblatt-Gimblett, "Introduction," in *Life*.

41. Carol Zemel, "Imagining the Shtetl: Diaspora Culture, Photography and Eastern European Jews," in *Diaspora and Visual Culture*, ed. Nicholas Mirzoeff (New York: Routledge, 2000), 193–206.

"The *Shkotsim* Were Even Worse Than the Dogs"

YIDDISH MEMOIRISTS AND THE REIMAGINING OF THE EASTERN EUROPEAN JEWISH EXPERIENCE IN POSTWAR AMERICA

Gil Ribak

In 1962, one of the leading figures of Labor Zionism in America, Borekh Tsukerman, published the first volume of his Yiddish memoir. Born in 1887 to a Hasidic family in a small town by the name of Kurenitz, near Vilna, Tsukerman immigrated to America in 1904. In his memoir Tsukerman describes how drunken peasants tore a prayer book from his father's hands, made fun of it, and assaulted his father. Another time, "two big, Polish youths" struck his father, since Tsukerman's father did not take off his hat near a big church in Vilna. For Tsukerman, the name "Christ" implied hatred toward Jews.[1]

Various observers have examined American Jewish popular culture (ethnography, literature, theater, and film), arguing that a static, ahistorical imagery of Jewish life in pre-Holocaust Eastern Europe, mostly epitomized by the shtetl, emerged in the postwar years. Critics attacked what they saw as American Jews' attempt to create a nostalgic, saccharine version of the Jewish past in Eastern Europe. Writing in 1954, in *Commentary* magazine, author Midge Decter lambasted the stage production of *The World of Sholem Aleichem*, a collection of one-act plays based on I. L. Peretz and Sholem Aleichem stories, transformed into a socialist call to solidarity with the downtrodden. Decter argued that the play fabricated "just the kind of Never-Never-Land American Jews like to think they came from." In her scathing opinion, "American Jews can afford to be pleased" by an ahistorical depiction of Jewish life in the old world, with the luxury to "enjoy the ghetto by retroactively making of it something it was not quite." For her, the play shows "the Jewish past as we like to think it," so laden with stereotypes that "some of the clichés escape me right now."[2]

Writing a decade later in *Commentary* as well, literary critic Irving Howe accused *Fiddler of the Roof* (1964) of creating "the cutest shtetl we've never had," which served as an "irresistible bait for the nostalgia-smitten audience." Howe saw the Broadway production not just as "nostalgia prompting a lack of critical standards," but also as a possible sign that "'Jewishness' as we have understood it is reaching an end".[3] Other works of the postwar era also augmented the image of Jewish life in the old world as a still picture of piety, poverty, and above all authenticity, such as Roman Vishniac's late-1940s photographic collection of Polish Jews (The Vanished World, 1947); Abraham Joshua Heschel's eulogy for the murdered Eastern European Jewry, *The Earth Is the Lord's: The Inner World of the Jew in Eastern Europe* (1950); and Mark Zborowski and Elizabeth Herzog's anthropological study of the shtetl, *Life Is with People* (1952). Barbara Kirshenblatt-Gimblet has defined those works as "the mode of memory work signaled by the term 'vanished world.'"[4]

Whether or not one agrees with the critics' charges of an overriding nostalgia and sentimentality in many of those cultural works, or points to earlier, pre-Holocaust nostalgic examples[5], it is clear that postwar Yiddish memoirists created their own depiction of the Old Country. This article demonstrates that years before *Fiddler on the Roof*, or even the 1953 production of *The World of Sholem Aleichem*, Yiddish autobiographers put forward a version of the Jewish past, which underlines violence and conflict—through their own personal histories—and by doing that, reimagined that past according to lessons from the annihilation of European Jewry. Looking back at their personal histories, those writers sought to show that the Holocaust was not an exception but rather a perpetuation of deep-seated anti-Jewish enmity. Writing in Yiddish, the memoirists directed their message at a Yiddish-speaking readership in America, which to their minds might not have fully realized (or had already managed to forget) the depth of Gentile hatred of Jews.[6]

Tsukerman's memoir was published in the early 1960s, hence making it a late example of a wider postwar phenomenon: the large group of Yiddish memoirists—Zionists, socialists, traditionalists, and nonpartisans—who came to America decades before the Holocaust and published their recollections in the two decades after the war. In their portrayal of their own lives—and Jewish life in general—in Eastern Europe of the late nineteenth and early twentieth centuries, these memoirists often oversimplify the complex and nuanced details of Jewish existence in order to fit it into a more generalized and rather one-dimensional picture of Jewish life. Undoubtedly, anti-Jewish hatred, persecution, and violent assaults were a reality in Tsarist Russia, Romania, and to a lesser degree in Habsburg Galicia in the late nineteenth and early twentieth centuries; yet patterns of everyday peaceful coexistence existed as well. In depicting the relations between Jews and their Gentile surroundings, nonetheless, many memoirists emphasize the antagonistic nature of these encounters.

Incontrovertibly, the readership of Yiddish writings in postwar America was far smaller than the public that watched Broadway productions about the Old Country.[7] Nevertheless, these memoirs are important to consider in terms of how Yiddish-speaking immigrants who actually lived in Eastern Europe began recreating their own past stories in light of the Holocaust. Despite the assertions by the abovementioned critics (among others), generalizations about Jewish life in Eastern Europe did not start with American-born Jews; rather Eastern European Jewish immigrants themselves promulgated generalizations about the Old Country. These depictions, however, contrasted sharply with the sentimental version circulating in American popular culture.

Market scenes, which pitted Jews against Christian peasants, were a staple of many memoirs. Avrum Pinkhes Unger, a garment worker and organizer for the International Ladies' Garment Workers' Union (ILGWU) was born in 1880 and raised in the town of Strykov (near Lodz) before immigrating to America in 1910. Unger's memoir, *Mayn heymshtetl strykov* (My Hometown Strykov) was published in 1957 by the socialist fraternal order, *Arbeter Ring* (Workmen's Circle). Unger recalls how during local fairs peasants sometimes got drunk and began shouting "beat up the Jews," with fights breaking out. Both the Russian police constable and the judge, in Unger's account, protected the Jews and chastised the peasants. A similar experience is mentioned in the memoir of a member of the socialist Bund, Meyer Kushner, who was born in 1881 in the industrial city of Kremenchug in Ukraine and immigrated to New York City in 1906. Kushner, who was also active in the ILGWU, published his autobiography in 1960. Kushner recounts that when the peasants came every Sunday to the city's churches, the Jews were frightened, since the peasants "were easily agitated to a pogrom."[8]

Socialist organizer Shneyer Yafe grew up not in a shtetl but in a village in northern Lithuania (near Kopishok). He was born around 1885, immigrated to America in 1906, and published his memoir in 1953. Since he lived in a village, he had to walk a long way to the *kheyder* each day. On his way back, the peasants' dogs often attacked him, but the "shkotsim were even worse than the dogs," as they kept beating him up so that "my young life was constantly in danger." In the summertime Yafe's father used to lease orchards and sell their fruits; once, he had a dispute over a certain transaction with a few Russian buyers. Yafe comments, "With some Gentiles you can still come to an understanding, but with Russians—it's bad," before describing how enraged Russian clients were looking to settle the score with his father.[9]

Other memoirists do not focus on physical assaults but rather on Jewish unsympathetic perceptions of their Gentile neighbors. Like Yafe, Yiddish poet Yoysef Rolnik grew up in the 1880s in a small village, Zhukhovitsh (near Minsk), where "eight–nine Jewish families lived." Rolnik published his memoir in 1954, in which he describes how his pious mother was "good to people," including the Gentiles, though she used *lehavdl* (differentiation) language, calling "a non-Jewish child—a 'bastard,' and a non-Jewish corpse—a 'carcass'." The poet portrays the neighboring peasants as crude: they swam in the local river in "a primitive way, kicking their thick feet and quickly exhausting themselves," and the women rode horses "spread-legged, like men." A similar differentiation between Jews and surrounding Gentiles appears in the recollection of New York socialist and labor organizer Morris (Moyshe) Goldovsky, who grew up in the 1880s and 1890s in Loyev (near Minsk). He recalls how his mother explained to him that "pork-eating shkotsim are healthy and can walk around barefoot without catching a cold, but Jewish children are weak and must not walk barefoot." When the young Moyshe felt that one of the Jewish children was siding with the "shkotsim" as they played, he went to the child's parents to complain about him.¹⁰

Similar recollections can be found in many *yizker-bikher* as well. Hundreds of such books were written and published after the war by Holocaust survivors or refugees, dedicated to the commemoration of specific towns and their destroyed Jewish communities, as discussed earlier in this volume by David Slucki and Eliyana Adler. Jack Kugelmass and Jonathan Boyarin consider those books "the single most important act of commemorating the dead on the part of Jewish survivors." *Yizker-bikher* were largely written in Yiddish or Hebrew, reflecting the sensibilities of the writers and editors, as well as a readership that hailed from a particular town.¹¹

No less important, some of those books viewed relations with Gentiles via the lens of the ultimate destruction of their communities, thus tending to emphasize themes of persecution and harassment over peaceful, mundane coexistence. Pogroms, violence, Gentile drunkenness, volatility, and crudeness often characterize most of the spectrum of Jewish-Gentile relations in those postwar memoirs. Isaac Englard-Wasserstrom of Brooklyn decisively describes his native shtetl, Kortshin (Korczyna, Southern Poland), as a place where "No friendship existed" between Jews and non-Jews: "Jews never got together with Gentiles," he reports, and the groups had "no relation with one another." Though until World War I Jews tended to live in peace with their neighbors, Englard-Wasserstrom recalls "two opposing groups without common social or cultural interests."¹² In the Vitebsk *yizker-bukh*, Aleksander Rapaport asserts, "Jews were socially separated from the non-Jewish population by an immovable wall." In terms of livelihood, "Christians had to buy from Jews and the Jews had to buy farm produce from the peasants." Still, "apart from the business ties, both the Jew and the non-Jew were distant from one another."¹³

The pattern of emphasizing the antagonistic aspects of Jewish-Gentile relations and Jewish insularity appeared also in English-language memoirs of Eastern European, Yiddish-speaking Jews, such as labor leader Philip Zausner, who published his recollections during the war. The would-be leader of the Jewish painters' union in New York grew up in the 1890s, not in a shtetl, but rather in the big city of Lemberg (Lviv), whose Jewish population underwent profound acculturation processes (first to German culture, and then to Polish). Yet Zausner remembers that the masses of Jews "lived 'their own' life, segregated from the rest of the city's population." Evidently Zausner's family was not so segregated, since the family's traditional patriarch feared his daughters were growing up to resemble "peasant women, like the goyim." A later memoir was that of philosopher Morris Raphael Cohen, who hailed from the town of Neshwies (Niasviž) in Byelorussia, immigrated in 1892 with his family at the age of twelve to America, and later taught for many years at the City College of New York. The philosopher's memoir was published posthumously in 1949. Cohen recalls, "As the majority of Goyim (Gentiles) whom one met in Neshwies were peasants or poor city dwellers, some of them former serfs, few of them literate, the Jews generally regarded them as an inferior race." Cohen also reveals, "My first attitude toward non-Jews—*Goyim*—was that they were not fully human beings. Those I saw were ignorant peasants and I heard of generals and *pritzim* (lords) who were our persecutors. I did not understand their ways and they did not understand mine." Cohen's memoir, which was written during the war and/or shortly afterward, unquestionably echoes both deeply-seated sentiments within traditional Jewish society as well as the philosopher's own critical evaluation of such parochialism. More important is Cohen's juxtaposition of the primitiveness of Eastern European Gentiles and the advancement of Gentile Americans: "The world that we faced on the East Side at the turn of the century presented a series of heartbreaking dilemmas.... We learned that all non-Jews were not mere soulless heathens. We found that the Jews had not been the only conservators of wisdom and civilization."[14] Even for Cohen, who criticizes the cultural milieu of traditional Jewish society in relation to Gentiles, the horrors of the war reverberate in the distinction between the crude Eastern Europeans and the advanced Americans.

It is important to mention that one cannot, of course, verify that the incidents actually happened as the memoirists relayed them. The fact that immigrants of different backgrounds, regions, and political convictions had communicated a pattern of hostile Jewish-Gentile relations, however, attests to the potency of their attitude in the postwar years. No less noteworthy, episodes of anti-Jewish enmity, harassment, and violent attacks seemed to be fairly common in Eastern Europe in the late nineteenth and early twentieth centuries.

Yet at the same time, lapses of memory and an ideological agenda often haunt the memoirs and other testimonies of older people, and a retrospective twist may have been given in order to impart a larger meaning. Later events mostly reinforced stereotypes rather than overturning them. Just as the rise of Nazism and the Holocaust clouded recollections about Germans that related to the 1890s or 1900s, the widespread pogroms in Ukraine after World War surely darkened, in some reminiscences, the image of Gentiles from decades beforehand.[15]

How can one determine whether it was the Holocaust per se that caused postwar memoirists to convey a more one-dimensional picture of their younger years? In some memoirs, the Holocaust is indirectly mentioned in recounting the years previous to it, with the application of postwar terminology about Nazism/fascism in reference to earlier events. Borekh Tsukerman, for example, describes how Socialist Zionists were among those who initiated the American Jewish Congress movement during World War I, combining what he sees as the healthy elements of both socialism and nationalism. But in more recent years, Tsukerman laments, the very term "National Socialism" had been defiled by the Nazis, in the same way that in America the name "Bund" had been tainted by the homegrown Nazi German-American Bund. Meyer Kushner details Jewish-Italian tension within the ILGWU in 1911 and 1912, at a time when the Italians workers demanded the creation of a separate, Italian-speaking locale. Kushner refers to the Italian leader as "a regular fascist"; apparently all that "fascist" wanted was to form a separate Italian-speaking division within a union where many of the meetings were held in Yiddish.[16]

A direct reference that ties together the prewar Jewish past and the Holocaust appears in the memoir of Yiddish journalist and humorist Khone Gotesfeld, who grew up in the 1890s in Skala on the River Zbrucz (in Eastern Galicia), and later enjoyed a prolific career in the *Forverts* and on the American Yiddish stage. In 1960 Gotesfeld published his memoir, which opened with his gratitude to God for giving him a father like his, a Jew called Shmuel. Gotesfeld portrays his father as "a simple Jew . . . who was not a learned man, not a scholar, and even not a great businessman." His father, in his view exemplified "all the virtues and shortcomings of a simple Jew . . . who live[d] in a Galician shtetl." But Gotesfeld also affectionately praises him: "He was good to all children . . . he never let a child cry, but sang to him, danced and jumped around.... He did not let anyone yell at a child. For him children were not just beloved, but also holy." Gotesfeld's love for his father, however, finds expression through a more general comparison between Shmuel and other potential fathers: "I could have been born to a hooligan of a father, a Ukrainian pogromist, from whom I would have learnt how to beat up Jews. I could have been born to a German antisemite of a father, a Nazi, may his name be erased, a Gestapo man, who tortured Jews, and I would have forever been ashamed that I am descended from such a murderer." That reference to antisemitism and the Holocaust allows Gotesfeld to tell a larger story about the purported nobler character of Jewish fathers in comparison to non-Jewish ones.[17]

The way in which the Holocaust had eclipsed earlier impressions can be vividly seen in the memoir of the leading critic of the Yiddish theater, A. Mukdoyni (pseudonym of Aleksander Kapel, 1878–1958). He immigrated to America in 1920 and published two volumes of his memoirs in 1955. Looking back at his experience in Warsaw prior to World War I (1909–1914), Mukdoyni notes, "The Pole is the most unusual Slav, he has all the shortcomings of the Slavs, but not even one of their virtues." Mukdoyni argues that the Pole "can cry like a child and torment people like a dreadful sadist"; the Pole "must hate" since it is "his second nature." He relates that "a Pole, whether a man or a woman, will not go out on the street without gloves, but under their fingernails there is a dark line of filth." Perhaps Mukdoyni deems this graphic portrayal to be necessary as a preface to his attack against the Polish culture and intelligentsia: "If you scratch a Polish revolutionary or radical, an antisemite or reactionary jumps out." During World War I, Poles "collaborated with their biggest enemy [Tsarist Russia] in order to torment their weak, defenceless neighbour, the Jew." And with regard to "the time of Hitler's occupation, we have scores of books by Jewish survivors about the close partnership of Poles with Hitler's murderers." Moreover, the Germans "tormented [the Poles] almost as much as they did to the Jews ... but the Poles helped Hitler's murderers to exterminate Jews." Mukdoyni concludes, "Yes, after Hitler the Pole would remain our historical *Amalek* [the biblical sworn enemy of the Israelites], which partnered with the murderers of Jews."[18]

One of the leading Jewish theologians of the twentieth century, Rabbi Abraham Joshua Heschel, provides a notable and early example of the

Eastern European Jewish past rendered as a timeless, monolithic totality in its relations with the outside world. In 1945 Heschel delivered a lecture in Yiddish at the annual conference of the Yiddish Scientific Institute (known by its Yiddish acronym YIVO) in New York City. That lecture's expanded version was published in 1950 in book form as *The Earth Is the Lord's: The Inner World of the Jew in Eastern Europe*. The lecture was published in Yiddish already in 1945 in the periodical *YIVO bleter*, and a year later Schocken Books published it as a booklet, titled *Der mizrekh-eropeyisher yid* (The Eastern European Jew). In that essay Heschel delineates the different eras of Jewish history, and asserts that "In the Ashkenazi era the spiritual life of Jews happened in seclusion. The people lived on its own among primitive Germanic and Slavic masses. Spiritually and mentally Jews stand higher than their neighbors." Heschel stresses what he saw as Jewish seclusion and claims that Eastern European Jews "borrowed no forms and no ideas from other cultures." Moreover, Heschel refers to the people of "the small Jewish communities in Eastern Europe," arguing that "progress had not deceived them. The spell of the twentieth century had not blinded them."[19]

To be sure, Heschel underlines profoundly important aspects and conditions of Eastern European Jewish life and captures the Jewish self-image vis-à-vis the non-Jewish surroundings. Nevertheless, Heschel presents a rather rigid portrayal, dismissive of the many-sided interactions between Jews and their neighbors, wherein Jews borrowed not only components from their Gentile neighbors' cuisine, garb, and language, but also elements from their social structure, literature, and even religion. Memoir accounts that underscore hatred, friction, and insularity hardly comprise the whole gamut of interactions that took place between Jews and non-Jews in Eastern Europe. As several scholars have reminded us, later events should not have a monopoly on interpretations of the history that preceded them. The relations between Jews and their non-Jewish neighbors were much more dynamic than what many of those postwar recollections suggest; as Lucy S. Dawidowicz aptly wrote in 1966, "East European Jewry was not, as the sentimentalists see it, forever frozen in utter piety and utter poverty."[20]

The dynamic nature of Jewish-Gentile relations in Eastern Europe can be seen in Yiddish folklore: despite an evident anti-Gentile streak, it often portrays non-Jews as down-to-earth, no-nonsense people, whose directness and simplicity were uncorrupted, in comparison with the tortuous ways, casuistry, and nervousness among Jews: "a good Gentile is better than a good Jew"; "a Jewish shrew is worse than a Gentile one"; "when a Jew has a lot of money and a Gentile just a little, he lives better than the Jew"; "sometimes it's harder to depend on a Jew than on a Gentile." Another pattern was to present Gentile shortcomings side by side with Jewish ones: "it's better to fall in the hands of Gentiles than in the mouths of Jews"; "it's better to live among Gentiles and die among Jews"; "God save us from Jewish arrogance and Gentile lust." The Gentile was earthy, coarse, and simple, but he was not suffering from *goles* (exile) complications and lived happily on his land. A vocal yearning for normalcy, to be *ke-khol ha-goyim* (like all other peoples) in economic and cultural life was noticeable by the closing years of the nineteenth century, as was the desire to break free from the traditional way of life.[21]

Furthermore, external influences permeated most facets of Jewish life, and closer personal relations were formed in spite of religious and social inhibitions. Some shtetl or city Jews employed non-Jewish maids and servants, who lived with them and brought a Gentile presence into the Jewish domestic sphere. Those Christians often became very attached to the family and learned to speak fluent Yiddish. Female maids sometimes said the blessings with the children and referred to other Gentiles as "goyim." Growing up in Vitebsk (Byelorussia) in the 1870s, revolutionary and Yiddishist Chaim Zhitlovsky remembers a Christian maid at his parents' house called Yulke, who was "assimilated": she spoke spicy Yiddish, called the local janitor an *orl* (derogatory for Gentile), and before Passover she warned that he might contaminate the house with *khomets* (the janitor answered her with a folksy Yiddish swearword). Similarly, Yiddish linguist Alexander Harkavy, who grew up in the 1860s–1870s in Novogrudok (Byelorussia) recalls a house maid by the name of Yustine, who spoke fluent Yiddish, served as the *shabbes goy* and knew some of the prayers. Playwright and theatrical designer Mordecai Gorelik, who grew up in a small shtetl near Minsk after the turn of the twentieth century, recalls how the local Gentiles spoke Yiddish and even went to the Jewish bathhouse. The regular hiring of Gentiles to perform necessary work on the Sabbath also made certain Gentiles very familiar with Jewish customs. Yiddish novelist Israel Joshua Singer, who grew up in a Polish shtetl at the turn of the twentieth century, mentions Gentiles who used to perform various chores in the shtetl, and who spoke fluent Yiddish and said the Jewish blessings. One of them even warned Jewish women to hide the kosher wine when he was around, "so he wouldn't make it *treyf* with his eyes." The level of closeness with those Gentiles rendered Jewish-Gentile relations more complex, revealing a level of friendliness and even intimacy with the next-door and household Gentiles.[22]

The multifaceted coexistence of Jews and non-Jews even made its way into memoirs that drew more attention to conflict and enmity between the groups. While Yoysef Rolnik presents peasants as crude and stresses how different they were from Jews, his own account includes another layer. Rolnik's parents employed a few Gentile workers for various tasks around the house, and he recalls that they were "truly Talmudists": "Once, as they covered the suke [sukkah], I heard how Matshi had an argument with Yezev, since Matshi said that the sky should shine through the thatch during daytime, and Yezev said the stars should sparkle through the thatch at nighttime. Both are the words of the living God." This last sentence—a Talmudic quote referring to a dispute between the schools of Hillel and Shammai—is probably meant to provide an amusing anecdote of how two Gentile domestic workers argued about the finer details of Jewish tradition, but the example also reflects the depth of familiarity between Jews and Gentiles.[23]

Other accounts that also belie the more negative characterization of Jewish-Gentile relations in Eastern Europe appeared already during the war. In May 1942 YIVO Institute issued a call for an autobiography-writing contest among Jewish immigrants, with the theme "Why I left Europe and what I have accomplished in America." More than two hundred Jewish immigrants from across America (and even from a few other countries)—housewives, shopkeepers, blue-collar workers, communal activists, and writers—sent their life stories in response, ninety percent of which were written in Yiddish. The scope of destruction and details about the Final Solution were still largely unknown in mid-1942, and as Jocelyn Cohen and Daniel Soyer have rightly observed, it is difficult to know what role, if any, the events in Europe had in motivating the participants to write.[24] In addition, even without World War II in the background, the wording of the competition's topic lent itself to an adverse view of the European past, combined with praise of the American present.

Hence, anti-Jewish hostility, violence, and pogroms indeed occupy an important place in many of the memoirs that were sent to the competition.[25] Nonetheless, more amicable and intimate relations between Jews and Gentiles are also a common feature in many memoirs. Bessie Moskowitz grew up in the Romanian city of Iasi in the 1870s and recalls that "people used to speak constantly about the Gentiles who beat up and murder Jews." Yet in her neighborhood, the few non-Jews she met spoke Yiddish and lived peacefully with their Jewish neighbors. An immigrant from Berditshev, S. Schreibman, remembers how older peasants warned him that the young *shkotsim* were "wild," and indeed some of them destroyed parts of a Jewish-owned inn. But on the next day, the same lads came to repair what they broke. An immigrant who identifies as "Ish Ikor" reminisces about friendly relations with the neighboring non-Jews when he grew up in Bessarabia in the 1880s and 1890s, but blames the Tsarist government for making Jews feel in exile due to its evil decrees.[26]

Still, such nuances do not appear in the bulk of the post-Holocaust recollections under review. Interestingly, the memoirists' portrayal of viscerally hostile Jewish-Gentile relations in Eastern Europe stands in contrast to the paradigm presented by scholars such as Dan Miron and Israel Bartal. Miron has analyzed the image of the shtetl in the writings of classic Yiddish writers such as Sholem Yankev Abramovitsh (commonly named after one of his main literary creations, Mendele Mokher Sforim), Sholem Aleichem, and other writers. Miron has explored what he calls "an influential tradition, a potent form" in Yiddish literature that "demanded the radical Judaization of the image of the Eastern European shtetl," imagining it as a purely Jewish cosmos. That tradition erased most, if not all, Gentile presence in the shtetl, and when Gentile characters did make their appearance, they were half-Judaized and defined by their Jewish function— the *shabbes goy*, for instance, or a Russian gendarme who happens to be a converted Jew. Many of those towns—Abramovitsh's Kabtsansk and Glupsk, Sholem Aleichem's Kasrilevke, some of the towns in Peretz's stories—are ahistorical, hermetic Jewish universes.[27]

More recently, Israel Bartal has also discussed maskilic and classic Yiddish literature with its "all-Jewish shtetl," arguing that those writers' ethno-geographic segregation—the Jews in the center of town and the Gentiles in the outskirts and villages—held a kernel of truth, but that did not mean the center of town was exclusively Jewish. In the same vein, Barbara Kirshenblatt-Gimblett has noted in her discussion of Zborowski and Herzog's *Life Is with People* (1952) that this postwar ethnography drew on the literary tradition that rendered the shtetl Judaized and frozen in time. That tradition led them to conflate the shtetl (town) with the *Kehile*, the corporate Jewish community, which historically sometimes had jurisdiction over the Jewish population in a number of places. Zborowski even observed in 1949 that the shtetl was "not a place but a state of mind."[28]

Post-Holocaust memoirists in America, on the other hand, tended to emphasize the presence of Gentiles, highlighting patterns of conflict, violence, and animosity between Jews and non-Jews. As the Italian philosopher and historian Benedetto Croce argued in 1938, "all history [has] the character of 'contemporary history'."[29] Memoirs and autobiographies are at least as much a creation of the time when they were written as they are a report of what the authors felt and experienced at the time they describe. The Holocaust served as a new prism through which memoirists reviewed their own prewar experiences, providing time and again an overgeneralized version of the complex and nuanced details of Jewish life in Eastern Europe in order to fit it to a sweepingly negative picture of Jewish-Gentile relations. To be sure, the hatred and violence toward Jews in Eastern Europe were hardly invented by the memoirists; but in the years following the greatest catastrophe to befall the Jewish people in the modern era, those elements seemed to trump anything else.

In that respect, the Holocaust was not unique. Jewish memoirists from Eastern Europe had been reviewing and reinterpreting their early life in light of later events many years prior to the *khurbm* (Holocaust in Yiddish). Memoirs written in the 1920s and 1930s bear the marks of the widespread pogroms of 1917–1922. In the civil war that wreaked havoc from late 1917 on, across the former Pale of Settlement (especially in Ukraine), hundreds of Jewish communities were attacked while Reds fought Whites, Poles fought Ukrainians, Poles fought Bolsheviks, and Ukrainians fought amongst themselves. "White" (counterrevolutionary) armies, Polish forces, Ukrainian nationalists under Semyon Petlyura, and marauding bands of peasants and Cossacks massacred tens of thousands of unarmed, non-combatant Jewish families. Famed Russian-Jewish writer Isaac Babel, who traveled with a Red Army cavalry unit as a war correspondent, described "naked seventy-year-old men with their skulls bashed in and tiny children with their fingers hacked off."[30] Borekh Tsukerman, who directed relief efforts in Eastern Europe after the Great War on behalf of *Poalei tsiyon* (Workers of Zion), witnessed the 1919 slaughter of Jews in Pinsk and linked it to the Holocaust. Psychological accommodation "to the idea that Jewish blood is free for all" and "the later willingness of the Poles, Ukrainians, Byelorussians, Latvians, Lithuanians, and other nations to collaborate with Hitler" were, in Tsukerman's view, "demonstrated already then."[31]

The extreme and prolonged outburst of murderous anti-Jewish violence in those years affected interwar Jewish memoirists in a way that is very similar to the early post-Holocaust recollections. Yisroel Binimetsky (later Beneqvit), who became active in the anarchist movement in America, grew up in the town of Belotserkov in Ukraine in the 1870s and 1880s, immigrated to America in 1888, and published his autobiography in 1934. Beneqvit recalls how the local Jews refrained from using the regular verb *shtarbn* (to die) when talking about the death of non-Jews; instead, they applied the word *peygern* (which denotes the death of an animal). The Gentiles did not eat but "devoured". Their family members were "fatheru, motheru, sisteru," a way of mocking Ukrainian pronunciation. The long shadow of the pogroms is evident in Beneqvit's story about a violent childhood friend who kicked him so hard that he lost consciousness: "I am strongly convinced that displaying such ferocity at a time when he considered himself my friend can only a Gentile do—a Slav." Beneqvit added that "only a Slav can spill blood cold-bloodedly, without a shudder, cause terrible misery, and callously look on when somebody is tormented." Other autobiographers in the interwar period, such as Yiddish editor and writer Mordkhe Spektor and Zionist leader Shmaryahu Levin, also underscore the cruelty and volatility of the Gentile masses, or in Spektor's words, "the beastly faces of the peasants and town's hoodlums."[32]

Memory is often deceptive. It reflects the ways in which present concerns and attitudes determine what components of the past one remembers and how one remembers them. Personal recollections can be at times ahistorical, since to understand a certain event historically is to be aware of its complexity, accept its ambiguities, and make an attempt to view it from multiple perspectives. Historical understanding also focuses on the historicity of events: that they took place then and not now, and grew out of circumstances different from those that exist in the present. But personal memories, especially in the wake of a cataclysmic event such as the Holocaust, often filter events from a committed perspective, exhibit impatience with ambiguities, and have no sense of the passage of time. More recent episodes tend to overshadow previous ones, and to define a more rigid identity for the members of your group and their enemies. That does not imply the abovementioned memoirs and autobiographies are not valid historical sources—they illustrate incidents of anti-Jewish hatred, persecution, and violent assaults that we know occurred in Eastern Europe, as well as common Jewish attitudes at the time—yet one must acknowledge those recollections' challenging character.[33]

The post-*khurbm* world seemed grimmer not only to Holocaust survivors, but also to people who were raised in Eastern Europe but left decades before the war. The overwhelming collapse of civilization in Europe during the war, and the participation of virtually all European nations in the atrocities, led Jewish memoirists to reconsider their own lives in light of the "Jewish catastrophe." That collapse prompted the writers to look for the seeds of evil in earlier years, and to demonstrate that the Holocaust was a direct continuation of European life and culture rather than an aberration. Writing in Yiddish, it was important for them to convey this message to other Jews, namely Yiddish speakers in America and elsewhere. That message was intended to disabuse their readership of dreams of universalism and brotherhood of all people, as well as of the nostalgic, soppy view of life in the Old Country. For the memoirists, the fact that they did not live under Nazi rule did not diminish the validity or authenticity of their insight; if anything, they looked for and found the precursor of Nazism and murderous antisemitism in their earlier experiences.

Critics have focused on how American-born Jews sentimentalized the Jewish past in Eastern European in a host of cultural products—books, theater and musical productions, and movies—but postwar Yiddish memoirists largely preceded them in providing the flipside, or the darker opposite, of that sentimentality.[34] They represented the Jewish past in Eastern Europe as a life in which antisemitism, hostility, persecution, and pogroms prevailed. Those memoirists wrote for a Yiddish-speaking readership and remained marginal to most American Jewish readers, not only because they wrote in Yiddish, but because their glum vision of Jewish life in the old world clashed with the romanticized imagery of that very life that pervaded American culture after the Holocaust. As American-born Jews flattened the image of the Old Country to a saccharine version of shtetl life, Yiddish-speaking immigrants who actually lived in Eastern Europe also flattened that image but in the opposite direction: in the shadow of the Holocaust, they redrew their own past into a dark tale of Jewish insularity in a hostile Gentile world.

Notes

1. Borekh Tsukerman, *Zikhroynes* (New York: Yidisher kemfer, 1962), 1: 22–23, 47–48, 131. At the time of publication, Tsukerman lived in Israel. On Tsukerman's important role in the Labor Zionist movement in America, see Mark A. Raider, *The Emergence of American Zionism* (New York: New York University Press, 1998), 137–39; and J. Zipper, "Baruch Zuckerman: The Man of Deed and Vision," in *Viewpoints: Canadian Jewish Quarterly* 6 (1972): 41–49.

2. Midge Decter, "On the Horizon: Belittling Sholom Aleichem's Jews—The Falsification of the Ghetto," *Commentary* 17 (April 1954): 389–90, 392. The play's title referred to a 1943 book by Romanian-born Zionist intellectual Maurice Samuel. See also Bennett Muraskin, "Sholem Aleichem's Show Biz Triumph," in *Jewish Currents* (Spring 2014), accessed June 2, 2015, http://jewishcurrents.org/sholem-aleichems-show-biz-triumph-30162.

3. Irving Howe, "Tevye on Broadway," *Commentary* 38 (Nov. 1964): 74. Alisa Solomon has rejected Howe's and others' critique of *Fiddler on the Roof* in *Wonder of Wonders: A Cultural History of Fiddler on the Roof* (New York: Metropolitan, 2013), 2, 42, 119. Jeffrey Shandler has shown that certain postwar films drew on prewar conventions of what shtetl life looked like: Shandler, *Shtetl: A Vernacular Intellectual History* (New Brunswick, NJ: Rutgers University Press, 2014), 131. See also Stephen J. Whitfield, "Fiddling with Sholem Aleichem: A History of *Fiddler on the Roof*," in *Key Texts in American Jewish Culture*, ed. Jack Kugelmass (New Brunswick, NJ: Rutgers University Press, 2003), 105–25.

4. Barbara Kirshenblatt-Gimblett, introduction to Mark Zborowski and Elizabeth Herzog, *Life Is with People: The Culture of the Shtetl* (1952, reprinted New York: Schocken, 1995), 20. That text was accessed on June 10, 2015, via www.nyu.edu/classes/bkg/web/liwp.pdf (pagination follows the online version). See also Kirshenblatt-Gimblett, "Imagining Europe: The Popular Arts of American Jewish Ethnography," in *Divergent Jewish Cultures: Israel and America*, ed. Deborah Dash Moore and S. Ilan Troen (New Haven: Yale University Press, 2001), 155–91. Roman Vishniac, *Polish Jews* (New York: Shocken, 1947). *Life Is with People* had informed the creators of *Fiddler on the Roof*—see Shandler, *Shtetl*, 77–78. See also, Elie Wiesel, "The World of the Shtetl," in *The Shtetl: New Evaluations*, ed. Steven T. Katz (New York: New York University Press, 2007), 290–306.

5. See, for example, Shandler, *Shtetl*, 39–40.

6. David G. Roskies has discussed post-Holocaust Yiddish writers' "collective need to commemorate." David Roskies, *A Bridge of Longing: The Lost Art of Yiddish Storytelling* (Cambridge, MA: Harvard University Press, 1995), 310–11.

7. On postwar Yiddish readership in America, see Jan Schwarz, *Survivors and Exiles: Yiddish Culture after the Holocaust* (Detroit: Wayne State University Press, 2015), 143–237.

8. Avrom Pinkhes Unger, *Mayn heymshtetl strykov* (New York: Arbeter Ring, 1957), 49–50. Meyer Kushner, *Lebn un kamf fun a kloakmakher* (New York: Published by a committee from local 9, International Ladies' Garment Workers Union, 1960), 56. There are many other examples of such market scenes: see also the wartime memoirs of the "Mohilev Carpenter," in American Jewish Autobiographies Collection, hereafter AJAC (YIVO), #83: 2; Yisroel Kerdman, AJAC, #105: 4; and an earlier example, a recollection by Hillel Katz-Blum, in *Di yidishe sotsyalistishe bavegung biz der grindung fun 'bund,'* ed. Elias Cherikover (Vilna: YIVO, 1939), 350. Cf. Aliza Grinblat, *Baym fentster fun a lebn* (New York: by the author, 1966), 10; Shalom Muhlstein, "At the Market," in *From a Ruined Garden: The Memorial Books of Polish Jewry*, ed. and trans. Jack Kugelmass and Jonathan Boyarin (1983, 2nd edition, Bloomington: Indiana University Press, 1998), 58–64.

9. Shneyer Yafe, *Epizodn fun mayn lebn* (Boston: By the author, 1953), 24, 26–27.

10. Yoysef Rolnik, *Zikhroynes* (New York: With the help of the David Ignatoff Fund, 1954), 7, 19, 21–22, 33. Morris Goldovsky, *Fun vayten amol un haynt: mayne 60 yor lebn un kamf in der arbeter bavegung* (New York: Published by a Committee, 1959), 15, 26. On the *lehavdl* language, see Max Weinreich, *History of the Yiddish Language*, trans. Joshua A. Fishman (Chicago: University of Chicago Press, 1980), 193–94; Israel Bartal, "Ha-lo yehudim ve-chevratam be-sifrut 'ivrit ve-yidish be-mizrach 'eropa bein ha-shanim 1856–1914" (PhD Dissertation, Hebrew University, Jerusalem, 1980), 257–59. Similar examples from other recollections are in I. A. Beneqvit, *Durkhgelebt un durkhgetrakht* (New York: Kultur federatsye, 1934), 1: 104–5; and Morris Raphael Cohen, *A Dreamer's Journey* (Glenco, IL: Free Press, 1949), 27–28, 219. See also the recollection of Zionist thinker Ahad ha'am (Asher Ginzberg) in *Kol kitvey ahad ha'am* (Tel Aviv: Dvir, 1953), 467 (Hebrew pagination).

11. Kugelmass and Boyarin, "Introduction," *From a Ruined Garden*, 1, 5–6; Shandler, *Shtetl*, 74–75. See also, Rivka Parciak, "The *Others* in Yizker Books," in *Memorial Books of Eastern European Jewry: Essays on the History and Meanings of Yizker Volumes*, ed. Rosemary Horowitz (Jefferson, NC: McFarland, 2011), 222–43. The problem of trying to depict a town but instead recalling only the relatives whom the Germans murdered is explained by Ben tsiyen Gold, "Zikhroynes vegn svir", khanokh Svironi (Druts) (ed.), *Unzer shtetele svir* (Tel Aviv: 'Irgun yots'ei svir be-medinat yisrael, 1959), 106.

12. Isaac England-Wasserstrom, "Dos tsuzamenlebn un farhaltn zikh fun yidn un nisht-yidn mit 100 yor tsurik, bizn Ershtn velt krig," in *Kortshin (kortshina) sefer zikaron/gedenk-bukh*, ed. Morris Zucker and Isaac Wasserstrom (New York: Kortshiner yizker bukh komitet, 1967), 59–60. On the appearance of Polish antisemitism even among its progressive intelligentsia, see Rafael Federman, "Sholem Ash, a"h, in unzer amolikn tshenstokhov", in *Tshenstokhov: Nayer tsugob-material tsum bukh tshenstokhover yidn*, ed. S. D. Singer (New York: United Czenstochov Relief Committee in New York, 1958), 173–74. See also Velvel Ze'ev Lefkovitsh, "Der mark zuntik," in *Bobroysk: yizker-bukh far bobroysker kehille un umgegent*, ed. Yehuda Slutsky (Tel Aviv: Tarbut ve-chinukh, 1967), 1: 638–40.

13. Aleksander Rapaport's "Bletlekh zikhroynes," in *Vitebsk amol*, eds. Gregory Aronson, Yankev Leshtsinsky, and Abraham Kohn (New York: H.A. Abramson, 1956), 502. See

also, the pre-Holocaust memoir of revolutionary and Yiddishist Chaim Zhitlovsky, who grew up in Vitebsk about a decade before Rapaport: his account has a wealth of information on relations between Jews and different groups such as Germans, Poles, and Russians. *Zikhroynes fun mayn lebn* (New York: Zhitlovsky's Jubilee Committee, 1935), 1: 120–21, 160–67.

14. Philip Zausner, *Unvarnished: The Autobiography of a Union Leader* (New York: Brotherhood Publishers, 1941), 3–4, 23. Cohen, *A Dreamer's Journey*, 27–28, 98, 219. On the growing acculturation of Jews in Lemberg (and Galicia in general), see Albert Lichtblau and Michael John, "Jewries in Galicia and Bukowina, in Lemberg and Czernowitz: Two Divergent Examples of Jewish Communities in the Far East of the Austro-Hungarian Monarchy," in *Jewries at the Frontier: Accommodation, Identity, Conflict*, ed. Sander L. Gilman and Milton Shain (Urbana, Ill.: University of Illinois Press, 1999), 29–38; Joshua Shanes, *Diaspora Nationalism and Jewish Identity in Habsburg Galicia* (New York: Cambridge University Press, 2012), 50–61. On the Jewish middle class in Lemberg and its early affinity to German culture, see Michael Stanislawski, *A Murder in Lemberg: Politics, Religion, and Violence in Modern Jewish History* (Princeton, N.J.: Princeton University Press, 2007), 31–32, 49–50, 69; Rachel Manekin, "'Daychn", polanim, 'o "ostrim': dilemat ha-zehut shel yehudei galitsia (1848–1851)", *Zion* 68 (2003): 223–62. On Cohen's life and influence, see Irving Howe, with the assistance of Kenneth Libo, *World of Our Fathers* (1976, reprinted New York: Schocken, 1989), 283–86. See also the memoir of pianist Samuel Chotzinoff, *A Lost Paradise: Early Reminiscences* (New York: Knopf, 1955), 67, 85–86.

15. Jill Ker Conway, *When Memory Speaks: Reflections on Autobiography* (New York: Alfred A. Knopf, 1998), 3–18, 60–86. Melissa R. Klapper, *Jewish Girls Coming of Age in America, 1860–1920* (New York: New York University Press, 2005), 9–10. Virginia Yans-McLaughlin, "Metaphors of the Self in History: Subjectivity, Oral Narrative, and Immigration Studies," in *Immigration Reconsidered: History, Sociology, and Politics*, ed. Virginia Yans-McLaughlin (New York: Oxford University Press, 1990), 254–90. On the influence of later events on the portrayal of Germans, see Gil Ribak, *Gentile New York: The Images of Non-Jews among Jewish Immigrants* (New Brunswick, NJ: Rutgers University Press, 2012), 20–24. On a particularly problematic autobiography see E. G. Stern, *My Mother and I* (New York: Macmillan, 1917); and Ellen M. Umansky, "Representations of Jewish Women in the Works and Life of Elizabeth Stern," *Modern Judaism* 13 (1993): 165–76. On the autobiography as a genre among Jewish writers, see Marcus Moseley, *Being for Myself Alone: Origins of Jewish Autobiography* (Stanford, CA: Stanford University Press, 2006), 50–66; and Michael Stanislawsky, *Autobiographical Jews: Essays in Jewish Self-Fashioning* (Seattle: Washington University Press, 2004), 3–17.

16. Tsukerman, *Zikhroynes*, 2: 54. Kushner, *Lebn un kamf*, 110–11. On the conflicts between Jewish and Italian immigrants in the ILGWU, see Charles Anthony Zappia, "Unionism and the Italian American Worker: A History of the New York City 'Italian Locals' in the International Ladies' Garment Union" (PhD diss., University of California-Berkeley, 1994), 163–172, 182–188, 197; Susan A. Glenn, *Daughters of the Shtetl: Life and Labor in the Immigrant Generation* (Ithaca, NY: Cornell University Press, 1990), 186–99; Ribak, *Gentile New York*, 103–25.

17. Khone Gotesfeld, *Vos ikh gedenk fun mayn lebn* (New York: Fareynikte galitsyaner yidn in amerike un yidish galitsyaner farband in argentine, 1960), 9–10. On Gotesfeld's prewar visit (1937) to his home shtetl of Skala, see Daniel Soyer, "The Travel Agent as Broker

between Old World and New: The Case of Gustave Eisner," in *YIVO Annual: Going Home* 21, ed. Jack Kugelmass (1993): 352–53.

18. A. Mukdoyni, *In varshe un in lodzh: mayne bagegenishn* (Buenos Aires: Tsentral farband fun poylishe yidn in argentine, 1955), 2: 7–11, 13, 19. On Mukdoyni's role as a critic and clash with other critics, see Faith Jones, "Sex and Scandal in the Encyclopedia of the Yiddish Theater," in *Inventing the Modern Yiddish Stage: Essays in Drama, Performance, and Show Business*, ed. Joel Berkowitz and Barbara Henry (Detroit, MI: Wayne State University Press, 2012), 251–74.

19. Avrom Yehoshua Heschel, *Der mizrakh-eropeyisher yid* (New York: Schocken, 1946), 7–8, 37–38. See also Kirshenblatt-Gimblett, introduction, 2–3; Deborah Dash Moore, preface to *East European Jews in Two Worlds: Studies from the YIVO Annual* (Evanston, IL: Northwestern University Press and YIVO Institute for Jewish Research, 1990), viii; Jeffrey Shandler, "Heschel and Yiddish: A Struggle with Signification," *Journal of Jewish Thought and Philosophy* 2 (1993): 245–99; Edward K. Kaplan, *Spiritual Radical: Abraham Joshua Heschel in America, 1940–1972* (New Haven, CT: Yale University Press, 2007), 57–60, 102–5.

20. Lucy S. Dawidowicz, introduction to *The Golden Tradition: Jewish Life and Thought in Eastern Europe* (Boston: Beacon, 1967), 6. One can mention only a handful of the scholars who have made that argument: Benjamin Nathans, *Beyond the Pale: The Jewish Encounter with Late Imperial Russia* (Berkeley: University of California Press, 2002), 13–14; Steven J. Zipperstein, *Imagining Russian Jewry: Memory, History* (Seattle: University of Washington Press, 1999), 88–105; Antony Polonsky, "Introduction—The Shtetl: Myth and Reality," *Polin* 17 (2004): 5–10. See also David Biale, "A Journey between Worlds," in *Cultures of the Jews: A New History* (New York: Schocken, 2002), 839–40.

21. The quotes are from I.L. Cahan, *Der yid: vegn zikh un vegn andere in zayne shprikhverter un rednsortn* (New York: YIVO, 1933), 25–32; Nakhum Stutchkov, *Der oytser fun der yidisher shprakh* (New York: YIVO, 1950), 167–68; Ignatz Bernshteyn, *Yudishe shprikhverter un rednsarten* (1908, reprinted Wiesbaden, Germany: Fourier, 1988), 53; Israel Steinberg, *Mima'ayan ha-khokhma shel 'am israel* (Tel Aviv: I. L. Peretz, 1962), 80–81. About the later aspiration to be like all other nations, see Anita Shapira, *Yehudim chadashim, yehudim yeshanim* (Tel Aviv: 'Am 'oved, 1997), 155–74; Oz Almog, *The Sabra: The Creation of the New Jew* (trans. Haim Watzman, Berkeley: University of California Press, 2000), 76–79; and David Biale, *Power and Powerlessness in Jewish History* (New York: Schocken, 1986), 130–33.

22. Zhitlovsky, *Zikhroynes fun mayn lebn*, 1: 120–21. Alexander Harkavy, *Prakim mechayay* (New York: Hebrew Publishing, 1935), 6–7. Mordecai Gorelik, *William Wiener Oral History Library of the American Jewish Committee* (New York Public Library), 8. Y. Y. Singer, *Fun a velt vos iz nishtu mer* (New York: Matones, 1946), 53, 109. See also the memoir of Kalman Marmor, *Mayn lebns geshikhte* (New York: IKUF, 1959), 1: 158; and the 1908 report from Vilna by A. Litvin on Christian maids in Jewish households, *Forverts*, Oct. 26, 1908: 4. See also Tuvya Bruk, "Goyim ke-yehudim," *Yeda-'am* 8 (1962): 84. Jacob Katz, *The "Shabbes goy": A Study in Halakhic Flexibility* (trans. Yoel Lerner, Philadelphia: Jewish Publication Society, 1989).

23. Rolnik, *Zikhroynes*, 16. On that Talmudic reference, see Avi Sagi, "'Both Are the Words of the Living God': A Typological Analysis of Halakhic Pluralism," *Hebrew Union College Annual* 65 (1994): 105–36.

24. On that competition and autobiographies collection, see Jocelyn Cohen and Daniel Soyer, eds. and trans., "Introduction: Yiddish Social Science and Jewish Immigrant

Autobiography," in *My Future Is in America: Autobiographies of Eastern European Jewish Immigrants* (New York: New York University Press, in conjunction with the YIVO Institute for Jewish Research, 2006), 4–17.

25. Only a few can be mentioned here—see the writer who identified as "Mohilev Carpenter" on how Gentiles attacked Jews during fairs, and the Jews fought back. American Jewish Autobiographies Collection (YIVO), #83: 2. See also H. Yermiyahu Cohen, #104: 20; and Israel Kerdman (Ben Eliezer), #105: 4. See also two detailed descriptions of the 1905 pogrom in Yekaterinoslav, in Bella Lewis, #80: 4–5, and Samuel Dinerstein, #159: 28–34.

26. Bessie Moskowitz, American Jewish Autobiographies Collection (YIVO), #50: 2–3. S. Schreibman, #154: 8–9. Ish Ikor, #162: 4–5. His name might mean "The Peasant," or it might signify that he was associated with the pro-Soviet Organization for Jewish Colonization in Russia (IKOR was its Yiddish acronym). See also the recollection of Max Davis, #129: 3. Similar examples of friendly relations with the surrounding peasantry are to be found in the autobiography of the socialist politician and attorney Louis Waldman, *Labor Lawyer* (New York: E.P. Dulton, 1944), 11–12; and Soviet-affairs expert Maurice Hindus, *Green Worlds: An Informal Chronicle* (Garden City, NY: Doubleday & Co., 1947), 70–71. The latter two memoirists' positive view of the peasantry reflects their ideological and professional agenda.

27. Dan Miron, *The Image of the Shtetl and Other Studies of Modern Jewish Literary Imagination* (Syracuse: Syracuse University Press, 2000), 1–4. For a classic example of that attitude, see Sholem Aleichem, "Di shtot fun di kleyne mentshelekh," *Kleyne mentshelekh mit kleyne hasoges* (Berlin: Menorah, 1948), 7–15. See also Shandler, *Shtetl*, 27–32; and Ruth R. Wisse, introduction to *A Shtetl and Other Yiddish Novellas* (1973, repr. Detroit: Wayne State University, 1986), 14–18.

28. Israel Bartal, "Imagined Geography: The Shtetl, Myth, and Reality," in *The Shtetl: New Evaluations*, ed. Steven T. Katz, 179–92. Zborowski is indirectly quoted in Kirshenblatt-Gimblett's introduction, 4–5. As Kirshenblatt-Gimblett has rightly observed, that claim was made earlier by sociologist Louis Wirth, *The Ghetto* (1928, reprinted New Brunswick, NJ: Transaction, 1998), 8.

29. Benedetto Croce, *History as the Story of Liberty*, trans. Sylvia Sprigge (London: George Allen and Unwin, 1941), 19.

30. Isaac Babel, "The Killers Must Be Finished Off," in *1920 Diary*, ed. Carol J. Evins, trans. H. T. Willetts (New Haven, CT: Yale University Press, 1995), 106. Oscar Kleinman from Bialystok recalls how the Red Army treated the Jews better than the Poles, but it was no "panacea" either. *Voices From Ellis Island* (Library of Congress), #1: 2. See M. Sadikov's contemporary accounts of the pogroms, *In yene teg* (New York: no publisher mentioned, 1926), 32–43. Committee of Jewish Delegates, *The Pogroms in the Ukraine Under the Ukrainian Government, 1917–1920* (London: John Bale, Sons & Danielson, 1927). N. Gergel, "The Pogroms in the Ukraine in 1918–1921," *YIVO Annual of Jewish Social Science* 6 (1951): 237–52. Peter Kenez, "Pogroms and White Ideology in the Russian Civil War," in *Pogroms: Anti-Jewish Violence in Modern Russian History*, ed. John D. Klier and Shlomo Lambroza (Cambridge, UK: Cambridge University Press, 1992), 293–313. Norman Davies, *God's Playground: A History of Poland* (New York: Columbia University Press, 1984), 2: 393–401.

31. Tsukerman, *Zikhroynes*, 2: 161–62. On the Pinsk massacre, see also Carole Fink, *Defending the Rights of Others: The Great Powers, The Jews, and International Minority Protection, 1878–1938* (Cambridge, UK: Cambridge University Press, 2004), 173–86. See also Meyer Weisgal, *So Far: An Autobiography* (New York: Random House, 1971), 19.

32. Beneqvit, *Durkhgelebt un durkhgetrakht*, 1: 13, 104–5, 110, 113. Mordkhe Spektor, *Mayn lebn* (Warsaw: Achisefer, 1927), 3: 65; and Shmaryahu Levin, *Me-zichronot chayai* (translated by Z. Vislevsky, Tel Aviv: Dvir, 1935), 1: 102; 2: 116–18. See also Yoysef Margoshes, *Erinerungen fun mayn lebn* (New York: Max Mayzel Farlag, 1936), 232.

33. Peter Novick, *The Holocaust in American Life* (New York: Houghton Mifflin, 1999), 4–5. Berel Lang, "Holocaust Memory and Revenge: the Presence of the Past," *Jewish Social Studies* 2 (1996): 1–20. David Patterson, *Sun Turned to Darkness: Memory and Recovery in the Holocaust Memoir* (Syracuse: Syracuse University Press, 1998), 1–22. See also Deborah E. Lipstadt, "America and the Memory of the Holocaust, 1950–1965," *Modern Judaism* 16 (1996): 195–214; Alon Confino, "Collective Memory and Cultural History: Problems of Method," *American Historical Review* 102 (1997): 1386–1403.

34. An excellent study of American Jewish textbooks is by Jonathan Krasner, "Constructing Collective Memory: The Re-envisioning of Eastern Europe as Seen through American Jewish Textbooks," *Polin* 19 (2007): 229–55.

Constructing the Eastern European Jewish Past in Post-Holocaust Children's Literature (1950–1975)

Ellen Kellman

IN THE author's note to her 1959 juvenile biography of a classic Yiddish writer, entitled *Keys to a Magic Door: Isaac Leib Peretz*, first generation American Sylvia Rothchild invited readers to "choose a key from the collection Peretz left for us and it will open a door to the past. One turn—and we are back in a world where most Jewish grandparents grew up."[1] Other Yiddish-speaking authors of post-Holocaust children's literature expressed similar ideas about the efficacy of literature in maintaining cultural continuity or recreating it where it had been lost. In the preface to *The Magician and Other Stories from the Yiddish*, an anthology he edited in 1957, Yiddish educator Itche Goldberg offered a wish that young readers would "learn to love these works and their creators, who gave voice to the life, sufferings, joys, dreams and hopes of your grandmothers and grandfathers."[2] And in the foreword to his first collection of short fiction for children, *Zlateh the Goat and Other Stories* (1966), Isaac Bashevis Singer opined that "literature helps us remember the past with its many moods. . . . In stories time does not vanish . . . For the writer and his readers all creatures go on living forever. What happened long ago is still present."[3]

Overview

In translating and adapting classic Yiddish stories and folk tales, or composing original fiction, memoirs, and biographical works in English for a reading audience of children born in North America after 1945, these authors produced works that exemplify what the cultural historian Jeffrey Shandler has dubbed "post-vernacularity." The term refers to creative expression based in a particular language and culture, in this case Yiddish, and which addresses readers who do not speak the language natively. Shandler has observed that people who have "an affective or ideological relationship with Yiddish without having a command of the language" have become the primary consumers of Yiddish culture in the post-Holocaust era.[4]

Recognizing that the Yiddish language was no longer a vernacular for the great majority of North American Jewish youth, Rothchild, Goldberg, and Singer seem to have made a pragmatic choice to try to transmit Yiddish literature to the post-Holocaust American generation by adapting and translating it into English. Thus, with other writers, editors, and illustrators who spoke Yiddish natively, they created a body of Yiddish children's literature for non-Yiddish speakers. Their ostensible objective was to imaginatively present the old country in such a way that juvenile readers would be drawn to the confluence of Eastern European Jewish culture and the American Jewish culture in which they were growing up, and would thus develop an affective attachment to it.

Every translator is faced with seminal choices vis-à-vis the interpretation of linguistic, stylistic, literary, and cultural elements in a given text. Translation theorist Lawrence Venuti writes of the complex and freighted nature of translation:

> [A] foreign text is the site of many different semantic possibilities that are fixed only provisionally in any one translation, on the basis of varying cultural assumptions and interpretive choices, in specific social situations, in different historical periods.... The aim of translation is to bring back a cultural other as the same, the recognizable, even the familiar; and this aim always risks a wholesale domestication of the foreign text, often in highly self-conscious projects, where translation serves an appropriation of foreign cultures for domestic agendas, cultural, economic, political.[5]

With respect to the works discussed here, I will endeavor to elucidate and compare the choices made by writers, translators, and illustrators in service of the objective of making Eastern European Jewish culture accessible to the child addressee in post-Holocaust America. Although these works contain no direct references to the *khurbn*, the fact that they represent the recently decimated culture gives them a greater valence than they might otherwise have. They thus attest to Hasia Diner's assertion that "the European catastrophe wound its way into [American Jewish] culture organically, yoked to Jewish texts."[6]

The present article undertakes a preliminary investigation of what I have designated the "Old World" sub-genre of Jewish children's literature. While it can be demonstrated that some authors and educators contributed to the genre even before mid-century, the preponderance of works began to appear in the postwar years.[7] I have chosen to focus on "The Magician," an illustrated adaptation by Uri Shulevitz (1935–) of a story by the Yiddish classic writer Yitskhok Leyb Peretz (1857–1915), and on the collection *Zlateh the Goat and Other Stories* by Isaac Bashevis Singer (1904–1991), translated and edited by Elizabeth Shub (1914–2004) with illustrations by Maurice Sendak (1928–2012).

It is apparent that the authors, translators, editors, and illustrators who created the Old World sub-genre were also motivated by personal and family history. Literary scholar Marianne Hirsch coined the term "postmemory" to describe how the perceptions, dreams, and emotions of children of Holocaust survivors may become dominated by their parents' memories of trauma. According to Hirsch, "Postmemory is a powerful and very particular form of memory precisely because its connection to its object or source is mediated not through recollection but through imaginative investment and creation."[8] The idea of imaginative investment is key here, and may be applicable to at least some of the originators of the Old World sub-genre. Hirsch believes that postmemory "may usefully describe other second-generation memories of cultural or collective traumatic events and experiences."[9]

For the purposes of the present discussion, I propose to extend the term "second-generation" to include people who descended from Eastern European Jewish civilization, and for whom its decimation during the Holocaust was traumatic, even if not experienced directly. With the exception of Peretz, the creators of the works considered here were either Yiddish-speaking immigrants to North America or, in the case of Sendak, the child of such immigrants. All were born in the first four decades of the twentieth century.

The concept of postmemory may shed light on what motivated these individuals' creative responses to the perceived endangerment of Eastern European Jewish culture after the Holocaust. While this is a mixed group (some with direct experiences of trauma, some with indirect experiences), the broad objectives of the adaptations and translations considered here—memorialization and cultural transmission—were held in common.

The time period under consideration in this volume is the immediate aftermath of World War II and the decades of the 1950s and 1960s. The earliest examples of books from this Old World sub-genre date from the latter years of the 1950s.[10] They tend to portray a safe, orderly, ethical world in which children thrive in loving, if impoverished, families. Powerful magic may exist in this imaginary world, but its potential destructiveness is contained. Elements of folk and spiritual wisdom, and of humor, are utilized extensively. Etchings, woodcuts, and line drawings are the predominant graphic media in these works.

With few exceptions, references to antisemitic attitudes and behaviors on the part of Christians are avoided. The authors also fail to mention the Holocaust in their introductions and treat ethnic and racial oppression as a tragic but universal human failing that must be continually combated. It appears that, for the purpose of fashioning an inviting world into which children could enter imaginatively, and thus form emotional bonds with it, these authors, editors, and illustrators elected to minimize the disorderly and disturbing aspects of that world.

Itche Goldberg and the Kinderbuch Anthologies of Yiddish Stories

Among the authors, editor-translators, and illustrators whose works are considered here, Itche Goldberg is an outlier with respect to Venuti's notion of "domestication" of texts in the process of translation in that, for the most part, he avoided adapting or abridging them. Goldberg edited two illustrated anthologies of English translations of Yiddish stories intended for a juvenile reading audience. These were published outside the mainstream book market, in 1957 and 1966. A Yiddish educator and publisher who had been active in the Jewish Communist movement for many years, Goldberg was born in Opatów (Apt), Poland in 1904. During World War I, he lived with his mother and younger siblings in German-occupied Warsaw, where the family suffered malnutrition. They immigrated to Canada in 1920.

During the early 1920s, the young Goldberg taught Yiddish literature in the socialist Workmen's Circle schools, first in Toronto and later in Philadelphia and New York. By 1926, he was part of the pro-Communist group that broke away from the Workmen's Circle, establishing the International Workers' Order (later renamed the Jewish Peoples' Fraternal Order—JPFO) in 1930. He served as national director of the JPFO schools for over two decades, during which time he wrote, edited, and published textbooks in Yiddish for use in the schools.[11]

As early as 1952, Goldberg acknowledged that many children who were attending these schools came from families where Yiddish was not spoken in the home.[12] Although they received instruction in Yiddish in school, such children did not have a strong enough command of the language to read Yiddish literature in the original, so that English translations were required for classroom use. Under Goldberg's editorship, *The Magician and Other Stories from the Yiddish* was published in a bound mimeographed edition in 1957 by Kinderbuch Publishers.[13]

The illustrated collection contained sixteen stories translated and adapted from the Yiddish, including seven by Sholem Aleichem and six by Yitskhok Leyb Peretz.[14] After eight mimeographed reprints, Goldberg expanded the collection and published it in book form in 1966 as *Yiddish Stories for Young People*, adding ten stories, including "Hershele" by Sholem Abramovitsh (otherwise known as Mendele the Bookseller), three folk tales, and three additional stories by Peretz. The books were distributed primarily to pupils in the national network of left-wing Yiddish schools.

In his introduction to *Yiddish Stories for Young People*, Goldberg emphasized the universal appeal of the works of the classic Yiddish writers—Abramovitsh, Peretz, and Sholem Aleichem—who "touched on themes in the life of their people, and of mankind generally, which have ever remained constant in man's search for a life of dignity, meaning, happiness."[15] Discussing the role of Yiddish literature in mirroring and interpreting the social upheavals of the nineteenth century, Goldberg wrote, "The heroes of this literature were the common folk,"[16] and he asserted, "The life that comes through in [it] pulsates with warmth and hope. The people suffer—but are never disheartened; they may walk in tatters—but always with dignity; though at times lost—they are forever searching, weighing, questioning the ways of man and the world."[17]

The stories included in these anthologies reflect Goldberg's left-wing political orientation and the educational goal of motivating juvenile readers to embrace their cultural heritage. In the preface to *The Magician and Other Stories* (which was reprinted in *Yiddish Stories for Young People*), he forewarned readers that the material in the book might take them out of their comfort zone as juvenile readers:

> Some of the stories in this collection are sad, some even heartbreaking, for they reveal a difficult life. Yet, if you read carefully you will find that none of them was really unhappy. No matter how poor and difficult life was, it was never hopeless. . . . The life of the children who grew up to be your grandparents was a hard one, but we need not pity them. They were too courageous and loved life too much to be pitied. You will learn to respect and love them.[18]

For the most part, the classic Yiddish writers did not write for a juvenile reading audience, although many stories *about* children are found among their works. The majority of stories that Goldberg selected for *Yiddish Stories for Young People* feature child protagonists. Several of these, such as Sholem Aleichem's "The Simchas Torah Flag" and two chapters from the series *Motl, the Cantor's Son*, feature first-person narration. As they are humorous tales of boys' misadventures, they seem to be the most easily accessible stories in the collection for the intended audience. Several others that feature child protagonists, such as "The Fast" and "What the Moon Told" by Peretz, "Hershele" by Abramovitsh, "Raisala" by Avrom Reisen, and "Motke Won't Suckle a Rag" by Sholem Asch portray the pernicious effects of extreme poverty on the lives of Jewish children in Eastern Europe. Two of the stories—"In Those Days" by Yehudah Steinberg and "A Country Passover" by Sholem Aleichem—foreground antisemitism and tensions in Jewish-Christian relations. As he stated in the preface to

The Magician and Other Stories, Goldberg did not regard the physical deprivation and violence portrayed in these stories as inappropriate for young readers.

Several of Y. L. Peretz's stories in the collection, such as "The Magician," "Seven Years of Plenty," and "The Little Hanukah Lamp" imitate Yiddish folk tales about the miracle-working Elijah the Prophet, while the well-known story "If Not Still Higher" recasts a popular Hasidic hagiographic legend, injecting a heavy measure of irony into it.[19] Since many of Peretz's stories may, at first glance, appear to be variants of authentic folk tales, a reader needs to be familiar with Eastern European Jewish beliefs and customs in order to understand the subtleties and ironic elements contained in them.

Goldberg was undoubtedly aware of the possibility that such complexities in Peretz's stories would go over the heads of school-aged readers, yet he considered them suitable for children because of their emphasis on Jewish ethical values, such as helping people in need. He deeply admired Peretz's short fiction, and believed that it could be successfully presented to children from kindergarten to high school. In an article entitled "Y. L. Peretz and the Jewish Child," he wrote that

> Although Y. L. Peretz's language is often difficult and his style is sometimes complicated, [his work] has always been a treasure-trove of values for the secular school. Peretz appeals to the child and gives the child what he is looking for in literature.... In addition to [enjoying] a good story, the child seeks to understand the ideas that underlie it. Peretz' imagination ... fascinates the child and keeps him in suspense.... His fast-paced writing style captivates the child, who follows [the stories] with delight.[20]

Although the stories in the two anthologies are neither abridged nor adapted, explanatory phrases are occasionally inserted, and a three-page glossary containing some of the culturally specific terms found in the stories is appended to the book. In designing *Yiddish Stories for Young People* for classroom use, Goldberg evidently intended that unfamiliar cultural contexts and literary devices would be explained to pupils by their teachers.[21] Himself deeply rooted in the culture he sought to impart to American-born children through literature, he published what he considered to be faithful (if not entirely literal) translations, confident that the works would be accessible to school-age readers in secular Jewish supplementary schools.

Uri Shulevitz's Picture Book Adaptation of Peretz's "The Magician"

While Itche Goldberg made very few alterations to the texts of stories by Peretz in *Yiddish Stories for Young People*, Uri Shulevitz adapted and abridged the well-known story "The Magician" for younger children.

A distinguished American author-illustrator of children's books, Shulevitz was born in Warsaw in 1935. He and his parents fled Poland during the German invasion and bombing of Warsaw in September, 1939. Escaping to the Soviet Union, they spent the war years suffering hunger and physical deprivation in the city of Turkestan in Central Asia. After the war, the family moved to France before settling in Israel in 1949. Shulevitz came to the United States in 1959. His first book for children was published in New York in 1963. He won the Caldecott Medal in 1969 for his illustration of a Russian fairy tale, *The Fool of the World and the Flying Ship*. He has also earned three Caldecott Honors: for *The Treasure*, his adaptation of a Yiddish folk tale (1979); *Snow* (1999); and *How I Learned Geography*, a memoir of his childhood in Turkestan (2009). Among other books with Eastern European Jewish content, Shulevitz illustrated Isaac Bashevis Singer's *The Fools of Chelm and Their History* (1973) and *The Golem* (1982). In 1978, he translated, adapted, and illustrated the story "Hanukah Money" by Sholem Aleichem.

In 1973, Macmillan published Shulevitz's adaptation of Peretz's story "The Magician," illustrated with detailed pen and ink drawings in the style of woodcuts. The drawings depict Jewish townspeople in a shtetl—with its streets, the exteriors and interiors of simple houses, and domestic animals. The figure of the magician is whimsical with his bulky, wrinkled clothing and clumsy movements, which resemble those of a marionette. Other subtle humorous touches add a measure of verisimilitude to the highly stylized drawings, such as the finger of a small girl reaching up to pick her nose while she stands near the magician, and the varied facial expressions of people who watch him do his tricks.[22]

Although Shulevitz never lived in a shtetl like the one depicted in *The Magician*, he created a lively, reverent interpretation of his own vision of a nineteenth- or early twentieth-century Eastern European Jewish community. In generational terms, Peretz could have been Shulevitz's grandfather or even his great-grandfather. An heir to the vanished world that Peretz's characters inhabited, Shulevitz tapped his own artistic imagination to re-envision it, utilizing forms inspired by folk art, yet creating distinctive characters by means of facial expressions and visual jests.

The original text of "The Magician" contains a full measure of the irony that is characteristic of Peretz's reimagined folk tales. A formerly wealthy man, now impoverished, who has lost his social status in the town, refuses to ask for money from the community poor fund, which provides destitute members of the community with Passover necessities: matzah, candles, and wine. After his wife finds a single silver spoon in a corner of their dwelling, he sells it and donates the proceeds to the poor fund, deluding himself that he is not as needy as those who receive such funds. He dismisses his wife's plea that they accept this charity with a brusque "God will provide." As a result of his pride and obduracy, his wife suffers terribly from shame because she is unable to prepare a Passover seder, and seethes with anger at her embarrassing predicament. As Passover begins, the husband finally admits to his wife that, in order to fulfill their obligation to celebrate the holiday, they must ask another family for a charitable invitation to their seder. In the next moment, however, Elijah the Prophet, disguised as a magician, appears at their door and conjures a sumptuous meal with all the ritual trimmings for them to enjoy. They are thus spared the embarrassment of having to ask for charity.

Folk tales featuring Elijah the Prophet usually involve Elijah's rewarding pious individuals, especially those who give charity to others, with special gifts. "The Magician" ironically questions whether a man who insisted that others needed charity more than he, just to save face, deserves such a rich reward.

Shulevitz condensed the plot of the story sufficiently to make it accessible to an early elementary school-aged child. The majority of the illustrations in the book depict the magician, his tricks, and the sumptuous seder he conjures up for the destitute couple. The selling of the silver spoon, the conflict between the husband and wife, the wife's anger and resentment at her husband, the gender inequality in their relationship, and the man's self-involved pride have been largely omitted. The resulting adaptation is a charming story that reads like a folk tale about Divine reward for simple piety and faith. In Shulevitz's version, on Passover eve, only one house in the shtetl, the home of the impoverished couple, remained dark: "They had no food and not even a single candle. Yet they would not ask for help. 'There are people who are worse off than we are,' the old man said. 'We will manage.'" Shulevitz's text retains a bit of the wife's resentment at not being able to prepare her own seder: "Night came. 'Happy holiday,' the old man said to his wife. 'Happy holiday,' she replied. But she could not help adding: 'Passover is here and we still have nothing.'"

On hearing his wife's reproach, the husband admonishes her for failing to trust in God's protection: "The Maker of the Universe does not abandon his creatures,' the old man said. 'And if God does not want us to have our own Passover feast, then we must bow to his will and attend someone else's. Come, we will be welcome at our neighbor's.' As in the Yiddish original, the husband's decision to ask for charity triggers the appearance of Elijah, disguised as the magician: "At that moment the door opened and a voice said, 'May I be your guest for Passover?'" However, the cultural valence of the man's decision is de-emphasized, and the link between his bowing to the will of God and being rewarded for doing so is entirely missing.

The shtetl in which the story takes place is small, insular, and homogeneous. No non-Jews appear to be present there, obviating any portrayal of the inter-religious conflicts that often occurred in real life during the Passover and Easter holidays. Shulevitz's adaptation of the original story downplays the complexities of human relationships depicted there and evokes a secure, harmonious world where good deeds and piety are rewarded through benevolent magic.

In distilling the text down to its plot, Shulevitz creates a well-paced tale. His masterful use of light and shadow in many of the illustrations focuses the reader's attention on the ambiguous boundary between good and evil magic. In addition, where the text is minimal, light and shadow are used to evoke the emotional states of the impoverished couple.

Shulevitz created a compelling interplay between pictures and text in this adaptation of Peretz's story. A good example of this is found in the final three drawings in the book, which depict the radiant light cast by the holiday candles in the couple's dwelling and the abundant starlight in the sky above the shtetl. These images symbolically resolve the conflicted emotions of the husband and wife and dramatize the triumph of "good magic" over "evil magic." Beneath a drawing of the night sky filled with stars above the shtetl, the text on the final page reads, "Only then did they know it was not a magician but the prophet Elijah himself who had visited them." While the moral subtleties and interpersonal nuances present in the original text were abridged for an elementary school-aged audience, Shulevitz's illustrations restored the emotional contours of the relationships portrayed there.

Artistic Synergy: Zlateh the Goat and Other Stories

The contributions of Isaac Bashevis Singer, together with his co-translator and co-adapter, Elizabeth Shub, shaped the Old World sub-genre more than those of any other writer of this pioneering group. Beginning with *Zlateh the Goat and Other Stories* in 1966 and concluding with *The Golem* in 1982, Singer produced fifteen children's books in English, with pictures by a number of distinguished illustrators, including, in addition to Sendak and Shulevitz, Nonny Hogrogian, Margot Zemach, William Pène du Bois, and Eric Carle. Singer's 1984 anthology, entitled *Stories for Children*, collected many of these previously published texts. In the author's note to the volume, he stated that he had never intended to write for children until his friend Elizabeth Shub, a children's book editor and translator, convinced him to try his hand at it.[23]

Isaac Bashevis Singer was born in Leoncin, Poland in 1904, and was raised in a religiously observant home. His father was a rabbi with close ties to Hasidic culture, and his mother, the daughter of a *misnagdish* (non-Hasidic) rabbi, was also highly educated for a traditional woman of her generation. Singer broke with his parents' way of life as a teenager and began writing fiction and literary criticism in Yiddish, publishing his first short story in 1925. He worked as a literary translator during the early years of his career, completing ten book-length translations between 1928 and 1932.[24] Singer's first novel, *Der sotn in Goray* (Satan in Goray) was published in Warsaw in book form in 1935, the year Singer left Poland to settle in New York City. Through his older brother, Israel Joshua Singer, who was already a well-known Yiddish writer, he found employment with the *Forverts* (Jewish Daily Forward) newspaper, where he published fiction, literary criticism, and reportage throughout his American career.

Although Singer knew English quite well, he wrote all of his fiction in Yiddish, relying on translators for stylistic refinement of his prose, and collaborating with them to produce works that could appeal to a post-vernacular audience. His work became known to an English-reading audience beginning in the mid-1950s. By 1966, the year *Zlateh the Goat and Other Stories* appeared, Singer had already published four novels, numerous short stories, and memoirs in English translation.

Elizabeth Shub was born during World War I in Vilna, the daughter of Shmuel and Bessie Charney. Shub's father, who was known by the pen name Sh. Niger, was a leading Yiddish literary historian and critic, and a dedicated cultural activist. In 1919, Niger narrowly escaped execution by the Polish army and soon thereafter emigrated with his family, settling in New York. He was a regular contributor to *Der tog* (The Day), a leading New York Yiddish newspaper, and numerous other Yiddish periodicals.

The Charney home in New York was steeped in Yiddish culture, and became a gathering place for Yiddish writers. Shub met Singer there in 1935, just after his arrival from Poland, and they formed a lasting friendship.[25]

Zlateh the Goat and Other Stories was Singer's first book for children, and the first translation project Singer and Shub undertook together. At the time, she was a juvenile editor at Harper and Row. In her study of Singer's works for children, *Isaac Bashevis Singer: Children's Stories and Childhood Memoirs*, Alida Allison discusses the importance of Shub's role both in encouraging Singer to write for children and in helping him to craft highly effective English versions of his stories. Three of the children's books she translated with Singer garnered Newbery Honor Awards.[26] Their collaboration produced ten children's books between the years 1966 and 1973.

Although Singer claimed that he had never considered writing for children until Shub suggested the idea to him at some point in the mid 1960s, literary historian Chone Shmeruk's research shows that although Singer disdained the idea of writing children's literature at the outset of his career and for many years thereafter, he became interested in it beginning in the late 1950s, when he visited Buenos Aires and Montreal, and was surprised to find that Yiddish schools in those cities were effectively educating a new generation of readers. He was thus, much belatedly, inspired to write in Yiddish for them.[27]

Unlike some of Singer's translators, Shub knew Yiddish well, although she could not decipher the author's Yiddish handwriting. As a result, according to Allison, when they worked together, Singer would begin by reading a draft of a story aloud to her in Yiddish, and she would type up an English translation as he read. Unfortunately, I have seen only two Yiddish texts of stories in the *Zlateh the Goat* collection, so I have not been able to analyze changes made to the other five stories during this first stage of adaptation. A Yiddish manuscript of "The Devil's Trick" (*Dem tayvls shtik*) has been preserved in the Harry Ransom Humanities Research Center at the University of Texas at Austin. A Yiddish version (presumably the original) of the story entitled "The Mixed-Up Feet and the Silly Bridegroom" (*Der narisher khosn un di farbitene fis*) was published in the *Forverts* on November 16, 1965.[28] These two texts are compared with Singer and Shub's translations in the following pages.

The first stage of editing would be followed by three or four additional rounds in which author and translator critiqued each other's wordings and made further corrections to the text.[29] Their collaborative method produced synergistic results.

In several of his essays about writing, and in interviews with journalists and critics, Singer repeatedly emphasized that he drew the *shtof* (substance, subject matter) of his writing from the Polish-Jewish milieu in which he was raised. In his view, authentic (and thus effective) writing had necessarily to be grounded in a writer's experience. Singer culled extensively from Eastern European Yiddish folklore in crafting his stories for young readers. In the afterword of *Stories for Children* (1984), he asserted:

> Folklore plays a most important role in children's literature.... Many modern writers have lost their roots. They don't belong and they don't want to belong to any special group. They are afraid of being called clannish, nationalistic, or chauvinistic. Actually, there is no literature without roots.... In literature, as in life, everything

is specific. Every man has his actual and spiritual address.... The more a writer is rooted in his environment, the more he is understood by all people; the more national he is, the more international he becomes. The events I related did not happen in no-man's-land but in the little towns and villages I knew well and where I was brought up. My saints were Jewish saints and the demons Jewish demons.[30]

Not surprisingly, Singer's intended reading audience was not limited to children of Jewish heritage: "When I began to write the stories of my collection *Zlateh the Goat*, I knew that these stories would be read not only by Jewish children but by Gentile ones as well. I described Jewish children, Jewish sages, Jewish fools, Jewish bridegrooms, Jewish brides.... And this book has been translated into many languages.... Without folklore and deep roots in a specific soil, literature must decline and wither away."[31]

Singer claimed that, beginning in childhood, he had read many works of world literature in translation.[32] He was especially partial to the fiction of the nineteenth century French and Russian realists, and believed, with them, that a well-constructed work of literature should have universal appeal.[33] Thus, when asked by author Laurie Colwin in a 1978 interview if he felt that he was preserving "the last part of a vanished culture" in his writing, Singer took exception to the idea:

> People tell me this, and while they tell me this I have a moment of feeling, yes, it is so. But I never sit down to write with this idea. I wouldn't be a writer if I would sit down to preserve the Yiddish language, or life in Poland, or make a better world or bring peace. I don't have all these illusions. I know that my story will not do anything but entertain a reader for half an hour. And this is enough for me.... The great writers of the 19th century—Tolstoy and Dostoevsky and Gogol and Dickens—were great entertainers.[34]

For Singer, the only authentic source of *shtof* for his fiction was his own cultural tradition. Nonetheless, in a talk entitled "On Writing for Children" given at the University of Connecticut in 1977, Singer stipulated, "I don't take all my stories from Yiddish folktales because I invent stories myself."[35]

While there are innovative adaptations of Yiddish folk tales in *Zlateh the Goat and Other Stories*, such as "The Snow in Chelm" and "Grandmother's Tale," other pieces in the collection, such as the title story and "The Devil's Trick," appear to be entirely original. Singer set most of the stories in the collection at Hanukah time, apparently for the purpose of marketing the book.[36]

Maurice Sendak's illustrations for *Zlateh the Goat and Other Stories* create a different kind of dynamic synergy. Although Sendak was hired to illustrate the book only after the manuscript had been completed, the images he made seem intrinsic to the reading experience, amplifying and informing meaning in the way words and images are meant to interact in a graphic novel. Born in Brooklyn in 1928 to immigrant parents from Poland, Sendak became a successful illustrator of children's books in his early twenties, winning the Caldecott Medal in 1964 for his widely acclaimed picture book *Where the Wild Things Are*, published by Harper and Row. According to Shub, Sendak saw the manuscript of *Zlateh the Goat* on an editor's desk at Harper and Row in 1966 and asked to illustrate the book.[37] As he had done with Shub, Singer read the original Yiddish stories aloud to Sendak, who knew Yiddish from having spoken it at home. Sendak later wrote, "It was extraordinary to work with Singer on *Zlateh the Goat*." He was surprised that Singer's Yiddish was "cultivated and very beautiful" in comparison to his parents' Yiddish, which was "rough-and-tumble." Sendak's parents had read Singer's work in the *Forverts* and were "enormously proud" of their son's involvement in the project.[38]

In contrast to Singer, who claimed that he set his stories in Eastern Europe and peopled them with Jewish characters simply because it was artistically impossible for him to do otherwise, Sendak expressly intended his illustrations for *Zlateh the Goat* to commemorate the lives of family members who had been killed in the Holocaust. In an interview entitled "Maurice Sendak: A Western Canon, Jr.," Sendak said:

> Both my parents lost everybody, practically, in the Holocaust. And Isaac meant a great deal to us, because he was a survivor and he was a great artist. And many of the pictures in *Zlateh* are portraits taken from photograph albums of people I never knew, because they died in concentration camps.... I gave some of the characters

their faces so I could surprise my parents. They were deeply touched because they recognized this one and that one. Those lost people were alive again in the book, they would always be alive in the book, they would always be characters in Isaac Singer stories.[39]

Although neither Sendak nor his parents suffered the trauma of the Holocaust directly (and Singer, too, was not a survivor, having arrived in the United States in 1935), his childhood perceptions of their familial histories and anguished losses of family members resemble second-generation postmemory as defined by Marianne Hirsch in *Family Frames: Photography, Narrative and Postmemory*. In 1970, Sendak was awarded the Hans Christian Andersen Medal, and he delivered his acceptance speech in Bologna, Italy in April of that year. In the speech he considered the sources that merged to form his artistic inspiration:

Mine was a childhood colored with memories of village life in Poland, never actually experienced but passed on to me as persuasive reality by my immigrant parents. On the one hand, I lived snugly in their Old Country world, a world far from urban society, where the laws and customs of a small Jewish village were scrupulously and lovingly obeyed. And on the other hand, I was bombarded with the intoxicating gush of America in that convulsed decade, the thirties.... For me, childhood was *shtetl* life transplanted, Brooklyn colored by Old World reverberations and Walt Disney.... My wish is to combine—in words and pictures, faithfully and fantastically—my weird, Old Country-New Country childhood; my obsession with shtetl life, its spirit; and the illuminating visions especially loved artists have shown me.[40]

The remarkable synergy between Singer and Shub's text and Sendak's illustrations belies the fact that Sendak did not collaborate directly with them in creating the book. Singer and Shub were fairly close in age and shared a birthplace, but Shub and Sendak both grew up in New York and shared the experience of being reared by immigrant parents while becoming immersed in Anglo-American culture. As Hirsch suggests, the "imaginative investment" that Sendak made in his drawings for *Zlateh the Goat and Other Stories* enabled him to forge a powerful personal bond with his family's past, at the same time enlarging and enriching the reader's experience of Singer's stories.

"Zlateh the Goat" is a tale about a boy whose unemployed father sends him on a terrible errand just before Hanukah. He must bring the beloved family goat to be sold to the town butcher in order to get money to feed the family. As the boy leads the goat to her fate, a blizzard suddenly blows up, obscuring the road to the town. The boy perceives that it is the work of evil forces:

> The snow grew thicker, falling to the ground in large, whirling flakes . . . Aaron realized that . . . . he had gone astray. . . . The wind whistled, howled, whirled the snow about in eddies. It looked as if white imps were playing tag on the fields. A white dust rose above the ground. . . . Aaron . . . knew . . . that if they did not find shelter they would freeze to death. This was no ordinary storm. It was a mighty blizzard . . . . Zlateh's bleating began to sound like crying. . . . Aaron began to pray to God for himself and for the innocent animal.[41]

Then Aaron notices a snow-covered haystack in a field, and boy and goat take refuge inside it, where they survive together for three days, the goat eating hay from inside the stack and the boy drinking milk from her teats, warming himself next to her body and taking comfort in her affectionate companionship. Their perfect mammalian symbiosis comes to an end when the weather finally clears up. They return home, and Aaron's relieved parents resolve never to sell the goat that saved their son from freezing to death. The threat to life is averted through a rebalancing of human and animal agency: boy and goat are shown to be equally beholden to one another for survival. Sendak's highly realistic drawing of Aaron and Zlateh inside the haystack emphasizes their bond. The child's idiosyncratic facial features—sunken eyes; broad nose; and full, serious mouth—suggest that the artist modeled his face after a photograph.

Three tales in the collection, "The First Shlemiel," "The Snow in Chelm," and "The Mixed-Up Feet and the Silly Bridegroom" were Singer's first contributions in English to the genre of anecdotes about the foolish inhabitants of the town of Chelm, the humor of which consists in creating a chain of ridiculous suppositions and illogical conclusions. Other illustrated English translations of Chelm stories had already popularized the genre among juvenile readers,[42] but Singer's versions were different from those taken directly from folkloric sources, which rarely foreground individual Chelmites.[43] In writing these stories, Singer invented characters, added dialogue and descriptive passages, and combined folkloric tropes. For instance, he placed a *shlemiel* (foolish, inept person) in Chelm, along with his wife and family. The resulting story, "The First Shlemiel," is a comedic enactment of the maskilic critique of the unproductive Jewish husband and his long-suffering, shrewish wife.[44] In Sendak's three drawings for the story, the faces of Shlemiel, his wife, and their baby are richly detailed and expressive. According to Selma G. Lanes, author of *The Art of Maurice Sendak*, the face of Shlemiel is modeled on that of a relative from the Sendaks' family album, while the animated face of the apprehensive Baby Shlemiel is based on photographs of the artist himself as an infant.[45]

There are many known variants of "The Snow in Chelm."[46] Singer's version embellishes the basic tale. In his retelling, the Chelmites are enchanted by the brilliant whiteness of newly fallen snow in the shtetl, and they imagine that a treasure of silver, pearls, and diamonds has fallen from the sky. Since the town is poor and much in need of such a treasure, they decide that no one must walk on the snow, lest it be trampled, so they send a messenger boy to warn the townspeople to stay indoors that day. Soon realizing that the messenger's footprints will ruin the pristine snow, and thus the treasure they imagine it to be, they revise their plan and send four people to carry the boy on a table. The story concludes on this absurd note.

"The Mixed-Up Feet and the Silly Bridegroom" combines two tale types. The first, found in both German and Turkish folklore, involves four sisters who share a bed and wake up one morning with their feet hopelessly entangled. The Elder of Chelm prescribes an effective remedy: unexpectedly whacking the girls' feet with a stick. Their mother performs the whacking, and the girls jump screaming from the bed, each regaining control of her own feet in the process.[47] The second part of the story is a long anecdote about the eldest sister's foolish bridegroom, whose illogical thinking causes him to lose a series of engagement gifts. Its humor, easily understood and appreciated by a child reader, lies in the very predictability of each loss.⁴⁸ The detailed, idiosyncratic faces in Sendak's three pen-and-ink illustrations for the story have a distinctive photographic quality.

Singer created other Chelm stories with the same cast of characters. Among these are "The Fools of Chelm and the Stupid Carp"; "The Elders of Chelm and Genendel's Key"; "Dalfunka, Where the Rich Live Forever"; and "Shlemiel the Businessman"; all of which are found in the 1984 collection *Stories for Children*.

According to bibliographer Roberta Saltzman, Singer published fourteen individual stories and one seven-part series about the fools of Chelm in the *Forverts* between 1965 and 1976. (Eleven of these appeared in a single year—1967.)⁴⁹ In spite of their absurdly silly humor, which is usually associated with literature for children, we can presume that most of Singer's Chelm stories that appeared in the *Forverts* were originally intended for an adult audience. Chone Shmeruk discussed this in his article "Yitskhok Bashevis: der mayse-dertseyler far kinder," observing that many of the original versions of Singer's stories, which had been "written earlier and published in the *Forverts* without specifically intending to address a young readership, are far from identical to versions published later in English, in books for children."⁵⁰

It appears that Singer co-opted the Chelm folktale type for his own literary purposes, creating parodic works about shortcomings in modern-day human thinking that were filled with references child readers would not understand. It was thus necessary to adapt as well as to translate them into English for the juvenile book market. The prime example of such an adaptation is *The Fools of Chelm and Their History*, in which Singer endeavored to show the uselessness of political action by creating a parodic story about a revolution in Chelm that destroys the social hierarchy in the town and results in the women of Chelm, who are no fools at all, taking over as its leaders. *The Fools of Chelm and Their History* was translated and adapted from a series of thirteen stories about the history of Chelm that ran in the *Forverts* from October 11, 1966 until March 16, 1967, and was signed with one of Singer's pseudonyms, Dovid Segal. Written for an adult audience, the series parodied various aspects of modern Western thought and culture, such as the "Big Bang" theory of the creation of the universe and Charles Darwin's theories of evolution, as well as totalitarianism and nationalism. In February and March, 1972, a seven-part series entitled "Nokh vegn di Khelemer khakhomim" (More about the Sages of Chelm), which carried the subtitle "kinder-mayses" (children's stories) ran in the *Forverts*. This series, which was signed Yitskhok Bashevis (Singer's best-known pseudonym), contained an adaptation of the 1966–67 series. With Shub's participation, Singer translated and further adapted the 1972 Yiddish series. The result was *The Fools of Chelm and Their History*, which was published by Farrar, Straus and Giroux in 1973, with illustrations by Uri Shulevitz.

Singer's version of another widely known Chelm story, about a Chelmite who sets out for Warsaw on foot but is tricked into returning to Chelm, concludes with a verse that succinctly conveys the author's philosophy about the limitations of human intelligence and the futility of humanity's strivings toward "progress": "Those who leave Chelm/ End up in Chelm./ Those who remain in Chelm / Are certainly in Chelm./ All roads lead to Chelm./ All the world is one big Chelm."[51]

Two other stories in the collection, "Grandmother's Tale" and "The Devil's Trick," contain supernatural elements. "Grandmother's Tale" is framed as what folklorists term a *memorat*, or a personalized tale, in which the teller attests that the story "really happened," as told by a living elder, or passed down over several generations. In this case, Grandmother Leah tells a story to entertain her grandchildren one evening during Hanukah, about eight sisters and brothers who stay up after their bedtime to play dreidel. Suddenly a devil appears at the family's door, disguised as a handsome, well-dressed *maskil* (enlightener) and plays dreidel late into the night with them, losing all his silver coins in the game. Finally, the children notice that their guest casts no shadow, the clock strikes thirteen, and the demon reveals himself to them—growing to twice his original height; sprouting horns; and spinning around like a dreidel, making the house spin with him. The children are horrified, but then the fiend sprouts wings and disappears without doing them any harm. Sendak renders the image in realistic detail to augment the visual impact of the terrifying figure, who is dressed in typical clothing for a shtetl inhabitant, and stands next to a table on which candles burn in a Hanukah menorah. His maleficent stare and protruding tongue, his wings, horns, and cloven hooves disclose his evil nature, as do the portly elfin *shretelekh* (imps) who dance at his feet.

Children's book critic Selma Lanes judged the picture to be "among the most inventive and commanding of the illustrations," [and] the perfect graphic incarnation of Singer's lines."[52]

In "The Devil's Trick," the dark forces are much more threatening. A poor boy's parents disappear just before Hanukah and he is left in charge of his baby brother. He lights the first Hanukah candle and leaves the family's hut to search for his parents. Goblins chase him, and he realizes the extremity of the danger. But then his ill fortune reverses itself, since, according to the story's narrator, "heaven and earth have vowed that the devil may never succeed completely in his tricks. No matter how shrewd the devil is, he will always make a mistake, especially on Hanukah. The powers of evil had managed to hide the stars, but they could not extinguish the single Hanukah candle."[53] The boy runs toward the light and reaches his hut just ahead of the devil. When he slams the door behind him, the devil's tail gets caught, and the boy boldly strikes a bargain—he must return the boy's parents in exchange for his tail. As a final gesture, the boy singes the devil's tail with the Hanukah candle and admonishes him: "Now, Devil, you will always remember, Hanukah is no time for making trouble."[54]

A Yiddish typescript entitled "Dem tayvls shtik" (The Devil's Trick) is preserved among Singer's papers in the Harry Ransom Research Center at The University of Texas. It is very likely that this is the original text from which Singer and Shub fashioned the English version. A comparison of the two texts reveals both differences in tone and the additions the author and translator made to the text, apparently for the purpose of amplifying the importance of Hanukah as a religious holiday.

The translation tones down some of the more frightening aspects of the story. For instance, a reference to the baby sleeping in its cradle as "a living orphan" is eliminated from the seventh paragraph of the translation, as is the question "Has the devil succeeded in exterminating an entire family?" In the same paragraph, the word "*sheydim*" (Yiddish: demons) is translated as "goblins," a term that American children associate with Halloween, with its make-believe forms of evil.

References to the holiday of Hanukah are added at several points in the story. The sentence at the end of the seventh paragraph of the translation reads, "No matter how shrewd the devil is, he will always make a mistake." The translators added the phrase "especially on Hanukkah" to the sentence.

The second to last paragraph was also altered to emphasize the holiday. In the Yiddish original, David forces the devil to write a promise in blood that he will stop playing evil tricks on people, while in the translated version, he singes the devil's tail with the Hanukah candle and tells him: "Now, Devil, you will always remember, Hanukkah is no time for making trouble." These changes may have been made both for the purpose of marketing the book as a holiday gift, and as a means of softening its frightening qualities.

Although Singer was admittedly pessimistic about the human condition, and made metaphorical use of devils and tempters in his adult fiction to accentuate this point of view, he made deliberate choices not to frighten child readers. Asked why his stories for children always have happy endings, he replied, "I know how sensitive a child is. If you tell a child that a murderer or thief was never punished . . . the child feels that there is no justice in the world . . . and I don't like children to come to this conclusion, at least not too soon."[55]

Conclusion

In evaluating examples of the Old World sub-genre of Jewish literature for children produced in the English language between 1957 and 1973, I noticed commonalities of approach in the inclusion of humor, detailed representation of shtetl culture, and limited portrayals of non-Jews, as well as in the downplaying of antisemitism, and a focus on child protagonists and the loving family constellation. These commonalities undoubtedly resulted, in part, from the deep personal, familial, and cultural connections the creators felt with the world they were depicting; from their desire to make that world interesting and comprehensible to American-born children; and from their need to respond to the loss of the culture, through what Marianne Hirsch has termed "imaginative investment." It is possible, too, that in the decades immediately following the Holocaust, writers, translators, and illustrators made deliberate choices to portray Old World Jewish culture as it was lived, rather than to focus on its destruction. In the works examined here, we have seen ample evidence of Lawrence Venuti's assertion that a translator is obliged to "domesticate" the text in certain ways in order to create a translation that allows readers significant access to a foreign culture.

Notes

1. Sylvia Rothchild, *Keys to a Magic Door: Isaac Leib Peretz* (Philadelphia: Jewish Publication Society, 1959), xi.
2. Itche Goldberg, *Yiddish Stories for Young People* (New York: Kinderbuch Publishers, 1966, 20). The 1966 edition is an expanded version of the 1957 collection and contains a reprint of the original preface.
3. Isaac Bashevis Singer, *Zlateh the Goat and Other Stories* (New York: Harper Collins Publishers, 1966), unnumbered page.
4. Jeffrey Shandler, *Adventures in Yiddishland* (Berkeley: University of California Press, 2006), 4.
5. Lawrence Venuti, *The Translator's Invisibility: A History of Translation* (London and New York: Routledge, 1995), 18.
6. See note 21 in the introduction to this volume.
7. In recent decades, literature for young people has openly addressed the Holocaust, but folklorized material of the type that was popularized by Peretz and later by Singer continues to be widely used. The *Jewish Publication Society Guide to Best Jewish Books for Children and Teens* (2010) lists forty children's books based on Eastern European Jewish folklore published in the 1990s and 2000s.
8. Marianne Hirsch, *Family Frames: Photography, Narrative and Postmemory* (Harvard University Press, 1997), 22.
9. Ibid.
10. The biweekly children's magazine *World Over*, published by the Jewish Education Committee of New York, anticipated the development of the sub-genre. See Jonathan Krasner, *The Benderly Boys: American Jewish Education* (Waltham: Brandeis University Press, 2011), chapter 11. The sub-genre blossomed beginning in the second half of the 1960s and sustained itself into the 1970s and 1980s.
11. See Isaiah Trunk, "The Cultural Dimension of the American Jewish Labor Movement," in *YIVO Annual of Jewish Social Science*, XVI, 381–387.
12. Itche Goldberg, "A kultur—mit undz oder on undz?" (A Culture—With Us or Without Us?), *Yidishe kultur*, March 1952, 24.
13. Kinderbuch was administered by the Service Bureau for Jewish Education, the successor organization to the JPFO.
14. Five translators contributed to the volume: Benjamin Efron, Henry Goodman, Sol Liptsin, Jack Moskowitz, and Max Rosenfeld. The collection was illustrated by Herb Krukman.
15. *Yiddish Stories for Young People*, 12–13.
16. Ibid., 14.
17. Ibid., 17.
18. Ibid., 19.
19. An English version of the original legend about the *rebbe* of Sasov is found in *The Hasidic Anthology: Tales and Teachings of the Hasidim*, ed. Louis I Newman (New York, Bloch Publishing Co., 1994), 209.
20. Itche Goldberg, "Y.L. Peretz un dos yidishe kind" (Y. L. Peretz and the Jewish Child), *Yidishe kultur*, April 1955, 16.

21. In Summer, 2015, I was fortunate to interview two former pupils of Yiddish schools administered by Itche Goldberg in the New York area. Michael Katz and Karen Rosenberg each recalled reading and discussing Peretz's stories in class. Both remember finding Peretz's fiction compelling for them as child readers precisely because it called upon them to engage with challenging ethical questions. Neither recalled feeling puzzled or alienated by the unfamiliar cultural contexts presented in the stories.

22. These images are found on the second and third pages of the un-paginated story book.

23. Isaac Bashevis Singer, "Author's Note," *Stories for Children* (New York: Farrar/Straus/Giroux, 1984), ix.

24. See David Neal Miller, *Bibliography of Isaac Bashevis Singer 1924–1949* (New York: Peter Lang, 1983), 233–239.

25. Paul Kresh, *Isaac Bashevis Singer, the Magician of West 86th Street*, 372–373 (citing a memoir by Elizabeth Shub originally published by the Children's Book Council in its *Calendar*, Spring-Summer 1975).

26. Alida Allison, *Isaac Bashevis Singer: Children's Stories and Childhood Memoirs* (New York: Twayne Publishers, 1996), 24. The award-winning books were *Zlateh the Goat and Other Stories* (1966), *The Fearsome Inn* (1967), and *When Shlemiel Went to Warsaw and Other Stories* (1968).

27. See Chone Shmeruk, "Yitskhok Bashevis: der mayse-dertseyler far kinder" (Isaac Bashevis: the Storyteller for Children), in *Oksforder Yidish III*, ed. Hirshe-Dovid Katz, 1995, 238–239, 244–248. Shmeruk remarked upon "the sad paradox" that Singer had disdained the idea of writing for children when there were "large numbers of child readers in Eastern Europe and in other parts of the diaspora," and only later, when "there were practically no readers for his children's stories," did he come to understand the importance of writing for Jewish children. None of Singer's stories for children have been published in Yiddish in book form.

28. According to Singer bibliographer Roberta Saltzman, "Der narisher khosn un di farbitene fis" is the only story from *Zlateh the Goat and Other Stories* that appeared in the *Forverts*, Singer's main venue for publication in Yiddish. See Roberta Saltzman, *Isaac Bashevis Singer: A Bibliography of His Works in Yiddish and English, 1960–1991* (Lanham, MD: The Scarecrow Press, Inc, 2002), 150–51. It is possible that Yiddish typescripts of other stories in the collection may be extant among Singer's papers at the Harry Ransom Center.

29. Allison, 22–23. See also the reproductions of the edited manuscript of the story "Zlateh the Goat" on pages 25–27, which clearly show Shub's emendations to the English manuscript.

30. *Stories for Children*, 334–335.

31. Ibid.

32. See Shmeruk, 239–240.

33. When asked by an interviewer whether he wrote primarily for Jewish readers, Singer responded with disdain:

> I think it is completely false. It's as if you would say that a French writer cannot be appreciated by the English. In a way it is true that a [sic] people of your nationality, of your group, understand you a little better. If you mention a town, they might have been in the town; your language is their language. But just the same the great writers are

understood by all people all over the world. Isn't it a fact that Dostoevsky is admired all over the world, yet the whole world does not consist of Russians or of people who speak only Russian.... I myself read translations from Japanese or from Chinese or from Indian, Hindu or whatever, and if there is something good, I understand it and I appreciate it even though I don't know their way of living. In other words, I deny that this is true.

Grace Farrell, "Seeing and Blindness: A Conversation with Isaac Bashevis Singer," in *Isaac Bashevis Singer: Conversations*, ed. Grace Farrell (Jackson: University Press of Mississippi, 1992), 132.

34. Laurie Colwin, "I. B. Singer, Storyteller" in *Isaac Bashevis Singer: Conversations*, 156.

35. Isaac Bashevis Singer, "On Writing for Children," *Children's Literature*, vol. 6 (1977), 9–16.

36. Kresh, 375 (citing a memoir by Elizabeth Shub originally published by the Children's Book Council in its *Calendar*, Spring-Summer 1975).

37. Ibid.

38. Maurice Sendak, "Visitors from My Boyhood," in *Worlds of Childhood: The Art and Craft of Writing for Children* (New York: Houghton Mifflin Company, 1990), 28–29.

39. Marion Long, "Maurice Sendak: A *Western Canon*, Jr." http://www.homearts.com/depts/relat/sendakfr.htm

40. Maurice Sendak, *Caldecott & Co.: Notes on Books and Pictures* (New York, Farrar, Straus and Giroux, 1988), 169–70.

41. Isaac Bashevis Singer, *Zlateh the Goat and Other Stories* (New York: Harper Collins, 1966), 81–82.

42. See, for example, Solomon Simon, *The Wise Men of Helm and Their Merry Tales* (New York: Behrman House Publishers, 1945); Samuel Tenenbaum, *The Wise Men of Helm* (New York: Thomas Yoseloff, 1965). Chone Shmeruk provides an extensive bibliography of Chelm stories in "Yitskhok Bashevis: der mayse-dertseyler far kinder," 260–261. For a treatment of the folkloric roots of Yiddish Chelm stories, see Ruth von Bernuth's book, *How the Wise Men Got to Chelm: The Life and Times of a Yiddish Folk Tradition* (New York: New York University Press, 2016).

43. For comparison, see tales 81–93 in *Yiddish Folktales*, ed. Beatrice Silverman Weinreich. (New York: Pantheon Books, 1988).

44. Shlemiel and Mrs. Shlemiel appeared in several other Chelm stories by Singer, notably "When Shlemiel Went to Warsaw" and "Shlemiel the Businessman," in the 1968 collection *When Shlemiel Went to Warsaw and Other Stories*.

45. Selma G. Lanes, *The Art of Maurice Sendak* (New York: Harry N. Abrams, Inc., 1984), 140.

46. One variant is found in *Yiddish Folktales*, 228 (tale number 89). Three others are included in Noyekh Prilutski's 1912 collection, entitled *Noyekh Prilutskis zamlbikher far yidishn folklor, filologye un kulturgeshikhte* (Warsaw: Nayer farlag, 1917), II, 198–199.

47. This tale type is found among stories attributed to the German prankster Till Eulenspiegel and the Turkish trickster Nasreddin Hodja. Noyekh Prilutski included a tale of this type entitled "Der makhshef" (The Sorcerer) in his 1912 collection, entitled *Noyekh Prilutskis zamlbikher far yidishn folklor, filologye un kulturgeshikhte* (Warsaw: Nayer farlag, 1917), II, 199–200.

48. A Yiddish text (presumably the original version of the story) entitled "Der narisher khosn un di farbitene fis" (The Foolish Bridegroom and the Changed Up Feet) was published in the *Forverts* on November 16, 1965, page 2, under one of Singer's pseudonyms, Yitskhok Varshavski. One notable difference between the story that appeared in the *Forverts* and "The Mixed-Up Feet and the Silly Bridegroom" is that the first paragraph of the Yiddish version identifies it as one that Singer's mother transmitted to him: "Among the stories that my mother told me was the story of the foolish bridegroom. The story took place not far from Chelm." This attribution locates the story in the broad context of Eastern European Yiddish folklore and implies that Singer's creative role was limited to retelling his mother's tale.

49. See Roberta Saltzman, *Isaac Bashevis Singer: A Bibliography of His Works in Yiddish and English*, 86, 102–05, 108–09.

50. Chone Shmeruk, "Yitskhok Bashevis: der mayse-dertseyler far kinder," 254.

51. The story, entitled "When Shlemiel Went to Warsaw," appeared in the 1968 collection *When Shlemiel Went to Warsaw and Other Stories*, with illustrations by Margot Zemach.

52. Selma G. Lanes, *The Art of Maurice Sendak*, 140.

53. Isaac Bashevis Singer, "The Devil's Trick," in *Zlateh the Goat and Other Stories*, 72.

54. Ibid., 73.

55. Singer, "On Writing for Children," 12–13.

"You Have Known Them with Your Eyes"
DUSK IN THE CATSKILLS AS POSTWAR LITERARY LEGACY

Holli Levitsky

THIS ESSAY examines literary writing about the experiences of Jews in the Catskills during the Holocaust. Two phenomena fostered my interest in this subject. First, I was involved in a breathtaking project that did not come to fruition, a photo-exhibition and book called *Last Days of the Four Seasons*. Related to Andrew Jacobs' film *Four Seasons Lodge*,[1] the large-scale photo-exhibition, book, and film all showcase a group of survivors as they decide the fate of the Catskills' bungalow colony they collectively own during its last summer in operation. The strength and creativity of the "lodgers" captivated me, as I came to see them as a unique contribution to Catskills history and, more broadly, to Holocaust studies. The second factor was a deep appreciation of Reuben Wallenrod's novel *Dusk in the Catskills*.[2] Once I began to think about how people in the Catskills lived during the Holocaust, I understood that Wallenrod portrays this experience in a fashion unparalleled by others. Certainly Wallenrod's eloquent juxtaposition of genocide and pleasure makes for a jarring, yet necessary, understanding. But more than that, Wallenrod tells his story over the entire season of the Rosenblatt Hotel, from pre-season preparation all the way to post-season closing down. In the process, he records the life not just of a hotel, but of a people.

The Holocaust was a looming issue facing Jews during the Jewish Catskills' heyday. As Jews in the Catskill mountain resorts, hotels, bungalow colonies, and private homes began learning about the extent of the atrocities committed against the Jews of Europe, how did they respond?

What was spoken and understood? What was left unspoken and incomprehensible at that moment in time? How much did Jewish Americans know about what happened to their fellow Jews in Eastern Europe? Wallenrod's novel is joined by a critical mass of literary writings about the war and post-war eras that directly address the situation of the Jews in Europe and the aftermath of the war. These writings forge a sense of connection between Jews in America and their European co-religionists, identify conflict within the hearts and souls of Jewish Americans in their inability to act upon those feelings of connection, and articulate a deep commiseration with the European Jews' plight. Evocative and compelling, these literary writings offer the non-witness an opportunity to witness the horror of the time. It is a particular kind of witnessing, active rather than passive, with literature mediating the testimonial experience through the construction of sites of memory. These powerful literary texts help us understand the ways American Jewry in the postwar era utilized literary texts and images in order to better understand the people and places that were destroyed. Probing themes that stage connections between Jews in the United States and those who were trapped in or were survivors of war-ravaged Europe, the stories create sites of memory through which to explore internal conflicts that shamed some to silence. They also probe the degree to which literary and artistic reconstructions reflected the historical reality and needs of the present time. In writing these texts, the authors move private memory into public space. These literary acts, in turn, serve as a memorial to the murdered Jews of Europe and the destruction of Jewish European life. The ongoing concern, specifically in Wallenrod's novel, about the decline of Catskills Jewish life also telegraphs the horror and disbelief about the destruction of European Jewry taking place alongside it (though offstage, so to speak). The horrible contradiction is that the Jews of Europe are being slaughtered while the Jews in the Catskills continue to laugh and dine and enjoy the bounty of life.

The history of the Jewish Catskills begins with farmlands located in Ulster, Sullivan, southern Greene, and a tiny sliver of southeastern Delaware Counties. The year-round Jewish population of chicken and dairy farmers had a hard time making a living on the poor soil there, and thus began taking in boarders. Eventually many made that into their main enterprise. Some boarding houses became *kuchalayns* ("cook for yourself"), rooms rented in a boarding house with shared kitchen and dining room. These facilities housed ten to forty guests at a time. *Kuchalayns* frequently developed into bungalow colonies, in which individual small cottages were rented out, complete with kitchen. Some *kuchalayns* later turned into hotels. *Kuchalayns* and bungalow colonies provided a familial milieu: people were together the entire summer, forming very close connections.

By the 1950s few *kuchalayns* remained, all but replaced by bungalow colonies and hotels. The small (50–250 guests) and medium-sized hotels (250–500 guests) retained the *kuchalayns'* intimacy. The owners, often a pair of in-law couples, were always present. They mingled with guests, many of whom were relatives and friends. Even in large hotels with 500–1,000 guests, owners, guests, and staff often knew each other. Smaller hotels frequently employed "solicitors" to recruit guests from their city neighborhoods, and hotels acquired a local culture that continued into the rest of the year. Guests returned year after year, and often from generation to generation—a child in the day camp might later be a junior counselor, then work as a busboy or waiter in the dining room, and return once again as a guest with spouse and children. Guests developed a loyalty to the hotel and its owners, based on family and friendship and the opportunity to participate in a miniature society where relationships were amplified by proximity. Many of the workers developed close bonds with each other, with the owners, and with longstanding guests, and many friendships lasted beyond the summer. Staff-guest romances often developed.[3] Yiddish was a commonly spoken language.

Some hotels and bungalow colonies were thoroughly Yiddishist, even into the 60s. The best known was the *Grine Felder* (Green Fields) literary colony in Woodridge, a major center of Yiddish writers, including Isaac Bashevis Singer. Merging both socialist and Yiddishist traditions, *Grine Felder* had bungalows named Emma Goldman, Karl Marx, and Mendele Moykher Sforim. Singer's Catskills background and literary interest shows through in his writings, including in *Enemies: A Love Story*[4] and in the short story "The Yearning Heifer,"[5] which features a traditional small farmer putting up boarders from the city. His experience with the Catskills began in 1938—just three years after he immigrated to New York from Poland. The visit was an opportunity to join his young friend and budding theater director Zygmunt Salkin at the Woodridge, New York bungalow colony, where he would oversee the rehearsal in English of I.L. Peretz's *At Night in the Old Marketplace*. *Grine Felder* was pioneered (and staffed) by a number of notable Yiddishists, including David Pinski, Mendl Elkin, Nahum Stutchkoff, Samuel Charney, Peretz Hirshbein, Jules Fainberg, Lazar Weiner, and Moishe Rudinow. The community also included prominent Zionists and Socialists such as Joseph Schlossberg, and Polish and Russian refugee poets, writers, dramatists, directors, producers, and critics, such as Maurice Schwartz, Alexzander Mukdoiny, Abraham Shiffrin, Sidor Belarsky, and Rosina Fernhoff (whose father, Dr. William Fernhoff, was an Austrian-Jewish immigrant who made house calls in the Catskills to colonies such as *Grine Felder*).[6]

Stemming from the strong radical traditions of many Eastern European Jews, the Catskills also became a location for leftists of varying types, some preparing to return to Eretz Yisrael, and others seeking to build different visionary societies. For those who wanted to build the Promised Land, Hashomer Hatzair's Camp Shomria, Camp Hemshekh, and other labor Zionist/socialist Zionist groups set up training camps in the Catskills to recruit and prepare Jews for aliyah to Israel. Vladimir Jabotinsky, the Zionist-Revisionist leader, died of a heart attack while visiting Camp Betar near Hunter, New York, in August 1940. The campers were members of the Zionist-Revisionist youth organization known as Brith Trumpeldor.

Other hotels were pointedly leftist. At Maud's Summer Ray, most guests were leftists in the pre-World War II era, ecumenically composed of socialists, communists, and Trotskyists. At Chester's Zunbarg, radicalism met fine entertainment, and shows featured Pete Seeger, the Weavers, Woody Guthrie, Paul Robeson, Leon Bibb, Ossie Davis, and Rubie Dee. Arrowhead Lodge in Ellenville was very closely affiliated with the Communist Party and its adult education Jefferson School, a non-credit school in New York City. The radical Furrier's Union even built the Fur Worker's Resort, later called White Lake Lodge, which began in 1949 and was sold to a Jewish camp six years later. Paul Robeson was a regular singer and speaker, and novelist Howard Fast was among the eminent lecturers there. Green Acres Hotel, owned by Socialist New York State Assemblyman

Elmer Rosenberg, sponsored local socialist activities and hired blacklisted show business figures like Zero Mostel.[7]

Woodridge, a town whose year-round population had a Jewish majority, bought an ambulance to send to the Spanish loyalists in the Civil War. Workmen's Circle chapters were founded in several towns, with their combination of socialism, union organizing, Yiddishist culture, and benevolent associations. In the 1930s when some Jews supported the Soviet Union's plans for a Birobidjan homeland for the Jews, camps in the Catskills trained people for that failed effort. Late 1940s and 1950s Catskills activism included local efforts on behalf of the progressive 1948 Henry Wallace campaign for president, as well as crossing the Hudson to attend the famous 1949 Paul Robeson concert in Peekskill, where the singer and his audience were pelted with stones, while state and local police looked on with encouragement and then arrested the victims.[8]

Even before the Holocaust, American popular culture represented the Catskills' mountain life as offering a home away from home for Jews. Generations of writers in America have documented, as witnesses and participants, the life of the Jewish mountain dwellers, while others have poetically re-imagined the world as a perfect confluence of people and place, culture and time. In the earlier literature, like Abraham Cahan's 1917 American masterpiece *The Rise of David Levinsky*, we get a glimpse into that particularly Jewish domain, which hosted an entire range of Jewish society, more in line with Theodore Dreiser than with Cahan's Yiddish speaking-and-writing ancestors.[9]

By the time more contemporary American writers such as Art Spiegelman, Allegra Goodman, Thane Rosenbaum, and others wrote about the Catskills, in the 1980s and beyond, the genre of Jewish Catskills literature had developed identifying characteristics. Its narratives present landscapes upon which reside a deeply connected community of Jews who remain wary of others, mostly gentiles, and segregate themselves from those others. In the stories that take place before the 1960s, segregation from the American mainstream was often a result of antisemitic practices barring Jews from other hotels and resorts.

In general, characters in all of the narratives by the more recent writers on the Catskills—including those about communities of religious Jews, socialists, and Holocaust survivors—voluntarily isolate themselves from a world that poses existential threats to their belief systems or frames of reference. The desire to be in the mountains also signals an alienation from the city and a Romantic appreciation for the natural world. These characters are drawn away from the metropolis and out into rural, small-town America. The stories present a landscape rich with human contact, in a culturally Jewish place.[10] It is nostalgic, to be sure, but nostalgia evokes yearning for a real as much as an ideal past. There are extensive descriptions of food purchases, meal preparation and consumption, exuberant and lusty sexuality, family politics, friendly and not-so-friendly bickering, and the ubiquitous tummlers (entertainers) with their uniquely humorous ways. All of this abundant life is carried out within a world both synchronic and diachronic, deeply present in and upon its own landscape and inescapably pressed into chronological time, affectively clothed as nostalgic.

As each decade of Jewish American life is woven into these Catskills stories, it becomes increasingly clear that Catskills Jewish life mirrors and reflects the larger state of Jews in American life and the issues they confronted. For example, what became known as "the Borscht Belt" (a term often used by journalists but which veterans of the culture rarely, if ever, used)—characterizing the Catskills era from the 1930s to the early 1970s—was in fact crafted out of institutional and tacitly practiced antisemitism: discriminatory practices of the twentieth century that kept Jews and other so-called undesirable groups away from housing in certain neighborhoods, as well as from membership in country clubs and mainstream centers of recreation. Socialists, Bundists, Communists, and others in the Catskills had a way to collectively congregate and practice their beliefs away from more mainstream American Jews—and from the rest of America. Ultra religious Jewish groups looking for a way to keep their community insular re-created a kind of shtetl life in the Mountains. The atmosphere of the Catskills today is greatly influenced by growing numbers of religious Jews.

From this leitmotif of Jewish separateness, we can identify at least three distinct and common themes in Catskills literary writing. The characters are drawn to the small-town, rural life that the Catskills Mountains offers, but remain segregated from the gentile world there; the mood is one of exuberance in appetites: for food, sexuality, humor, and entertainment; and the setting, though localized, tends to reflect the larger issues facing Jews in America.[11]

Dusk in the Catskills

While it is worthwhile to examine all of the literary writing about the Catskills and the Holocaust, such as it is, the primary focus of this essay is a detailed analysis of Reuben Wallenrod's novel *Dusk in the Catskills* and its central role in Catskills Holocaust history. Wallenrod was born in 1899, in the small town of Wizna, Poland. His mother died when he was fifteen, after which he spent several years with his grandparents. He was educated as one of just a few Jews at the boy's classical gymnasium in nearby Slutsk, a town at the center of Zionist activity. He and his sister Myriam emigrated to Palestine in 1920, leaving behind the entire remaining family. He left Palestine the following year, staying in Paris for two years, and finally arriving in America in July 1923. He studied first at NYU, followed by an MA from Columbia Teacher's College, with degrees in education and French. After teaching at various Jewish schools, he returned to France to complete a dissertation on John Dewey. Unable to find work in Palestine, his preferred home, he came to America with his wife, Rae, and began a career teaching Hebrew Language and Literature at Brooklyn College. He published significantly during the 1940s and 1950s, producing articles and books, fiction and non-fiction.

The literary imagination of Reuben Wallenrod is not unique in merging historical fact with a writer's fancy. According to his family, the setting for *Dusk in the Catskills* was the actual Hotel Rosenblatt in Glen Wild, called Hotel Brookville in the novel (Wallenrod was a "writer in residence" at the hotel, probably around 1939). The novel's focus on the inner life of hotel keeper Leo Halper helps to create a sharp tension between the stories of violence and destruction coming from Europe and the Jewish immigrant's comfort in the calming, panoramic Catskills' landscape. Guided by both linear, chronological time and the cyclical time of seasons and associative memories, our reading experience is directed by Halper's thoughts, but also by the larger story of Catskills resort life and Halper's (and likely Wallenrod's) own memories of his childhood village in Poland.[12] Halper can neither imagine what has been lost in Europe nor what that loss will mean to him personally, in his Catskills haven. But he suffers deeply from his concern.

Part of the fascination of *Dusk in the Catskills* is that it was written twice: first in Hebrew between 1941–44 and published in 1946 as *Ki Fanah Yom* (Because the Day Turns), and then translated by the author into English and published by the Reconstructionist Press of Wyncote, PA in 1957. Wallenrod's lamentations in Hebrew offer some notable differences from the English version, only a few of which I will discuss here.[13] According to his daughter, Naima Prevots, Wallenrod felt "it was essential to preserve Jewish identity not through religion or Yiddish, but by encompassing Hebrew as a living language, thus forging a bond with an historical tradition and with a future homeland in Palestine"[14]. Although no longer well-known, Wallenrod was part of a group of writers known as "Jewish Nationalists" or "Hebraists," Jews whose core identity was neither American nor Jewish American but ardently and nationalistically Jewish. An accomplished novelist and literary critic, he published in Hebrew a number of books and studies on Hebrew language and literature.[15]

Dusk in the Catskills follows hotel owner Leo Halper over the course of one full year, from the end of one summer season to the following autumn. During this period, the United States has entered the war in Europe. Halper, like Wallenrod, a Jewish immigrant from Eastern Europe, is acutely and painfully aware of the atrocities happening to the Jews in Europe, which are likely occurring to his family, friends, neighbors, and former acquaintances. At the same time, he simply and unabashedly loves his little hotel in the Catskills, and the rich life it has given him, his family, and other European émigrés. He ruminates about this perplexing state, which includes both deep sorrow and utter pleasure. The beauty of the landscape only inflames the texture of his memories and thoughts, and Wallenrod's third-person limited narration exposes Halper's thoughts as they are happening, directly engaging the reader.

The fact that there are two versions of the novel lends the story a prophetic air. In the first (Hebrew) version, Wallenrod still had limited knowledge about the scope of the catastrophe. Written over ten years after the Hebrew, the English version provides an opening epigraph from Jeremiah 6.4: "Woe unto us! For the day declineth,/ For the shadows of the evening are stretched out."[16] Written well after the war, the English novel sends back a warning, announcing the imminent arrival of a long period of dark and deadly days for the Israelites. It was a warning that should have been a call to arms. Although Wallenrod was not a religious man, he was obligated to his people and to their teachings. He felt it necessary to reveal, to witness, to testify about the disaster, as Jeremiah (the "weeping prophet") had. The idea of warning one's "flock" is tied to the writer's mission on behalf of his people, his nation, and the surrounding world. And this warning was confirmed by time. *Dusk in the Catskills* then stands—with Jeremiah—as a prophet's lamentation at the suffering of his people, even as he sees some expression of divine verdict in their exile. Exiles can still be reached by God.

We learn in the course of the story that Halper is joined in the Catskills by other exiles. Who are these foreign friends and peers who also made the Catskills their new Jerusalem? Halper offers the reader his limited and shared point of view on their lives. Much like real hotelkeeper Rosenblatt, most of the fictional Halper's associates are other European Jewish immigrants, many of whom left Eastern Europe first for pre-state Palestine, where, like Halper and Wallenrod, they helped build the modern country. Most of them also spoke Hebrew. These intellectuals, writers, and artists came each summer to his little hotel; they valued Hebrew over English in language, art, and culture. There was an understanding that they lived amongst a Jewish American public alienated from authentic Judaism. Their American Jewish peers seemed unable or unwilling to learn and read Hebrew, or to know Jewish texts or practice Jewish rituals. These American Jews would likely not read their works or invest in their intellectual climate. Thus they formed their own culture-in-exile in the Catskills, where Halper's hospitality offered them a world of their own.

As a small hotel owner, Halper has many domestic concerns that consume him. He has a longstanding payment arrangement with his elderly neighbor, a banker, to keep his hotel afloat; the banker's son, however, threatens to change the terms of the note because the hotel is losing money. During the lean war years, fewer visitors have been staying at the hotel, yet he continues to have mounting bills that need payment. He worries that he might lose his hotel. He worries that the world of the Jewish Catskills is fading. He worries that the many immigrant writers and artists who depend upon him each summer season will lose that community. The reader follows Halper's fears as they emerge and grow larger by the day.

While he bemoans what he imagines may be the imminent demise of this domestic serenity, a larger and more poignant worry grows even larger within him, hidden from his family and friends. He is deeply troubled by the atrocities committed against the Jews of Europe, the horrifying details about which he comes to know more and more during the course of the novel. He enjoys family time, the ongoing literary salon with his fellow exiles, and the verdant surroundings, even as he obsesses in his mind over the destruction of European Jewry. His thoughts turn to his childhood, his home and village and family. He remembers his early years in this village, a rural landscape not unlike the Catskills. He remembers discrete moments with boyhood friends that shaped him into the nature-loving man he has become: running in the many fields and swimming in the ponds, but also—with his classmates and teachers—learning the texts and the religion that he loves. He recognizes that these people from his memories are being threatened with torture and death. Halper feels more than sympathy for their plight; he is existentially connected to his co-religionists in Europe, and this connection rouses him to an almost feverish state of anxiety over his helplessness.

While he walks the grounds of the hotel, these memories of his youth crowd his mind. He remembers particular people—neighbors, teachers, individuals he once saw daily. By the end of chapter IV, fragments of childhood memories emerge in Leo's consciousness with regularity. He ruminates over these people from his past, observing that even at the movies, the pain of remembering was only halted, not stopped. Wallenrod writes that for Halper, "It was bad when they started coming. They crept from outside and from inside, from yourself. They seemed to speak somewhere in your consciousness."[17] The flocks of clouds and light wind in the trees bring one memory vividly to mind:

> Somewhere in the distance of time there were sunbeams in a window and big square columns of golden dust; then there were unbuttoned coats, joyous shouting, drying paths which bore the fresh imprints of human feet and animal hoofs. In those memories there came at times a joyous youthful exalted roar and the heart overflowed with happiness. But then the joy subsided, the happiness was gone and longings pressed his heart as if with tongs.[18]

As he strolls past the hotel casino, he notes with wonder the disparity he feels between life and death, memories of a past now disappearing, and the vibrant life he created in the Catskills stretching out before him. Watching young people dancing in the casino, he reflects on this tension:

> The heart knows well that there is another great wide, threatening world outside you, but you are afraid to stop your dancing and think of that world. Such knowledge may well break up the charm of the circle, it may well break up your very being, all of you.... They come, however, those people and stand before you. You see among them men and women you actually knew. You have known them with your eyes and you have known them in your imagination.[19]

An interesting narrative switch occurs here. Wallenrod moves between third-person omniscient and third-person limited narration, referring both to the young people dancing and to himself with the pronoun "you." Of course in English there is no plural for this pronoun, so the reader must accept that Halper is inclusive here, that they are all one in imagining this disaster of their people. The rhythm of the language in this scene moves the way a sermon or a rabbinical blessing or command might, striking at the heart of the reader, demanding a witness. Like the leader of a congregation, Halper the hotel keeper bears responsibility for his people and believes that they may not know what is best, or how to act, or how to see the deeper catastrophe. This passage conveys the strength of the connection between all Jews: the younger generation, who cannot help but know about the developing destruction in Europe, joyously dance together in the casino, because that's what young people do; meanwhile images of Halper's family and friends in the old country flood his heart and stand before his eyes. In the merging of the pronoun, from the "you" of others to the "you" of himself in both passages, all Jews become connected to one another. Whether they came from the old country or were born in the new one no longer matters: the crisis emerges from consciousness with the potential to crack open the entire Jewish world.

We don't always know which particular historical event is being depicted in the novel as Halper thinks about these things. He began the novel in 1941, early in the war; thus he writes history as he himself is learning it. It is possible the lack of clear and correct details about particular events is deliberate; but deliberately vague or not, Wallenrod shares specific information coming from Europe. The reader learns of the general mayhem, and the particulars of roundup, torture, deprivation, and murder as Halper reads his daily *New York Times,* or listens to radio broadcasts from his living room. The characters share this information amongst themselves, but our point of view is through Halper, and it is Halper who dwells on the terrible details coming from abroad. Still, there is an ambivalence that he cannot shake. He wants to help the cause, like other immigrant and American Jews; he donates to the Jewish National Fund and other sources willingly, to help the new Israeli refugees resettle in the land. He continues to struggle with feelings of satisfaction and pleasure, yet, as soon as he feels grateful to have escaped the bleakness and death, fear and torture, he also feels shame. He is deeply conflicted, and his anxiety breaks down into three main feelings: frustration at not being able to help family and friends in Europe; shame for being safely away from the atrocities; and guilt over the feelings of joy his life brings him. He isn't willing to sacrifice his daily comfort. But he has whole memories of a world now being destroyed, and he lives in a liminal state between shame and joy. Wallenrod beautifully captures that ambivalence in the following passage:

> He was gnawed by the thought that he and Lillian were hiding here between the mountains in a sheltered den. There, across the mountains, terrible things were going on. People were being driven with whips in the cold and wind; little children stood helplessly on the side of the road like forsaken sheep, and near them and from above them came fearful shrieks through the storm. And he, Leo Halper, was hiding here between the walls of his house in the Catskill Mountains. It was awesome and shamefully pleasant in the shelter.[20]

Writing this story from 1941–1944, when so many atrocities were being committed against the Jews of Europe, but when the full extent was not yet known, Reuben Wallenrod wrote what he knew then.[21] When he returned to the story a decade or so later, writing in English, much more was known and could be written back into the novel. In both the Hebrew and English versions, Wallenrod laments the atrocities so that they are voiced, and thus remembered. Revealed only to the reader, this private form of commemoration is associated with Halper's ambivalence about feeling safe while his co-religionists are dying in Europe. In a novel of almost 300 pages, the reader is asked to think about the war in Europe and its Jewish victims in every chapter, on almost every page. It is neatly and elegantly drawn into the larger story of the fading Jewish Catskills, but it is a story in its own right. The terrible facts are just surfacing in the 1940s for author Reuben Wallenrod; for narrator, hotel owner, and European Jewish immigrant Leo Halper, they are happening in real time. This passage neatly places Halper quietly sitting at his radio, conflating the winter storms outside his living room window with the raging storm troopers destroying Europe's Jews:

> The window panes trembled, the trees hummed, the voices on the radio told of terrible storms across the mountains and the oceans. There people fled in terror, hid in snow pits; men and women left the houses in which they had lived all their lives and ran like frightened animals. There, across the mountains and the oceans, wild beasts laughed and mocked and threatened, and here a man sat and listened to the radio.[22]

From the beginning of the novel, Halper is a reliable narrator who commands the reader's sympathy and respect, and thus his inner monologues about the victims in Europe offer a site of remembrance that is authentic and reliable. His self-reflective nature offers us ongoing access to his inner thoughts, so we are intimate with this ineffable desire to commemorate the suffering of his coreligionists. We feel his frustration over the lack of understanding among his gentile neighbors. He wants to reach everyone with his tender feelings, but he is ashamed to feel blessed at the same time. Wallenrod has Halper lean toward, but ultimately avoid, extreme identification with the victims, which would lead to an excess of empathy and an inability to discern between himself and those Jews caught in Europe. Halper is aware of his own privileged position vis-à-vis the stories he hears and recognizes the implications of over-identification. In his poetic and percipient musings on the atrocities, the hotelkeeper substitutes feelings for facts, while Wallenrod conveys the facts. As a story, then, *Dusk in the Catskills* undercuts the myth of silence and alienation that this volume addresses.

In remembering those who lived—and died—through his fictional account, Wallenrod's very private narrator presents a public and thus shared memory of the Holocaust. Indeed, the novel operates as a commemoration of the Holocaust in the Catskills, which resonates with more recent historical research about the postwar years. This position forcefully rejects the belief that the war years and immediate postwar years were barren of memory and memorialization of the Holocaust. These new studies shift our understanding of that period, as does Wallenrod's novel, and indeed, so does the body of literary and commemorative writings that come from or describe Jews in the Catskill mountains.[23] It's unlikely that during those years American Jews deliberately avoided talking or writing about the Holocaust. The irony for *Dusk in the Catskills* is that reviewers at the time of publication did not necessarily highlight the Holocaust-related elements. A 1957 *Jewish Currents* review says the novel "tells a simple story about a hotel-keeper, a summer hotel, the people who work there and the guests who visit."[24] Though the reviewer calls it "compassionate and readable," he fails to acknowledge the atrocities referenced by Wallenrod, and he may well have found their presence in the story unremarkable. In 1957, they are still a part of the history of the time in which they occurred. Wallenrod can say of Halper, "You have known them with your eyes," because both author and protagonist emerged from the burning villages. The reviewer, similar to most American Jews, most likely did not share that historical context.

We must also note that Halper's personal financial concerns are tied to his fear that the whole Catskills Jewish culture was declining. The potential loss of the Jewish Catskills is parallel, though of course not comparable, to the large-scale destruction of Jewish life in Europe. The loss of Jewish life and culture is part of a millennia-old narrative of destruction and exile, and this is a point we can take from *Dusk in the Catskills*. Just as Wallenrod's novel became a memorial to a culture he thought was disappearing, so too did the Jews of the United States shape, from the ground up, a memorial culture during the war. They had to: there was no recent Jewish or American historical precedent for this sort of commemorative culture. Wallenrod's novel, and others like it in this genre, shows that

Jews of all traditions made room for the Holocaust in large and small ways, that they "wove the catastrophe deeply into the basic fabric of community life and that they considered what they said and did as monuments to Europe's destroyed Jewish world."[25]

The communal life of Jews in the Catskills bears out this thesis. It offers a powerful example of Jews finding ways to release their rising fears and ongoing anxieties during and after the war years by engaging in community life while living away from the disaster. The ubiquitous entertainers—hired to amuse and distract the guests at every large hotel, and many of the small hotels as well—were as conscious as other Jews about what was happening overseas. Their acts often included jokes about the war. The social climate of the Catskill mountains addressed a lighter side of life: an abundance of pleasures in the form of food, sex, dancing, and humor. Surrounded by carnality, it would not have been seemly to speak directly and publically about the state of European Jewry. But it was surely within the hearts and minds of Jews who dwelled there.

Reuben Wallenrod lost his father, his sister, and her two children in the Holocaust. His book honors their memory, closely examining, through the loneliness of Leo Halper, the terrible crisis of being removed from one's family as they faced their death. Halper feels fearful, joyful, and ashamed all at once. Wallenrod must also have felt that he escaped a fate so many of his dear family and friends did not; as Halper's memories return to those people and his former life "over there," he is tortured by an inability to act. And yet his memories become a blessing, a monument to those people and places. *Dusk in the Catskills* memorializes the several fields of loss in its beautiful evocation of those worlds. Halper's thoughts are private memory; but the book is shared and public, and openly expresses sorrow and sympathy in its lamentation.

Notes

An earlier version of this essay was first published in *Summer Haven: The Catskills, The Holocaust, and the Literary Imagination* (Boston: Academic Studies Press, 2015).

1. *Four Seasons Lodge*, directed by Andrew Jacobs (2008; New York: Rainlake Productions), Film.
2. Reuben Wallenrod, *Dusk in the Catskills* (New York: The Reconstructionist Press, 1957).

3. Phil Brown, *Catskill Culture: A Mountain Rat's Memories of the Great Jewish Resort Area* (Philadelphia: Temple University Press, 1998).

4. Isaac Bashevis Singer, *Enemies, a Love Story* (New York: Farrar, Straus and Giroux, 1972).

5. Isaac Bashevis Singer, "The Yearning Heifer," in *The Collected Stories of Isaac Bashevis Singer* (New York: Farrar, Straus, and Giroux, 1982).

6. Martin Boris, "The Catskills at the End of World War II," in *In the Catskills: A Century of the Jewish Experience in "The Mountains,"* ed. Phil Brown (New York: Columbia University Press, 2002).

7. Ibid., 91.

8. Ibid., 93.

9. Abraham Cahan, *The Rise of David Levinsky* (New York: Harper & Brothers, 1917).

10. Michael Weingrad, *American Hebrew Literature: Writing Jewish National Identity in the United States* (Syracuse: Syracuse University Press, 2011).

11. Weingrad, *American Hebrew Literature*.

12. Jill Aizenstein, "Engaging America: Immigrant Jews in American Hebrew Literature" (PhD diss., New York University, 2008).

13. It is important to note, as I did earlier in the essay, that there are two versions of this novel, both written by Reuben Wallenrod, The extent of differences between the two novels is too large to pursue in this essay. However, several significant differences should be mentioned, the first of which is the epigraph in the English version that does not appear in the Hebrew version.

14. Levitsky and Brown, *Summer Haven*, 89.

15. Wallenrod's books in Hebrew include the following: *B'diyota hashelishit* (Tel Aviv: Dvir, 1937); *Ki fanah yom* (New York: Ohel, 1946); *Derakhim v'derekh* (New York: Ohel, 1950); *Bein Homot* (New York: Mosad Bialik, 1952); *Be'ain Dor* (Tel Aviv: Am Oved, 1953); *Mesaprei Amerika* (Tel Aviv: Dvir, 1958); and *Bayit B'kfar* (Tel Aviv: Dvir, 1965).

16. Jeremiah 6:4 (Hebrew Bible)

17. Wallenrod, *Dusk in the Catskills*, 256.

18. Ibid., 64.

19. Ibid., 151–52.

20. Ibid., 24.

21. In an extended email exchange I conducted with Naima Prevots, Reuben Wallenrod's daughter, she indicated that her father monitored the war against the Jews in Europe as it was happening.

22. Wallenrod, *Dusk in the Catskills*, 63.

23. Hasia R Diner. *We Remember with Reverence and Love: American Jews and the Myth of Silence After the Holocaust, 1945–1962* (New York: New York University Press, 2009).

24. Frank Cantor, "Book Review: *Dusk in the Catskills,*" *Jewish Currents* (1957) 26.

25. Ibid., 9.

Leon Uris's *Mila 18*, Muscular Judaism, and the Warsaw Ghetto Uprising in American Culture

Samantha Baskind

> I had to come face to face with a problem that many Jewish writers write about. There came that day of reckoning when I had to say ... "I am a Jew and what am I going to do about it and how am I going to live with it."[1]
>
> Leon Uris, 1961

LEON URIS's novel *Mila 18* (1961) stands as one of the most public and popular cultural projects about the Holocaust from the early postwar decades. In this fictional account of life in the Warsaw Ghetto and the legendary uprising that took place there, Uris aimed to highlight a Jewish fighting spirit. I am interested in how assiduously Uris orchestrated his novel, down to the book's artistic program, which augmented the author's narrative purpose: to use the uprising as a grand statement to refute a larger view, both by Jews and non-Jews, of Jewish passivity during the Holocaust. Uris wrote *Mila 18* to underscore defiance and dignity rather than meekness, anguish, and shame. By looking carefully at *Mila 18* as well as a few related projects, and especially the visuals that accompany them, I explore how the events in the Warsaw Ghetto were constructed by Uris not so much as a means of Holocaust remembrance but rather as a way to shape postwar perceptions of Jews.

Mila 18 and Uris's earlier novel about the founding of Israel—*Exodus* (1958)—provide keen depictions of muscular Judaism, the pervading theme in each book, highlighting military skill in particular.[2] The wildly popular *Mila 18* functioned as Jewish propaganda by elevating the so-called courageous Jew over the unfortunate yet pervasive canard that Europe's Jews went submissively to the gas chambers like sheep to their slaughter. The bestseller's success came about in part because of the pride it instilled in the American Jewish public, while also changing perceptions of Jews among non-Jewish readers. As the dust jacket announces, "The hero of *Mila 18* . . . is the Jewish people as represented by this handful of doomed men and women. It was fortitude and heroism like theirs that led to the creation of the state of Israel and the fulfillment of a two-thousand-year destiny. It was a proud moment in the history of Jews."[3]

Anchored by the passionate, fearless Andrei Androfski, who mobilizes the resistance, *Mila 18* weaves a multi-layered tale based on the actual events of the establishment and ultimate liquidation of the Warsaw Ghetto, and of course the uprising too—the seminal event that served the author's cause. Uris provided his own resistance by employing the resistance to counter essentialist versions of Jewishness, but in doing so he creates a version of "the Jew" that is just as essentialist. An assimilated Jew, like many mid-century Jewish Americans who finally lived in the mainstream rather than on the margins, Uris felt sure-footed in his efforts to question and undermine longstanding Jewish categorizations.

The covers of *Mila 18* and *Exodus* function as a paratext, which Gérard Genette defines as a threshold, "a zone between text and off-text, a zone not only of transition but also of *transaction*: a privileged place of pragmatics and a strategy, of an influence on the public, an influence that . . . is at the service of a better reception for the text and a more pertinent reading of it."[4] That is, Genette refers to elements that accompany a narrative, that "surround it and extend it, precisely in order to *present* it . . . to ensure the text's presence in the world, its 'reception' and consumption in the form of a book."[5] Some of these devices' power and influence shape the reader's experience, and others help us to understand the reception of a book over time. Among the many paratexts that Genette explores in detail are prefaces, dedications, epigraphs, and book jackets. Of interest to Genette, and to me, are the epitexts, which Genette delineates as "any paratextual element not materially appended to the text within the same volume but circulating, as it were, freely, in a virtually limitless physical and social space . . . anywhere outside the book."[6] Epitexts relevant to this essay include Uris's correspondence, presentations, and lectures. Both paratext and epitext, as demonstrated here, shed light on the cultural history and context of Uris's novels.

With this in mind, let us turn first to the book jacket for *Exodus* (figure 1). Designed by Sidney Butchkes with a drawing by Harlan Krakowitz, the cover of *Exodus* reveals a representation of the militant Jew, and thus the reader is invited to consider the implications of that image before reading the novel. Extending across the vertical length of the cover is a strapping freedom fighter in army fatigues, with his gaze cast to the distance. There is nothing nonchalant about his posture. Assuredly he holds his rifle, which points upward, guiding the viewer's eye to the author's name. (While not directly influenced by Uris, the movie poster by graphic designer Saul Bass, also Jewish, exploits the same motif: five arms stretched upward with one holding a rifle aloft). The fighter's gun lies against his leg, at the mid-section of his right thigh. That gun, poised upward in defiance, connotes a man's erect penis—namely, his virility. This iconic figure and pose appear at center amid a typeface that evokes a typical Hebrew font, traditionally thick, bold, and blocky with an occasional flourish (such a "Jewish" style print was banned by the Nazis). In white capital letters, the typography complements the blue background of the cover, creating an obvious reference to Zionist hues with a dash of gold, the color used for Uris's name. Beneath these essential details, in smaller white letters, stands the tagline "A Novel of Israel." Uris was so enamored of his book's cover that he had Francis Whitaker, an esteemed blacksmith who helped renew the art of modeling iron for aesthetic purposes, design a wrought-iron freedom fighter gate based on the *Exodus* cover for the entrance of his Aspen, Colorado home (figure 2). Whitaker took the two-inch high original figure and enlarged him to forty-two inches tall. Graceful radial lines accentuate the fighter and his gun as they converge at the figure's waist. Whitaker's interest in negative space, that space created by the iron and not just the design itself, is readily apparent by the twin Stars of David on the side panels of the gate and the shadows created by the figure's clothing.[7]

The cover of *Exodus*, and the heroic story about the founding of Israel told within, derive from negative constructions about the Jew's supposed disinterest and inability to participate in the military. Troubled by this shibboleth, over the course of his long career Uris tenaciously concentrated on Jewish leaders in fighting scenarios, aiming to counter ideas about Jewish cowardice and deficient Jewish bodies, which he, and the general public, encountered in numerous venues. Even a late nineteenth-century

Figure 1. Cover of Leon Uris's *Exodus*, 1958.

volume on diseases chronicles the Jewish failure to fight: "Since they were conquered they have never from choice borne arms nor sought distinction in military prowess. . . . To be plain, during their most severe persecutions nothing told so strongly against them as their apparent feebleness of body."[8]

Mark Twain, in an essay in *Harper's Monthly* from 1899 that mostly defends Jews, points out that a Jew may be "a frequent and faithful and capable officer in the civil service, but he is charged with a [sic] unpatriotic disinclination to stand by the flag as a soldier."[9] Upon discovering statistics to the contrary, revealing that Jews participated in American wars, Twain

Figure 2. Francis Whitaker, wrought-iron freedom fighter gate, 1975. Aspen, Colorado.

rescinded this insult in a postscript, penned a few years later and titled "The Jew as Soldier": "I was not able to endorse the common reproach that the Jew is willing to feed upon a country but not fight for it . . . That slur upon the Jew cannot hold up its head in presence of the figures of the War Department. It has done its work, and done it long and faithfully, and with high approval: it ought to be pensioned off now, and retired from active service."[10] Even so, before and after Twain's qualification, the slur persisted. In 1895, Simon Wolf, a lawyer and activist, wrote a book called *The American Jew as Patriot, Soldier and Citizen*, intent on dispelling the claim that Jews reneged on their military obligations in American wars, above all in the Civil War, but also in the War of 1812 and the Mexican War. Wolf records the fact that Jewish soldiers, in both the north and south, exceeded their proportions in the general population.[11] Yet still, a 1903 article in *Popular Science Monthly* perpetuates the falsehood that "Jewish immigrants of a military age who could pass our army requirements for recruits are comparatively rare."[12]

By mid-twentieth-century, Jews wrote non-fiction apologetics aimed at touting Jewish accomplishments in the military. Among these were Ralph Nunberg's aptly named book *The Fighting Jew* (1945), which at the onset noted, "Jewish membership in the armed forces of our country is 40 per cent higher than that of the non-Jews!"[13] Mac Davis's author's note in *Jews Fight Too!* (1945) melodramatically sets the stage for the larger argument within:

> Jews have fought, bled, and died on all the far-flung fronts around the globe. They were in the battle for Africa...in the battle for Britain...at Pearl Harbor...at Stalingrad...at Dunkirk...in the steaming jungles of Guadalcanal...at Tarawa...in the skies over Berlin...on the bloody beaches of Italy...and on D-Day, in the Invasion of France. Everywhere, Jews took up the challenge and fought.[14]

The third and final chapter of Rufus Learsi's *The Jew in Battle* (1944), titled "The Jew Fights for America," reads as a defense of Jewish loyalty to their adopted country. Such participation and sacrifice, Learsi argues, should be acknowledged as a "splendid record" and "shining record" as well as a "truth" that "should be displayed if only to save Christians of good-will from being infected by the anti-Semitic virus."[15] Several photographs of Jewish soldiers punctuate Learsi's points.

Allied with the notion of the weak, un-soldierly Jew is the stereotype of the effeminate Jew. As Paula Hyman has observed, "By caricaturing Jewish men as feminized, antisemites and their fellow travelers attempted to strip them of the power and honor otherwise due them as men."[16] Advancing this analysis, Sander Gilman connects the male Jew's alleged femininity to circumcision, confirming the ritual affirmation of Jewishness as emasculating in Gentile eyes: "the mutilation of the penis was a feminizing act."[17] Gilman explains, for example, that late nineteenth-century Viennese slang used the word "clitoris" to connote Jew, and female masturbation was deemed "playing with the Jew."[18] The rite of circumcision,

Freud suggests, commonly associated in the Christian mind with Jews, is also "unconsciously equated with castration" (Freud then relates this castration anxiety to the "roots of anti-Semitism").[19] The idea of the Jewish man as emasculated, or as a woman—certainly inadequate and powerless because of his circumcised penis—provides insight into why some gentiles have connected sexuality and masculinity with Jewish victimization, and this history appears to have influenced the freedom fighter's conspicuously erect gun on *Exodus*'s cover.

Indeed, modern psychoanalysis has identified the belief that a penis makes one sex "better" than the other. Freud articulates this idea by stating that from certain standpoints "what is common to Jews and women is their relation to the castration complex."[20] Freud's case history of little Hans illustrates the regrettable notion of woman as less than man. Hans, an eight-year-old boy obsessed with genitalia, comes to a shocking conclusion when he realizes that women have different genitalia from men. Freud paraphrases his conversation with Hans: "Could it be that living beings really did exist that did not possess widdlers? If so, it would no longer be so incredible that they could take his widdler away, and, as it were, make him into a woman!"[21] Uris attempted to rebut the canard of the sexually inferior Jewish man in *Exodus* with his characterization of the main character of Ari, and later Androfski in *Mila 18*—both handsome, virile lovers who engender the devotion of beautiful gentile women. Uris was married to a non-Jew, Betty Beck, at the time he wrote *Exodus* and *Mila 18*, and in two subsequent unions (although his third wife Jill converted to Judaism), a point he noted publicly, perhaps with the same aggrandizement by which he celebrated Jewish manliness in fiction. Androfski embodies sexiness, both in his actions and his physical prowess, which translates into a well-muscled body. To put it bluntly, Androfski's body and person afford a foil to the pale, scrawny, yeshiva boy and the sexually frustrated Jewish neurotic like Philip Roth's Alexander Portnoy or Paul Bronski in *Mila 18*. A bookish Jew collaborating with the Nazis, Bronski loses his wife Deborah to the Gentile Christopher di Monti, who is in favor of resistance. This view of the Jewish male as effeminate, physically sub-standard, and Other because of his so-called truncated penis and impotence finds visual form in the counter-trope on the first edition book jacket of *Exodus*, and as we will soon see in a subtler way on the *Mila 18* cover.

It is worthy of mention that the author photograph on the back cover of *Exodus* conveys Uris's own self-image as a tough, confident Jew (figure 3). Like the freedom fighter on the front, Uris wears military clothing and holds a large machine gun aimed upward, although more vertically, his hand casually placed near his pocket in front of an army jeep. A caption underneath his name reads, "With a patrol in the Negev Desert." As Uris later recalled, "I was in the Negev Desert with a patrol of Israeli paratroopers. You'll see on my dust jacket picture on the back of the book I'm hanging onto a machine gun. This appears romantic, but the fact is it was 127° in the shade and if I were not holding on, I would have collapsed."[22] Such a confession comes as a surprise, considering it nullifies Uris's conscious mythmaking in this image of ruggedness, but the average reader would be unaware of the truth behind the photograph. Confession aside, the author photograph conveys Uris's identification with the idealized Israeli soldier; suggests his pride in Israeli militancy, made especially manifest during the War of Independence and then a few years later during the Six Day War; and offers a visual accompaniment—bolstered by many examples in his written documents—of how profoundly the author's work was infiltrated by the fighting consciousness so central to Israel's military ideology. It is relevant to note that Uris's personal view of himself as an aggressive Jew not only informed *Exodus* and the subsequent *Mila 18*, but several of his other novels. Uris was a veteran of the United States Marine Corps who served for four years in the Pacific. From his first work of fiction, a story about the Marine Corps titled *Battle Cry* (1953), Uris demonstrated his special focus on robust Jews serving in the military. In *Battle Cry*, the Jewish Captain Max Shapiro dies bravely.

Turning now to *Mila 18*, Uris's portrayal of Androfski centers on his strength and intrepid nature, especially in battle. He is a man imbued with "mystic power," who defies the hackneyed platitude of the cowardly, scrawny Jew.[23] The twenty-six-year old Androfski, based on uprising leader Mordecai Anielewicz, offered Uris a chance to depict Jewish valor and physicality for all to read about once again, considering the international success of *Exodus*—in both print and film—and as such, to advance interest in his publications. Early on Androfski's strong, athletic body is detailed; the reader learns that when he kicks, "leg muscles [are] fairly rippling through his trousers."[24] He has played for the national soccer

Figure 3. Back cover of Leon Uris's *Exodus*, 1958.

team; won the light heavyweight wrestling championship of the Polish Army; and, according to his own account, can throw a javelin farther and jump a horse higher than almost any man in Poland."[25] Androfski's high rank in the Polish army also receives immediate mention.[26] Before he meets his love interest, Gabriela, she sees him from afar and recalls that he is nicknamed "The Tarzan of the Ulnays."[27] After making his acquaintance, Gabriela is "consumed by his great and wonderful power. . . . to her, Andrei was like David of the Bible . . . He was a giant who lived his life for a single ideal. . . . He was a symbol of strength to his friends."[28] Examples of Androfski's physical supremacy appear again and again, carrying through the entire novel—from battles in the Polish Army where his peers tolerate him for his strength, despite his Jewishness, all the way to the climatic uprising. As the fighting winds down and weapons are scarce, Androfski engages in hand-to-hand combat and manages to survive to nearly the end, in part, because his "eyes could penetrate the darkness with the sharpness of the large cat he was when he moved in the night."[29]

Androfski provides the most forceful example of the type of Jewish warrior advocated by Uris, but his compatriots also demonstrate their heroism, markedly during the uprising, which Uris manages to make suspenseful even though readers already know the outcome. Preceding this climactic event, Nurse Susan Geller goes to the death camps with the children under her care in the ghetto's orphanage rather than let them perish, terrified, on their own—a parallel to ghetto doctor Janusz Korczak's real life heroics. Wolf Brandel, Alexander Brandel's teenage son and an idealistic leader of the resistance, and his girlfriend Rachel Bronski, Wolf's equally idealistic girlfriend and the daughter of Paul and Deborah Bronski, mature physically and emotionally in the novel, discovering an inner strength in addition to their love for each other. Wolf volunteers as a runner, a Jew who sneaks out of the ghetto onto the Aryan side to distribute information about conditions in the ghetto, to smuggle in food and weapons, and to perform other tasks. During the uprising Wolf, promoted to Androfski's first lieutenant, is one of the primary resistance leaders. After the ghetto suffers its final defeat, Wolf and Rachel guide the ghetto's twenty-some starving, exhausted survivors through the sewers in chest-high water to safety. Most forcefully, as the story climaxes on the dramatic eighth day of fighting, Uris broadly describes Jews who "turned savage" fearlessly "hurling themselves into German ranks as living grenades and torches. Cornered, out of ammunition, they fought with rocks and clubs and bare hands.... They fought like maniacs."[30] The fictionalized news accounts declare: "Tales of the fantastical Jewish courage dribbled out. The myth of Jewish cowardice was burst."[31]

In the midst of these final fighting scenes, Alexander Brandel—a pacifist who only slowly comes around to a strategy of armed resistance—chronicles in his diary: "Our boys and girls still fight fiercely.... I will die with pride."³² Androfski reiterates this point in one of his last utterances to his troops, paraphrasing the January 22, 1943 call to resistance by the Jewish Fighting Organization (Żydowska Organizacja Bojowa, or ZOB)—"Let everyone be ready to die like a man!—with his own words: "Now hear me. So long as your lungs breathe, you fight."³³ Here, as in many other areas of the book, the characters' actions mirror reality; the underground Polish Jewish newspaper *Biuletyn Informacyjny* (no. 17, April 29, 1943) pronounced the uprising, in a late April 1943 article titled "The Last Battle in the Great Tragedy," as "a victory in [the fighters'] eyes if the forces of the enemy were weakened just a little: and finally—it was a victory in their eyes to die while their hands still grasped arms."³⁴ Building on this historical perspective, the last words of *Mila 18*, penned by the surviving Gentile Christopher de Monti, who paraphrases Brandel in the final journal entry from December 1943, read, "I die, a man fulfilled. My son shall live to see Israel reborn. I know this. And what is more, we Jews have avenged our honor as a people."³⁵ Such a "heroic death," as David Ben-Gurion coined it in reference to the smaller January rebellion in Warsaw, negated misconceptions about deficient Jewish bodies and spirits, while simultaneously restoring dignity through a new Jewish ideal.³⁶

The cover for *Mila 18* (figure 4) just as persuasively continues the theme inherent in Uris's *Exodus* cover, which also amplified the story's objective: Jewish might, masculinity, and battle readiness. As with *Exodus*, Harlan Krakowitz again drew the jacket image, although here Al Nagy designed the cover. A drawing of a young partisan with a rifle strapped on his back, heavily shadowed on the right side of his body, takes up the top half of the cover. He prepares to throw a bottle bomb, alit with a dash of red—the only color in this otherwise black and white rendering. Like the weapon carried by the *Exodus* freedom fighter, the ghetto rebel's rifle stands tall, as does the Molotov cocktail he stalwartly grasps in his hand. To the left of him one finds the author's name and titles of two earlier bestselling books, *Battle Cry* and *Exodus*, in a simple red typeface. The title is rendered in large print, in blue and black, accompanied by a short description, indicating that the novel relays a story about the uprising. Uris and his colleagues judiciously chose the color scheme. Uris addressed this matter in a letter from October 31, 1961 to Tim Seldes:

Figure 4. Cover of Leon Uris's *Mila 18*, 1961.

I was really impressed with the way that *Exodus* is still selling and how in the planning of the dust jacket of *Mila 18* we so carefully reversed the colors so that every bookstore I went in had the two books side by side on display, invariably it was the most eye-catching item in the store. They really looked beautiful together, and amusingly enough, every bookseller who had the two books side by side believed he thought it up all by himself. I think our advance planning to make them companion features has really started to pay off.[37]

Uris's planning extended beyond that of the book's cover. Crucially, when reviewing the galley proofs for *Mila 18*, he marked up the opening page, suggesting that the freedom fighter on the cover of *Exodus* be reproduced to the left of the title page, along with the list of other books by him. Indeed, the subsequent foundry proof and published book include the freedom fighter, gun in hand, deliberately pointing toward the titles of Uris's earlier novels.[38] Uris shrewdly capitalized on this well-recognized figure in American culture that denoted his beloved earlier book to move copies of his newest novel. Just as shrewdly, the repetition of this figure on an opening page of *Mila 18* further emphasized the defining ideal of the vigorous, fierce, and proud Jew. The freedom fighter became Uris's surrogate signature, appearing on the left of the title page in future books, pointing to the titles of previous novels.

The fighter's pose on the cover of *Mila 18* conspicuously recalls that of another great Jewish fighter: the biblical David as sculpted by Gianlorenzo Bernini in 1623–24—notably the most masculine of the trio of renowned sculpted Davids from art history and the only David sculpted in the midst of battle. Certainly, Michelangelo's *David* (1501–4) possesses chiseled musculature, but he appears introspective as he prepares to fight and is meant to be admired as much for his physical beauty as for his bravery. While shown victorious in battle, Donatello's bronze David (after 1420) is a smirking adolescent rather than a mature man. The cover designer for *Mila 18* adapts the dynamic corkscrew spiral of Bernini's David's torso as it twists with extreme effort while he prepares to release his weapon. Recounted in 1 Samuel 17:48–51, David's unlikely victory over the giant Goliath provided a perfect analogy for *Mila 18*. With an inferior weapon, David managed to defeat his powerful foe. Similarly, Warsaw's Jews possessed inferior weapons, and while they did not win their battle against the heavily armed Nazis, they put up an epic effort. Further, David's pose, and by extension the Warsaw Ghetto resister's pose, has an even older precedent in the *Borghese Gladiator*, from around 100 BCE. This Hellenistic marble sculpture, which inspired copies in various locations in Europe and America, portrays a warrior engaged in combat.

Before Uris began writing *Mila 18*, he voiced his admiration for John Hersey's treatment of the same subject in *The Wall*, a bestselling work of historical fiction from 1950 about the Warsaw Ghetto, and a winner of the National Jewish Book Award. As he wrote in a 1957 letter to his father, albeit with a jab, *The Wall* was "the finest novel I ever read. Hersey, as a boy was a very sophisticated anti-Semite. It's hard to believe. I feel he is our most underrated novelist."[39] Reviewers and fans also made logical connections between the two historical novels. A fan letter sent just one month after *Mila 18*'s publication lauded Uris's book over *The Wall*. Perhaps unconsciously influenced by Hersey's outsider status as a non-Jew and Uris's position as the son of a father who immigrated from Poland (the family's original surname was Yerushalmi), the fan wrote, "You might enjoy hearing that I found your book exciting, stimulating, and thoroughly moving. Though I'd read Mr. Hersey's "The Wall," it remained for your pen to humanize the Warsaw Ghetto story!"[40] *Kirkus Reviews* mentioned the two books in the same breath, not favoring one over the other. Both are praised for "employing the same unbelievable proof of man's capacity for suffering and ability to endure and fight and live, to tell it in a broader frame of reference, and to build, on factual details, a tremendous saga of adventure and heroism."[41] *Library Journal* "highly recommended" Uris's novel "as a book to stand beside Hersey's 'Wall.'" Apparently swayed by Uris's Jewish heritage over Hersey's gentile background, the reviewer adds, "because of Uris's advantage of his more personal involvement, his book may well outrank the earlier classic."[42]

The representation of strength and resistance on the cover of *Mila 18* vividly contrasts with the original cover of *The Wall* (figure 5). An ominous wall dwarfs the tiny Jewish figures, only lightly drawn in white, nearly fading out of existence in front of our very eyes, a precedent that Uris surely wanted to eschew. Another instructive comparison is the cover of Mary Berg's diary, published in English in 1945, at war's end (figure 6). The original book jacket comprises a giant monolith of bricks, blood red rather than the more realistic hue of bricks, with the book title submerged in a burned patch at the center.

In October 1962, Bantam Books released a paperback edition of *Mila 18*, following four printings of the hardcover version and various honors, including selection for the Book-of-the-Month Club in January 1962 and the Doubleday Dollar Book Club in April 1962, and a Commonwealth Club silver medal awarded in San Francisco in May 1962. Uris's publisher

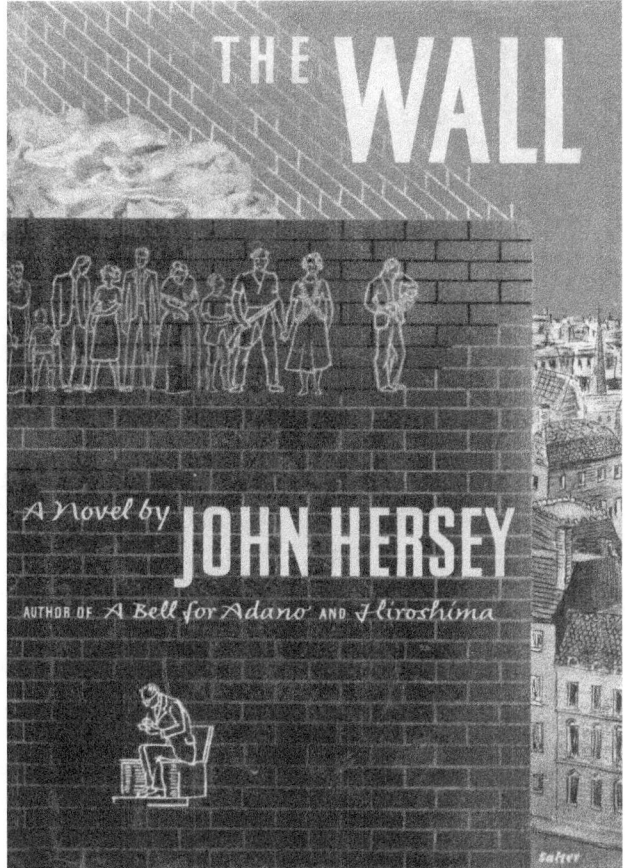

Figure 5. Cover of John Hersey's *The Wall*, 1950.

estimated that the paperback would sell between two to 2.5 million in the first year. Earlier that year, in June, Uris wrote to his father that he had approved the cover of the paperback, noting, "it looks very fine."[43] The 95-cent paperback cover varies slightly from the image on the cloth edition (figure 7). The same Zionist blue color Uris favored for the hardcovers of *Exodus* and *Mila 18*, as well as the paperback of *Exodus*, is used for the title. Underneath, a black-and-white rendering of a determined looking man holds a Molotov cocktail in one hand, similar to the cloth edition's cover. The paperback, though, further emphasizes the partisan's fighting nature with a gun slung down his back. Twisting his body with effort akin

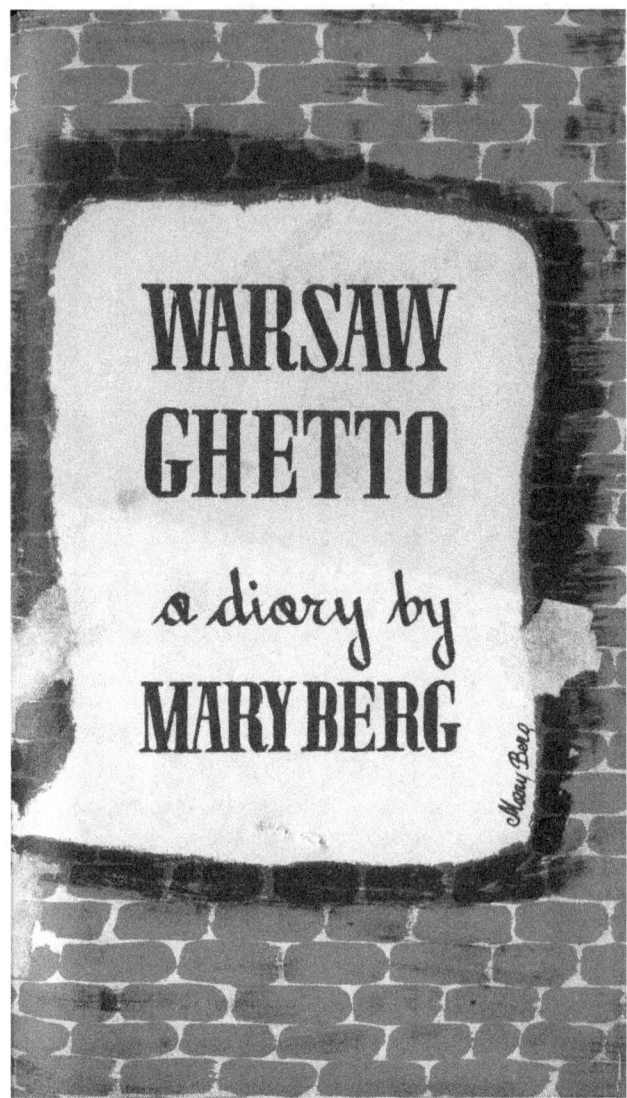

Figure 6. Cover of Mary Berg's *Warsaw Ghetto: A Diary*, 1945.

to the hardcover figure, the rebel's fighting nature is even further underscored by a second gun in his left hand. Also added is a woman sitting near the man's foot, grasping a gun, and a menacing tank off to the right. On the back cover, this same representation is displayed in a mirror image, with text declaring that the first edition of *Mila 18* spent thirty-three

Figure 7. Cover of paperback edition of Leon Uris's *Mila 18*, 1962.

weeks atop the national bestseller list. Below the title, again partially colored Zionist blue, a blurb in all caps histrionically declares that inside a reader will find "The soaring story of the uprising which defied Nazi tyranny and Wehrmacht tanks with homemade weapons and bare fists in the most heroic struggle of modern times."[44] A reprinted review excerpt from the *Chicago Tribune* praises the book as "Tremendous! Magnificent! Uris has written a great angry torrent of a novel!" While these acclamations were common, not all reviews of *Mila 18* were positive. *Atlantic Monthly* derided *Mila 18* as "comedy, but not by the author's conscious design. Leon Uris has written 500-odd pages of melodramatic hoop-la about a small group of beleaguered fighters making a determined stand against superior forces.... It is to be hoped that Mr. Uris' travesty of their achievement will be quickly forgotten."[45]

In contrast to Hersey's and Berg's book jackets, Uris's *Mila 18* covers were unabashedly meant to signal fighting and strength rather than oppression and destruction. Uris's books were among the first to feature the figure of a tough Jew, but as Paul Breines observed, "Rambowitz novels" showcasing fighting Jews gained ground especially after the mid-1970s. In a revealing discussion of numerous books highlighting Jewish aggressors, Breines hypothesized that while the 1967 Arab-Israeli War initiated "the Jewish American cult of both Israel and tough Jewish imagery," there was a pause in the release of this material until the 1973 Yom Kippur War.[46] At that time, with Israel showing some vulnerability even in victory, Jewish potency needed to be reasserted, hence the emergence of Breines's designated "Rambowitz novels," books like Uris's that tell stories about self-reliant, untroubled Jews without a hint of timidity or schlemiel-like qualities. Obviously *Exodus* and *Mila 18* predate the period Breines investigates, and I would add that perhaps the positive reception of Uris's novels in this vein spurred subsequent writers in that direction. The Munich massacre at the 1972 Olympics may have played a role in the upsurge as well. Another fictional retelling of Jewish courage, John Fredman's *The Wolf of Masada* (1978) chronicles that great showdown on the mountaintop, with a dust jacket depicting resistance leader Simon ben Eleazar as a chiseled Greek God with massive muscles, clad in armor.

Overlooking the kibbutz Yad Mordecai in southern Israel, a larger than life-sized sculpture of Mordecai Anielewicz (1951) by Nathan Rapoport (who sculpted the Warsaw Ghetto Monument on the site of the uprising) similarly attempts to convey such fortitude. While he wore glasses and was on the thinner side, Anielewicz—with a slightly open shirt to show his heavy musculature and holding a grenade in his right hand—gazes over his left shoulder, resolutely and un-bespectacled into the distance, his face in three-quarter view. No doubt this pose was influenced by

Michelangelo's *David*, representing a Jew who also fought against a vastly stronger opponent. On a stone plaque beneath the sculpture are Anielewicz's words: "My last aspiration in life has been fulfilled, the self-defense turned into a fact. I am content and glad that I was among the first of the Jewish Fighters in the Ghetto." The kibbutz houses a museum about Anielewicz and the uprising.

A pre-publication article written by Uris came out in the November 1960 issue of the periodical *Coronet*. Titled "The Most Heroic Story of Our Century," the article told a vivid, shortened version of *Mila 18* seven months prior to its publication, and explained how Uris conducted some of his research. Four accompanying drawings advance a similar agenda to *Mila 18*'s subsequent book covers. The first drawing conveys the Nazi reaction to the type of Jewish partisan who ultimately graced the cover of *Mila 18*. A caption reads, "the Nazi became a flaming torch as the fire bomb smashed into him. Then the rebels opened fire."[47] Three Nazis appear flabbergasted by the Jewish siege; the Nazi struck by the firebomb staggers backwards, losing control of his rifle; another one runs away; and a third looks upward in shock. A second illustration shows a Jewish man and woman fighting side by side, makeshift weapons in hand as a tank approaches. The caption reads, "Men, women and children charged tanks barehanded—refused to be taken alive."[48] The final two illustrations show a man and a woman wading through the underground sewers toward escape while grasping rifles, and lastly a group of captured Jews, hands in the air in defeat. Nevertheless, this caption announces, "A handful of survivors were rounded up—but the spiritual victory was theirs."[49]

As has been clearly noted, Uris found the thought of the cowering Jew anathema to his vision. He countered this idea repeatedly and in an extreme, sometimes hyperbolic fashion, as evidenced by his single-minded focus in *Mila 18*, *Exodus*, and also in his personal correspondence. Just before the publication of *Exodus*, Uris wrote a letter to his father about his recent reading of *The Diary of Anne Frank*:

> I was tremendously shaken up by seeing it. But in the final analysis must temper my feelings with one of anger and resentment. I do not like to see Jews hiding in attics and feel there is something far more decent about dying in dignity which is of course the

choice that every Jew had. They did this in the Warsaw Ghetto....
ANNA FRANK was badly received in Israel, for they have a
strong feeling about Jews who will not fight back.[50]

Three years after the publication of *Mila 18*, Uris again disparaged this icon of the Holocaust in a different letter: "I did not see the Anne Frank television show, but speaking in generalities I am against the sentimentalizing of her death. She is, to me, the symbol of the passive Jew who died quietly and as you know from my writings this goes strongly against my grain. I like my Jews mean and fighting."[51]

Uris exploited the success of *Mila 18* in some unexpected ways. In the late 1980s, Uris and his wife Jill began "performing" an enactment of the uprising titled "The Rising of the Warsaw Ghetto." This is not a reading from *Mila 18* but rather a presentation grounded on the actual occurrences during the uprising. Reading from a script penned by Uris, the pair alternately speak as they offer a dramatization of the events in the ghetto, in the manner of radio plays on the same subject written during the war, such as "The Second Battle of the Warsaw Ghetto" and "Battle of the Warsaw Ghetto," which both aired in 1943. Uris so identified with the ideal of the muscular Jew that remarkably, and problematically, near the end of this presentation he and his wife take on the personas of another married couple, Antek Zuckerman and Zivia Lubetkin. Two surviving leaders of the actual uprising, Zuckerman—Anielewicz's deputy commander—and Lubetkin met with Uris during the research phase of his book. Uris and Jill used the survivors' exact words from accounts they gave of the uprising. The reading ends with Uris speaking: "If the Warsaw Ghetto marked the lowest point in the history of the Jewish people, it also marked the point where they rose to their greatest glory, for from the rubble of the ghetto they avenged and redeemed their honor as a people."[52] Among other venues, his often requested presentation was given for Judaic Studies departments and at Yom HaShoah events, accompanied by a more conventional speech from Uris.

Another project by Uris offers a similarly blatant interest in muscular Judaism: *Exodus Revisited* (1960), a photo essay published a year earlier than *Mila 18*, meant in part to reiterate the themes of *Exodus*.[53] Akin to *Exodus* and the soon-to-be-released *Mila 18*, *Exodus Revisited* tells a story—in this case non-fiction but certainly biased—from a Zionist viewpoint of Jewish persecution, the Jews' fighting sprit, and Israel's founding. *Exodus Revisited* is illustrated with over three hundred black-and-white photographs. To establish a precedent for Jewish might, a spread juxtaposes two earlier revolts at Bar Kochbha and Masada.[54] Uris follows this material with biblical references to Samson and David and Goliath, thereby calling to mind implausible Jewish victories.[55] A large section of the photo essay is devoted to the Warsaw Ghetto uprising, beginning with a portrait of Antek Zuckerman.[56] The caption underneath his smiling yet pensive bust-length photograph states, in part, "This man is a living legend . . . He and his comrades staged the first rebellion against the Nazis and sounded the great trumpet that signaled the return of the Jewish people to their Biblical tradition as great fighters."[57] What follows is the longest verbal passage of *Exodus Revisited*: Zuckerman's recollection of the uprising, standing alone with no need of imagery beyond his vivid account.[58] Immediately following Zuckerman's reminiscence are words from Zivia Lubetkin, described by Uris as "a heroine of the Warsaw uprising."

It is important to point out that prior to *Mila 18* other American cultural producers also purposefully depicted the Warsaw Ghetto and the uprising. In the immediate years after the uprising, even before the war ended, the rebellion was used to demonstrate that Jews were anything but passive, and thus the revolt became a compelling point of Jewish pride. These earlier projects had diverse goals. To offer a few examples: Barely a year and a half after the courageous exploits of the Warsaw Ghetto fighters, on October 10, 1944, the New Jewish Folk Theatre (formerly the Yiddish Art Theatre) debuted its inaugural production, highlighting the epic fight. The Yiddish-language play by H. Leivick (the pen name of Leyvick Halpern), boldly titled *The Miracle of the Warsaw Ghetto* (*Der nes in geto*). A poet who gained renown for *Der Goylem*, Leivick's drama was billed on the play's poster as a "great artistic production . . . about heroic resistance in Warsaw" that "must be seen by every Jew." The play was written solely for a Jewish audience considering the language spoken by the actors, and so its message—one of inspiration and optimism—must be seen as geared to Jews. *The Miracle of the Warsaw Ghetto* ran in New York for twenty weeks and then traveled to other cities. A Jewish fighting spirit, Jewish honor, and the bravery of the "comrades," as the characters call themselves, pervade the play. Jewish militancy was even featured in a promotional photograph of star Ben-Ami, which portrays him resolutely staring forward and decisively grasping a large rifle. At different points the characters lament the murders of their brethren and vow not to be similarly slaughtered. At the play's denouement, most of the rebels obviously die, but not before their lionhearted battle. The play was so well received as a symbol of courage and hopeful affirmation that soon after the war Leivick was sent to Europe by the World Jewish Congress, along with Emma Lazaroff-Shaver, an opera soprano and folk singer, and a delegate from the International Red Cross. As the *Jewish Telegraphic Agency* euphemistically reported, the trio's visit was meant "to help sustain the morale of the thousands of Jews in the displaced persons camps whose physical and mental condition has been endangered by the long series of trials to which they have been subjected."[59]

Artist Arthur Szyk, a Polish Jew who immigrated to the United States in 1940, also explicitly foregrounded a message of heroism and Jewish strength in several images. A compilation of several of Szyk's satirical, antiAxis political cartoons was published soon after the war's end. Titled *Ink and Blood: A Book of Drawings* (1946), this book included several images published earlier, accompanied by new material, with seventy-five illustrations in all. Carefully placed at the end of *Ink and Blood*, one of seven color plates in the book, *Battle of the Warsaw Ghetto* portrays male and female fighters, young and old, conquering an SS officer, who lies on the ground with his helmet and gun strewn uselessly around him. One of the Jewish fighters mockingly holds up a sign that reads "Eastern District, Order to the Troops: All Jews must be killed." Other armed Jews populate the background, which includes a glimpse of the ghetto's infamous wall, and one proudly holds aloft a Zionist flag. To augment his point, Szyk inscribed words on all four highly decorated borders of the image, inspired by Persian-style miniatures. At bottom is a dedication to "Samson in the Ghetto" referring to the biblical figure in Judges, which overtly links Warsaw's Jews with this strongman who killed his Philistine oppressors at the cost of his own life (recall that Uris invoked Samson in *Exodus Revisited*). The words "MY PEOPLE" appear inside a Star of David. A phrase around the border proclaims, "To the German people, sons of Cain, be ye damned for ever and ever amen."

On the second anniversary of the uprising, with the war continuing on, the Jewish Labor Committee organized an exhibition at the Valentine Gallery in New York City, called *Martyrs and Heroes of the Ghettos*, which showed from April 19 to May 25, 1945. The organizers had a very clear agenda; they invited many dignitaries to the opening, including the Minister of Denmark, the Ambassador of the Union of Soviet Socialist Republics, and the Peruvian Embassy Ambassador (none of them attended), to lend credence and importance to the events in the ghetto and the truth of the war, which was emphasized not only in the catalog, but in official statements in both writing and speeches at the event. Planning documents reveal the objectives of the exhibition explicitly laid out; one document describes the "aim of impressing on the American public at large the brutality and ruthlessness with which the Nazis have undertaken to exterminate the Jews, the *heroism* with which the Jews have attempted to *resist*, and the necessity for prompt and effective aid to those who survived."[60] The fifteen-page accompanying exhibition catalog explains, "This pictorial exhibit aims to pay tribute to the *heroes* of the Warsaw Ghetto."[61] The introduction continues pointedly, "*The Jews in the ghettos did not go silently to the slaughter.* Forgotten by the world, left alone to their fate by all the nations, unprotected, unarmed, the Jews of the ghettos launched an open battle against the mighty Nazi arms."[62] The narrative ends with a plea: "The exhibition presented by the Jewish Labor Committee is dedicated to the *heroes* and martyrs of the ghettos. Let us pay them honor, They have not perished in vain, The blood of 5,000,000 victims cries for vengeance; demands justice! The world, humanity, owes a great debt to the old and suffering people of Israel."[63]

Unlike earlier representations of the Warsaw Ghetto such as those by Szyk, H. Leivick, and the Jewish Labor Committee, Uris's novel was not explicitly crafted toward a political end, save for his ever-present desire to demonstrate why the State of Israel was of vital importance, a secondary goal in *Mila 18* as opposed to *Exodus*. Rather, *Mila 18* was meant to serve a social purpose, to once again undermine the view of Jews as weak and unresponsive, an ever-prevailing misrepresentation that unfortunately continued into the late 1950s and early 1960s, when Uris penned his novel and after its release. *Mila 18*, and the vast audience it reached, represents a watershed moment in the canonization of the Warsaw Ghetto uprising in Jewish American culture during the postwar years.

Uris's portrayal of muscular Judaism at one particular moment is even further fleshed out when looking at *Mila 18* in relation to later representations of the ghetto, which did not always—or even often—engage the ideal of the fighting Jew. Issue #247 (1981) of Joe Kubert's war comic series *The Unknown Soldier*, about a young child's miraculous escape from the ghetto, unfolds with the resistance as merely the backdrop. The savior here is the non-Jewish Unknown Soldier, not militant Jews. Similarly, in *Superman: The Man of Steel #82* (1998) the desperate Jewish inhabitants of the Warsaw Ghetto do not save themselves, but rather Superman swoops in to rescue them. When director and Holocaust survivor Roman Polanski decided to address the Holocaust, he did not opt for a story about the concentration camps (his mother died in Auschwitz) or the resistance, but rather chose to tell one man's survival story in the festering, oppressed Warsaw Ghetto. Polanski's filmic adaptation of Wladyslaw Szpilman's memoir *The Pianist* (2002) makes manifest the severe deprivation in the insular ghetto, with the uprising as a small episode. Further, while Szpilman's wits, and a great deal of luck, enabled his survival, his ultimate savior was a German soldier. I would argue that the *need* for constructed representations such as that by Uris—and later eschewed by Kubert, the makers of *Superman: The Man of Steel*, and Polanski—was subverted by the growing reputation of Israeli might in battle and the prominence of this New Jew in widespread venues.

Uris's shaping of the Warsaw Ghetto uprising to suit his purposes certainly tells us something about who he was as a man, a Jew, and a writer. In reference to Jewish identity, Barbara Kirshenblatt-Gimblett insightfully asks, "Perhaps the question should be rephrased: not, What is Jewishness? but rather, When does an individual foreground his identity as Jewish, by what means, and to what ends? What is the cultural content of this social differentiation? What is the display of Jewishness counterposed to? Who are the relevant others?"[64] For the many Americans who welcomed the author's conception of the twentieth-century Jew, Uris tendered a display of Jewishness that was counterposed to a pre-Holocaust and Holocaust Jewishness, and as such the overwhelming popularity of *Mila 18* also offers a perspective on postwar perceptions of the Holocaust held by Jews and non-Jews. In *Exodus*, Ari affords a positive example of a post-Holocaust Jew, while in *Mila 18* Androfski serves to illustrate that such masculine Jews existed during the Holocaust. In his two sweeping, Jewishly inflected novels, these idealized types were constructed, in both text and image, to "prove" that Jews cannot and did not inherit a faint-hearted nature. Accordingly, *Mila 18* is not so much about the loss of Jewish life in Europe, even if most of the characters in it die, nor is it a book conceived with a memorializing function. To state it plainly, Uris staged the events in the Warsaw Ghetto with the aim of influencing postwar views of Jews, aspiring to reinvent and reinvigorate Jewish identity.

Let me end by sharing two fan letters, of the many Uris kept in his files, that demonstrate two representative responses to *Mila 18*'s counter narrative. As one Jewish admirer wrote to Uris in 1961, "I have always decried the Jew who ran from his oppressor and prayed for deliverance instead of standing and fighting like a man. The State of Israel of course to our joy, has changed this picture of the cringing Jew. *Mila 18* gave us the reincarnation of the ancient Hebrew, the brave and powerful warrior when he had to be."[65] The writer signs off by suggesting that Uris write a book about the Maccabees. In October of that same year, another admirer wrote from a Christian perspective:

> I have neither the eloquence of Alexander Brandel nor the wisdom of Rabbi Solomon; I have only the quality of being grateful. I am grateful for being able to read both *Exodus* and *Mila 18* ... I am grateful as a Christian to be able to say to my Jewish brethren, "We shall die before we allow a people to be so persecuted because of their religious persuasion." *Mila 18* has opened my eyes in another way. It is hard to realize the struggle for survival so engrained in the soul of man; you have demonstrated in your writings the spirit which has enabled the Jewish culture to survive thousands of years of persecution and to emerge victorious and even more strong. It is my hope that the many thousands of people who have read and will read *Exodus* and *Mila 18* will better be able to understand their Jewish brethren.[66]

The awakening of consciousness to what Jews had suffered and what they had stood up against over the centuries stands at the core of Uris's work, initiated by his distaste for the deeply engrained categorization of the Jew as weak and cowardly, accompanied by his effort to subvert this epithet, redeem the Jewish image, and create a new conversation. The novel's reach was tremendous, extending even to bookstore browsers who may only have encountered *Mila 18* (and *Exodus*) as they casually walked past the persuasively propagandistic covers displayed on a shelf. For readers who did not know about the Warsaw Ghetto and the uprising, *Mila 18* not only apprised them of it, but solidified a particular representation in time and memory—of dignified and defiant Jews, who went to their deaths fighting back.

Notes

1. Leon Uris, "About 'Exodus,'" in Martha Boaz, ed., *The Quest for Truth* (New York: Scarecrow Press, 1961), 126–27. Ellipses in original. Uris delivered the lecture that included this quote as part of a series at the University of Southern California's School of Library Science. All invitees were charged to speak about their personal connection to their writing. Other notable lecturers include William Saroyan and Leonard Wibberley.

2. For a broad overview of Uris's oeuvre, including a chapter discussing each of his novels through 1988's *Mitla Pass*, see Kathleen Shine Cain, *Leon Uris: A Critical Companion* (Westport, CT: Greenwood Press, 1998). See also Ira B. Nadel's in-depth study, *Leon Uris: Life of a Bestseller* (Austin: University of Texas Press, 2010).

3. Leon Uris, *Mila 18* (Garden City, NY: Doubleday and Company, 1961).

4. Gérard Genette, *Paratexts: Thresholds of Interpretation*, trans. Jane E. Lewin (Cambridge: Cambridge University Press, 1997), 2. Emphasis in original.

5. Ibid., 1. Emphasis in original.

6. Ibid., 344.

7. Francis Whitaker, *Beautiful Iron: The Pursuit of Excellence* (self-published, ca. 1997), unpaged.

8. Benjamin Ward Richardson, *Diseases of Modern Life* (New York: Bermingham and Company, 1882), 98. The author goes on to praise Jews for their unlikely survival despite such diminished capacity: "In the course of centuries the most powerful nations have died out, and empires of perfect physical beauty and chivalric fame have passed away. But through all these vicissitudes one race [Jews], cultivating none of the so-called athletic and heroic qualities . . . has held its irrepressible own."

9. Mark Twain, "Concerning the Jews," in Charles Neider, ed., *The Complete Essays of Mark Twain* (Garden City, NJ: Doubleday and Company, Inc., 1963), 240.

10. Mark Twain, "The Jew as Soldier," in Neider, 250.

11. Simon Wolf, *The American Jew as Patriot, Soldier and Citizen* (Philadelphia: Levytype Company, 1895), 10.

12. Roger Mitchell, "Recent Jewish Immigration to the United States," *Popular Science Monthly* (February 1903): 342. As cited in Robert Singerman, "The Jew as Racial Alien: The Genetic Component of American Anti-Semitism," in David A. Gerber, ed., *Anti-Semitism in American History* (Urbana: University of Illinois Press, 1986), 109.

13. Curt Reiss, "Introduction," in Ralph Nunberg, *The Fighting Jew* (New York: Creative Age Press, Inc., 1945), viii.

14. Mac Davis, *Jews Fight Too!* (New York: Hebrew Publishing Company, 1945), 13. Ellipses in original.

15. Rufus Learsi, *The Jew in Battle* (New York: American Zionist Youth Commission, 1944), 60, 63. On Jews and the military, across continents and in conjunction with Jewish ideas about fighting, beginning with biblical and rabbinical commentary, see Derek J. Pensler, *Jews and the Military: A History* (Princeton: Princeton University Press, 2013).

16. Paula E. Hyman, *Gender and Assimilation in Modern Jewish History: The Roles and Representation of Women* (Seattle: University of Washington Press, 1995), 134.

17. Sander L. Gilman, *Freud, Race, and Gender* (Princeton: Princeton University Press, 1993), 85. For a fascinating discussion of different views on Jewish circumcision, see especially chapter two (49–92), "The Construction of the Male Jew." Also essential reading, and influential on my work, is Sander Gilman, *The Jew's Body* (London: Routledge, 1991).

18. Gilman, *Freud, Race, and Gender*, 39.

19. Sigmund Freud, "Leonardo Da Vinci and a Memory of his Childhood," *The Complete Standard Edition of the Works of Sigmund Freud*. Vol. 11, trans. James Strachey et al. (London: Hogarth Press, 1957), 95–96 (n. 3).

20. Sigmund Freud, "Analysis of a Phobia in a Five-year-old Boy," *The Complete Standard Edition of the Works of Sigmund Freud*. Vol. 10, trans. James Strachey et al. (London: Hogarth Press, 1955), 36 (n. 1).

21. Ibid., 36.
22. Uris, "About 'Exodus,'" 128.
23. Leon Uris, *Mila 18*, 518.
24. Ibid., 15.
25. Ibid., 38, 34, 39.
26. Ibid., 15, 34.
27. Ibid., 34.
28. Ibid., 45–46.
29. Ibid., 506, 504.
30. Ibid., 493.
31. Ibid.
32. Ibid., 502.

33. The entire ZOB call to resistance can be found in Yitzhak Arad, Israel Gutman, and Abraham Margaliot, eds., *Documents on the Holocaust*, eighth ed. (Lincoln: University of Nebraska Press, 1999), 301–302. Uris, *Mila 18*, 518.

34. Arad, Gutman, and Margaliot, eds., "The Last Battle in the Great Tragedy," in *Documents on the Holocaust*, 320 (entire reprint on 319–320).

35. Uris, *Mila 18*, 539.

36. David Ben-Gurion as quoted in Israel Gutman, *Resistance: The Warsaw Ghetto Uprising* (Boston: Houghton Mifflin Company, 1994), 257. Ben-Gurion's remarks were made in February 1943, at a commemoration honoring the battle at Tel Hai. This statement was preceded by a nod toward the legacy of Tel Hai for the Warsaw Ghetto rebellion, quoted in further depth: "The death of the defenders of Tel Hai was not in vain. Six days ago news reached us that our comrades in Warsaw—the tiny remnant of Jews still there, decided to fight for their lives and organized small groups to rise up and defend themselves.... [the fighters in the Warsaw Ghetto] have learned the new lesson of death which the defenders of Tel Hai and Sedgera have bequeathed to us—the heroic death."

37. Letter from Leon Uris to Tim Seldes, November 13, 1959, Leon Uris papers, Harry Ransom Center, University of Texas at Austin, box 135, folder 7 (hereafter Uris papers).

38. *Mila 18*, final galley proof, Uris papers, galley files.

39. Letter from Leon Uris to William Uris, June 20, 1957, Uris papers, box 137, folder 8.

40. Letter from George (first name unclear) J. Jaffe to Leon Uris, July 5, 1961, Uris papers, box 139, folder 2.

41. "Mila 18," *Kirkus* (June 1, 1961): 370.

42. George Adelman, review of *Mila 18*, *Library Journal* (June 15, 1961): 2339. Uris had Israeli relatives that survived the camps, including an uncle who published more than one memoir about the Holocaust, although this fact was not known until later. See, for example, Eliezer Yerushalmi, *Pinkas Shavli: Yoman mi-geto Litai* (Jerusalem: Yad Vashem, 1950). In Hebrew.

43. Letter from Leon Uris to William Uris, June 15, 1962, Uris papers, box 137, folder 8.

44. Leon Uris, *Mila 18* (New York: Bantam Books, 1962).

45. Phoebe Adams, "Warsaw Ghetto," *Atlantic Monthly* (August 1961): 94.

46. Paul Breines, *Tough Jews: Political Fantasies and the Moral Dilemma of American Jewry* (New York: Basic Books, 1990), 175. A bibliography of "tough Jewish novels," as Breines terms them, can be found on 265–267. This subgenre peaked in the early 1980s. Daniel Boyarin offered a rejoinder to Brienes, Hyman, and other research on the New Jew. Examining written and visual texts, he demonstrates that pre-modern, traditional, and thereby marginalized Jews were offended by values surrounding the fighting Jew, and did not see themselves as weak, but rather as prizing a gentle and intellectual nature. He views later masculinization, instigated by the modern Jewish experience, as less traditionally "Jewish" than that of the more common "rabbinic," bookish male. See Daniel Boyarin, *Unheroic Conduct: The Rise of Heterosexuality and the Invention of the Jewish Man* (Berkeley: University of California Press, 1997).

47. Leon Uris, "The Most Heroic Story of Our Century," *Coronet* (November 1960): 173. Importantly, *Mila 18* was written before the Eichmann Trial, and thus it had no impact on Uris's narrative, nor did critics or fans make correlations between the book and Eichmann's prosecution.

48. Ibid., 174.

49. Ibid., 175, 177.

50. Leon Uris to William Uris, March 4, 1958, Uris papers, box 137, folder 8.

51. Leon Uris to William Uris, December 22, 1964, Uris papers, box 137, folder 10.

52. Leon Uris, "The Rising of the Warsaw Ghetto," 5, Uris papers, box 181, folder 7.

53. Leon Uris and Dimitrios Harissiadis, *Exodus Revisited* (Garden City, NY: Doubleday, 1960).

54. Ibid., 38–39.

55. Ibid., 40.

56. Ibid., 255.

57. Ibid.

58. Ibid., 257.

59. "World Jewish Congress Sends Cultural Delegation to Jews in Displaced Camps in Germany," *Jewish Telegraphic Agency* (December 28, 1945), accessed February 12, 2012, http://archive.jta.org/article/1945/12/28/2869174/world-jewish-congress-sends-cultural-delegation-to-jews-in-displaced-camps-in-germany.

60. "Jewish Labor Committee records, 1943–47," reel 32, frame 311. United States Holocaust Memorial Museum, RG 67.001M. Author's emphasis.

61. Ibid. Author's emphasis.

62. Ibid. Author's emphasis.

63. Ibid. Author's emphasis.

64. Barbara Kirshenblatt-Gimblett, "The Folk Culture of Jewish Immigrant Communities: Research Paradigms and Directions," in Moses Rischin, ed., *The Jews of North America* (Detroit: Wayne State University Press, 1987), 87.

65. Letter from Gerri Kalb to Leon Uris, September 28, 1961, Uris papers, box 139, folder 2.

66. Letter from an illegible signature to Leon Uris, October 31, 1961, Uris papers, box 139, folder 3.

Part III: Politics
MOBILIZING FOR THE FUTURE

Purim, Passover, and Pilgrims
SYMBOLS OF SURVIVAL AND SACRIFICE IN AMERICAN POSTWAR HOLOCAUST SURVIVOR NARRATIVES

Rachel Deblinger

ON NOVEMBER 15, 1945, the American Jewish Joint Distribution Committee (JDC) announced a supplies collection project that called on American Jews to help "our suffering brethren overseas."[1] The program, Supplies for Overseas Survivors, sought to collect clothing, shoes, medicine, canned food, toys, and other material goods to be sent directly to Jewish victims of Nazism in the Displaced Persons camps of Europe. It was advertised widely to American Jews and non-Jews as SOS. The name alone communicated a sense of urgency, and SOS publicity materials cast American Jews as the saviors of European Jewry, the crucial line of support that could save Jewish lives and preserve a Jewish future.

SOS was just one of many communal programs that directed American Jewish aid to survivors abroad, all of which appealed to donors by tying the fate of Jewish survivors to the heroic and generous actions of American Jews. The initial SOS appeal letter articulated this relationship, telling donors, "You can save Jewish lives and rebuild hope from the rubble of despair," as donations of new and used goods would allow a million and a quarter Jews to "start life again."[2] American Jews overwhelmingly responded to the call that they take responsibility for the survival of European Jewry. Between January 1946 and December 1949, SOS collected 26,000,000 pounds of relief goods, sending to Europe 14,000,000 pounds of food, 11,000,000 pounds of clothes (including 3,000,000 pounds of layette materials), more than 1,000,000 medical drug items, thousands of religious items, and over 170,000 toys—enough for each surviving Jewish child.[3]

The rhetoric that enabled this kind of philanthropic success defined European Jews, most of whom had survived some aspect of the Holocaust, as desperate but hopeful victims, dependent on financial and material aid from American Jews to rebuild their lives. At the same time, American Jews were represented as the necessary benefactors, protectors, and rescuers. Public expressions of this relationship linked American Jews with their European brethren through philanthropy and inspired a diverse American Jewish population to donate to programs like SOS. Stories about the surviving Jews of Europe and references to their ongoing suffering were thus collected and crafted for use in fundraising pamphlets, letters, posters, short films, campaign events, radio programs, and advertisements. As a result, the efforts of the organized American Jewish community to aid survivors abroad shaped an early American understanding of the Holocaust through the public rhetoric of campaign appeals. As will be seen, the relationship between the savior and the saved that defined these appeals was expressed through stories about survivors that focused on the loss and devastation that followed the war and reflected American postwar values rather than the unique experiences of Jews under Nazism.

The urgency of these appeals successfully inspired Jewish action, serving to challenge the idea that American Jews willfully ignored the Holocaust or remained silent in their pursuit of mainstream, suburban American lives.[4] Philanthropic projects like SOS enabled American Jews to respond to the Holocaust in ways that reflected their Americanness and—at the same time—a deep commitment to Judaism, Jewishness, and Jews around the world. Responding to Jewish destruction through American Jewish communal activity was, in fact, a continuation of the impulse that founded the JDC and other organizations during and after World War I.[5] After World War II, this work yielded an unprecedented philanthropic response that affirmed American Jewish knowledge of and deep concern for Jews who survived Nazi persecution.

Yet, the cultural ephemera of communal groups have been long overlooked as a source for understanding an initial American Jewish encounter with the Holocaust. As the Holocaust took on new resonance and wider cultural relevance in the 1960s and 70s, these efforts and the narratives that publicized them were largely forgotten. These same organizations moved on to the crises of the Cold War, and scholars turned their attention to projects of Holocaust remembrance. Nonetheless, the philanthropic response of American Jews in the postwar period serves as an early site of Holocaust representation that preserves a significant mode of knowledge dissemination in the wake of the war.

As such, this essay relies on the public materials of Jewish communal organizations to consider how American Jews first encountered Jewish Holocaust survivors and offers a close consideration of the kinds of narratives that inspired American Jews to act after the Holocaust. These sources reveal a range of postwar narratives, shaped by both Jewish and American interests, that reflect the overlapping identities of American Jews at the time and point to ways in which American Jewish communal organizations participated in broader postwar American discourse. Not only did Jewish organizations echo America's new position as the leader of the postwar world, but they picked up the rhetoric of "winning the peace" through humanitarian aid as an initial approach to the emerging Cold War. Narratives crafted for fundraising efforts, political advocacy campaigns, and volunteer projects blended these American tropes with Jewish ones. Survivors became Pilgrims and American Jews became the biblical Esther and the biblical Moses—one given refuge and the others acting as rescuers. Through these evocative and historically resonant narratives, Jewish groups, such as the JDC and United Jewish Appeal (UJA), intermingled American values and motifs with Jewish heroes and myths to render European stories about Nazism into stories about triumph and survival for American audiences.

This essay traces these symbols in postwar Jewish philanthropic campaigns as they were expressed through the stories of Purim, Passover, and Thanksgiving to understand how America and the myths Americans tell about themselves played a central role in an early understanding of the Holocaust. The public rhetoric of SOS serves as a jumping-off point for considering the relationship between American Jews and their European brethren in the context of postwar American abundance and consumerism. I then introduce the United Nations Clothing Collection (UNCC) drives of 1945 and '46 to juxtapose efforts of a broader American public to send needed material goods abroad. American Jews, alongside their non-Jewish neighbors, recognized philanthropy as a weapon in the postwar battle for peace and participated in these collection campaigns as a performance of patriotism. American Jews also participated in the annual campaigns of the UJA to respond to particularly Jewish concerns in the wake of the Holocaust, and this essay takes up the 1946 "Year of Survival" and 1947 "Year of Sacrifice" campaigns to explore these intersecting themes; only through American Jewish sacrifice—real sacrifice—could Jews around the world survive. Finally, I consider the transformation of Jewish survivors into American Pilgrims as a rhetorical tool used by advocacy organizations focused on reforming American Jewish immigration laws. Representing Displaced Persons as Delayed Pilgrims aligned Jewish immigration needs with a long American history and evoked the central myth of America as a site of haven for all in need.

Throughout, this essay reflects a deep concern with the narrative transformations that resulted from postwar efforts of American Jewish communal organizations to motivate action in response to the unprecedented suffering of Jews under Nazism. Recognizing such an immediate response to the Holocaust calls attention not only to the construction of early survivor representations, but also to the postwar modes of communal engagement that allowed American Jews to publicly perform their Jewishness alongside their Americanness. For American Jewish women, in particular, participation in clothing drives like SOS enabled meaningful commitment to Jewish life while adjusting to new suburban lives.

The organizations that collected, translated, and transmitted survivor narratives for American audiences in the aftermath of the war did so in order to provide necessary relief for Jewish survivors—relief that was not provided by American or international bodies. By depicting American Jews as the necessary saviors of Jewish lives, a Jewish future, and Judaism itself, the fundraising and collection campaigns of the JDC and the UJA constructed reciprocal stories about American Jews and European survivors. As a result, the narratives that informed American Jews about the plight of Jews abroad reflected the continued displacement and devastation of Jewish survivors while signaling their potential to become good Americans. These narratives also affirmed American Jews as leaders of the postwar Jewish world, a role they continued to accept throughout the postwar period by giving ever greater amounts of money to Jewish causes.

American Jewish Saviors: SOS, Women, and Postwar Consumerism

SOS employed all available media to appeal to its audience, recording radio spots, sending out printed letters, and sponsoring SOS days in cities across the country, all of which repeated the central idea that American Jewish donations of food, clothing, and home goods were lifesaving and sustaining for the Jews of Europe. As this 1947 brochure depicts (figure 1), the JDC took literally the idea that American Jews were the lifeline to survivors. In this central image, a rope encircles survivors eating and receiving new clothing, shoes, toys, and books, all materials supplied by SOS donations.[6] This appeal detailed the immediate needs of survivors, linking these urgent demands not only to American Jewish intervention, but also to the viability of a strong Jewish future. The caption here reflects this association between past destruction, present need, and future renewal: "In the ruined towns and cities of Europe, thousands . . . are bravely picking up the threads of life again. . . . But, in order to build for the future, Europe's Jews must have help in the present."

As this appeal demonstrates, American Jewish communal groups asserted that Jewish survival and a renewed Jewish future relied upon the participation of American Jews. Such appeals, however, painted generic portraits of survivors, reflecting postwar hunger, disease, and homelessness without detailing any experiences under Nazism. Survivor representations in philanthropic appeals of this kind successfully depicted a general story about the war and its aftermath, urging American Jewish action in response to the most pressing problems of the day rather than individual suffering. Narratives and images like those in this SOS brochure employed survivor representations not for memorial or historical purposes, but to draw public attention to the ongoing homelessness of Jewish orphans, to hunger and disease in DP camps, and to the continued displacement of Jews in Europe. These depictions were meant to tug at the heartstrings of donors and inspire financial generosity, not to document and commemorate Jewish persecution.

At the same time, appeals for postwar Jewish aid told dynamic stories about American Jewry, depicting acts of generosity as active forms of postwar response. Ruth Litin, the SOS chair of the National Federation of

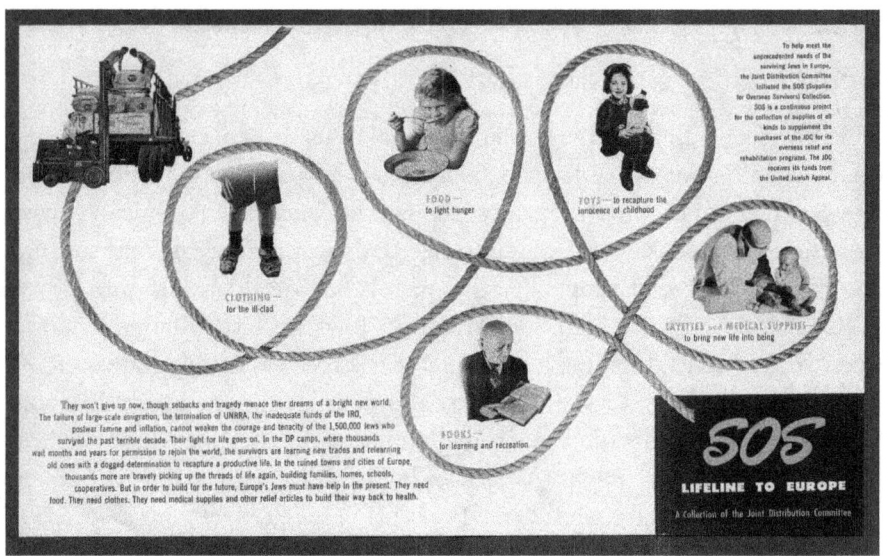

Figure 1. 1947 JDC brochure.

Temple Sisterhoods, recognized a particular heroism in this participation by painting American Jewish women as modern-day Esthers in honor of Purim.[7] She wrote, "If there is any festival that glorifies the woman in Israel, it is Purim. We recall with pride, Esther, the Queen, the savior of her people. Today, with our SOS campaign . . . we are enacting a similar role."[8] Litin may have overestimated the role Americans played in saving the Jewish people through clothing and food collection, but she did so within the scale of other SOS public statements. In brochures and public speeches, SOS leaders, both men and women, congratulated American Jews for "the lives you saved . . . the hope you gave."[9] Such expressions of emotional support were woven into the aid sent through SOS; the goods collected by individuals could, as Blanche Gilman, the first SOS chairman told volunteers, "provide food for only a week" but restore hope and faith "for a much longer time."[10]

To fulfill these roles, American Jewish women were called upon to clean out their closets and form knitting circles. The gendered nature of this volunteerism reflected the initiative of American Jewish women to help survivors in the postwar period in whatever ways they could. SOS was originally founded by a diverse coalition of women's groups determined to send food, clothing, knitted items, and other necessities to survivors.[11] When JDC took over SOS, they increased the scope of collection by establishing a gifts-in-kind campaign that engaged manufacturing and grocery industry leaders. This campaign eventually accounted for fifteen percent of all goods sent abroad through SOS, but women remained central to the leadership and community of volunteers that made the project successful.[12]

This kind of feminized participation in the postwar relief effort, and participation in organizations such as the National Council of Jewish Women, Hadassah, Organization for Relief through Training (ORT), and Pioneer Women more broadly, allowed Jewish women in the postwar period to build social networks within their new suburban surroundings. As Hasia Diner notes, these organizations also served as political associations, providing American Jewish women with access to and a venue for understanding local, national, and international politics.[13] Like their non-Jewish neighbors, American Jewish women relied on voluntary associations, particularly all-female associations, to engage in the pressing movements of the day.[14] In the immediate aftermath of the war, affiliation with projects like SOS allowed American Jewish women to respond to particularly Jewish concerns within the gendered spaces of the suburbs; even as expectations about women's domestic roles returned to prewar conservatism, philanthropy remained open to them for engagement in the public sphere. The stereotype of postwar suburban domestic life, in which a housewife stayed home "to rear children, clean house, and bake cookies" obscures the active roles women played in political life through participation in communal groups.[15]

Building on the work started by Jewish women's groups in 1945, SOS continued to appeal to American Jewish women through their traditional gendered roles as consumers and homemakers. Religious and secular, members of Zionist and non-Zionist groups, Jewish women across the American Jewish landscape sought to help (and were called upon to help) Jews in Europe through traditional activities—namely making, purchasing, and collecting household goods like food and clothes. Rendering humanitarian aid through consumerist terms in this way reflected a broader trend in American Jewish philanthropy. According to Jeffrey Shandler, Jewish consumerism in the early twentieth century took on philanthropic possibilities when buying Jewish products became a way to support the *Yishuv*, and Jewish women in particular invested in Zionism by buying wine, almonds, and cigarettes.[16]

This kind of consumerism—understood as an expression of loyalty—was also embedded in a celebration of postwar American prosperity. Consumption was promoted as a way to enhance economic recovery so that more Americans could pursue their own American dream. Lisbeth Cohen suggests that American consumerism in the postwar period took on both economic and political meaning as Americans across the country believed that mass consumption promised a more equitable political system. In the wake of the war, she asserts, "citizens had a patriotic responsibility to consume."[17] For American women, in particular, shopping became a way of affirming and expressing an American way of life.[18] These values were reflected in the campaign materials of SOS that urged American women to donate old items to make room for new goods as a means of saving Jewish lives in Europe.

Winning the Peace: Philanthropy as a Cold War Weapon

That the Jews of America were particularly responsible for this work was, perhaps, best articulated by Frieda Schiff Warburg, who said of the Jewish survivors, "Their lives depend upon the help that can come only from America."[19] Warburg's idea that Americans provided the only hope for Europe's Jews echoed mainstream postwar American sentiments. As early as December 1945, this idea found popular expression in a *Saturday Evening Post* article, titled "World Relief is America's Job," which explained that America was "the only country still capable of producing in quantity what the world needs" and, therefore, must act as "Santa Claus" and "Clara Barton" at once—sending material goods, medicine, and good cheer.[20]

The depiction of Americans as the saviors of the postwar world was explicit in political discourse of the time as well, particularly in recognizing the fight for peace that followed the end of the war. In August 1945, President Truman asserted that American aid abroad was the only way to secure a lasting peace: "Victory in a great war is something that must be won and kept won. It can be lost after you have won it—if you are careless or negligent or indifferent.... If we let Europe go cold and hungry, we may lose some of the foundation of order on which the hope for world peace must rest."[21] In pursuit of securing peace, Truman supported aid projects that sent American goods around the world and, with those goods, exported American optimism and friendship.

Philanthropy thus became an important expression of American patriotism, and efforts like SOS allowed American Jews to display their American loyalty and Jewishness at the same time. In fact, American Jews performed this kind of humanitarian patriotism by participating not only in SOS, but also in the United National Clothing Collection (UNCC) campaigns. The United Nations Relief and Rehabilitation Administration (UNNRA) sponsored the first UNCC in April 1944, mobilizing 18,000 communities across the country to collect over 150,0000,000 pounds of clothing.[22] This effort was so successful that another nation-wide campaign was launched at the end of the war and the Victory Clothing Collection amassed nearly a hundred million pieces of clothing in January 1946. In both instances, JDC organized the efforts of Jewish organizations for UNCC, coordinating collection by the Council of Jewish Federations and Welfare Funds, Women's American ORT, B'nai B'rith, and the National Council of Jewish Women, among others.[23]

Like SOS, the UNCC urged Americans to donate used clothes, canned foods, and other home goods in order to live up to their potential as saviors. The ubiquitous slogan of both the UNCC and the Victory Clothing Collection asked, "What can *you* spare that they can wear?" Just as JDC outreach sought to make American Jewish donors feel like only they could save Jews abroad, publicity materials for the nationwide clothing drives crafted a reciprocal relationship between Americans and "war victims" around the world. Only if Americans gave generously could the rest of the world receive the necessary goods to rebuild their lives after the devastation of war.

Yet, the publicity campaigns for UNCC did little to convey to American donors the personal experiences of these devastated war victims. Like the generic images of Jewish survivors depicted in the SOS Lifeline brochure, victims of wartime destruction were undefined in UNCC public appeals.

This is particularly true for images of Jewish Holocaust survivors. A *Time* magazine article about the Victory Campaign from January 14, 1946 serves as an example. The article featured an image of concentration camp survivors in their striped prison uniforms behind barbed wire, and the caption read, "Memo to the US: With a feeling that some Americans had already begun to forget the war, the committee in charge of the Victory Clothing Collection last week sent out this picture of prisoners liberated from a German Concentration camp at Ebensee, in the Austrian Tirol. To help clothe them and 300 million other war starvelings, the Victory Collection needs 10,000,000 garments, plus shoes and bedding."[24] Such public appeals for participation and volunteerism conveyed the urgency of clothing collection to American audiences without communicating any Jewish particularity or specificity about life in concentration camps. Rather, images of destitute and helpless victims signaled the larger postwar crisis and reinforced the need for Americans to act as saviors.

These kinds of public appeals also projected humanitarian aid as central to the American way of life. Wendy Wall has argued that by celebrating diversity and highlighting examples of American consensus, efforts to win the peace through humanitarian aid depicted a postwar American ideal that benefited American society, communities, and individual families.[25] At the same time, Stephen Ross Porter argues, humanitarian projects, particularly those related to refugees and relief (like the UNCC and the Victory Clothing Collection), served as "outward projection[s] of American authority onto a global arena."[26] These volunteer efforts, then, enacted soft diplomacy in the early stages of the Cold War—sending friendship through clothing around the world—while reinforcing domestic harmony.

The public rhetoric of these projects reflected the potential of Americans to act as saviors and secure the peace through small acts: Americans placed friendly notes into the pockets of donated clothes for the Victory Clothing Collection, knitted layettes for newborn babies in Displaced Persons camps, and canned fresh fruit and vegetables to be sent around the world.[27] Through these acts, Americans understood their voluntary efforts to be both a public display of patriotism and an extension of the war effort.[28] As an August 1945 UNCC press release stated, "Now that Europe's guns have cooled, food must continue the fight for freedom if starving millions are to survive and justify the price paid in freedom's name."[29] In this way, Americans became the saviors not only of war-torn victims, but of freedom around the globe.

Ensuring a Jewish Future: The Year of Survival and the Year of Sacrifice

SOS offered a particularly Jewish version of securing peace abroad, and Blanche Gilman voiced the Jewish element of SOS work, saying, "We could not restore to Europe's Jews the six million fathers and mothers, brothers and sisters slain by the Nazis. But we can be thankful that we could and did help them with the supplies they needed to begin life again."[30] Here, Gilman recognized the limitation of American intervention in the experience of Jewish survivors. She did not make American Jews into the Esthers of the Holocaust. Rather, she echoed President Truman in suggesting that material donations from American Jews could send hope to desperate victims and support rehabilitation.

Yet, the relationship between American and European Jews was essentially different than between Americans and war victims around the world. SOS acted not just to secure peace through comfort and stability, but to secure a Jewish future by prompting Jews to act for their "brethren overseas." As such, "overseas survivors" were often described as "our survivors." The use of "our" as the central pronoun conveyed a common identity that was woven into all aspects of SOS work. At the January 1948 SOS annual dinner, Gilman drew out this idea. Her emotional speech evoked "our displaced persons," "our second remnant," "our people," "our 40,000 souls," and "our overseas survivors."[31] Her speech catalogued just some of the nomenclature used about survivors at this period and underscored how American Jews understood their responsibility to aid Jews abroad.

Of course, for many American Jews, the use of personal pronouns reflected real family relationships. So the idea of "our survivors" was, for American Jewry, both a personal and a collective idea, which was used in communal materials outside the SOS context, notably in the title of Adele Levy's 1946 UJA report, "Our Child Survivors."[32] Levy, the daughter of famed philanthropist Julius Rosenwald, was a founder of UJA, and she became the first chairwoman for its National Women's Division. In this capacity, Levy toured the orphanages of postwar Europe and documented the work of UJA with child survivors. Her report offers another way to understand how American Jews conceived of themselves as the saviors of European Jews.

In addition to saving Jewish lives, Levy asserted that American Jews were also responsible for the preservation of a Jewish future. She wrote, "If we save the children, we save the Jewish people for generations to come. If we fail to help adequately we may be faced with the tragic prospect of the disappearance of the Jews of Europe."[33] With this dramatic declaration, Levy suggested that the future of the Jewish people rested with American Jewish action—only they could "adequately" prevent further destruction and the disappearance of European Jewry. By pointing to the potential of American Jews to make a difference in the lives of Europe's Jews, Levy also contended that American Jews had the power to "finish Hitler's work" in destroying the rest of European Jewry. As such, Levy condemned American Jewry for any inaction in the postwar period (and perhaps, too, during the war) and called on them to "make sacrifices to assure [survivors] that they will never again be subjected to the horror and sorrows of the past decade."[34] This sacrifice, her report insisted, could only be demonstrated through giving to the $100,000,000 1946 UJA campaign.

Levy thus linked the survival of Jewish lives and the future of the Jewish people to the financial generosity of American Jews. Other organizations, such as the Orthodox Rabbinical organization Vaad Hatzala, additionally asserted that American Jews were responsible for saving Judaism itself.[35] The anxieties of America's organized Orthodox Jews highlighted the blow to religious Judaism in the wake of the Holocaust and again offered American Jewish philanthropy as the answer. American Jews could save more than the Jewish people and the Jewish future: they could save Judaism by supporting Vaad Hatzala, the only organization that funded kosher kitchens, Jewish education, and yeshivot in postwar Europe.

Recognizing the spectrum of responsibilities placed on the shoulders of American Jews in the postwar period points to the huge increase in Jewish fundraising—not just in the name of Zionism as has often been asserted, but to all the constituent groups of the United Jewish Appeal that supported Jewish life in Palestine, Europe, America, and around the world.[36] The call for American Jewish aid, as articulated in the examples laid out thus far, was part of an unprecedented response of American Jews to the postwar reality of world Jewry. In the year 1946 alone, the UJA succeeded in raising the "ridiculous" sum of $100,000,000 and raised more than $150,000,000 in 1948.[37] These amounts reflect a dramatic increase over Jewish fundraising during the war, when UJA raised nearly $100,000,000 between 1939 and 1945.[38] In the wake of the war, UJA totals soared, amounting to over $750,000,000 between 1945 and December 1952.[39] For another comparison, the Red Cross, an organization with over 18 million members in the 1940s, also set a fundraising goal of $100,000,000 in 1946.[40]

The campaigns of the UJA during this period appealed to the Jews of America by insisting upon the same kind of sacrifice articulated by Levy. As the 1946 UJA Speaker's Manual explained, "Any failure on our part to provide the help needed will condemn the survivors to the fate of the 6,000,000 who perished in the death camps and gas chambers."[41] Again, the ongoing survival of Jews in Europe became the responsibility of American Jews, as the life or death immediacy of wartime extended into the postwar era. To further aid volunteers in drawing connections between fundraising and Jewish survival, the manual for the "Year of Survival" campaign scripted the following key phrases: "The remnants have been saved from extermination. They have not yet been saved from hunger, disease, homelessness and suffering. . . . The $100,000,000 UJA Campaign is our strongest weapon in the battle for survival." The description of survivors as "remnants"—hungry, diseased, and suffering—offers a sense of how liberation failed to alleviate the precarious existence of European Jews, and echoes Truman's call to fight for peace through donations of food and clothing.

This appeal also echoed Levy's charge of complicity against American Jews: if they did not act in the postwar period, they would be responsible for the death of the survivors. The idea that American Jews held the power of life and death for survivors after the war resonated throughout American Jewish philanthropic appeals and worked to evoke the kind of guilt that Yehuda Bauer has identified as the root of postwar philanthropic activity.[42] While Bauer notes that "more accurate, and frightening" information and better developed fundraising techniques also contributed to the increased postwar fundraising totals, he pointedly remarks, "suddenly, American Jewry found it had the money which, had it been found in 1936–1942 might have saved many, many lives."[43] Organizations across the political and religious spectrum appealed to Jews by asserting that failure to act after the war would, indeed, recommit the crimes of Nazism. However, these organizations were armed with more than just guilt; as Bauer argues, increased access to information supported a growth in fundraising, and organizations employed stories about Jewish loss and survival in their appeals to inspire and motivate.

These stories and the impact of coming face-to-face with the survivors of European Jewry played a significant role in activating postwar Jewish philanthropy. Additionally, such postwar activity reflected the larger cultural scene, and organizational rhetoric made this connection clear. Postwar philanthropy that aided war victims around the world was patriotic, pervasive, and, significantly, optimistic. Integrating Jewish stories with American themes strengthened such organizational appeals and provided a framework for narratives that highlighted hope and freedom.

A radio appeal by actor Paul Muni gave voice to how sacrifice in support of Jewish survivors was presented as an American ideal. In the 1948 radio drama *Displaced*, Muni played Kurt Maier, a survivor of Auschwitz, Ohrdruf, Sachsenhausen, and Buchenwald, and a recent new American.[44] At the end of the broadcast, Muni spoke directly to the listening audience as himself, saying of the survivors overseas, "Whether they live to breathe the air of freedom and health and happiness or sink into despair and death is for *us* to decide. The *choice* is *ours*."[45] As a means of provoking action among the American audience, Muni invoked the New Testament story of the good Samaritan who stops to help a fallen stranger, and ended by claiming, "it is for us to choose, remembering for that choice, we stand accountable to our conscience and to God."[46] Muni's appeal reiterates the idea that Americans (here, he spoke to all Americans, not just American Jews) were individually responsible for the lives and deaths of Jewish survivors and further suggests that Americans were forced to choose between generosity and complicity.

The 1946 UJA-produced film *Battle for Survival* similarly asserted the relationship between the survival of European Jews and the sacrifice of

American Jews. The film was narrated by Orson Welles and depicted the Jewish DPs of Europe as ragged and destitute, evoking the trope of the Wandering Jew as it opened on barefoot Jews marching aimlessly down a dusty road. Towards the end of the film, Welles narrates, "Once, Hitler had the decision of life or death. Now, that decision is ours."[47] American Jews were prompted to act not in response to the atrocities of Nazism, but because the decision of life and death was now in their hands. In this way, *Battle for Survival* presented its titular battle; the DPs survived liberation but continued to struggle, and only American donations and generosity could ultimately save them.

The urgency around fundraising created through the film reached a crescendo in the final scene, filmed at the annual UJA meeting in Atlantic City. Adele Levy, the evening's only female speaker, shamed the assembled leaders and the film audience for not sacrificing enough for the cause of Jewish survivors. Levy passionately delivered the core of her speech to resounding applause:

> Unless you care enough, and unless I care enough, we cannot succeed in this great undertaking ... not one of us, including myself has ever made one real sacrifice for this cause. Some of us have felt very good. Some of us have felt that we have given generously.... Has one of us sacrificed something that we really wanted in a material sense? For these are suffering, bleeding, starving persecuted people. And I think the answer is no.[48]

Following this call to action, Welles ends the film by asking, "Can we spare it?" With this ending, the film explicitly appealed for American Jewish donations by demanding a "real sacrifice" for the sake of Europe's surviving Jews.

Levy's accusation that American Jews had not sacrificed materially for the cause speaks not only to the presence of postwar guilt, but also to the imagined ideal of sacrifice that permeated American society during the war.[49] Americans on the home front viewed themselves as a crucial part of the war effort—sacrificing at home so that the "American way of life" could be secured around the world.[50] In the subsequent cultural memory of World War II, this ideal has loomed even larger: central to the notion of the Greatest Generation is the sacrifice made by soldiers abroad and their families at home.[51] According to Mark Leff, the notion of sacrifice "decisively shaped the discourse of wartime politics" even if most Americans had not made any "real sacrifices."[52] He argues, "In common parlance, sacrifice did not require suffering a terrible loss. It instead comprehended a range of activities—running the gamut from donating waste paper to donating lives."[53] Put more bluntly, expressions of sacrifice, more often than not, involved small gestures that limited growth rather than the kinds of sacrifices (through destruction, loss, and devastation) experienced by victims of World War II.

The call for "real sacrifice" by Levy and the UJA illustrates Leff's claim and suggests that the efforts made during the war by American Jews appeared superficial as news of the Holocaust reached American Jewish homes. The postwar campaigns demanded more significant action, and Jews around the world heeded this call. *Battle for Survival* aired in Canada with an additional appeal to Canadian Jewry.[54] Samuel Bronfman, leader of the United Jewish Relief Agencies of Canada, sat stiffly behind a desk, looked straight at the camera and read:

> We were spared the horrors of war and the pictures we have seen must rend the heart of every thinking and feeling Jew in this country. They bring within our vision the plight of our wandering people, still wandering the face of Europe, still homeless. Those impoverished children's bodies little more than living skeletons ... cry out to us for help. Seeing is understanding, understanding is feeling. And to feel is to open our hearts and purses.[55]

In this way, Bronfman called attention to the images and stories of Jewish survivors that were essential for inspiring postwar aid. Such images juxtaposed the sacrifice of European Jews with that of Jews in Canada, who, like American Jews, lived out the war far from the reach of Hitler. Given this distance, philanthropic sacrifice was their only possible response, and the portrayal of homeless "skeletons" reiterated the importance of American (and Canadian) Jews in acting as heroes through financial donations.

In 1947, the UJA campaign picked up this call for "real sacrifice" and turned its attention from the survivors to the American donors during the

"Year of Sacrifice." This shift in focus reflects the central idea of this paper: that the American Jewish response to the Holocaust through philanthropic action crafted stories about survivors that reflected a new understanding of American Jewry. A campaign booklet for the 1947 welfare campaign in Los Angeles shows that the idea of sacrifice refracted the story of survivors through American action by declaring, "The years between 1933 and 1946 were years which witnessed the Jews overseas making sacrifice after sacrifice—they lost their homes, their hopes, their lives. Now 1947 has come—<u>our</u> year for sacrifice."[56] UJA national chairman Henry Morgenthau, Jr. reiterated the need for sacrifice and more explicitly expressed the identification American Jews should have with their European "brethren" when he wrote, "You and I—we cannot rest, we cannot enjoy the good things of life as long as we know that our brethren are wandering across the face of Europe, homeless and without permanent roots."[57] In this way, Morgenthau tied together the futures of American and European Jews, arguing that the good fortune and postwar prosperity of American Jews could help alleviate the suffering of the surviving Jews of Europe.

Even after the founding of the State of Israel, the narratives of Holocaust survivors were employed to motivate American Jews to action and served to unify fundraising efforts and philanthropic projects of a diverse American Jewish population.[58] The 1948 UJA campaign, the "Year of Destiny," reflected the new reality of the postwar Jewish world. For the first time, UJA directed more funds to Zionist interests than other projects, as the story of world Jewry turned to the creation of the State of Israel.[59] In this context, American Jews more overtly saw their philanthropic actions as heroic, and the relationship between survivors and American Jews continued to be defined in terms of the savior and the saved.

Even after this turn in international events, Jewish survivors remained central to UJA fundraising appeals. The 1948 JDC fundraising film serves as an example: *The Future Can Be Theirs* declared that survivors were "still alive *because* the JDC was there." The final scene of the film shows one family at a table, and then the camera pans out to reveal a long table in a room filled with long tables, with hundreds of people gathered for a Passover Seder. Invoking the story of Passover to depict the journey of Europe's surviving Jews during and after the Holocaust, the narrator declares, "We have helped bring them out of bondage. We have helped deliver them from death. We have promised them a future. Now we must help them still so that the future can be theirs."⁶⁰ As the film lingers on the DP Seder, the final line announces, "The story is not yet ended because the end is up to us." Just as the National Council for Jewish Women declared that American Jewish women acted like Esther by participating in SOS, JDC suggested that through support for UJA, American Jews also acted as Moses, bringing their fellow Jews out of bondage.

Delayed Pilgrims and Postwar Immigration Advocacy

Of course, the future of Jewish survivors could not only be supported through relief abroad. Securing a Jewish future meant securing emigration avenues for the surviving Jews of Europe, a political goal that determined Zionist and domestic advocacy campaigns. American organizations arguing for more lenient immigration policies, including groups like the United Service for New Americans (USNA) and the Citizens Committee for Displaced Persons (CCDP), employed American motifs of Thanksgiving to persuade others that America should live up to its history as a haven for the oppressed. These groups commonly referred to Displaced Persons as "Delayed Pilgrims," evoking the history of America's founding myth to advocate on behalf of Jewish and non-Jewish postwar refugees.

On November 27, 1947, the USNA aired a radio broadcast of a special Thanksgiving dinner event, which featured speeches by Jewish leaders, political figures, and New Americans (a common term for recently arrived Holocaust survivors). The broadcast aired on Thanksgiving Day as the *Delayed Pilgrims Dinner*.⁶¹ As this title indicates, the USNA aligned the immigration of Jewish survivors with the arrival of the pilgrims, who sought freedom from religious persecution. A series of well-known speakers confirmed this rhetorical connection at the event. Actor Raymond Massey, whose ancestors landed at Salem, addressed the collected new immigrants as "fellow pilgrims," and New York City Mayor William O'Dwyer, who served as the Director of the War Refugee Board in 1945, said, "I greet those who so recently arrived from the Displaced Persons Centers of Europe . . . to start new lives in America . . . a country which itself started as a refuge for those who needed shelter."⁶²

Jonathan Sarna has asserted that Thanksgiving tropes were commonly adapted for Jewish purposes throughout American Jewish history.[63] In fact, he argues that American Jews regularly integrated a range of American themes into Jewish stories as part of both conscious and subconscious efforts to show that American and Jewish values were not only compatible, but mutually enhancing. For organizations concerned with Jewish immigration, Thanksgiving took on particularly political dimensions in the postwar period as the extent of DP administration and possible quota reform were debated in Congress. By referring to the Jewish DPs as Delayed Pilgrims, Jewish and other immigration advocacy groups called attention to those still in need of saving and appealed to America's historical imperative to act.

The survivor voices in *Delayed Pilgrims Dinner* also integrated America into their stories of the Holocaust, embracing the idea of Thanksgiving by expressing gratitude for America's freedoms and the potential for prosperity. Such stories affirmed the work of Jewish organizations in the postwar period and upheld America's own perception of itself as a site of promise. In the broadcast, Mr. Israel Burkenwald, a recent immigrant learning English at night school to feel "more American," was invited to address the crowd and the listening audience. With a noticeable accent Mr. Burkenwald said, "I have many reasons to be thankful on this Thanksgiving. I was only fourteen when I was taken to Auschwitz. After years of forced labor, you can understand what it means for me to have a home, a job, a country that I can call my very own."[64]

By juxtaposing the loss and oppression of Nazi Europe with the freedom and possibility of America, the *Delayed Pilgrims Dinner* exemplified how American motifs were integrated into early Holocaust representations, particularly how the trope of the Pilgrim was used to tell survivor accounts. Other programs similarly celebrated this association: an episode of *The Eternal Light* that aired on November 23, 1947, the Sunday before Thanksgiving, titled "The Late Comers," told the history of immigration to America, beginning with the Pilgrims and ending with the DPs after World War II. *The Arrival of Delayed Pilgrims* chronicled the debates over the DP Act in 1948.[65] American Jewish communal organizations sponsoring these broadcasts relied on the rhetoric of freedom and the symbolism of Thanksgiving to appeal to non-Jewish American audiences as a way of building emotional connections and to argue that the European Jewish survivors would make successful Americans. Just as SOS called on American Jews to serve as the lifeline to their brethren overseas, and UJA demanded a greater sacrifice of Jewish donors, organizations appealing for immigration reform employed motifs of Thanksgiving to inspire action.

This political device allowed organizations like the USNA and the CCDP to advocate for suspended immigration quotas and temporary legislation that would allow more displaced persons to legally enter the United States. The Citizens Committee, founded in 1946 by the American Jewish Committee and the American Council for Judaism, contended that America had now to take on a larger share of the world's problems, declaring, "After the nightmare of Nazism and Fascism, after the holocaust of World War II, we owe it to ourselves and to the world to be the guardians of freedom and peace. We owe it to ourselves and to the world to take action in solving problems that threaten the peace. The leading problem today is that of the displaced persons!"[66] As this demand makes clear, the use of American values, particularly the recurring ideals of freedom and peace, were used to tell stories about the Holocaust that made the crimes of Nazism apparent to American audiences and that asserted the responsibility of Jewish Americans and all Americans to participate in the postwar fight for peace.

Conclusion

The discursive transformation of Holocaust survivors into Pilgrims enabled Jewish organizations to cast European Jews as good Americans and to heighten the emotional urgency for postwar aid. By employing this essential American myth, Jewish communal groups rendered the tragedy of the Holocaust as a story of freedom and possibility. At the same time, Jewish narratives that imagined American Jewish women as the biblical Esther and donors as the biblical Moses depicted American Jews as good Jews. These two narratives reinforced each other: only through the heroic philanthropic actions of American Jews could European Jews survive, and only by bringing the survivors to the U.S. could America live up to its historical legacy. In the public narratives that Jewish communal organizations told about themselves, then, both the savior and the saved upheld the American ideals that defined the postwar period.

In the decades since, the use of American ideals and themes to tell stories about the Holocaust has similarly conveyed an emotional resonance to American audiences. In the midst of the booming Holocaust culture of the 1990s, Michael Berenbaum affirmed that Jewish organizations reshaped stories of the Holocaust "to participate in the fundamental tale of pluralism, tolerance, democracy, and human rights that America tells about itself."[67] This process of Americanization, Berenbaum argues, adds value to our understanding of the Holocaust as we make sense of the Jewish persecution under Nazism in relation to contemporary American concerns. The integration of American values and motifs into early narratives about the Holocaust thus shaped initial representations of survivors according to the ideals and expectations of postwar American audiences.

This is true both for Jewish audiences and for a broader, more diverse American audience, and suggests that Berenbaum's assertions about the Americanization of the Holocaust in the 1990s started much earlier. Organizations in the second half of the 1940s hoped to influence contemporary political debate around immigration as a way to aid the DPs (both Jewish and non-Jewish) who waited for relief in the DP camps of Europe. By making DPs part of the long history of American immigration and declaring DPs to be future American citizens, these groups worked to sway Americans fearful of immigrants. As such, the telling of Holocaust stories through American motifs both defined an American discourse about the Holocaust and reaffirmed America's self-understanding as a site of refuge, even as American immigration policy limited possibilities for postwar immigration.

The projects of American Jewish communal organizations that tied the sacrifices of American Jews to the survival of their European brethren similarly drew on traditional Jewish tropes, evoking Esther and Moses to define American Jews as the saviors of the postwar Jewish world, responsible for Jewish lives around the globe. This kind of self-representation reflected the wider American rhetoric of the postwar period, but was specifically connected to the representation of Holocaust survivors and the Jewish experience under and after Nazism. Through the publicity of these programs and the appeals of national fundraising efforts, American Jews promoted the idea that they were responsible for the fate of the Jews in Europe and around the world and came to understand themselves as bearers of hope for the Jewish future.

Notes

1. Preliminary Announcement Letter, November 15, 1945, AR 45/54 File 1268, American Jewish Joint Distribution Committee Archives, New York (JDC).
2. Ibid.
3. "Three Years of Achievement," SOS Bulletin 8:1, April 1949, AR 45/54, File 1345, JDC Archives. "SOS Collected over 26,300,000 Pounds of Relief Supplies During Past Three Years," April 11, 1949, Jewish Telegraphic Agency online archive, http://archive.jta.org/article/1949/04/11/3018175/sos-collected-over-26300-pounds-of-relief-supplies-during-past-three-years.
4. Peter Novick, *The Holocaust in American Life* (Boston: Houghton Mifflin, 1999), especially Chapter 6: "Not in the Best Interests of Jewry," 103–23.
5. Yehuda Bauer, *My Brother's Keeper; a History of the American Jewish Joint Distribution Committee, 1929–1939*, 1st ed. (Philadelphia: Jewish Publication Society of America, 1974).
6. "They need these things to live!" Brochure, Item ID 646520, November 28, 1947, NY AR194554/3/5/9/1345, SOS Publicity Printed Materials, 1947–1949, JDC.
7. References to Esther were common in philanthropic efforts organized and conducted by women. As Melissa Klapper writes, "The reference to the biblical book of Esther, one of the few named for a woman, was not lost on an audience of Jewish women who believed that striving for peace was their heritage of old." Melissa R. Klapper, *Ballots, Babies, and Banners of Peace: American Jewish Women's Activism, 1890–1940* (New York: New York University Press, 2012), 123.
8. Letter from Ruth Litin, February 10, 1948, National Federation of Temple Sisterhoods (Women of Reform Judaism), MS 73, Box F-5, Monthly Folders, 1948, Circular File 1, American Jewish Archives (AJA).
9. "Three Years of Achievement," SOS Bulletin 8:1, April 1949, AR 45/54, File 1345, JDC.
10. Speech by Mrs. Isaac Gilman given at April 1949 luncheon in honor of SOS, 45/54 # 1330 [45/64 # 4369] Subjects: Relief Supplies: S.O.S., 1949, JDC.
11. JDC cites eight initial women's groups that led the charge, including Hadassah, the Women's Zionist Organization of America; the Council of Jewish Federations and Welfare Funds; Mizrachi Women's Organization of America; Women's Division of the Union of Orthodox Jewish Congregation of America; National Women's League of the United Synagogue of America; National Federation of Temple Sisterhoods; National Council of Jewish Women; National Jewish Welfare Board; Federation of Jewish Women's Organizations; Women's Supreme Council of B'nai B'rith; and the Ladies Auxiliary, Jewish War Veterans of the United States. These groups represented a range of political and religious affiliations: Hadassah was the largest Zionist organization in the country while National Council for Jewish Women remained politically neutral during this period. Religiously, Orthodox women were members of both the Mizrachi Women's Organization of American and the Orthodox Jewish Congregations Women's Division. NCJW, meanwhile, was comprised of mostly Reform Jewish women. "JDC Calls for contributions from National Groups," Press release, November 25, 1945, 45/54, #1268, JDC.
12. Initial Letter to Trade and Industry, SOS Manual, September 1948, 45/54, #1344, JDC Archives; Editorial by Fred A. Stern, July 23, 1948, 45/54, #1344, JDC.
13. Hasia R Diner, *The Jews of the United States, 1654 to 2000* (Berkeley: University of California Press, 2004), 302.

14. Kathleen D. McCarthy, "Parallel Power Structures: Women and the Voluntary Space," in *Lady Bountiful Revisited: Women, Philanthropy, and Power* (New Brunswick: Rutgers University Press, 1990).

15. Joanne Jay Meyerowitz, *Not June Cleaver: Women and Gender in Postwar America, 1945–1960* (Temple University Press, 1994), 3.

16. Jeffrey Shandler, "*Di Toyre fun Skhoyre*, or, I Shop therefore I am: The Consumer Cultures of American Jews," in *Longing, Belonging, and the Making of Jewish Consumer Culture*, ed. Gideon Reuveni and Nils H. Roemer (Leiden: Brill, 2010), 183–200, 188–89.

17. Lizabeth Cohen, *A Consumers' Republic: The Politics of Mass Consumption in Postwar America* (New York: Knopf: Distributed by Random House, 2003), 108.

18. For example, *Bride Magazine*'s handbook for newlyweds instructed newly married brides to buy American brands because "what you buy and how you buy it is very vital in your new life—and to our whole American way of living." Brett Harvey, *The Fifties: A Women's Oral History* (New York, NY: HarperCollins Publishers, 1993), 110.

19. "More than 3,500,000 pounds of contributed relief supplies shipped overseas by JDC's SOS Collection," Press Release, November 8, 1946, JDC International Offices Collection, IS 4/2, United States Holocaust Memorial Museum Archives (USHMM).

20. "World Relief is America's Job," *Saturday Evening Post*, December 22, 1945. Found in Scrapbook, Volume 2, Part 4, Collection of Clippings and other miscellaneous material on the United National Clothing Collection, 1945–46 (UNCC), Library of Congress (LOC).

21. Radio Report on the Potsdam Conference, President Truman, August 9, 1945, Truman Library Public Papers, accessed at www.trumanlibrary.org/publicpapers/index.php?pid =104&st=&st1.

22. Announcement from Dan West, June 19, 1945, Box 1, Folder: Correspondence, Collection of Coordinating Committee of National Jewish Organizations for the United National Clothing Collection for War Relief (CC-UNCC), American Jewish Historical Society (AJHS). "News for Chairmen," February 11, 1946, Microfilm Reel PI/1, Side 1, Folder: Victory Clothing Collection, Press Releases, UNRRA Records, Columbia University Rare Books and Manuscript Division.

23. The UNCC was led nationally by chairman Henry J. Kaiser and organized through the agencies registered with the President's War Relief Control Board, including Jewish institutions, union groups, churches, rotary clubs, scouting groups, and political associations. The full list of participating Jewish organizations included the following: the American Association for Jewish Education, American Committee of OSE, American Jewish Congress Women's Division, Women's American ORT, B'nai B'rith, Council of Jewish Federations and Welfare Funds, Hadassah, Junior Hadassah, HIAS, Jewish Labor Committee, Jewish War Veterans of the United States and Women's Auxiliary, JDC Junior Division, National Council of Jewish Women, National Jewish Welfare Board, Synagogue Council of America, and Mizrachi Women's Organization of America. JDC Announcement from Chairman, Louis H. Sobel, Box 1, Folder 1: "Special Information for local Communities," CC-UNCC/AJHS.

24. *Time*, January 14, 1946, found in Scrapbook Volume 2, Part 4, UNCC/LOC. The same image was featured in a press proof designed by UNCC, and a note attached explained that the proof was sent directly to newspapers. Radio Kit, December 1945, 6, Volume 1, Part 1, UNCC/LOC.

25. Wall writes that projects like the UNCC encouraged Americans to "find common ground capable of uniting increasingly estranged groups of Americans." Wendy Wall,

Inventing the "American Way": The Politics of Consensus from the New Deal to the Civil Rights Movement (Oxford; New York: Oxford University Press, 2008), 12.

26. Stephen Ross Porter, *Defining Public Responsibility in a Global Age: Refugees, NGOs, and the American State* (PhD diss., University of Chicago, 2009), 5.

27. In the announcement for the 1946 Victory Clothing Collection, President Truman acknowledged that many donations from 1944 had included personal letters and asked donors to include short notes of friendship in the pockets of their used items, calling such letters an "expression of international friendship" that "can bring peace to the world." Letter from Henry Kaiser in Victory Clothing Collection Information Bulletin 4: Educational Program and good-will letters, vol. 1, part 1, UNCC/LOC.

28. Susan A. Brewer, *Why America Fights: Patriotism and War Propaganda from the Philippines to Iraq* (Oxford University Press, 2009), particularly chapter 3: "The Good War: Fighting for a Better Life in WWII," 87–140.

29. Press Release, August 13, 1945, Reel PI/1, Side 1, Folder: United National Clothing Collection Press Releases, UNRRA/Columbia.

30. Speech by Mrs. Isaac Gilman given at April 1949 luncheon in honor of SOS, 45/54 # 1330 [45/64 # 4369] Subjects: Relief Supplies: S.O.S., 1949, JDC.

31. Letter from Mrs. Louis H. Dreier, read by Mrs. Blanche Gilman at January 3, 1948 SOS Dinner. Transcript of Dinner proceedings, AR 45/54, File 1343, JDC.

32. Adele Levy, *Our Child Survivors* (New York: United Jewish Appeal, 1946), YIVO library.

33. Levy, *Our Child Survivors*.

34. Levy, *Our Child Survivors*.

35. "Shall Judaism Survive?" Brochure, Box 7, Folder 61, Vaad Hatzala Papers, Yeshiva University Archives.

36. Oliver Zunz, *Philanthropy in America: a history* (Princeton, N.J.: Princeton University Press, 2012), 160.

37. Henry Montor, executive vice chairman of UJA, recalled the idea of a hundred million dollar goal sounding "ridiculous" at the time. Quoted in Marc Lee Raphael, *A History of the United Jewish Appeal, 1939–1982* (Chico, CA: Scholars Press, 1982), 21

38. Raphael cites the figure of $124 million as the amount *pledged* between 1939–1945. Raphael, *United Jewish Appeal*, Table 4:1, 136.

39. "Report from Dr. Schwartz," *UJA Reports*, December 18, 1952, Volume 7, 17, Box 39, Herbert A. Friedman Papers, AJA.

40. Foster R. Dulles, *The American Red Cross: A History* (New York: Harper & Brothers, 1950), 509.

41. 1946 UJA Speaker's Manual, Box 10, Nearprint UJA, AJA.

42. Yehuda Bauer, *Out of the Ashes: The Impact of American Jews on Post-Holocaust European Jewry* (Oxford: Pergamon Press, 1989).

43. Bauer, *Out of the Ashes*, xviii. Edward Shapiro also points to guilt to explain the increased amounts of giving in the postwar period. Edward Shapiro, *A Time for Healing: American Jewry Since World War II* (Baltimore: Johns Hopkins University Press, 1992), 63.

44. For more about Maier, *Displaced*, and the use of radio as a medium for conveying stories about the Holocaust to American audiences, visit Memories/Motifs, an online exhibit built to explore postwar Holocaust memory, accessed at http://memoriesmotifs.com/.

45. *Displaced*, sound recording, YIVO Sound Archive and Marr Sound Archives. Emphasis in original.

46. *Displaced*.

47. *Battle for Survival*, film, US Holocaust Memorial Museum Steven Spielberg Film and Video Archive.

48. Ibid.

49. Brewer, *Why America Fights*, 119.

50. See Inger L. Stole, "The 'Salesmanship of Sacrifice': The Advertising Industry's Use of Public Relations During the Second World War," *Advertising & Society Review* 2, no. 2 (2001), doi:10.1353/asr.2001.0008.

51. In a critique of the Greatest Generation, Kenneth Rose argues that the resurgence of patriotism in the wake of September 11, 2001 has only heightened the popular imagination of World War II as a heroic event, including the idealized nostalgia of sacrifice on the home front. He writes, "If there is a 'fog of war,' surely there is also a fog of nostalgia and forgetting that settles in after every war." Kenneth Rose, *Myth and the Greatest Generation: A Social History of Americans in World War II* (New York, London: Routledge, 2013), 6.

52. Mark H. Leff, "The Politics of Sacrifice on the American Home Front in World War II," *The Journal of American History* 77, no. 4 (March 1, 1991): 1296–1318, 1296. DOI: 10.2307/2078263. See also Kenneth Rose, "The Home Front and Its Discontents," in *Myth and the Greatest Generation*, 105–28.

53. Leff, "The Politics of Sacrifice," 1296.

54. The film archive at the USHMM has two copies of *Battle for Survival*. Tape 2296 includes this extra appeal that so clearly states the power and possibility of film. *Battle for Survival*. Tape 2296, USHMM Steven Spielberg Film and Video Archive.

55. Ibid.

56. "Here are the Facts about the 1947 Campaign," United Jewish Appeal of Greater New York (RG117), Box 206, Folder 2, YIVO.

57. *1947 United Jewish Welfare Fund of the Los Angeles Jewish Community Council Yearbook*.

58. Narratives and representations of survivors were especially used to contrast the past and the present, so that the tragedies of the Holocaust made life in Israel even more sweet. For example, a Passover skit performed by Pioneer Women's groups throughout the country, titled "From the Warsaw Ghetto to the Gates of Hope," featured two women acting as Holocaust survivors comparing past Passovers spent in despair to the freedom of spending the holiday in the Jewish state. Survivor stories employed in this way marked a journey from Europe to Israel and represented the completed promise of American philanthropy. "From the Old to the New," Pioneer Women, April Program Calendar, 5, Folder 252, Labor Zionist Organization of America, YIVO Archives.

59. Raphael, *A History of the United Jewish Appeal*, Table 4:1 "UJA Campaign Finances: 1939–1948," 136. See also Milton Goldin, *Why They Give: American Jews and Their Philanthropies* (New York: Macmillan, 1976), 196.

60. *Battle for Survival*.

61. *Delayed Pilgrims Dinner*, November 27, 1947, YIVO Max and Frieda Weinstein Archive of Recorded Sound.

62. Ibid.

63. Jonathan D. Sarna, "The Cult of Synthesis in American Jewish Culture." *Jewish Social Studies* 5 (1998): 52–79, 52.

64. *Delayed Pilgrims Dinner.*

65. *The Eternal Light*, "The Late Comers," November 23, 1947, WOR NY, YIVO Sound Archive; *The Arrival of Delayed Pilgrims*, WNYC, YIVO Sound Archive.

66. "Citizens Committee on Displaced Persons: A Brief Statement of Aims," Pamphlet, 1947, Historical Society Library Pamphlet Collection, 54-1522, Wisconsin Historical Society Archives.

67. Michael Berenbaum, *After Tragedy and Triumph: Essays in Modern Jewish Thought and the American Experience* (Cambridge: Cambridge University Press, 1990), 40–41.

Canadian Communist J. B. Salsberg and the Response to Soviet Jewry in the Wake of the Holocaust

Ann Komaromi

AUTHOR MORDECAI RICHLER wrote about Jewish consciousness in the postwar era. In one memorable episode of Richler's 1971 novel, *St. Urbain's Horseman*, protagonist Jacob (Jake) Hersh reflects on the curse of his generation:

> Wrong place, wrong time. Young too late, old too soon was, as Jake had come to understand it, the plaintive story of his American generation. Conceived in the Depression, but never to taste its bitterness firsthand, they had actually contrived to sail through the Spanish Civil War, World War II, the holocaust, Hiroshima, the Israeli War of Independence, McCarthyism, Korea, and, latterly, Vietnam and the drug culture, with impunity. Always the wrong age. Ever observers, never participants. The whirlwind elsewhere.[1]

Hersh enjoys moderate success as a TV and film director living in London with a beloved (non-Jewish) wife, but his Canadian Jewish origins and a sense of not living up to the standards of other generations haunt him. Hersh's mordant attitude toward his "American" generation suggests the broader unease of many North American Jews after the war, who enjoyed increasing prosperity and opportunities for assimilation but remained troubled by an apparent loss of identity and purpose. While Hersh's sensibility as outlined here seems neither particularly Canadian nor especially Jewish, this passage expresses merely the surface of his consciousness.

Richler writes from a profound sense of Canadian location: the title of the novel suggests the importance of Hersh's locale as a youth, growing up on St. Urbain Street in Montreal. The "horseman" of the title grafts the force of myth and legend onto that provincial place: Jake imagines his elusive cousin Joey Hersh to be a fantastic hero, a Nazi hunter and world traveller (although Joey's father questions the integrity of Joey's motives: "if he is actually searching for Mengele... and finds him... he won't kill him, he'll blackmail him," Joey's father shouts).[2] The horseman figure concentrates Jake's anxiety and longing, rooted in his Jewish heritage. The diary Joey has left behind includes a string of ambiguous quotes about Jews on horses, beginning with one from Isaac Babel's play *Sunset*: "When a Jew gets on a horse he stops being a Jew."[3] Babel's works probed the ambivalence of Jewish assimilation in the context of the Russian revolution, which eventually reduced Babel to silence. Jake Hersh's search for a Jewish hero transposes these themes into the postwar world.[4] Although the "holocaust" appears in lower case in the middle of Jake's litany of big historical traumas, the larger themes of the book make the Holocaust seem deliberately understated, like a buried center of Jake's consciousness.[5]

The Holocaust formed a partially buried center of drama in the life of another larger-than-life character, the Canadian politician J. B. Salsberg. Joseph Baruch Salsberg (1902–1998) rose from being a Polish immigrant kid to a Communist party leader, prior to his scandalous departure from the party in 1956. Salsberg's increasing concern about the fate of Eastern European Jews after the Holocaust led to a series of influential articles in which he exposed the problems Jews faced in the Soviet Union. Subsequently, Salsberg reoriented his efforts toward advocacy for Israel, Soviet Jews, and his brand of secular Yiddish values. Salsberg's trajectory shows how North American Jews found a voice—and a purpose—after the Holocaust, in part through the movement for Soviet Jewry. His story also illustrates the turn from a universalizing pursuit of social justice through revolutionary politics toward responsibility for particular Jewish concerns as part of that quest. Salsberg's biography illuminates some of the distinctive features of the Canadian Jewish experience. His conversion from Communist to Jewish activist provocatively highlights the role of individual experience and communal conscience in finding an authentic voice. At the same time, his story demonstrates the extent to which Jewish engagement with Eastern European Jewry, rooted in the experience of the Holocaust, was an international and collective effort, one not confined to the particular context of US politics.

Salsberg and a Jewish Approach to Revolutionary Politics

J. B. Salsberg, born in Łagów, Poland, came to Canada with his family in 1913. After informing his parents he wished to give up study of the Talmud at age sixteen, Salsberg began attending meetings of the *Yunge Poalei Zion*, the Young Workers of Zion, a branch of the left political party affiliated with labor groups in Palestine.[6] Having embarked on union work in the early 1920s, Salsberg left the *Yunge Poalei Zion* and joined the Communist Party of Canada in 1926. Salsberg biographer Gerald Tulchinsky described Salsberg's decision to join the Communist Party as "a radical break with the past," the consequence of having "rejected the Torah Judaism of his parents," as well as the Zionism and moderate trade unionism of his youth.[7] However, like many young Jews on the political left at that time, Salsberg likely felt a profound resonance between his Jewish identity and his Communist commitments. Many Jews of that generation believed that the Russian Revolution would eliminate antisemitism and the "Jewish question."[8] Salsberg clearly believed that Communism offered the best hope for Jews and a just world for all, and this belief led him to abandon the traditional religiosity of the world from which he had come and commit himself to new political possibilities. Salsberg's choice of modern secular engagements, his affiliation with the left's struggle for labor rights and social justice, reflected the currents of the time and provided this young immigrant boy from a small Polish town the scope of activity his talents and energy appear to have demanded.

Salsberg came from a marginal class of poor immigrants, uncomfortably lodged in the poor downtown Jewish district of a Protestant and prospering Toronto. Salsberg came naturally to represent the workers of the clothing industry, which employed many of this Jewish underclass, as well as other underprivileged members of Canadian society. However, Salsberg did not find it easy to work within the Communist Party. The Communist ethos demanded submission to Party discipline, and Salsberg struggled with some Party dictates. Salsberg's decision to leave his position with the Needle Trades Workers Union to become the Ontario organizer for the Workers' Unity League (WUL) angered comrades in the Party, who expelled him in December, 1929. However, even before being readmitted in 1932, Salsberg continued to work on behalf of Party initiatives. He proved useful in the Party's mission to radicalize workers. Although Salsberg's formal schooling was minimal, he was an effective orator. Salsberg was a man of the streets, who socialized easily and often with the members of his downtown district, and who largely through his own learning (rather than through formal education) developed both informed commitment to the Communist cause and impressive rhetorical prowess in spoken word and print. His effectiveness in this context stemmed from his ability to use language from the right authorities, Marx and Lenin foremost among them.[9] Salsberg gave a voice to the working class from within the discourse of the Party. While he chafed at times at its dictates, he almost always helped maintain a united front for outsiders, speaking at prominent public events and vigorously defending the Communist Party against the hostility of the larger society.[10]

At the time Salsberg began his public career, Canadian Jews still adhered to a relatively traditional type of establishment advocacy. The Canadian Jewish community was smaller than that of the United States, it was more institutionally centralized, and in the early decades of the twentieth century it had just begun to see a significant influx of Eastern European immigrants.[11] Salsberg's political affiliations and his outspoken advocacy of the cause of workers and the disenfranchised made him a new kind of modern activist, alien to the Jewish establishment. Jewish factory owners and other members of the Jewish elite in Canada felt little affinity for their poor cousins, recently arrived from Eastern Europe and carrying with them a provocative set of radical political ideas.[12] The establishment tended to follow a genteel British version of Jewish advocacy—*shtadlanut*. Such intercession by the elites on behalf of the whole Jewish community depended on the access by those in the upper echelons of Jewish society to non-Jewish persons in positions of power, and it functioned by means of closed-door meetings and little or no public discussion.[13] The strength of this correspondence between privilege and public voice helped reinforce hierarchical distinctions and affirm the position of those established at the head of the Jewish community. In this context, Salsberg represented a new, challenging force welling up from the lower classes.

By the mid-1930s, Salsberg acted on his political ambitions. He ran for a spot on the Toronto City Council in 1934 and 1935, although he did not prevail. Salsberg did win a seat on the council in 1938, and he won re-election as alderman in January 1943.[14] More importantly, in August, 1943, he won a seat in the Ontario provincial legislature as a member of the Labour-Progressive Party (LPP), the entity representing Communists in Canada between 1943 and 1959.[15] Salsberg served in the Ontario legislature for twelve years, until 1955.

As a provincial legislator, Salsberg did not advocate communism as such, but he did pursue political advocacy that reflected the universal nature of his commitment to justice for all. Moreover, he did so in terms that could be understood by his fellow legislators at City Hall and in the Provincial Parliament: that is to say, Salsberg for the most part jettisoned Marxist rhetoric to advocate on issues of general public concern.[16] He could be a colorful speaker, and he embraced his role as an opposition leader, declaring that his responsibility was "to stop [the government] from falling asleep, and wake them up when they begin to snore."[17] As a result of his effectiveness as an opposition member and his popularity among constituents, Salsberg won re-election in 1945, 1948, and even 1951, despite rising anti-Communist sentiments.

However, Canada saw Cold War tensions intensify early thanks to the Gouzenko Affair. Igor Gouzenko, a clerk in the Soviet embassy in Ottawa, defected in September, 1945, with documentation of a Soviet spy network. The scandalous case led to dozens of arrests in Canada and two major convictions—for Sam Carr, national organizer of the Communist Party, and Fred Rose, the only Communist member of the Federal Parliament. Rose was expelled from Parliament in January of 1947, and he spent over four years in prison. The Communist Party had been declared illegal twice in Canada, first in 1931 and again in 1940. A number of its members were arrested and detained, including Salsberg, who went into hiding before turning himself in to police and spending a few weeks in jail in 1942. Such events amounted to something like a rite of passage in revolutionary culture, and they were not seriously harmful to Salsberg's political prospects then. However, the Gouzenko affair was different. Historian

Merrily Weisbord argued that, "Because of the Gouzenko affair, the Canadian Communist Party had the dubious honour of being among the first Communist parties in the world to experience isolation and stagnation."[18] This early and intense experience of Cold War tensions formed the backdrop to Salsberg's growing concerns about how the Communist Party was handling the situation of Soviet Jews.

As Salsberg subsequently recounted it, he had become seriously concerned by 1939 about the closing of Jewish institutions in the USSR. However, Salsberg did not break ranks publicly on the issue.[19] Bowing to Party discipline, he also declined to challenge in public the Party's stance against war with Nazi Germany for the duration of the Molotov-Ribbentrop pact between Hitler and Stalin from 1939–41. It seemed clear that in order to stay in the Party, there was no other choice.[20] This logic remained in force in the early postwar period, too, when the dissolution of the Jewish Anti-Fascist Committee in 1948, and the sudden silence of Jewish intellectuals in the Soviet Union, provided further grounds for anxiety.

Like most Communist Party members at that time, Salsberg accepted the argument that fighting hostile bourgeois elements mattered more than challenging strict Party discipline. In one of the least inspiring moments in his political career, in March, 1953, Salsberg delivered a fulsome eulogy for Joseph Stalin on the floor of the House, declaring confidence that "the figure of Stalin will emerge and remain in history as one of the greatest among the great of all times."[21] Salsberg probably succumbed to serious pressure placed on him by the Party as the only Communist parliamentarian in the British Commonwealth, and thus felt duty-bound to make the speech. The effects for Salsberg proved to be politically devastating—in the context of the Cold War, and with demographic changes pushing Salsberg's constituency out of the downtown and to the more affluent suburbs, Salsberg lost the next election in 1955 to his Conservative and anti-Communist opponent.[22]

Finding a New Voice: Salsberg's Articles of 1956

The Holocaust had a big impact on Salsberg. He traveled to Poland in 1947 to witness the effects of World War II firsthand. Touring various communities, he was struck by the plight of Jewish refugees. He also visited his family's hometown of Łagów, Poland, and wrote in his notes about the "ghastly appearance of [the] town. Burned skeletons, fields where once houses [stood]."[23] Salsberg was told that his own grandmother had been taken away in a cart—"she was a little thing and far too old to walk—and they shot her by the side of the road." He recalled, "It was the first time I've ever lost control. I cried like a child."[24] Although Salsberg applied to visit the Soviet Union to investigate the Jewish situation there as well, he was refused permission on the grounds that the visit could attract the attention of Anglo-American intelligence and make the situation of Communists in Canada even worse.[25]

Although Jews in the central and eastern portions of the Soviet Union escaped the Holocaust, their situation after the war grew increasingly worrisome. By 1949, Soviet newspaper articles stressing the Jewish names and origins of the majority of those accused of being "cosmopolitans" showed Soviet Jews being systematically scapegoated.[26] On January 13, 1953, Soviet newspapers announced "The Arrest of a Group of Saboteur Doctors," physicians of Jewish origin who supposedly planned to murder Soviet leaders through harmful medical practices.[27] Salsberg's trip to Moscow in 1955, following his attendance at the World Peace Assembly in Helsinki, and at the World Jewish Conference Against German Rearmament, did little to quiet his fears. Soviet officials responded to his questions about the disappearance of Jewish intellectuals by admitting that innocent people had been arrested and even killed, though they insisted that mistakes were being rectified. Back home, the National Executive of the LPP declined Salsberg's proposal to challenge the Communist Party of the Soviet Union on the issue. Salsberg agreed to wait for Canadian leader Tim Buck's report.

Salsberg, like most Communist faithful, remained publicly quiet until after Soviet First Secretary Nikita Khrushchev's "Secret Speech," delivered at a closed session of the Twentieth Party Congress in Moscow on February 25, 1956. Khrushchev criticized the arbitrary purges that took place under Stalin and opened up the possibility of questions and critique among Soviet citizens and foreign observers.[28] While he did not mention Stalin's offenses against Jews in particular, international discussion immediately turned to Jewish issues as well.

The report by Leon Crystal, published in his New York Yiddish daily *Forverts* on March 7, 1956, about the execution of at least five major

Yiddish authors (David Bergelson, Itsik Fefer, David Hofshteyn, Leib Kvitko, and Peretz Markish were among those killed) on August 12, 1952, provided initial information about the violent dissolution of the Jewish Anti-Fascist Committee (JAC). A subsequent article in the Polish Yiddish newspaper *Folks-shtimme* on April 4, 1956, entitled "Our Pain and Our Consolation" (*Undzer veytik un undzer tryst*), came closest to an official acknowledgment of the truth of Crystal's report, and it shocked the left.[29] This was a watershed piece, an "opening blast" after the Twentieth Party Congress that, as one commentator put it, "set the tone, fixed the terms, and defined the limits of the enormous volume of criticism that flooded the Jewish Communist press" during the next few years.[30] In the Soviet Union, meanwhile, there was no public acknowledgment of the terrible events reported.

The fate of the Jewish Anti-Fascist Committee, along with the revelations of the "Secret Speech," became topics of heated debate. Members of Communist Parties abroad began to reconsider the structure of the Party and its expectations of unquestioning discipline. In Canada, Party members expressed new distrust of the Party leadership. In Montreal, the Jewish Section had become the largest part of the LPP, and many of them had joined the Party because, as Weisbord wrote, the Party was the "champion of religious and racial equality and [those Canadians who joined] believed that there was no anti-semitism in the Soviet Union." That had proved to be untrue: "Why didn't we speak out?" one woman asked in retrospect about her activity in the Party.[31]

While appearing firmly in line with the LPP's policies in public, Salsberg made waves behind closed doors: he appealed to the Canadian Communist Party leadership to interrogate Moscow officials on questions about the treatment of Jews, although he was initially rebuffed. His charge that Soviet officials were practicing antisemitism got him kicked out of the National Executive in the early 1950s. After the revelations of 1956, the National Executive of the LPP reinstated Salsberg to its committee.[32] They also sent him with three other Party delegates to Moscow in August, 1956. Perhaps the decision to send Salsberg came under pressure from the Party rank-and-file, who were skeptical of the leadership but believed that Salsberg—known internally for challenging Party leaders—could more objectively evaluate how thoroughly the Soviet government had overcome

Stalinism.³³ In any case, Salsberg had a specific mandate to ask about Soviet government policy toward Jews.

Salsberg met with the same evasive replies, and he found that Soviet leaders, while blaming past excesses on Stalin and his administration, continued to embody antisemitic attitudes, showing no awareness of ongoing problems. Stymied again by his own Party leadership, Salsberg chose to publish nine articles in the Toronto *Vochenblatt*, in Yiddish and English, in fall 1956. Salsberg's articles, in which he reflected on Party failings and continuing problems with post-Stalin leadership, were widely reprinted and excerpted.³⁴ In particular, Salsberg's articles were cited in a special issue of the leftist magazine *New Leader*, on "Jews in the USSR," in September, 1959. Moshe Decter, editor of *New Leader*, was working with a clandestine Israeli office called Nativ, or the Liaison Bureau (*Lishkat hakesher*), to advance the issue of Soviet Jewry in public discussion, particularly among left intellectuals in North America.³⁵ Nativ had also facilitated Leon Crystal's reporting for *Forverts* on the execution of Yiddish cultural figures in 1952.³⁶ The Nativ bureau chose Decter as its American emissary because of his close ties with Left intellectuals whom Nativ was eager to mobilize in a pointed—but not overtly anti-Soviet—campaign to aid Soviet Jews. The September 1959 issue of the *New Leader* had been assembled out of materials brought to Decter by his Nativ contact. It included "testimonies of former . . . Jewish Communists, in various languages . . . who confessed to their bitterness over their discovery of the plight of Soviet Jewry . . . and even more, their sense of culpability for having been silent about what they had known all along."³⁷ Salsberg was one effective spokesman among a whole cohort of disillusioned communists and socialists.

Salsberg's articles were important for their frank criticism of the Party's approach to the Jewish question in the USSR after Stalin. Plainspoken and straightforward, Salsberg forthrightly rejected Soviet authorities' explanations about the withering away of interest in Jewish institutions. He judged that "Soviet Jewish culture was completely destroyed."³⁸ Salsberg did not spare himself or the Party: he acknowledged his own "painful silence" over many years,³⁹ confessing, "We were always concerned, but we did not act."⁴⁰ Salsberg had become convinced during his 1955 trip to Moscow that the closing of Jewish institutions was, "as I had previously suspected—a brutal and terroristic act." Lacking much specific information, he believed then that in the case of the Jewish writers, "a great tragedy had occurred."[41] Salsberg looked back critically on his former belief that the only way to act was through the Communist Party. The dissonance between Salsberg's conviction and the inadequacy of the institutions in which he believed lent a poignant force to his account for the many left-leaning readers who had shared his hopes, fears, and allegiances. He offered a frank appraisal: "During my visit to Moscow in the summer of 1955 I could not escape the feeling that had the communist parties acted they might have been able to save the executed writers, both Jewish and non-Jewish. Perhaps. But they lacked that measure of real independent thinking in relation to the Soviet Union that was required."[42]

Salsberg's account derived authority from the fact that his small Canadian delegation enjoyed special access to the Moscow leadership. Salsberg noted, "no other party—to my knowledge—had ever placed this question [about Soviet Jewish life] as one of central importance requiring full discussion with the Soviet leaders." The Canadians participated in four official conferences with top leaders including Central Committee member Boris Ponomarev, Politburo member Mikhail Suslov, and First Secretary of the Party Nikita Khrushchev.[43]

Others had broken news of the terrible fate of the Jewish Anti-Fascist Committee under Stalin and the evisceration of institutional and communal Jewish life in the Soviet Union, but Salsberg's account resonated because it revealed the extent to which the leadership after Stalin refused to take responsibility in attempting to extirpate antisemitism from Soviet society. Salsberg reported that Soviet authorities had no plans for re-establishing any central Jewish organization or Jewish schools, newspapers, or other cultural institutions. Officials admitted that Jews had been expelled from positions because they were Jews, and that Soviet organs had censored the mention of Jews in print. Such actions contributed to the psychological dissonance of Soviet Jews who could never quite assimilate.[44] The American Jewish Committee cited Salsberg's articles as an important indication of the attitudes of Soviet leaders. They identified the "high point" of Salsberg's series as the account of casually antisemitic remarks made by Khrushchev about the characteristics of Jews as a people—that they were loath to clean up their own streets, disloyal and liable to defect, and prone to build a synagogue wherever they went.[45]

The articles created a scandal. For Salsberg and many others, the Jewish issue exposed fundamental problems. Blind subservience to the CPSU (the Communist Party of the Soviet Union) had proved to be a moral and political failing. There were other scandals at the time, including, notably, the brutal suppression of the Hungarian uprising in November 1956. Thanks to these and other factors, by the time Salsberg left the Party, in May 1957, hundreds of others had abandoned the organization. The Canadian Communist Party was broken.[46] After his departure from the Communist Party, Salsberg participated in the establishment of the New Fraternal Jewish Association, a party combining democratic socialism, secularism, and Zionism. The party would not become broadly influential in Canadian politics. Salsberg's political career was over, although he did not abandon his struggle for justice and on behalf of the Jewish people.

Canadian Jewish Inflections in a New Collective Voice

After World War II, Canadian Jews, like Jews south of the border, began to experience greater prosperity and increased integration into the surrounding society. Richler wrote about the longing of his generation to live up to the legacy of their forebears also in his novel *Joshua, Then and Now* (1980), in which he described the "double burden" of a Canadian Jew: "Canadian-born, [he] sometimes felt as if he were condemned to lope slant-shouldered through this world that confused him. One shoulder sloping downwards, groaning under the weight of his Jewish heritage . . . the other thrust heavenwards, yearning for an inheritance, any inheritance, weightier than the construction of a transcontinental railway, a reputation for honest trading, good skiing conditions."[47]

The Soviet Jewry movement, often depicted as a new exodus of Soviet Jews from enslavement to the "Red Pharaoh," answered the aspiration for something higher for North American Jews who were not entirely at ease with their integration and prosperity, and who remained haunted by the legacy of the Holocaust in the context of a continuing threat to Eastern European Jewry. The Soviet Jewry movement challenged traditional establishment activism, mobilizing people from all strata of the Jewish community. Canada did not have a civil rights movement like that in the United States. Therefore, the concerns of Holocaust survivors helped push the boundaries of acceptable strategies and topics for activism. Canadian Jews saw proportionally greater waves of immigration from Eastern Europe after the war, including a significant influx of Holocaust survivors. By 1961, Holocaust survivors and their descendants made up around fourteen percent of the roughly 255,000 Canadian Jews. This proportion far exceeded the approximately four percent of survivors among American Jews at that time.[48] Canadian Jews had also been more consistently and deeply Zionist, a commitment that informed the establishment agenda and united much of the community.[49] While the level of Zionist commitment did not change, the concerns of Holocaust survivors helped drive street demonstrations and grassroots initiatives that challenged the exclusive right of the Jewish establishment to set the agenda and strategies of the community. When people took to the streets to protest the visit of Nazi Party leader George Lincoln Rockwell in the fall of 1960, Canadian Jewish Congress head Saul Hayes complained about the new development, observing that, "Jews never marched on the streets of Montreal before."[50]

Such grassroots efforts would be employed in Canada—as in the States—on behalf of Soviet Jewry by the beginning of the 1970s. Part of a new phase of social movements and non-institutional activism prevailing generally in these decades, the Soviet Jewry campaign involved mass marches, public rallies, and theatrical displays keyed to media coverage.[51] Thus, during Soviet Premier Alexei Kosygin's visit to Canada in October, 1971, sixty rabbis with prayer shawls (*tallesim*) and prayer books (*siddurim*) marched from the Jewish Community Center to the Soviet Embassy in Montreal. When Kosygin and Prime Minister Trudeau arrived at the House of Commons, they saw the rabbis in prayer—one blew a shofar. The newspaper *The Montreal Star* featured a photo the next day of the rabbis at the Centennial Flame with Canada's Peace Tower behind them.[52]

The Six-Day War of June 1967 marked a turning point in the mobilization of Soviet Jews and their supporters abroad, who were further provoked by the infamous Leningrad Hijacking Trial of December 1970. The conclusion of that trial, in late December 1970, saw surprisingly harsh sentences, up to and including the death sentence, meted out to Jewish activists who attempted to commandeer a Soviet plane with unloaded weapons in order to fly out of the Soviet Union.[53] However, the colorful and highly media-driven campaign on behalf of Soviet Jews that ensued depended on groundwork laid in the immediate postwar decades. In this way, the Soviet Jewry movement resembled the public response to the Holocaust. Hasia Diner wrote, "In large part, the American Jews of the post-1967 era, who made and consumed the massive Holocaust project of their time, benefited from the spadework undertaken by their forebears of the postwar period."[54] J. B. Salsberg, who helped launch the Soviet Jewry campaign in Canada in the early 1970s, illustrates the advent of new forms of activism with roots in the *prise de conscience* of the 1950s and early 1960s.

Yiddish style and values informed this activism in Canada perhaps more than in the United States. After all, thanks to immigration patterns, it became common to say that Canadian Jews were one generation closer to the shtetl.[55] Salsberg in the 1970s headed the Yiddish Committee and chaired the Steering Committee for Soviet Jewry within the Canadian Jewish Congress (CJC).[56] The CJC, the establishment organization headed by Samuel Bronfman, who made his fortune with Seagram's Beverages, had excluded the socialist United Jewish People's Order for years—they were the "other side." However, times had changed. No longer was Salsberg the upstart socialist from a slum background tilting against the windmills of the upper-class Jewish establishment. We might suspect an element of accommodation or opportunism in the behavior of Salsberg, who was seeking new political relevance, just as we might suspect it of Jewish communities in North America during the Cold War era generally—Jews were anxious to demonstrate their bona fides and criticism of the Soviet Union was a good way to do so.[57] However, Salsberg's shift might also be seen as a harbinger of the new, less clearly ideological or binary model of activism that became characteristic of the postwar era. Salsberg and the establishment now worked in sometimes contentious concert.

Salsberg continued crusading on behalf of the oppressed from within the establishment. An article from 1971 reported that Salsberg objected to the way Henry G. Goodman and the United Jewish Welfare Fund he headed treated "the plight of the Jewish poor." Regarding the intention of the Fund to "assure [the Jewish poor's] needs are met," Salsberg ironically exclaimed, "Now that's very charitable, Henry!" He also said, "I'm not enamored by such words like 'deserving poor', 'underprivileged', the 'needy.'" Salsberg explained, "My complaint, Henry, is that the larger half of our community; the poor, the wage and salary earners and the little fellow generally, have lost their voice and influence in the shaping of the character of our community."[58] Salsberg's folksy style and direct address showed his disdain for hierarchy and signified the plain common sense of Yiddish wisdom.

Salsberg helped raise the profile of the date August 12, 1952, known as the "Night of the Murdered Poets," for Jewish activists in the 1970s. It became one of four cardinal dates of the Soviet Jewry campaign calendar.[59] On that night thirteen people associated with the Jewish Anti-Fascist Committee had been executed, including poets Itsik Fefer, Leib Kvitko, Peretz Markish, and other leading literary and intellectual figures from the Soviet Jewish elite.[60] Salsberg had proposed such a commemoration at least as early as August, 1971, and his Yiddish committee helped plan the event.[61] The date served as an emblem of the destruction of Jewish culture in the Soviet Union. As we saw, the process of initially publicizing this Stalin-era crime had been facilitated by the Israeli bureau Nativ. Salsberg had made the case that Soviet Jews continued to suffer repressions and injustice after Stalin, a point that Nativ's emissaries were glad to amplify as the Soviet Jewry movement gained momentum.

The complementary roles of Nativ and of persons like Salsberg, who for their own reasons engaged the problems of Soviet Jewry, illustrates a convergence of organized (state-sponsored) and individual (grassroots) interests. The contamination of positions formerly separated as binary poles runs throughout postwar activism like a leitmotif. Rather than sublimating the cause of Jewish liberation into a Communist struggle for universal emancipation, the Soviet Jewry movement represented an ongoing dialogue between the twin imperatives articulated by Hillel: "If I am not for myself who is for me; and being for my own self, what am I?"[62] Similarly, the future no longer excluded the past—Salsberg's postwar discourse illustrated the new value placed by this former Communist and others on the heritage of a lost Yiddish world. Thus, he counseled comfortable Canadian readers, "your Yiddish-speaking parents' lives included hard labour, struggle and resistance, but also cultural enrichment, commitment and *menschlichkeit* that needs renewal in our days."[63] The past became a source of strength for the future. Similarly, in this post-ideological context, the base and the establishment become more equal partners, often antagonistic, but sometimes constructively so: the base pushed the establishment to take on causes they initially resisted, and then grassroots efforts complemented those of establishment organizations to pursue a common agenda. In grassroots actions in particular, the antinomy of private vs. public spaces and identities, so key to the maskilic (enlightenment) understanding articulated by Yehuda Leib Gordon, "Be a man in the streets and a Jew at home,"[64] yielded in this postwar environment to a messier (and often fertile) blend.[65]

The sparks created by striking together formerly opposed categorizations helped forge a new type of Jewish unity. Western Jews and their Soviet brethren, like organizational representatives and grassroots activists, came together in a common cause. Religious and secular Jews, Zionists and former Communists worked together. Not that all differences dissolved: Salsberg, for example, maintained his own principled attachment to secular Yiddish values and denounced empty forms of synagogue affiliation in the surrounding community. He continued to be a gadfly to establishment attempts to dominate the discussion. Salsberg challenged the World Jewish Congress and Edgar Bronfman's claims to credit for the release of Prisoner of Zion Yosef Mendelevich in 1981. Bronfman's negotiations with Soviet Ambassador Anatoly Dobrynin deserved recognition, Salsberg acknowledged. However, he said:

> The real heroes of this successful accomplishment are in my view, the thousands of Jews—young and old—who kept up the determined struggle for the release of all Prisoners of Zion in the USSR; the committees for Soviet Jewry and their staffs around the world; the dedicated committees of 35 in many lands including Canada, who marched and demonstrated in the most difficult circumstances for the freeing of the imprisoned; the Jewish student groups who, for many years, were the shock-troops in the struggle; the countless committees for Soviet Jewry in the synagogues, in women's organizations, in societies of every sort; the thousands of our good people who assembled, who marched, who demonstrated in countless cities and towns in the Western world.[66]

In this spirit, released Prisoner of Zion Natan Sharansky recalled a KGB officer's derisive comment about mere "students and housewives" who supported him. Sharansky took over the formulation, asserting, "the army of students and housewives turned out to be mightier than the army of the KGB."[67] Among Canadian supporters, David Sadowski, leader of the student "caravan" traveling around to summer camps in 1971 to educate youth about Soviet Jewry, spoke of a feeling of profound connection with Soviet Jews, among whose ranks his family might have been if they had not left the Russian empire in 1884. He watched Sharansky, falsely accused of espionage and imprisoned for his rights activities, and thought, "There but for the grace of God go I."[68] Among the "housewives," the indomitable Genia Intrator, a native Russian speaker and militant activist, was often a thorn in the side of the Canadian establishment. Nevertheless, she received support from establishment organizations for telephone communications with Soviet refuseniks that furnished information for organizations worldwide.[69] Barbara Stern, member of the Canadian 35s, a branch of the grassroots organization formed by "housewives" who got out on the streets to protest and raise awareness, worked also with the CJC on shared goals: on a volunteer basis Stern compiled and typed the three volumes of information on hundreds of refuseniks that served as a critical reference work for negotiations during the Helsinki Process.[70] Along with the enormous set of materials on the Sharansky case prepared by lawyer Irwin Cotler (who later served as Member of Parliament and Minister of Justice), these volumes represented a significant Canadian contribution to an international effort to press the Soviet Union to keep its legal obligations with respect to Soviet Jews.

The Jews of Silence?

Salsberg lamented his "painful silence" during the years of not challenging the Communist Party on behalf of Soviet Jews. In part, evoking that silence—for which others also felt culpable—lent force to the act of breaking the silence, as Salsberg did with his powerful articles of 1956. Holocaust survivor Elie Wiesel wrote a decade later about the "Jews of Silence": "I went to Russia drawn by the silence of its Jews. I brought back their cry."[71] The Jews of the west could not remain silent, Wiesel insisted, calling on them to take responsibility for their Eastern European fellows. The slogan "Never Again," recalling the Holocaust, became a rallying cry for action on behalf of Soviet Jews.[72] The "silence" of North American Jews during the Holocaust—more properly characterized as their inability to save more of those who perished—constituted a particularly painful legacy in Canada, given the nation's abysmal record on Jewish immigration through the war years.[73] Talk of the "cultural genocide" of Soviet Jews linked their plight to the Holocaust, even as it distinguished the two situations: in most cases contemporary Soviet Jews were not threatened with physical destruction.[74]

Emil Fackenheim, the Jewish philosopher and theologian who fled Europe for Canada, grounded his philosophical and theological response to the Holocaust in the spontaneous, lived response that had been going on for decades around him.[75] Similarly, as we now realize, public Holocaust awareness after 1967 depended on a prior "vast unorganized spontaneous project that sought to keep alive the image of Europe's murdered Jews."[76] The Soviet Jewry campaign, one of the expressions of a postwar Jewish identity, built similarly on the efforts of previous decades, including that deeply-rooted response to the Holocaust. It meant more than simple tribalism or accommodation to the Cold War environment: the campaign presented a new and distinctively postwar way of being Jewish and conducting Jewish activism. The achievements of the Soviet Jewry movement in the 1960s–1990s resulted from years of preparation in the immediate postwar decades. The themes of silence and voice pervade discussions of the Holocaust and responses to it. Widely held convictions regarding the silence of Jews about the Holocaust in the decades immediately following WWII are hardly empirically founded, as Hasia Diner has convincingly shown.[77] Such convictions might be explained in part as a function of a changing political and media landscape, and in part as the result of rhetorical strategies: just as Salsberg's evocation of his earlier painful silence made his speaking out seem more urgent, Wiesel's description of the silence of Soviet and western Jews dramatically highlighted the task at hand. North American Jews found a new voice in the movement to aid Soviet Jewry, one that redressed to a certain extent the sense of responsibility left over from the Holocaust, while it also gave North American Jews new communal and political identity that countered to some degree the threat of materialism and conformity in the years of postwar prosperity. North American Jews needed Soviet Jewry as much as Soviet Jews needed them.

The Canadian contribution of this postwar Jewish voice had prominent Yiddish elements. This was true in the case of Canadian writer Mordecai Richler, whose literary style blended Yiddish inflections into English everyday speech as part of a distinctively localized satirical realism.[78] It was true for J. B. Salsberg, who brought his secular Yiddish values over from pre-war politics to postwar activism. Salsberg lost his Communist ideology and prominence, but he gained and contributed something else through his commitments to Jewish solidarity. In postwar articles written for the mainstream weekly the *Canadian Jewish News*, Salsberg regularly invoked a figure representing the wisdom of the previous generation of Eastern European immigrants: "Uncle Eliezer," described as a combination of Sholom Aleichem's Tevye and the legendary wit Hershele Ostropolyer. Uncle Eliezer's laconic remarks "frequently reflect widely held views on Bathurst Street," Salsberg wrote.[79] Salsberg's reference was local and concrete. Like downtown Spadina Street, the historic center of the Jewish immigrant community in Toronto where Salsberg got his start, Bathurst had become the place, metaphorically speaking, where Salsberg found his *Klal Yisrael*—the mix of "the religious and the secular, the affiliated and the unattached, people of all social and economic classes, and of all ages, and with wide-ranging political views."[80] That world, like the European Yiddish world from which it derived, was gone by the time Salsberg wrote about it. However, it remained in some sense Salsberg's home. That spirit of solidarity continued to shape Jewish identity and activism in the new, postwar context.

Notes

Thanks for advice, insight, materials, and support for this article are owed to many, including Donna Bernardo-Ceriz and the staff at the Ontario Jewish Archive, the archives of the Canadian Jewish Congress in Montreal, and the Queens University Archive. I am indebted to Soviet Jewry activists including David Sadowski, Marsha Slavens, Barbara Stern, and the Honorable Irwin Cotler; historians including Wendy Eisen, Pauline Peretz, Hesh Troper, and Gerald Tulchinsky; and to my perspicacious reviewers. Mistakes and omissions are my own.

1. Mordecai Richler, *St. Urbain's Horseman* (Montreal: New Canadian Library, 1989).

2. Ibid., 40.

3. The full line reads, "A Jew who climbs onto a horse stops being a Jew and becomes a Russian." From Scene one of *Sunset: A Play in Eight Scenes*, in *The Complete Works of Isaac Babel*, ed. Nathalie Babel, trans. Peter Constantine (NY: W. W. Norton & Company, 2002), 756–57. Richler, *St. Urbain's Horseman*, 40. The history of horse-mounted Cossacks victimizing Jews serves as a background for Babel's character, who feels ambivalent about his role with the Red Army amidst the suffering Jews of the war-torn Pale of Settlement.

4. Richler adapted Babel's play *Sunset* for BBC television in 1963 as *The Fall of Mendel Krick*. He considered Levka's statement about a Jew on a horse to reflect "the quarrel between the Israeli and Diaspora Jew." See Reinhold Kramer, *Mordecai Richler: Leaving St. Urbain* (Montreal: McGill-Queen's University Press, 2008), 174–75, 473. Therefore, the "horseman" of his novel might represent the anxiety of the Diaspora Jew to realize heroic potentials.

5. The Holocaust, Israel, and World War II in general "mesmerized" Richler (1931–2001) and informed his writing. Kramer, 224.

6. On Salsberg's origins, early life, and political career, see Gerald Tulchinsky, *Joe Salsberg. A Life of Commitment* (Toronto: University of Toronto Press, 2013).

7. Tulchinsky, *Joe Salsberg*, 20–21.

8. As fellow Canadian Joshua Gershman put it, "I became a Communist because I am a Jew.'" Quoted by Tulchinsky, *Canada's Jews. A People's Journey* (Toronto: University of Toronto Press, 2008), 263. Gershman also worked in the Needle Trades Workers' Union in Canada and later became editor of the Toronto Yiddish/English newspaper *Vochenblatt*, in which Salsberg's 1956 articles appeared.

9. For example, Salsberg cited Marx to the effect that "without being aware of it, [trade unions] become the focal points for the organization of the working class, just as the medieval municipalities and communities bec[a]me such for the bourgeoisie." Tulchinsky quoted this line from Salsberg's lecture and affirmed his "outstanding qualities as an orator." *Joe Salsberg*, 54.

10. On activity of the later 1920s to the early 1930s, see Tulchinsky, *Joe Salsberg*, 29–44.

11. Jewish emigration from Eastern Europe began to expand the small Canadian Jewish community in the 1880s–90s, which saw exponential growth in the early 1900s, growing to 126,201 by 1921, the overwhelming majority of whom were concentrated in Montreal and Toronto. See William Shaffir and Morton Weinfeld, "Canada and the Jews: An Introduction," in *The Canadian Jewish Mosaic*, ed. I. Cotler, W. Shaffir, and M. Weinfeld (Toronto: John Wiley & Sons, 1981), 10.

12. Tulchinsky noted that the Canadian Jewish community was more conservative than its US counterpart in two senses: the absence of a large German Jewish migration to introduce reform elements meant the basic religious culture remained more traditional, while the community as a whole felt the influence of a Canadian orientation to "Crown, established churches, and certain quasi-aristocratic trappings related to the British connection." As a result, "Canadian Jews ... saw themselves as defenders of the British tradition as well as of Jewish Orthodoxy." See Gerald Tulchinsky, "The Canadian Jewish Experience: A Distinct Personality Emerges," in *From Immigration to Integration: The Canadian Jewish Experience: A Millennium Edition*, ed. Ruth Klein and Frank Dimant (Toronto: The Institute for International Affairs, B'nai Brith Canada, 2001), 25.

13. Mindy Avrich-Skapinker described the Canadian Jewish community as highly organized, dominated by an upper-middle-class conservative leadership, and exhibiting a preference for *shtadlanut* political advocacy that continued to be the norm until the 1960s, in her thesis *Canadian Jewish Involvement with Soviet Jewry, 1970–1990: The Toronto Case Study* (University of Toronto: PhD thesis, 1993), 15–18.

14. Meanwhile the Communist Party of Canada had gotten one member elected to the Manitoba legislature in 1936, and it saw two Winnipeg city councillors elected from its ranks in 1938 (Tulchinsky, *Joe Salsberg*, 57–58).

15. LPP candidate A. A. MacLeod won election to the Ontario parliament the same year from the neighboring Bellwoods riding. Also, in 1943, Montreal LPP member Fred Rose won election to the federal House of Commons.

16. Tulchinsky discussed Salsberg's battle against discrimination of all kinds and his tireless work for fair pensions, among other issues. He won some real results and broad respect. *Joe Salsberg*, 72–74, 87–88, 93.

17. From a 1953 interview, quoted by Tulchinsky. *Joe Salsberg*, 87.

18. See Weisbord, *The Strangest Dream: Canadian Communists, the Spy Trials, and the Cold War* (Montréal: Véhicule Press, 1994), 204.

19. On others in the Jewish section of the Communist Party in the late 1940s who knew or suspected that bad things were happening to Jews in the Soviet Union but declined to speak publicly, see Albert D. Chernin, "Making Soviet Jews an Issue. A History," in *A Second Exodus: The American Movement to Free Soviet Jews*, ed. Murray Friedman and Albert D. Chernin (Hanover and London: Brandeis University Press, 1999).

20. Weisbord, *The Strangest Dream*, 98–99.

21. Tulchinsky, *Joe Salsberg*, 86–87.

22. Ben Kayfetz discussed the context for Salsberg's eulogy for Stalin and its impact on his career in "J. B. Salsberg—Charismatic 'Man of the People,'" in *Only Yesterday: Collected Pieces on the Jews of Toronto*, ed. Benjamin Kayfetz and Stephen A. Speisman (Toronto: Now & Then Books, 2013), 90.

23. Salsberg had visited Łagów and remaining family there in August 1939. Tulchinsky, *Joe Salsberg*, 96.

24. Ibid., 96–97. Tulchinsky quoted Salsberg's remarks.

25. Ibid., 97.

26. Yehoshua A. Gilboa discussed the anti-cosmopolitan campaign in light of Soviet postwar politics in *The Black Years of Soviet Jewry: 1939–1953*, trans. Yosef Shachter and Dov Benn-Abba (Boston: Little, Brown and Company). See in particular pages 158–59.

27. On the so-called "Doctors' Plot" and its relation to the campaign to discredit the JAC, see Iakov Etinger, "Stalin's Solution to the Jewish Question," in *Jews and Jewish Life in Russia and the Soviet Union*, ed. Yaacov Ro'i (Portland, Oregon: Frank Cass, 1995), 104–105.

28. The text of the speech, which Khrushchev asked Party members to keep confidential, got around quickly. The CIA received a Polish copy of the speech in early April, 1956, from Israeli intelligence, and they released it to the *New York Times*, which published it on June 4, 1956. See William Taubman, *Khrushchev: The Man and his Era* (New York, London: W.W. Norton & Company, 2003), 284.

29. The essay appeared in English translation as Document 74 in Benjamin Pinkus, *The Soviet Government and the Jews 1948–1967* (Cambridge: Cambridge University Press, 1984), 211–14.

30. A speaker characterized the *Folks-shtimme* essay this way in a paper entitled "The Jewish Communist Press Speaks Out on the State of Soviet Jewish Culture," for the Conference on the Status of the Soviet Jews, held October 12, 1963, in New York City. Text from the J. B. Salsberg Fonds, Box 13, File 11 at the Queen's University Archives (QUA), Kingston, Ontario. Moshe Decter organized this conference attended by Martin Luther King Jr., Robert Penn Warren, Norman Thomas and others. Paper author unknown.

31. Weisbord, *The Strangest Dream*, 216–217.

32. LPP officials acknowledged the Party leadership's unjustified intransigence and Salsberg's right to push the issue in a Party Statement on July 12, 1956 (QUA, Salsberg Fond, 9.4).

33. Weisbord, *The Strangest Dream*, 219. The 1956 Canadian delegation had been preceded by a group sent in 1955 by the Canadian-Soviet Friendship Society. That small delegation included leading Jewish communist Morris Biderman, who asserted that Soviet Jews faced no special problems or discrimination. Gennady Estraikh, *Yiddish in the Cold War* (London: Legenda, 2008), 17.

34. Salsberg's articles were reprinted in whole or part in the New York Yiddish communist daily paper *Morgen Freiheit*, in the Parisian Yiddish *Naie presse*, and the New York quarterly *Klorkeit*, as well as Tel Aviv's *Drahim Hadashot*. See Tulchinsky, *Joe Salsberg*, 108; and Yaacov Ro'i, *The Struggle for Soviet Jewish Emigration 1948–1967* (Cambridge: Cambridge University Press, 1991), 372, n. 81.

35. Salsberg was quoted in "The Absence of Cultural Freedom," *The New Leader* (Sept. 14, 1959): 9. On Decter and Nativ, see Gal Beckerman, *When They Come for Us, We'll Be Gone: The Epic Struggle to Save Soviet Jewry* (New York: Houghton Mifflin Harcourt, 2010), 52–55.

36. See Ro'i, *The Struggle*, 115–16; and Pauline Peretz, *Let My People Go. The Transnational Politics of Jewish Emigration during the Cold War*, trans. Ethan Rundell (New Brunswick, NJ: Transaction Publishers, 2015), 75.

37. Transcript of Decter's Oral History interview, May 10, 1990, 1–4, 1–5 (AJHS-Moshe Decter Papers, Box 3, F. 1).

38. Salsberg, "It's a Hangover of an Incorrect Policy," *Vochenblatt* 17, no. 841 (Dec. 13, 1956): 1. Vochenblatt has been preserved on microfilm at the Ontario Jewish Archives (OJA).

39. Salsberg, "Dissolution Began in the Late Thirties," *Vochenblatt* 17, no. 834 (Oct. 25, 1956): 1.

40. Salsberg, "We Were Always Concerned," *Vochenblatt* 17, no. 835 (Nov. 1, 1956): 3.

41. Salsberg, "My Moscow Discussions of 1955," *Vochenblatt* 17, no. 836 (Nov. 8, 1956): 3.

42. Salsberg, "We Were Always Concerned," 4.

43. Salsberg, "We Ask for a Statement on the Past—They Reply," *Vochenblatt* 17, no. 837 (Nov. 15, 1956): 3.

44. Zvi Gitelman outlined the widely discussed "psychological dissonance" created by the absence of Jewish culture in the USSR combined with the persistence of an often disadvantageous legal and social definition of Jews applied to citizens in the "nationality" category of Soviet passports. See his article, "Soviet Jews. Creating a Cause and a Movement", in *A Second Exodus*, ed. Friedman and Chernin, 86.

45. The American Jewish Committee, Library of Jewish Information: "Jews Behind the Iron Curtain," March 1957, 5. Salsberg related Khrushchev's remarks in "What Nikita Khrushchev Told Us," *Vochenblatt* 17, no. 840 (Dec. 6, 1956): 3.

46. Weisbord detailed the departure of Communist Party staff after the Canadian delegation returned from its 1956 trip: "It was the first time in the history of any communist party in the world that the leadership had abdicated en masse." Most remaining Party members left with them (*The Strangest Dream*, 220–223).

47. Mordechai Richler, *Joshua Then and Now* (Toronto: McClelland and Stewart Limited, 1980), 190–91; quoted by Avrich-Skapinker in *Canadian Jewish Involvement*, 12–13.

48. Franklin Bialystok wrote that between 30,000 and 35,000 survivors and their descendants had immigrated to Canada by 1961, in *Delayed Impact: The Holocaust and the Canadian Jewish Community* (Montreal: McGill-Queen's University Press, 2000), 73. The Jewish population in Canada was 254,368 in 1961.

49. The depth of Canadian Zionism, widely remarked and demonstrated in higher per-capita Canadian contributions to Israeli fundraising campaigns, might be explained on the basis of a conjunction of factors including the absence of strong German Reform influence; the perceived accord between Zionism and British imperialism early in the twentieth century; a relatively large number of immigrants from Eastern Europe; and the multi-national character of the Canadian Dominion, which did not exert the same pressure for assimilation as the United States. See Tulchinsky, "The Canadian Jewish Experience," 24–28.

50. The Canadian Jewish Congress, representing the Jewish establishment in Canada, did not sanction or support the anti-Rockwell demonstration. Congressional leaders also refrained from joining the march to commemorate the Holocaust and Liberation held by a survivors' group in May 1961. See Harold Troper, *The Defining Decade. Identity, Politics, and the Canadian Jewish Community in the 1960s* (Toronto: University of Toronto Press, 2010), 98–99; and Bialystok, *Delayed Impact*, 103–5.

51. Peretz borrowed Paul Burstein's characterization of "social movement organizations" to describe the grassroots elements of the Soviet Jewry Movement. Such organizations feature noninstitutional forms of political participation, that is, activities intended to be disruptive (whether legal or illegal). Peretz, *Let My People Go*, 116.

52. Wendy Eisen, *Count Us In: The Struggle to Free Soviet Jews. A Canadian Perspective* (Toronto: Burgher Books, 1995), 43–44. Shaul Kelner analyzed the use of ethnic and religious forms in Soviet Jewry activism as a new phenomenon in "Ritualized Protest and Redemptive Politics: Cultural Consequences of the American Mobilization to Free Soviet Jewry," *Jewish Social Studies: History, Culture, Society*, 14.3 (2008): 1–37.

53. Thanks to an international outcry, the two death sentences in the Leningrad Hijacking Trial were commuted. See Yuli Kosharovsky, *"We Are Jews Again": Jewish Activism in the Soviet Union*, ed. Ann Komaromi, trans. Stefani Hoffman (Syracuse, NY: Syracuse University Press, 2017), 88–95.

54. Hasia Diner, *We Remember with Reverence and Love: American Jews and the Myth of Silence after the Holocaust, 1945–1962* (New York and London: New York University Press, 2009), 374.

55. Shaffir and Weinfeld wrote, "Canadian Jews are roughly one generation closer to the Old World than are American Jews," "Canada and the Jews," 13.

56. OJA, Fonds 17, Series 3–1, File 2.

57. Diner discussed the pressure American Jewish communities felt to prove their anti-Communist loyalties in the Cold War era. *We Remember*, 287. Looking back, Henry Feingold evaluated the movement along these lines: "[A] concealed dividend of the campaign to 'free' Soviet Jewry may be the dissipation of the Judeobolshevik myth. Nothing could be

more effective in doing that than the photos of thousands of Jews arriving in Israel and their total disaffection from anything that smacked of Socialism." See Feingold, *"Silent No More": Saving the Jews of Russia, The American Jewish Effort, 1967–1989* (Syracuse, New York: Syracuse University Press, 2007), 16.

58. "JB' Fires Broadside . . . Refuses to Back Down," *Canadian Jewish News* (December 31, 1971), QUA, Salsberg Fonds, 18.2.

59. A report dated May 26, 1976, of the meeting of the Toronto Action Committee for Soviet Jewry, stated: "When we think of Soviet Jewry, four dates come to mind—Pesach, 'S'man Herutaenu'; Simchat Torah, when Jews dance in the squares; Human Rights Day; and August 12th. Why August 12th? In 1952 Stalin executed Soviet Jewish intellectuals on that day." OJA, Fonds 17, Series 3–1, File 8.

60. The exact details of the trial and executions long remained obscure. They can be found in *Stalin's Secret Pogrom*, eds. Joshua Rubenstein and Vladimir P. Naumov, trans. Laura Esther Wolfson (New Haven, London: Yale University Press, 2001), 5.

61. The May 26, 1976, report of the Toronto Action Committee stated that, "A committee, working with the Committee for Yiddish, will memorialize these murdered Jews on August 12th. Toronto is the only Jewish community to do so." OJA, Fonds 17, Series 3–1, File 8. The Toronto Committee may have been a Canadian leader, but Joel R. Sprayregen also pushed for commemoration of August 12 to NCSJ Director Jerry Goodman in a letter of April 16, 1971. AJHS, New York—NCSJ Records, Box 37, F. 5. The Americans mounted a well-publicized and orchestrated commemoration of the twentieth anniversary in 1972. AJHS—NCSJ, Box 37, F. 6.

62. Pirkei Avot I.15, as translated by Charles Taylor, in *Sayings of the Jewish Fathers, Comprising Pirqe Aboth and Pereq R. Meir*, ed. Charles Taylor (Cambridge: Cambridge University Press, 1877), 37.

63. From the *CJN*, April 1, 1977, quoted by Tulchinsky, *Joe Salsberg*, 124–25.

64. From Gordon's poem "Awake My People!" (*Hakitsah ami*, 1863). Anna Shternshis described the realization of this modern, maskilic ideal in the Soviet Union in the mid-1920s and 1930s. See her *Soviet and Kosher: Jewish Popular Culture in the Soviet Union, 1923–1939* (Bloomington and Indianapolis: Indiana University Press, 2006), 184–85.

65. Kelner talked about the blurred boundaries between conceptual dichotomies, including private and public, as well as religious and secular, expressive and instrumental, in Soviet Jewry activism. "Ritualized Protest," 3–4.

66. Salsberg, "Mad scramble for credit mars release of Mendelevich," *Canadian Jewish News*, March 12, 1981.

67. Natan Sharansky, *Fear No Evil*, trans. Stefani Hoffman (New York: Vintage Books, 1989), 170.

68. Interview with Sadowski (January 17, 2013; Toronto).

69. A brief profile appears in the obituary by Frances Kraft, "'Charismatic' activist fought for refuseniks," *Canadian Jewish News*, August 14, 2008, accessed June 19, 2012, www.cjnews.com/node/81594.

70. *A study of Jews refused their right to leave the Soviet Union* (Montreal: Canadian Jewish Congress, 1980–83), 3 vols, was initially undertaken as material for the Canadian delegation to the gathering convened in Madrid, 1980, of the Conference for Security and Co-operation in Europe. Interview and correspondence with Barbara Stern, May–June 2012.

71. Elie Wiesel, *The Jews of Silence: A Personal Report on Soviet Jewry* [originally 1966] (New York: Knopf, Doubleday Publishing Group, 2011), 1.

72. Pauline Peretz characterized the memory of the Holocaust and the provocative questions it raised about Jewish responsibility as "the single most important factor" in mobilizing Western Jewish communities on behalf of Soviet Jews, apart from the Israeli Nativ bureau efforts. *Let My People Go*, 93.

73. Irving Abella and Harold Troper documented the fact that between 1933 and 1945 Canada admitted fewer than 5,000 Jews. After the war and until the founding of Israel in 1948, just 8,000 more were allowed entry. After 1948, barriers to Jewish immigration began to be lifted. See Abella and Troper, *None is Too Many* (Toronto: Lester & Orpen Neys, 1983), xxii, 285.

74. Diner cited a few instances of the widespread use of the term "cultural genocide" with reference to Soviet Jews, in *We Remember*, 285.

75. Fackenheim is best known for his 614th Commandment: "the authentic Jew of today is forbidden to hand Hitler yet another, posthumous victory." See "The 614th Commandment" (orig. 1967), in *The Jewish Return Into History* (New York: Schocken Books, 1978), 22–23.

76. Diner, 11.

77. Ibid. A similar argument was made by Michael Rothberg, who insisted that "the early postwar period [of Holocaust memory] is richer and more complex than earlier studies, with their stress on a period of silence and repression . . . have allowed." See Rothberg, *Multidirectional Memory: Remembering the Holocaust in the Age of Decolonization* (Stanford: Stanford UP, 2009), 22.

78. See Kramer, *Mordecai Richler*, 4–5; and Adam Gopnik, "Introduction," in *Mordecai Richler Was Here: Selected Writings*, ed. Jonathan Webb (Toronto: Madison Press Books, 2006), 8–9.

79. Salsberg, "Yes, Uncle Eliezer, I will," *Canadian Jewish News*, September 10, 1971, QUA, Salsberg Fonds, 18.2.

80. Tulchinsky, *Joe Salsberg*, 124.

In the Presence of the Past

RABBI JOACHIM PRINZ, HOLOCAUST MEMORY, AND THE FIGHT FOR JEWISH SURVIVAL IN POSTWAR AMERICA

David Jünger

ON AUGUST 28, 1963, the president of the American Jewish Congress (AJC), Rabbi Joachim Prinz (1902–1988), had what he later recalled as "the greatest religious experience" of his whole life.[1] In front of an audience of more than two hundred thousand people, he delivered a speech at the March on Washington for Jobs and Freedom. Minutes before Martin Luther King, Jr. entered the stage and talked about his great "Dream," Rabbi Prinz addressed the audience with a similarly remarkable speech about his own political posture regarding the Civil Rights Movement and American Jewry after the Holocaust.[2]

In his speech, he insisted that it was not compassion for the plight of Blacks that had drawn him into the civil rights struggle, but rather the profound conviction that Jews and Blacks were deeply entangled in each other's destinies, struggles, and goals for civil liberties in the United States. In his words, it was "not merely sympathy and compassion for the black people of America that motivates us. It is above all and beyond all such sympathies and emotions a sense of complete identification and solidarity born of our own painful historic experience."[3] This identification derives, as Prinz further explained, from the mutual history of slavery and the mutual experience of racial discrimination in contemporary America.

In addition to these considerations, he also invoked his own personal story as a Zionist liberal rabbi, who was born in Imperial Germany, grew up under declining conditions for the Jewish community during World

War I and the Weimar Republic, and was expelled from Nazi Germany in 1937. "When I was the rabbi of the Jewish community in Berlin under the Hitler regime," Prinz said in his address at the March, "I learned many things. The most important thing that I learned under those tragic circumstances was that bigotry and hatred are not the most urgent problem. The most urgent, the most disgraceful, the most shameful and the most tragic problem is silence."[4] He finished his speech with an invocation of the American Dream and a demand for its immediate fulfilment: "America must speak up and act, from the President down to the humblest of us, and not for the sake of the Negro, not for the sake of the black community, but for the sake of the image, the idea and the aspiration of America itself."[5]

Joachim Prinz was one of the major figures of the AJC from the late 1940s through the 1960s. During this period, the Congress grappled with its self-conception, as well as with the meaning of Jewishness and with the prospect of a Jewish future in post-Holocaust America. At the same time, it played a leading role in the Civil Rights Movement and was, as an organization, one of the most important Jewish allies of Martin Luther King, Jr. The civil rights struggle and the quest for renewed Jewish meaning were closely connected to each other, and the man who best represented this connection was Rabbi Joachim Prinz. Time and again, he explicitly stated that the future of American Jewry depended crucially on its capacity to adapt to the conditions of a post-Holocaust world. In Prinz's understanding, these conditions were predetermined by the ubiquitous topic of civil rights in an America that needed to be transformed into a culturally pluralistic society. Even though Rabbi Prinz's contemporary and current reputation has been strongly connected to his participation in the March on Washington, his relationship to the Civil Rights Movement is more ambiguous than it seems to be. He was without doubt a fervent supporter of civil rights in America and also a reliable ally of Martin Luther King, Jr. and the Civil Rights Movement. But he also worried that the dominance of political issues within American Jewry could eventually lead to its disintegration. It was his conviction that the civil rights program must not be carried out at the expense of Jewish values and Jewish religion, but to the contrary, it had to be integrated into a program for the reconfiguration and strengthening of Judaism in the postwar world. In this way, the civil rights struggle could be a tool for the survival of the Jewish people. It is my argument in this article that Joachim Prinz's understanding of American pluralism, the Civil Rights Movement, and the legacy of the Holocaust were deeply rooted in his own personal experiences with Nazi oppression in the 1930s, when he was a famous Zionist rabbi in Berlin.

Even though the AJC was a major political force in American Jewry as well as in the civil rights struggle, its postwar history is almost unknown.[6] The same is true for its leading figure from the late 1940s to the 1960s: Rabbi Joachim Prinz.[7] Recovering this knowledge is especially crucial if one wants to explore the reasons for Jewish involvement in the Civil Rights Movement. The personal accounts of Jews participating in this struggle often named the legacy of the Holocaust as one of the major reasons to take part. The most famous allusion to the Holocaust within this context, besides Prinz's speech in Washington, might be the letter by the fifteen rabbis arrested in St. Augustine, Florida in June 1964, which reads, "We came as Jews who remember the millions of faceless people who stood quietly, watching the smoke rise from Hitler's crematoria. We came because we know that, second only to silence, the greatest danger to man is loss of faith in man's capacity to act."[8] There is a comprehensive literature on Black-Jewish relations in postwar America that deals with different aspects of Jewish participation in the civil rights struggle.[9] However, as yet, no cohesive study on the connection of Holocaust memory and the Jewish civil rights struggle has been carried out. Only a few articles elaborate on this topic.[10]

In this essay, I will emphasize how Prinz's personal experiences with oppression and persecution in Nazi Germany generated the moral foundation for his life as a political rabbi, and how this was connected to his involvement in the Civil Rights Movement and his understanding of the reconfiguration of American Jewry in the post-Holocaust world. Thus, this essay contributes to the growing field of American Jewish postwar studies that tries to more deeply elaborate on transnational encounters between American, European, and Israeli Jewry. It is my argument that the experiences of refugees from Germany and Nazi-occupied Europe are important to understanding the political developments of American Jewry after World War II.

DAVID JÜNGER

Between Admiration and Persecution: Formative Years in Weimar and Nazi Berlin

Joachim Prinz was born in 1902 in a small village in Upper Silesia, Germany, a region known for its mixture of different populations, mostly Germans, Poles, and Jews. After growing up in an assimilated Jewish family with an ardent German patriotic father, he discovered Zionism around 1918. In 1921, he started his rabbinical education at the Jewish Theological Seminary in Breslau and a year later began his university studies. In early 1924, he graduated with a PhD in Philosophy and also finished his rabbinical education, though he was not yet formally ordained as rabbi. He and his first wife Lucie Horvitz moved to Berlin in 1926.[11]

In early 1927, at the tender age of twenty-four, Prinz was inaugurated as rabbi of the liberal Jewish community *Friedenstempel* in Berlin.[12] Within a short period of time, he became one of the leading and most famous Jewish preachers in Berlin. During the first years of the Nazi regime, he was one of the most important Zionist voices in Germany, maybe second only to Robert Weltsch, the editor of the prestigious Zionist newspaper *Jüdische Rundschau*. He was also, after Leo Baeck, probably the most famous rabbi, at least of Berlin. His public speeches and sermons were attended by hundreds of (mostly) young German Jews. In recalling his childhood in Berlin, author Peter Wyden mentions the impact of Prinz: he writes that the Friedenstempel Synagogue "accommodated 1,500 people, and Rabbi Prinz was such a charismatic figure that sometimes on High Holidays the police had to block off the crowd of pushing people trying to enter."[13] Eva Samo, a friend who became acquainted with Prinz in Berlin in 1933, testified decades later, "He was to us what nowadays would be a rockstar."[14]

By the time the Nazis rose to power in 1933, Prinz was not only an acclaimed speaker but also a distinguished writer. His first book, *Jüdische Geschichte* (Jewish History), published in 1931, was already a great success, surpassed only by his famous work *Wir Juden* (We Jews), published three years later.[15] *Wir Juden* was a profound commitment to Judaism and Zionism and one of the most important Jewish books published during the Nazi era. The book triggered a heated internal Jewish debate about the meaning and prospects of Jewish existence in the modern world, as well as in Nazi Germany.

Prinz's rabbinical behavior was decidedly unconventional. He did not observe the Sabbath or the kosher dietary laws, nor did he socialize or communicate with the rabbinical establishment of his time or comply with the rules of rabbinical sermons, and, perhaps most radically, he overtly rejected monogamous matrimonial relationships. When he also publicly questioned the organizational structure of the Berlin Jewish community, he became an outcast and lost his rabbinate in 1935—a unique incident within the Jewish community during the Nazi era. The so-called Prinz Affair evolved during 1935 and sparked intense debates in newspapers and public panel discussions.[16] It was almost symbolic that Prinz gave his last sermon as a rabbi two days before the promulgation of the Nuremberg Laws.[17] Thus, in mid-September 1935, he was regarded twice as an outsider, first by the Jewish community of Berlin and then by the German nation. It was also around 1935 that Nazi authorities began to monitor Jewish speakers more severely.[18] Prinz came to the notice of the Gestapo and was detained a couple of times. Finally, after another two years in Germany, he decided to leave. In the summer of 1937 he immigrated to the United States, where he stayed till the end of his life.

German Experience and the Civil Rights Struggle

By the time Prinz arrived in America, he was already deeply affected by his own more than four years of resistance to the humiliations and denigrations of the Nazi regime. His early Zionist convictions, expressed in his famous 1934 book *Wir Juden*, had centered on concepts of Jewish *volk* and Jewish race, but shortly after publishing the book, he realized the limitations and dangers of this kind of racial thinking. He committed himself, as he later testified in his speech at the March on Washington, to never be silent in the face of injustice, discrimination, or oppression of any kind.

This conviction was challenged the very first time he reached American soil in early 1937, on his preparatory trip a few months before immigrating. His first encounter with America, and moreover with American Jewry and American Zionism, was for him "a great disappointment."[19] Unsettled by what he perceived in a slightly arrogant way as the simplicity of American Jewry, he was especially troubled by their approach to race relations. Whereas German Jewry—of which he was a part—had always been the minority in Germany, American Jewry was different. Prinz might not have fully understood American society on his first trip, but what he saw in New York City reminded him of the situation in Germany. Except that in this case, the American Jews, as he saw it, were part of the white supremacy, and the situation for the American Blacks resembled that of the German Jews.

After Prinz returned to Germany some months before his final immigration, he described his impressions of the trip in the German Jewish monthly *Der Morgen*:

> Strange, how our view has changed. We, who came here to look around, have a sharper view and deeper feelings. The Negroes of Harlem remind us of the times of *Uncle Tom's Cabin*. We therefore do not understand how the Jews there can look at Negroes with such utter indifference, or how they can be so arrogant.... We cannot do this. We understand them too well, the Blacks in the ghetto of Harlem.[20]

It was Prinz's conviction that the perspective of a German Jew living in the modern ghetto of Nazi Germany led to a different understanding of racial discrimination in other places. And he was unsettled that Jews could be part of racial discrimination against others, even while their brethren were persecuted for similar reasons in Europe. His anger was aggravated when he toured the American South in late 1937, a couple of weeks after his arrival as a new immigrant to the United States. A Zionist group had invited him to a gathering in Atlanta, but before going to the city, he first had a long talk with the black Methodist bishop Willis Jefferson King. When his Zionist hosts learned of this meeting, one of them approached Prinz and insulted King with racist terms. Prinz later wrote about this experience in his autobiography:

> I was completely speechless.... I was amazed to hear such words from a Jewish group welcoming a Hitler refugee whose people had been persecuted in the country of their birth because of their race. I added that I simply did not understand nor had I known that Jews, the classical victims of racial persecution, could themselves be

racists. I said that what was evidently happening to the black people of America was the very same thing that was happening to the Jewish people in Europe.²¹

This encounter with Jewish racism depressed Prinz, who later wrote, "Altogether, the American Jews were a great disappointment to me."²²

Almost three decades later, when Joachim Prinz stood in front of the Lincoln Memorial and drew the connection between his personal experience with Nazi antisemitism and his fight against racism in America, he reiterated his by then deeply rooted conviction of a mutual fight and shared destiny between Blacks and Jews, a conviction that dated back to his own first encounters with America and the American Jews of 1937.

Prinz spent his first years as a new American giving lectures on Jewish topics and on the Jewish catastrophe in Europe, which brought him to almost all the states and opened his mind to the American situation. He testified that his "experiences as a lecturer were of extraordinary importance," since they permitted him "to see much of America, traveling from coast to coast, meeting all kinds of people, Jews and non-Jews" alike.²³ What he learned step by step, and what puzzled him severely, was something he perceived as Jewish separatism: "What impressed me most negatively was the fact that the Jews lived among themselves. Although they were citizens of the United States and very proud of it, their life after six p.m. was restricted to their Jewish friends."²⁴ As someone who had admired the vivid urban life of Weimar Berlin and was ultimately ripped out of this lifestyle by the Nazi regime, he could not comprehend the self-estrangement and separatism he witnessed in American Jewry.

For Prinz's early career in America, his relationship to Stephen S. Wise, the prominent American Zionist and long-serving president of the American Jewish Congress, was crucial. They had been corresponding with each other since the early 1930s and had met for the first time at the Zionist congress in Lucerne in late 1935.²⁵ Wise had brought Prinz to America and, shortly after Prinz's immigration, managed, in 1939, to provide him with a congregation in Newark New Jersey, Congregation B'nai Abraham.²⁶ Within a short time, Prinz became a prominent figure of the American Jewish community. Wise also introduced Prinz into the AJC, where he soon held leading positions. In 1958 he was elected as its president and maintained this post until 1966. He also became a senior member of the World Jewish Congress (WJC), and from 1965 to 1967 was chairman of the influential Conference of Presidents of Major Jewish Organizations. In addition to being a close friend of Wise's, he also became good friends with Nahum Goldmann, the chairman of the WJC.

The 1950s and 1960s, when Prinz was a leading figure and the president of the AJC, was the heyday of the Civil Rights Movement as well as of the Black-Jewish "alliance."[27] The AJC was, from its beginning, an ardent supporter of the movement, and it was the first Jewish organization that publicly endorsed the turn from the legal battle to tactics of civil disobedience at the beginning of the 1960s.[28] It was also the Jewish organization that was the closest to the emerging hero of the Civil Rights Movement, Martin Luther King, Jr.[29]

Stanley Levison was the first and most important protagonist of this relationship. He was a communist and also a member of the AJC, and—according to Coretta King—Martin Luther King's closest white friend.[30] But even beyond Levison, many leading figures of the AJC perceived the civil rights struggle as the most important element of Jewish political activism in postwar America. The most audible and persistent civil rights propagandists of the AJC were Justine Wise Polier (Stephen S. Wise's daughter) and her husband Shad Polier. In a panel discussion with Prinz in 1958, Wise Polier asserted, "By dint of our heritage, our faith, the intuitive and all but instinctive reaction of the Jew against injustice or the violation of human dignity, we are committed to the battle for human freedom—whether it is or is not good for the survival of the Jewish people."[31]

This statement was intended to defend the civil rights agenda of the AJC against the criticism that it violated Jewish self-interest. It was said that the organization had abandoned its formerly Jewish content for the sake of human rights in general. The question was, as Milton Himmelfarb later argued, whether the AJC was "a Jewish organization with a civil-rights program or a civil-rights organization whose members are Jews."[32]

Wise Polier's statement stood in sharp contrast to Prinz's understanding of the imperatives for post-Holocaust Jewry. While Wise Polier deemed "Jewish survival" as less important than civil rights issues, Prinz opposed this kind of prioritizing. He replied to Wise Polier at the same debate: "Too many of us find refuge in the Congress civil rights program because it affords an opportunity to belong to a Jewish organization without being involved in a 'Jewish program.'" And he claimed that the AJC had to return to its old fight for Jewish survival and democracy, of which the civil rights struggle was only one aspect.[33]

Even though Prinz repudiated Wise Polier's understanding of Jewish survival and civil rights issues, he still supported the civil rights agenda of the AJC. This was demonstrated at the very same National Biennial Convention of the AJC in Miami Beach, Florida, in May 1958, where the aforementioned debate between Wise Polier and Prinz took place. At this convention, Prinz was elected president of the AJC for the first time, succeeding Israel Goldstein. For this event, he invited Martin Luther King, Jr. as his special guest speaker. It was the first time that King had spoken to a white audience south of the Mason-Dixon Line. In his speech, King echoed Prinz in his thoughts on the mutual destiny of Blacks and Jews. First, according to King, Blacks and Jews shared a common history: "My people were brought to America in chains. Your people were driven here to escape the chains fashioned for them in Europe. Our unity is born of our common struggle for centuries, not only to rid ourselves of bondage, but to make oppression of any people by others an impossibility."[34] Second, he stressed that both groups shared the same struggle since "the segregationists make no fine distinctions between the Negro and the Jew."[35] Thus, he concluded, "Our common fight is against these deadly enemies of democracy."[36] Coming to the end of the speech, he invoked the American Dream, just as Prinz would do about five years later at the March on Washington. King said, "America, the first nation to electrify the world with a new concept of man's capability of self-rule without monarchs or regents, must fulfill the promises of its constitution and Declaration of Independence."[37]

The collaboration of King and Prinz continued through the early 1960s. King was invited to speak in Prinz's synagogue, B'nai Abraham, in January 1963, while Prinz was invited a couple of months later, in August 1963, to be one of the key speakers at the March on Washington.[38] Time and again, King took a clear and overt stance against the growing antisemitism within the Black community and publicly defended the State of Israel, even beyond the Six Day War of 1967.[39]

American Diaspora, Israel, and the Holocaust

After his speech in front of the Lincoln Memorial, Rabbi Prinz received dozens of letters from people all over the world thanking him. For example, Julius Wildstein, a member of the AJC as well as of Prinz's congregation, wrote him in pride and gratitude: "I am sure that there will be a day in the future when my daughter will be asked by her children where we were on August 28, 1963, and the answer will be that we were in Washington, D.C., and were not one of the 'silent listeners' as it was so dramatically put in the wonderful speech of Rabbi Prinz—*our* Rabbi."[40] Not only the Jewish audience but also the leadership of the Civil Rights Movement were deeply impressed by Prinz's remarks. Roy Wilkins, executive director of the National Association for the Advancement of Colored People (NAACP), wrote to Prinz in a personal letter, "In the sober ruminations after the peak excitement of the day, the consensus among the many who have talked with me has been that 'the Rabbi' was among the two or three best. I join personally in that view and offer my thanks, not only for your speech at the Memorial, but for your cogent observations and guidance in the various conferences and radio and television panels."[41]

Due to his performance in Washington, for the following months, Prinz was acclaimed as the Jewish hero of the Black-Jewish alliance. After a while, however, this imaged blurred. "Posterity has been unfair to Joachim Prinz," writes Stephen J. Whitfield, who argues that in most of the major fields Rabbi Prinz worked in, there was always someone else who surpassed him in his reputation. In German rabbinate this was Rabbi Leo Baeck; in civil rights issues Abraham Joshua Heschel; and in New Jersey, where he lived and preached, Rabbi Arthur Hertzberg. This is the reason, according to Whitfield, why he has been forgotten by history: "Obscurity has dogged him . . . consigning to near oblivion the German-born rabbi who escaped Nazi Germany to find a home in the United States."[42] Many people who knew Prinz personally or know the history of Black-Jewish relations, however, have a different image, namely that of the splendid rabbi of Newark, NJ, who stood in front of the Lincoln memorial as the personification of a modern, progressive, and caring Judaism and its involvement in the civil rights struggle of the African-American community.

This image, however, is slightly misleading. The fact that he was the key Jewish speaker of the event was rather coincidental. Isaiah Minkoff of the National Jewish Community Relations Council was originally planned as speaker but was replaced by Prinz on very short notice.[43] And Prinz's stance towards the Civil Rights Movement was anything but pure altruism. Unlike Justine Wise Polier and Shad Polier, his opponents vis-à-vis civil rights issues in the AJC, he thought of the civil rights struggle not only in terms of its intrinsic value but also as a tool for more Jewish concerns. From the late 1950s until the early 1960s, he argued with both Poliers about the meaning of that struggle within the American Jewish agenda. The Poliers' belief that the civil rights struggle must rule out any other specific Jewish activities and should be the one and only political task of AJC was sharply repudiated by Prinz. In a letter to former AJC president Israel Goldstein, he complained bitterly about Shad Polier's attitudes.

> In a recent debate which I had with Shad, he said very clearly that the only kind of Jewish living he understands and is important is the participation of the Jews in the solution of the problem of the American Negro. I cannot possibly equate Jewish survival with the problem of segregation, and I refuse to admit that the American Jewish Congress cannot make a contribution to creative Jewish continuity, to alerting American Jewry to the problems inherent in Diaspora living, etc.[44]

As indicated in the letter, Prinz's involvement in civil rights issues was part and parcel of his general preoccupation with American Jewry in the post-Holocaust decades. The future of Judaism, American Jewry, or more generally the diaspora—condensed in the term "Jewish Survival"—was his major concern. His political life centered on three major issues that were mutually entangled, and which shaped his attitudes towards the Civil Rights Movement. The first was the catastrophe of the Holocaust in Europe, the second the founding of the State of Israel, and the third the meaning of the American diaspora in a post-Holocaust world.

The devastating effects of the Holocaust in Europe were his most personal concern. As early as 1934, in his famous book *Wir Juden*, Prinz proclaimed—as many other Zionists did—the end of the era of emancipation. This era, Prinz explained, was subject to the concept of Liberalism, which had declined throughout the whole of Europe. Furthermore, assimilation—which was for him tantamount to emancipation—he perceived as a process that had also failed entirely.[45] After arriving in the United States in 1937, he declared publicly, "There is no future for the Jews in Germany. . . . They are condemned to extinction. The last chapter in the history of German Jewry is now being written, and it is necessary to recognize this fact and to make no attempt to preserve any illusion about the matter."[46]

Although this was not a prophecy of the Holocaust, the German mass murder of European Jews indeed left a devastated continent and a German Jewry that was either murdered or dispersed. After World War II, Prinz would time and again reiterate his opinion that German Jewry would be lost forever. In 1949, he returned to Germany for the second time after the war in order to participate in the Heidelberg Conference on "The Future of the Jews in Germany." In a statement at the conference, he described his strange feelings of coming back to what was once his country: "A return after so many years to Germany means the discovery of a great deal of death and decay, of graves and tombstones, of broken houses and of a devastated people. This is the reality of Germany today and certainly of the Jewish community living here."[47] In this vein, he further declared that, "German Jewish life has nothing of the glory and the splendor of a real living Jewish organism. Although Jewish history was written in this country, the community itself is . . . no longer anything but the echo and the reflection of what was once a noble reality."[48]

Even though the Jewish community in Germany lived on, Prinz stood firm in his conviction that German Jewry could not be revived after the Holocaust and was doomed to extinction. Referring to the vivid debate of the late 1960s on the so-called German-Jewish symbiosis, he wrote in 1969, "The debate on the relationship between Germans and Jews which has taken place since the end of the Second World War has been conducted in the shadow of the events during the Hitler regime. The shadow was large and ominous. It was cast by the mass graves and the gas ovens. It took place in the shadow of Auschwitz."[49] Since these shadows were so strong and dark, he denied that what he called the "German-Jewish bridge" could be (re)built: "The bridge which was not built firmly enough during the course of sixteen hundred years of German-Jewish history will not be built by our generation. It will remain the Pont D'Avignon, the unfinished bridge, in Jewish history."[50] A few years earlier, in 1961, he had predicted the extinction of Germany Jewry within ten years.[51]

When it came to the reverberation of the Holocaust in Europe, Prinz went further in stating that it was not only German Jewry that had nearly vanished but almost the entire European and global diaspora, referring to the communities in Poland, the Soviet Union, the Middle East, and North Africa. These crucial alterations of the Jewish world, as Prinz declared in an article in 1970, had dire consequences for the American Jewish diaspora. Until the beginning of World War II, American Jewry had been consistently invigorated by European Jewry, either spiritually or personally. But after World War II, the vital forces of European Jewry had disappeared: "American Jewry has for a long time been nourished by the tradition of old communities. We are now totally on our own, and I am afraid there is no place in the world nor [a] Jewish community anywhere on the globe that can provide us with what once upon a time Vilna, Warsaw and Frankfurt did. . . . We are, in every sense of the word, orphans."[52]

But what about Israel? After World War II, American Jewry became perhaps the most important center of world Jewry, but a new center was emerging: the Jewish state of Israel. Its founding in 1948 changed the Jewish world fundamentally for a second time. The founding of Israel was, as Prinz called it, "the Jewish revolution of 1948."[53] This revolution meant that the multiple faces of Judaism were replaced by Israeli culture, arts, and politics, which was different from what Judaism used to be. As mentioned earlier, Prinz had been a committed Zionist when he was a rabbi in Berlin, but his Zionism was utterly different from the Zionism represented by the State of Israel. Because of its messianic, prophetic, and utopian meaning, Zionism, according to Prinz, had been the greatest force in Jewish history since the early days of emancipation. Looking back on his Zionist inclinations of the 1920s and 1930s, Prinz concluded in an interview given in 1980, "We didn't think of going to Palestine, because we didn't think the state could ever be created. As a matter of fact, the fact that it could not be created was part of our . . . ideology. The impossibility of Zionism was the beauty of it, that it could not be concretized. It was a very unconcrete, non-concrete, very idealistic, very romantic thing, a flag, a song.[54]

In this understanding, Zionism stood for the revival and survival of Judaism as a progressive religion. With the founding of Israel, the messianic, prophetic, and utopian character of Zionism had gone. Shortly after Israel's founding in May 1948, Prinz proclaimed at a convention in Philadelphia, "Zionism is dead, long live the Jewish people and Israel."[55] One year later he wrote, "The Zionist movement, however important its new functions may yet be, has lost its Messianic qualities. The dream has come true. It was good as long as it was unfulfilled. 'Next Year in Jerusalem' now means a telephone call to a travel agent. It means ticket and visa."[56]

Even if he adamantly defended Israel against its foes and considered it a haven for the Jewish people and a source of Jewish inspiration, he perceived the state as a crucial challenge, and to some extent even a threat for the American diaspora, which to Prinz meant it was a threat to Judaism in general. In the first years of Israel's existence, he had perceived and publicly defended the Jewish state as the most important stimulating factor for world Jewry.[57] He had also deplored the fact that "American Jewish relationships to Israel are defined by fundraising concerns and are conceived almost wholly in terms of philanthropy."[58] Thus, he warned that "if bridges are not created now between the two communities we shall be confronted by a yawning chasm. Indeed, we can now glimpse the widening gulf that divides the young American Jew and his Israeli counterpart."[59] The bridges were built but not firmly enough. Over the years, Israeli state representatives, primarily David Ben-Gurion, tried to negate the right of a Jewish diaspora outside the Jewish state. Friction arose between those Israelis who aspired to end what they believed was only a temporary Jewish exile, and the American Jews, whose perception of the *galut*, or the diaspora, had a more inner and eternal meaning.[60] Moreover, the "status quo" agreement between the state and the Orthodox community in Israel had rendered Orthodox Judaism both a state religion and the only Jewish denomination allowed to exist. In this sense, Prinz thought, Israel was not only limiting Judaism to its Orthodox branch, but also striving to influence American Jewry and make it its own hinterland. Over time, Prinz became more and more embittered over the American-Israel relationship. In 1972 he said in an interview, "I think that . . . the number one item on the agenda of the Jewish people [is] the relationship between the Jews of the Diaspora and the sovereign State of Israel. I'm very critical of the State of Israel trying to manipulate and manage Diaspora Jewry."[61]

Diaspora Jewry—namely American Jewry—became for Prinz the anchor of the Jewish future in a post-Holocaust world. The meanings of the American diaspora, the Civil Rights Movement, and the future of Judaism were in a sense closely connected to each other. In Prinz's perception, Judaism in the modern world stood at the edge of an abyss: Jewish life had been nearly wiped out in Europe, the Middle East, and North Africa—the prewar centers of Jewish existence—and Israel had emerged as a new and promising Jewish entity. But Judaism, or the Jewish religion in Israel, was at an impasse. Hence, Prinz assigned the preservation of Judaism exclusively to the American diaspora. Even though Zionism was declared dead by Prinz, its heritage was rich and meaningful: "Zionism is—for all practical purposes—dead. But it has bequeathed to the Jewish people a rich inheritance. . . . Jewish life today is the immediate heir of the Zionist movement."[62] But American Jewry itself faced a predicament. Right after World War II, the last barriers for Jews in America began to disintegrate. For the first time in their history, the Jews were about to fully enter American society. The centrifugal forces that drove Jews out of the fold became stronger and stronger. This process could already be discerned before the war, but it gained enormous momentum in the 1950s and 60s. Prinz explained that the vital forces for the preservation of Judaism no longer existed: not the vitalizing impact of the European diaspora, nor the prophetic vision of Zionism, nor even the antisemitism that had always forced Jews to stick together.

> Our problem is not antisemitism. Sometimes I wish it were, for we have seen the creative responses to persecution. It is indeed our problem, that, although we have learned to survive in adversity, we have not yet learned to survive in freedom. . . . I think that we can state bluntly . . . that we have not yet succeeded, nor do I know whether we ever will succeed in our battle against the organic process of assimilation which we all watch with such great apprehension.[63]

Prinz's phrase "to survive in freedom" referred to one of the major topics of American Jewry after the war: the question of so-called Jewish survival, which was also Prinz's main preoccupation throughout his political career.[64] The term "survival" can be found in almost all of his writings. In 1949, right after the founding of Israel, he wrote,

> We need a program for the survival of American Jewry and we need it badly. We need it badly because we are already in the midst of a movement of assimilation.... We deal here with a quiet, almost unnoticed phenomenon of beginning disintegration, of which intermarriage and conversion are only two of the symptoms. We are confronted with the complete de-Judaization of the children and grandchildren of even our leading Jews.[65]

This apprehension struck him severely. In his 1962 book *The Dilemma of the Modern Jew*, he wrote, "I admit that present conditions seem to speak against Jewish survival: the watering down of the Jewish heritage, the provincial mentality of Jewish organized religion, the laziness, the rebellion of many against any interference with comfort and convenience, the lack of the kind of heroism and stubbornness that are required for conscious survival."[66] Jewish survival, according to Prinz, would only be possible if the Jews revived Judaism as a living religion of humanity. He continued in this vein by declaring,

> In spite of all this, I believe that there will be a new kind of Jewish survival. Not one born of nightmares and fears. Not one born of dreams and illusions. But one born of a new twentieth-century understanding of man as he is, of all the factors, complexities, memories, drives and hopes that make of a human being something living, something so unbelievably rich and unique, so unlimited in desire and potential.[67]

When Prinz wrote these lines, he was already entangled in the civil rights struggle. He wanted this struggle to make Judaism a living religion of the twentieth century and hence to act as the remedy for Jewish survival. This understanding of humanity or ethical values as the main content of Judaism was close to the Reconstructionist Judaism of Mordecai Kaplan and the concept of "Judaism as a Civilization," elaborated in Kaplan's book of the same title.⁶⁸ This was one of the main reasons Prinz did not hesitate to align the AJC with the civil rights struggle, even if he disagreed with the Poliers about its centrality. A couple of years later, he again described the value of the civil rights struggle for Jewish survival:

> The only significant move in contemporary Judaism which, for the first time in the twentieth century, made Judaism relevant to the current generation, was the application of Jewish values to the problems of justice, equality, hunger and peace. Some of us tried to make our contribution to it, and there was a time at the March on Washington when hundreds of rabbis, ministers, priests, and nuns participated in what to me was the greatest religious experience of my life . . . . It indicated to the world that Judaism had returned to its prophetic teachings, and that it was no longer a museum of antiquity, but a living and acting religion of the twentieth century.⁶⁹

Beyond the Dream

By the time Prinz reevaluated the meaning of Jewish participation in the March on Washington in particular, and the civil rights struggle in general, Black-Jewish relations had become increasingly tense. The 1970s were characterized by a deepening rift between Blacks and Jews. The multiple reasons for this shall not be presented here, but it is enough to mention that Prinz felt embittered by both the increasing antisemitism within the Black community and the decreasing interest in civil rights issues in the Jewish community. Prinz's dream of Blacks and Jews joining together in a mutual fight for civil rights issues and a modernized America did not come true.⁷⁰

The political biography of Joachim Prinz is on the one hand a remarkable individual story, but on the other hand also a paradigm for the challenges American Jewry was confronted with in the post-Holocaust decades. The reverberations of the Holocaust for the Jewish community in the United States were tremendous. Before the war, America, Eastern Europe, and Western Europe were all major centers of World Jewry. After the war, only America was left. With the founding of the State of Israel, another center of Jewish life arose. Even if most American Jews and

American Jewish organizations had supported the founding of this state, with its creation, their status as diaspora Jewry was now fundamentally contested and had to be redefined. Prinz was one of many who adamantly defended the diaspora as the most important entity for Jewish survival in the modern world.

Rabbi Prinz's struggle for Jewish survival, for civil rights, for the future of the diaspora, for the future of Judaism and for the fulfilment of the American Dream were all part and parcel of the readjustment of American Jewry to the post-Holocaust era. Especially for those who had immigrated to the United States from Germany or other Nazi-occupied territories, this readjustment was infused by their own experiences with Nazi persecution. Prinz's biography is a clear example of this configuration: his understanding of the post-Holocaust world and his political activism were both shaped by this experience. Even if he was not someone who explicitly discussed the Holocaust and its immediate consequences, the memory of the past in Nazi Germany was always present for him.

Notes

1. Joachim Prinz, "An Agenda for the Jewish People," *Proceedings of the Rabbinical Assembly* 34 (1970): 15–28, quote: 28.

2. "The Issue is Silence," Address by Rabbi Joachim Prinz, President of the American Jewish Congress, at the March on Washington for Jobs and Freedom, Lincoln Memorial, Aug. 28, 1963.

3. Ibid.
4. Ibid.
5. Ibid.

6. There is only one comprehensive study of the AJC before 1950: Morris Frommer's *The American Jewish Congress: A History, 1914–1950* (PhD diss., Ohio State University, 1978). A recently published book compares three major American organizations (including the AJC) and one German Jewish organization and their patterns of contemporary politics: Sebastian Hoepfner, *Jewish Organizations in Transatlantic Perspective: Patterns of Contemporary Jewish Politics in Germany and the United States* (Heidelberg: Winter, 2012). There is only one article that deals with AJC's involvement in postwar civil rights issues: John P. Jackson's "Blind Law and Powerless Science: The American Jewish Congress, the NAACP, and the Scientific Case against Discrimination 1945–1950," *Isis* 91/1 (2000), 89–116.

7. At the time of writing, only Joachim Prinz's autobiography with the introduction by the editor Michael A. Meyer and a recently published article by Stephen J. Whitfield deal with Prinz's life and times, even though he is mentioned and cited a lot in other publications: *Joachim Prinz, Rebellious Rabbi: An Autobiography—The German and Early American Years*, ed. Michael A. Meyer (Bloomington and Indianapolis: Indiana University Press,

2008); Stephen J. Whitfield, "Joachim Prinz, the South, and the Analogy of Nazism," *Bulletin of the German Historical Institute. Supplement* 11 (2015): 99–117.

8. Jewish Women's Archive. "Why We Went: A Joint Letter from the Rabbis Arrested in St. Augustine." Accessed July 3, 2015, http://jwa.org/media/why-we-went-joint-letter-from-rabbis-arrested-in-st-augustine. Further examples: Michael E. Staub, ed., *The Jewish 1960s: An American Sourcebook* (Hanover, NH: Brandeis University Press, 2004), 1–34. A critique of the comparison of Nazi Germany and Jim Crow is offered by Robert E. Goldburg, "Ersatz Judaism," *Jewish Currents*, September 1963, 4–9.

9. To name just the most pertinent ones: Seth Forman, *Blacks in the Jewish Mind: A Crisis of Liberalism* (New York: New York University Press, 1998); Murray Friedman, *What Went Wrong? The Creation and Collapse of the Black-Jewish Alliance* (New York: Free Press, 1995); Cheryl Lynn Greenberg, *Troubling the Waters: Black-Jewish Relations in the American Century* (Princeton, NJ: Princeton University Press, 2006); Jonathan Kaufman, *Broken Alliance: The Turbulent Times between Blacks and Jews in America* (New York: Scribner, 1988); Melanie Kaye/Kantrowitz, *The Colors of Jews: Racial Politics and Radical Diasporism* (Bloomington and Indianapolis: Indiana University Press, 2007); Jack Salzman, *Bridges and Boundaries: African Americans and American Jews* (New York: Braziller, 1992); Debra L. Schultz, *Going South: Jewish Women in the Civil Rights Movement* (New York: New York University Press, 2001); Eric J. Sundquist, *Strangers in the Land: Blacks, Jews, Post-Holocaust America* (Cambridge, Mass: Belknap Press of Harvard University Press, 2005); Stuart Svonkin, *Jews Against Prejudice: American Jews and the Fight for Civil Liberties* (New York: Columbia University Press, 1997); Clive Webb, *Fight Against Fear: Southern Jews and Black Civil Rights* (Athens: University of Georgia Press, 2001).

10. Whitfield, "Joachim Prinz"; Johnpeter Horst Grill and Robert L. Jenkins, "The Nazis and the American South in the 1930s: A Mirror Image?," *Journal of Southern History* 58 (1992): 667–694; Atina Grossmann, "Shadows of War and Holocaust: Jews, German Jews and the Sixties in the United States, Reflections and Memoirs," *Journal of Modern Jewish Studies* (2014), 99–114; Michael Rothberg, "W.E.B. DuBois in Warsaw: Holocaust Memory and the Color Line, 1949–1952," *The Yale Journal of Criticism* 14:1 (2001): 169–189; Stephen J. Whitfield, "The South in the Shadow of Nazism," *Southern Cultures* 18:3 (2012): 55–75.

11. His early life can be traced in Prinz, *Rebellious Rabbi*, 1–63.

12. *Jüdische Rundschau*, January 7, 1927, 13.

13. Peter Wyden, *Stella. Novel* (Goettingen: Steidl, 1993), 37.

14. Trailer of documentary *I Shall Not Be Silent*, accessed July 28, 2016, https://vimeo.com/88013711.

15. Joachim Prinz, *Jüdische Geschichte* (Berlin: Verlag fuer Kulturpolitik, 1931); and *Wir Juden* (Berlin: Erich Reiss, 1934).

16. The Prinz Affair was covered in all Jewish newspapers, but most intensively in the *Jüdische Rundschau*, which published a series of articles throughout 1935. A short overview of the affair is given in "Verantwortlichkeiten," *Jüdische Rundschau*, June 21, 1935, 3.

17. "Dr. Prinz haelt Rueckschau. Abschiedspredigt im Friedenstempel," *Jüdische Rundschau*, September 17, 1935, 13.

18. Bayerische Politische Polizei, decree "Versammlung jüdischer Organisationen," February 20, 1935, in Hans Mommsen, "Der nationalsozialistische Polizeistaat und die Judenverfolgung vor 1938," *Vierteljahrshefte fuer Zeitgeschichte* 10/1 (1962): 68–87, decree: 79 f.

19. Prinz, *Rebellious Rabbi*, 195.

20. Joachim Prinz, "Amerika—hast du es besser? Notizen von einer Reise," *Der Morgen*, June 1937. Prinz uses the "we" in these sentences as *pluralis majestatis*. He means himself as the one who observes the scene, but also German Jewry in general as he sees himself as its representative.
21. Prinz, *Rebellious Rabbi*, 194 f.
22. Ibid., 195.
23. Ibid., 203.
24. Ibid., 202.
25. Ibid., 123–25.
26. "Berlin Rabbi Heads Newark B'nai Abraham," *New York Herald Tribune*, September 8, 1939, 19.
27. For a discussion of the appropriateness of the term "alliance" and its meaning, see Greenberg, *Troubling the Waters*, 1–9.
28. Ibid., 209.
29. Marc Schneier, *Shared Dreams: Martin Luther King, Jr. & the Jewish Community* (Woodstock, Vermont: Jewish Lights Publishing, 1999).
30. Friedman, *What Went Wrong?* 157–176; Schneier, *Shared Dreams*, 49–56.
31. Justine Wise Polier, "The Jewish Commitment," *Congress Weekly*, Vol. 25, June 16, 1958, 5 f., quote: 6.
32. Milton Himmelfarb, "In the Community," *Commentary*, Jan 1, 1960, 157–60, quote: 160.
33. Joachim Prinz, "Ideology and Program," *Congress Weekly*, Vol. 25, June 16, 1958, 3–5, quote: 3.
34. Martin Luther King, Jr., "Address Delivered at the National Biennial Convention of the American Jewish Congress," May 14, 1958, in *The Papers of Martin Luther King, Jr., Vol. IV: Symbol of the Movement, January 1957—December 1958*, ed. Clayborne Carson et al (Berkeley and Los Angeles: University of California Press, 2000), 406–410, quote: 407.
35. Ibid., 408.
36. Ibid.
37. Ibid., 410.
38. Robert Wiener, "A Church and a Synagogue Seek Memories of a Visit by Dr. King," *New Jersey Jewish News Online*, May 17, 2007, http://njjewishnews.com/njjn.com/051707/njChurchAndSynagogue.html.
39. Schneier, *Shared Dreams*, 159–80; Greenberg, *Troubling the Waters*, 214.
40. Julius Wildstein to Joachim Prinz, September 4, 1963, American Jewish Archives, MS-673: Joachim Prinz Papers, Box 4, Folder 4: W, General (following: AJA/MS-673/4/4).
41. Roy Wilkins to Joachim Prinz, September 5, 1963, AJA/MS-673/4/4.
42. Whitfield, "Joachim Prinz," 99.
43. Friedman, *What Went Wrong?* 199.
44. Joachim Prinz to Israel Goldstein, May 27, 1959, Central Zionist Archives, Box A364: Israel Goldstein, 1896–1986, Folder 1220: American Jewish Congress, Corr. w. Dr. Joachim Prinz, 1956–1960 (following: CZA/A364/1220).
45. Prinz, *Wir Juden*, 19–72.
46. "British Parliamentarian, Robert Szold Hit Partition as Hadassah Ends Parley," *Jewish Telegraphic Agency* (JTA), November 1, 1937.

47. Heidelberg Conference, July 31, 1949, "The Future of the Jews in Germany," Minutes edited by Harry Greenstein, Advisor on Jewish Affairs, The United States Military Government in Germany, September 1, 1949, Leo Baeck Institute New York Archives, MS 168. MSF 14, p. 45.

48. Ibid., 46.

49. Joachim Prinz, "Germans and Jews—Is there a Bridge?" in *Jubilee Volume dedicated to Curt C. Silberman*, ed. Herbert A. Strauss and Hanns G. Reissner (New York: American Federation of Jews from Central Europe, 1969), 48–59, quote: 48. For the debate on the German Jewish symbiosis, see *The German-Jewish Dialogue Reconsidered: A Symposium in Honor of George L. Mosse*, ed. Klaus L. Berghahn (New York et al: Lang, 1996); Manfred Voigts, *Die deutsch-jüdische Symbiose. Zwischen deutschem Sonderweg und Idee Europa* (Tübingen: Max Niemeyer, 2006). Compilations of original sources include *Deutsche und Juden. Beiträge von Nahum Goldmann, Gershom Scholem, Golo Mann, Salo W. Baron, Eugen Gerstenmaier und Karl Jasper* (Frankfurt: Suhrkamp, 1967); Ritchie Robertson, *The German-Jewish Dialogue: An Anthology of Literary Texts, 1749–1933* (Oxford and New York: Oxford University Press, 1999); *Deutschtum und Judentum. Ein Disput unter Juden aus Deutschland*, ed. Christoph Schulte (Stuttgart: Philipp Reclam jun., 1993).

50. Prinz, "Germans and Jews—Is there a Bridge?" 59.

51. "End of Jewish Population in Germany Seen in 10 Years, Only 25,000 Left at Present," *The Montreal Gazette*, October 18, 1961.

52. Joachim Prinz, "An Agenda for the Jewish People," *Proceedings of the Rabbinical Assembly* 34 (1970): 15–28, quote: 16.

53. Joachim Prinz, "This Jewish Revolution, *Congress Weekly*, Vol. 16, April 4, 1949, 5–8, quote: 5.

54. Interview with Joachim Prinz, September 4, 1980, Leo Baeck Institute New York Archives, AR 25385 (following: LBINY/AR 25385), p. 14.

55. Interview with Joachim Prinz, by Michael Schwarzschild, June 1970, LBINY/AR 25385, p. 2.

56. Prinz, "This Jewish Revolution," 7.

57. Ibid.

58. Joachim Prinz, "Beyond the Zionist Dream," *Congress Bi-Weekly*, Vol. 28, No. 2, January 16, 1961, 5–7, quote: 6.

59. Ibid., 7.

60. Melvin I. Urofsky, *We Are One! American Jewry and Israel* (Garden City, N.Y.: Anchor Press, 1978), 235–319.

61. Interview with Joachim Prinz, by Michael Schwarzschild, June 1970, LBINY/AR 25385, p. 2.

62. Prinz, "Beyond the Zionist Dream," 6.

63. Prinz, "An Agenda for the Jewish people," 25 f.

64. Edward S. Shapiro, *A Time for Healing: American Jewry since World War II*, i.e. *The Jewish People in America*, Vol. V, ed. Henry L. Feingold (Baltimore/London: John Hopkins University Press, 1992), 27; Jonathan Woocher, *Sacred Survival: The Civil Religion of American Jews* (Bloomington: University of Indiana Press, 1987).

65. Prinz, "This Jewish Revolution," 7.

66. Joachim Prinz, *The Dilemma of the Modern Jew* (Boston and Toronto: Little, Brown and Company, 1962), 216.

67. Ibid., 216 f.

68. Mordecai M. Kaplan, *Judaism as a Civilization: Toward a Reconstruction of American-Jewish Life* (New York: Macmillan, 1934). It is difficult to locate Prinz's religious views within American Judaism, but it seems that Reconstructionism was the closest to his beliefs, though he never affiliated with any Jewish denominational organization, neither personally nor with his congregation, B'nai Abraham. I am grateful to Rabbi Gary P. Zola and Rabbi Clifford M. Kulwin of Temple B'nai Abraham for calling my attention to Prinz's relationship to organized Jewish religion.

69. Prinz, "An Agenda for the Jewish people," 27 f.

70. For an analysis of the problems, see: Greenberg, *Troubling the Waters*, 205–255.

Haunted by History, Fueled by the Present

AMERICAN-JEWISH EFFORTS TO HALT POLAND'S ANTI-ZIONIST CAMPAIGN

Rachel Rothstein

ADDRESSING THE participants of an American Jewish Joint Distribution Committee (JDC) Young Leadership Mission to Europe and Israel in 1970, JDC Director-General Louis Horowitz declared, "Not since Hitler's time have I found the Jewish condition as troubled as now. In the course of one generation, the Holocaust has been blotted out of the world's memory and age-old prejudices have quickly returned in some countries with creeping insidiousness."[1] The fallout from Israel's Six Day War in June 1967 impacted Jews worldwide. For Jews in Poland, the consequences were life-altering. Horowitz referred in his speech to the Jews who had been forced to leave Poland as a result of a state-sponsored anti-Zionist campaign that began in March 1968. International Jewish leaders were horrified by the post-1967 Six Day War exodus that forced more than seventy thousand Jews to leave their homes in the Middle East and Eastern Europe, but Poland was singled out as being particularly brutal, given the country's recent past. The Holocaust had ended less than twenty-five years earlier, yet, according to Jewish leaders, government-sponsored antisemitism was being unleashed once again.

For the Polish Jewish community, 1968 constituted a moment of intense shock that continues to resonate today. Much of the region experienced a spike in anti-Zionist, antisemitic sentiment as a result of the Soviet Union's pro-Arab stance during the 1967 Six Day War. With the exception of Romania, the communist bloc countries followed Moscow's support for the Arab countries in the Middle East, subsequently cutting off diplomatic ties with Israel.[2] The Polish government, however, took the anti-Zionist sentiment to an extreme. On June 19, 1967, Poland's First Secretary of the Polish United Workers' Party (PZPR), Władysław Gomułka, delivered a speech to the Trade Union Congress in which he warned about an emerging fifth column in Poland that supported Israel. He then suggested that those people emigrate. Following the speech, the state security apparatus began to out alleged Zionists from within the Party ranks and civil services. By March 1968, conditions were ripe for an organized antisemitic campaign under the guise of an anti-Zionist campaign. While antisemitism was incompatible with socialist ideology, Jews could be targeted on charges of anti-Zionism, and thus the Party emphasized that it was targeting Zionists, not Jews. When students began to rebel against the government in March 1968, the government blamed Zionist student instigators. Shortly after, Polish Jews, including those best described as Poles with Jewish roots, since they may not have even been aware of or identified with their Jewish roots, were removed from their jobs and the Party ranks. While the tensions in the Middle East provided a cover for the attack on Polish Jews, the campaign was really the result of internal divisions within the Polish government. More nationalist elements used the opportunity to attack Jews and liberals within the Party, hoping that once they were gone from prominent positions, a new, more conservative leadership would emerge.[3]

The anti-Zionist campaign had a profound impact on Poland as a whole and the Jewish community in particular. By the time the March campaign was in full-swing, Polish Jews were limited in how they could respond. The Social-Cultural Organization of Polish Jews (TSKŻ) faced what was essentially a choiceless choice—denounce Israel or cease to exist. Having chosen the former, it, along with the religious community (which, as a religious body, was not forced to denounce Israel), ensured that Jewish life continued in Poland even after much of the remaining Jewish population left. For most individuals, however, staying in Poland was not an option. As the situation deteriorated and Jews lost their jobs, many had no choice but to leave. The campaign, then, ushered in an era of forced emigration. Between thirteen thousand to twenty thousand Jews left Poland as a result of the campaign, giving up their Polish citizenship and rebuilding their lives in Scandinavia, the United States, and Israel.[4]

This essay illustrates how a rise in government-sponsored Polish antisemitism, beginning in the summer of 1967 and climaxing with the outbreak of the anti-Zionist campaign in March 1968, mobilized American Jews like the JDC's Horowitz to respond. Moved by the recent memory of the Holocaust and Cold War affairs, American Jews rallied against the campaign on individual, communal, political, and religious fronts. While scholars have written about the Soviet Jewry Movement in the United States, few have looked at American involvement within the Soviet bloc countries.[5] The events of 1968 loom large in Polish Jewish collective memory, yet 1968 and its aftermath has been largely forgotten in diasporic Jewish collective memory and historiography. Despite this absence in the historiography, the American Jewish community was well aware of what was occurring in Poland and actively responded to the situation through a multitude of American—and American-based international—Jewish organizations. From issuing public statements and organizing protests, to calling for the revocation of Poland's Most-Favored-Nation (MFN) status as well as for special allowances for Polish Jews wishing to immigrate to the United States, American Jews from across the religious and political spectrum did not sit idly by while the Polish government pursued its antisemitic campaign.[6] The campaign thrust Polish Jewry into the larger arena of Jewish issues during the Cold War, and it should be included in the literature of the period. While the Polish-Jewish response was mostly limited—people either acquiesced to the Party line or were forced to emigrate—American Jews could publicly protest in an attempt to end the campaign.

The Initial Response

Within a few days of the campaign's launch, the leaders of several major American Jewish organizations spoke out against the Polish government's antisemitic attack on Polish Jewry.[7] Their initial response can be characterized as more focused on public opinion than on policy, though later efforts would reverse this emphasis. The leaders' methods varied. Some used inflammatory rhetoric to incite people to action, comparing the current antisemitic campaign to prior instances of state-sponsored antisemitism.

Others, like Morris Perlzweig, a World Jewish Congress (WJC) representative, argued that a more tempered approach was necessary, given the geopolitics of the Cold War. Viewing the campaign through the lens of recent—and not so recent—history, Jewish leaders based in America compared the campaign to the Tsarist repression of freedom, the Stalinist purges, and the Nazi regime. Dr. Joachim Prinz, the chairman of the American Jewish Congress's Commission on International Affairs (see David Jünger's essay in this volume for more on him), demanded that the Polish Government "repudiate the incitement to primitive racial and religious hatred and halt their scurrilous and racist appeals to latent anti-Semitism."[8] He understood the historical roots of the attack, as well as the potential for the government's position to spread to the masses and create an even more precarious situation for the Jews in Poland.[9] Rabbi Jacob Philip Rudin, the president of the Synagogue Council of America, declared that "no amount of slanderous anti-Zionist rhetoric can hide from the world the moral degradation of a regime that would invoke racial animosity, in a manner reminiscent of Nazi tactics, against a community of 20,000 Jews who represent the pathetic remnant of three million Polish Jews butchered by the Nazis."[10] Rudin's charged rhetoric linking the contemporary events to the Holocaust attempted to stir the masses, Jewish and otherwise, against the Polish government.

It is hardly surprising that Rudin compared the Polish government's antisemitism to that of the Nazis, but his mention of race is striking, as is Prinz's. Both men referred to "racial" hatred and animosity long after it had become taboo to refer to Jews by using the language of race. The Polish government was framing its campaign on nationalist, not racial, grounds. Rudin and Prinz were both active in the American Civil Rights Movement, and it seems as though American Jewish leaders were turning not only to Jewish history in Europe, but also to their own circumstances in the United States in order to support their stance. Furthermore, neither they, nor the other leaders, relied on Zionist rhetoric to fight the anti-Zionist campaign. This demonstrates that the American Jewish leadership immediately understood this as an antisemitic, *not anti-Zionist*, campaign, and therefore treated it as such.

American Jewish communities reacted at the local level as well. In Los Angeles, the Jewish Federation-Council of Greater Los Angeles

Community Relations Committee issued a resolution condemning the policy of the Polish regime "in using Jews as scapegoats in a desperate effort to maintain political control."[11] While such a condemnation may not have reached Poland, a Jewish Federation-sponsored resolution had a high likelihood of gaining press coverage in local Jewish newspapers, receiving mention in rabbinical sermons, and mobilizing Jewish youth groups, to name just a few of the possible outcomes. Furthermore, in Los Angeles the campaign became part of the official twenty-fifth anniversary commemoration of the Warsaw Ghetto Uprising. This was the case throughout the United States as the Federation-based National Community Relations Advisory Council strongly encouraged Jewish communities to combine their observance of the anniversary of the Warsaw Ghetto Uprising with protests and demonstrations against the contemporary antisemitic policies of the Polish government.[12]

In Washington, D.C., for example, the opening of a YIVO Institute for Jewish Research exhibit commemorating the twenty-fifth anniversary provided an important venue for leaders to speak out against the Polish campaign. New York Congressman Emanuel Celler used the opportunity to state publicly that it was "sadly ironic that Warsaw, the very city which saw so heroic a manifestation of man's indomitable spirit, is now once again the scene of anti-Semitic outrages."[13] Comparing the ghetto fighters' heroism to the liberal segments of Polish society then under attack, he argued, "'the decent and liberal elements in Poland' will gain the freedoms they seek and 'thus vindicate the cause for which the martyrs of the Warsaw ghetto gave their lives.'"[14] Celler recognized that the campaign, though targeted against the Jews, was really more about domestic issues in Poland.

The World Jewish Congress's Perlzweig shied away from a strong "us vs. them" approach. After meeting with the Polish ambassador to the United States, he wrote to the WJC Paris office that, "the habit of Jewish organizations to conduct diplomacy at the top of their voices is not helpful."[15] Explaining this in more detail, he continued, "The President of the mysterious American Committee for Soviet Jewry has publicly demanded the abrogation of the most favored nation status accorded by the United States to Poland in economic matters. This can only have the result of infuriating the State Department, which has important interests in Poland."[16] Responding to the statement that his own organization had issued,

Perlzweig wrote, "I fully realize that some statement should have been made, and I agree with the tenor of the statement, though I am as usual against the abundant use of adjectives in it."[17] His observation that the loud, and at times threatening, Jewish response to Poland's antisemitic campaign could have highly negative consequences demonstrates a nuanced understanding of the Cold War politics of the time. While the knee-jerk reaction for so many Jewish organizations was to protest vocally against the Polish government, Perlzweig understood that it was important to take into account potential long-term repercussions for the relationship between Jewish leaders, the American government, and the Polish government.[18]

While the first response to the campaign included the issuance of statements condemning the Polish government, American Jewish leaders also mobilized to convince their own government to take direct action. As they had during previous periods of crisis, American Jewish leaders appealed to both the US and Polish governments to bring an end to the Polish campaign through letter writing, protests, and petitions. At the local level, Jewish communities, mostly represented by local Jewish Federations, issued appeals or public statements about the events and urged their community members to take action, often through letter writing campaigns.[19] Cleveland's Jewish Federation, for example, issued a call to Jews in Cleveland, asking them to write protest letters to the Polish Embassy in Washington, DC.[20]

On March 20, B'nai B'rith issued a memo to its regional and local leadership, as well as to its Board of Governors, regarding the situation in Poland. Providing a detailed explanation of the "Polish Crisis," namely the domestic issues in Poland unrelated to the local Jewish population, B'nai B'rith's President, William A. Wexler, pleaded with its leaders to take action:

> B'nai B'rith is determined that this contemptible tactic of using the Jews as scapegoats shall not succeed. It is necessary that each of you undertake to see that as many letters as possible—from Jews and non-Jews alike, from private persons and organizations—go to your newspapers and to the Polish embassy in your country protesting this dangerous development in Polish affairs. As you

know, the more individual the letters, the more effective the protest. In the United States, address your letters to His Excellency Jerzy Michalowski, the Polish Ambassador to the U.S.[21]

Wexler firmly believed in the power of the written protest. His plea that local leaders initiate a wide campaign, which included asking their friends, family, colleagues, and acquaintances (both Jewish and not) to write, indicates his strong conviction that if enough people voiced their opposition, they could turn the tide of antisemitism in Poland.

A little over a week later, B'nai B'rith's Executive Vice President, Rabbi Jay Kaufman, reiterated Wexler's call to action in a memo directed to the organization's district secretaries:

> The situation in Poland is still critical and volatile . . . there is a struggle between reactionaries and liberals throughout Eastern Europe. A victory over the reactionary anti-Semites in Poland will permit Jews to breathe more freely in all these countries of Eastern Europe. A defeat will worsen their situation. The need is urgent, therefore, for an effective follow-through on Dr. Wexler's appeal of March 21st to 600 key B'nai B'rith leaders to get letters from Jews and non-Jews to newspapers and Polish Embassies.
>
> Some of you had already begun your own public opinion campaigns. Congratulations and thanks! I hope now that each of you will make *at least* six telephone calls to people who can write impressive letters to newspapers and the Polish Embassies. Ideally, some of these letters should be from non-Jews.[22]

Wexler and Kaufman both viewed the letter writing campaign as essential for their fight against the Warsaw government's anti-Zionist campaign. They understood the need to spread the word and galvanize Jews and non-Jews alike in their fight against the antisemitic reactionaries who were attacking not only the Jews, but Polish liberals as well. If the reactionaries won, Polish Jewry would be in danger. The leaders were careful not to make this an issue that concerned only Polish Jews. Presented in terms of reactionaries versus liberals, this was an appeal based on Cold War sensibilities and fears.

The letter writing campaign was one of B'nai B'rith's primary responses to the campaign, but it did not leave the letter writing solely up to its members (or members' acquaintances). On April 3, Wexler wrote directly to Pope Paul VI, asking him to fulfill an earlier promise that the Pope had made to speak out against persecution targeting Jews. Wexler acknowledged that the Polish government also discriminated against the Church, but thought that the religious commitment of so many Polish individuals might be able to help sway the government to "ameliorate, if not reverse the anti-Semitic campaign of the Polish government."[23] He also implored the Pope to convince other influential Catholic leaders to put pressure on the Polish government.[24] Wexler's appeal to the Pope demonstrates that he understood the situation in Poland to be serious enough to appeal to one of the most influential leaders in the world, although ultimately it was an unsuccessful appeal.

In addition to issuing statements and writing letters, some Jewish organizations turned to organized protests for community members to voice their opposition to Poland's campaign. The North American Jewish Youth Council and the Conference of Presidents of Major American Jewish Organizations organized a protest in March, demanding an end to the antisemitic campaign.[25] Attended by hundreds of college students and others, the protest in front of the Polish Mission to the United Nations fit in well with the mood of late 1960s America, when Jewish students were engaged politically as an identifiable group. This protest further demonstrates that the concern for Polish Jewry percolated throughout multiple generations of American Jews, ranging from senior leaders to students.

Yet another mode of protest included circulating and signing petitions. In early April, the Jewish Telegraphic Agency reported that the Jewish Labor Committee sent a petition, co-signed by a number of Jewish organizations, including other labor and Holocaust survivor groups, directly to President Johnson, urging him to "instruct the American delegation on the United Nations Human Rights Commission to call for an emergency session of that body to deal with the Polish Government's campaign against the Jewish minority."[26] It is unclear whether Johnson paid heed to their call, but it demonstrates that the JLC believed this to be of the utmost importance.

Jewish leaders also arranged meetings with American government representatives and Polish officials at the Embassy in Washington, DC. The President of the Synagogue Council of America, Rabbi Rudin, met with the United States Under Secretary of State, Nicholas Katzenbach, the same week that the campaign broke out. Rudin expressed his concern that the latest events in Poland were reminiscent of the early attacks on Jews in Nazi Europe. According to the State Department's memo of this meeting, "Rabbi Rudin said the group had come to express the deepest kind of concern over what it saw as the 'utilization of the most brazen, cold-blooded kind of anti-Semitism' in recent statements by the Government of Poland and to voice the hope that everything was being done which could be in order to prevent the repetition of the events of Hitler's time."[27] Other representatives of leading American Jewish organizations, such as the American Jewish Committee, met with Polish Embassy officials, hoping that their concerns would be conveyed to the government in Warsaw. At least one American Jewish leader, Rabbi Herschel Schachter, chairman of the Conference of Presidents of Major American Jewish Organizations, met directly with Ambassador Jerzy Michalowski on March 25.[28] Memos between the Embassy in Washington, DC and the Polish government in Warsaw indicate that the persistence of the American Jewish leaders made an impact. The minutes from private Embassy meetings reveal that Polish officials believed Poland was under attack and that something had to be done to counter the "smear campaign of the Zionist centers."[29]

Increased Pressure

By mid-summer 1968, as it became increasingly clear that the Polish government's anti-Zionist campaign was not weakening, the American Jewish response became more forceful. Wexler turned to Congress to try to revoke Poland's Most-Favored-Nation (MFN) status, which would end Poland's favorable trade conditions with the United States. This was not the first call to revoke Poland's status. Immediately after the campaign began, the Jewish Labor Committee had called an emergency meeting to pass a resolution calling for the US government to revoke Poland's MFN status, and numerous other individuals called for the revocation, demonstrating the "knee-jerk" response the WJC's Perlzweig had criticized.[30] The Embassy in

Washington, DC was aware of the calls to revoke MFN and reported to Warsaw that American Jews were trying to blackmail Poland through economic sanctions. This would not intimidate the Polish government, however. According to an Embassy report, "There is no doubt that trade relations are certainly very important for our national economy, but not at any price."[31]

Warsaw's reluctance to respond to these threats did not deter B'nai B'rith from continuing to push for MFN revocation. Their Board of Governors passed a resolution in May 1968, which appeared in the June 4, 1968 Congressional Record, with an introductory statement from Virginia Senator Harry F. Byrd, Jr. Byrd pointed out that Poland was granted MFN status with the hope that Poland would become increasingly independent from the Soviet Union.[32] This, Byrd argued, had not played out. Instead, Poland was benefiting from favorable trade relations with the United States, while simultaneously following Moscow's line and sending arms to North Vietnam. Thus, he believed, Poland's MFN status needed to be reevaluated.

B'nai B'rith's resolution, which appeared directly below Byrd's call to reconsider Poland's MFN status, read as follows:

> In 1958, Congress authorized the President to extend the most-favored-nation tariff benefit to Yugoslavia and Poland, whose governments were then moving away from Soviet domination and were seeking closer relations with the West. Poland continues as one of only two nations of East Europe that enjoys the privilege of its exports entering the United States at the lowest duties imposed by the tariff act. Ironically, Rumania and Czechoslovakia, substantially independent and genuinely seeking better relations with the West, have not been granted this economic advantage.
>
> In view of the Polish government's encouragement of anti-Semitism and hostility to the West, B'nai B'rith calls upon the President of the United States to declare that the conditions which led to granting most-favored-nation benefits to Poland no longer exist and that therefore this preferential status be rescinded.

> A systematic, government-organized campaign of anti-Semitism can no longer be regarded as simply a matter of domestic concern. Our generation knows too well the ultimate cost in lives and civilized standards. The governments of the world must speak out against this reactionary menace.[33]

By highlighting that the original reason Poland had been granted MFN status, namely its desire to move closer to the West, was no longer relevant, the B'nai B'rith Board of Governors hoped that the US government would reconsider. Also calling attention to the fact that Romania and Czechoslovakia did not have this status, though they had strengthened their ties to the West, further indicates that the B'nai B'rith leaders viewed this as a Cold War issue, not only a Jewish issue. Because of the geopolitics of the time, it appears that Wexler believed couching the need to revoke Poland's MFN status in Cold War terms might help convince the government to take action.

Yet, this was also a Jewish issue, as the resolution indicated at the end. Jewish leaders, recognizing that they could perhaps more effectively influence policy by presenting this as a Cold War issue, also believed that the Holocaust, which had ended only a little over twenty years before, still resonated with American government leaders. The perception that America had not done enough to save European Jewry was real. Thus, while the appeal to Cold War sensibilities was practical, highlighting the Jews' distress in Poland in 1968 also appealed to the emotions and consciences of America's leaders.

On June 12 and 13, Herman Edelsberg, the director of B'nai B'rith's International Council, went before the House Ways and Means Committee and the Senate Banking and Currency Committee to read Wexler's statements regarding Poland's MFN status.

> Poland has clearly moved away from the West and is more subservient to Moscow than ever. The Poland of 1968 is not the Poland of 1963; she no longer qualifies as an "independent." The economic benefits of 1968 are nonetheless still tailored to the Poland of 1963. In view of Poland's government inspired anti-Semitism and her

consistent aping of her Soviet master, Congress should rescind the tariff benefits.

There are two kinds of precedent in our history to guide us. In the 1930's as the Hitler menace grew with one conquest after another, and his appetite was whetted by appeasement, the West continued business as usual. The tragic verdict of history is, as the book "While Six Million Died" reminds us, that the American governmental indifference, apathy and inaction—inaction that was reflected in other Western states—permitted the Nazi crematoria to murder hundreds of thousands—perhaps millions—who might have been saved.

There is, however, another precedent and another guide. In the first decade of the century, the pogroms and brutal discriminations of Tsarist Russia shocked the conscience of Americans. Protests mounted in the press and in the Congress. President Taft refused at first to take any action, claiming that the larger American interest was in continued trade with Russia. But on December 13, 1911, the House of Representatives in an action that redounds to its eternal credit, voted 301 to 1 to direct the President of the United States to terminate its commercial treaty with Russia, which had been in force since 1832. And the treaty was scrapped....

It is, we submit, contrary to America's national interest to grant economic privileges to this Polish government, which by its shameful conduct has forfeited the right to such privileges. Congress, we earnestly hope, will so declare and rescind most-favored-nation treatment for Poland.[34]

Wexler's statement, far blunter than any of his previous statements, stated loudly and clearly that America had a moral obligation to revoke Poland's MFN status. Additionally, it was important to remember the earlier precedent set by Congress, rather than to continue "business as usual" when it came to dealing with European antisemitism.

Wexler did not stop with these two Congressional committees in his push to have Poland's MFN status revoked. He also appealed to individual members of Congress, writing letters to those he believed he could convince to support his fight. Wexler had reason to believe that some of them would be willing to help, as several had spoken out immediately after the campaign began. Representative Seymour Halpern spoke out before Congress to protest the Polish government's campaign, alongside Representative Edward J. Derwinski. Both commented on the irony of the proximity of the events to the twenty-fifth anniversary of the Warsaw Ghetto Uprising, which they saw as a powerful and politically provocative coincidence. The following day, Representative Leonard Farbstein linked the Polish campaign to historical Polish pogroms, claiming that "it was an old tactic in Eastern Europe to divert the masses by use of anti-Semitism."[35] American politicians continued to speak out against the campaign. On July 15, Connecticut Senator Thomas J. Dodd wrote to Wexler, thanking him for his interest in Dodd's resolution proposing the revocation of Poland's MFN status and expressing great pleasure that B'nai B'rith had previously endorsed such a move.[36]

Wexler believed that the press would be an important avenue through which to promote their cause. Earlier he had asked B'nai B'rith members to write, and to ask others to write, letters to newspapers and the Polish Embassy. In a series of letters to the editor of the *New York Times*, Wexler himself explained why revoking Poland's MFN status was in the best interest of the American public. He wrote that President Johnson's renewal of MFN was based on the hope that doing so would help drive a wedge through the Moscow-Warsaw relationship, and that it would lead to greater Polish independence. Yet, he wrote:

> The events of this spring showed dramatically that our confidence in the present Polish government was altogether misplaced. The Poland of 1968 is, with the possible exception of Eastern Germany, the most servile of the Moscow satellites. When the students of Poland petitioned for an end to Moscow-dominated censorship of their theater and their press, and for greater freedom generally, they were put down with police clubs and fire hoses. When it seemed that the general Polish population, long dissatisfied over the Soviet Union's domination of Poland's economic and foreign policy, might join forces with the students, this Polish government resorted to the shameful device of scapegoating the Jews, in an effort to confuse and divert the upsurge for freedom.

> Our trade policy should reflect the realities of 1968, not our hopes of 1964. It should recognize that Czechoslovakia and Romania at considerable risk have moved away from Soviet domination and towards more normal relations with the West; yet they do not enjoy most-favored-nation status. It must recognize too that the present Polish government has flouted the West and has deliberately embarked upon a campaign of anti-Semitism.
>
> Throughout the Eastern European bloc, there are hundreds of thousands of young people and liberals who yearn for greater freedom and independence and better relations with the West. If the United States thoughtlessly continues most-favored-nation treatment for Poland, it turns its back on these potential friends of the West. It says, in effect, that it makes no difference that their efforts have been crushed by brute force and by no less brutal government-inspired anti-Semitism; America will do business as usual.[37]

Not dealing with the situation in Poland, he claimed, would be turning America's back on potential allies in the fight against Moscow and communism. Here, too, he underplayed the Jewish issue, instead revealing the far more serious repercussions, at least from the perspective of most *New York Times* readers, in the larger Cold War battle.

While Wexler remained committed to fighting for the revocation of Poland's MFN status, the upper echelons of the American government were unwilling to budge. William B. Macomber, Jr., the Assistant Secretary for Congressional Relations, made this statement in mid-May:

> Most-favored-nation treatment for Polish imports is subject, of course, to review in the light of changing conditions. We have concluded, however, that the withdrawal of most-favored-nation treatment from that country at this time would not contribute to an improvement of the situation.... It would be more likely to jeopardize what ability we have to influence events and would be damaging to United States interests and policy objectives as a whole.[38]

Macomber's response claimed that the government could not put aside its larger interests in Poland at the present time. Furthermore, he argued that revoking Poland's MFN status might be against the Polish Jews' interest, given that another major challenge for Jewish organizations involved working to ensure that the Jews who were leaving Poland could resettle in the United States. The American government, too, was focused on facilitating immigration. When US Congressman Joshua Eilberg inquired as to whether the US government had warned Poland that their continued attack on the Jews would lead to stronger demands to revoke Poland's MFN status, Macomber replied, "we have been mindful of the importance of facilitating, so far as we are able to, emigration of those Jews who wish to leave Poland. Provocative public statements or official acts of severe retaliation against Poland—such as the withdrawal of MFN treatment—could be counterproductive in effect by causing the Poles to cut off the flow of emigration."[39] Thus, revoking Poland's MFN, which only a few years later would be a major card dealt to the Soviet Union at the height of the Soviet Jewry Movement, was not considered to be in the best interests of either the US government or the Jews in Poland, and it was subsequently rejected. The US government was reluctant to issue any harsh statements or levy sanctions against the Polish government, despite pressure to do so from American-Jewish leaders.

Offering Refuge in America

As Macomber noted, Poland's doors, unlike those in the Soviet Union, were open for a Jewish exit. The Polish government generally allowed Polish Jews to emigrate, given that they were, according to the government, a disloyal fifth column. However, the decision to leave Poland at this moment came at a heavy price—the forfeiture of one's Polish citizenship. Officially, immigration to Israel was the only option permitted (those who expressed a desire to go to Western Europe or the United States while still in Poland were often denied the possibility to emigrate). Yet, the great irony of the anti-Zionist campaign—namely that many of those who were attacked were not Zionists—meant that Israel was often not their desired destination. An internal JDC memo by a Geneva staff member to the New York office predicted that this would be the case.

> Should Poland start issuing travel documents for Israel in large numbers, it may be an answer to many, but not to all of the people

who would like to leave. All kinds of Jewish officials who have been fired from the Civil Service, from the Army, from industry, and from the Party, and who rightly object that they didn't deserve such treatment because they are devoted Party members and patriotic Poles, that the accusation of their "Zionism" and double loyalty is absolutely unfounded, may find it hard, after their dismissal, to go to the Militia station to renounce Polish citizenship in order to go to Israel.[40]

As difficult as it was psychologically, however, over fifteen thousand Jews renounced their citizenship, though most had no intention of going to Israel. A March 1969 telegram from the United States' Embassy in Vienna estimated that about eighty percent of the emigrants waiting in transit in Vienna wished to go to the United States.[41] Thus, the American government became a major player—albeit seemingly involuntarily at first—during this wave of emigration from Poland.

As early as the first week of April, New York Congressman Bertram Podell recognized that many would prefer to immigrate to the United States rather than to Israel. Therefore, he introduced a bill that would raise the number of visas for Jews who wished to emigrate from Poland.[42] Explaining that such a bill would demonstrate that America welcomed refugees from oppression, Bertram was, undoubtedly, reminding his fellow congressmen of the last time that America had failed to provide enough visas during a time of persecution.

Leaders of American Jewish organizations were also involved in the immigration conversation. The American Jewish Committee sent a delegation to meet with Polish Ambassador Michalowski to confirm that exit permits would be granted. The delegation also met with the State Department to request that US Embassy officials "speed up emigration procedures at the U.S. Embassy in Warsaw so that Jews desiring to proceed to the United States could be processed by the Polish emigration authorities."[43]

On May 15, Under Secretary of State Katzenbach sent President Lyndon B. Johnson a secret memorandum entitled "Jews in Poland." Noting that the Polish antisemitic campaign, "masquerading under the guise of anti-Zionism," was largely an internal power struggle, Katzenbach wrote, "the fact still remains that many Jews are suffering persecution and that

Jewish opinion outside Poland—and particularly in the United States—has been aroused."[44] Katzenbach believed that the "cautious course" the United States had followed up to that point was no longer sufficient. His memo noted the difficult place the US Government was in at the time. Because Soviet policy prevented Jews from emigrating, there was a legitimate concern that the Polish government might change its own policy and impose similar restrictions. When Katzenbach asked the US Ambassador to Poland, John Gronouski, for advice, Gronouski warned him that active interference could potentially jeopardize the Polish government's willingness to allow Polish Jews to emigrate, and that it was best not to intervene too forcefully.[45]

Thus, rather than ask Johnson to issue any kind of public statement, Katzenbach believed that the most appropriate course of action would be to make changes to American immigration policy in favor of those who might wish to immigrate as "refugees from religious persecution in Poland."[46] According to the memo, Katzenbach believed that the United States should be willing to go so far as to "accept any Polish Jews who might wish to emigrate to the United States."[47] Realizing that American Jewish leaders would continue to demand more action, Katzenbach asked the President for permission to "authorize the Attorney General to be prepared to invoke the parole provisions of the Immigration and Nationality Act to admit additional refugees (as we have done in the case of the Cuban refugees) when the visa 'numbers' run out."[48] Furthermore, noting that he and Gronouski planned to meet with the Conference of Presidents of Major American Jewish Organizations the following week, he knew that he must have a clear response regarding the official US stance on immigration. He wrote to Johnson, "Right though I think our stand is, it simply will not wash with the vast majority of the American Jewish Community. Too many American Jews are extremely sensitive to our Government's failure to lower immigration barriers during the Nazi period. They see our silence now as a repetition of our stand during the 30's and 40's." Thus, he also asked for Johnson's approval to tell the Conference of Presidents of Major American Jewish Organizations that Johnson had decided to "set aside all numerical limitations on the immigration of Polish Jews to the U.S."[49]

While this appeared to be a generous offer, in fact, Katzenbach noted, there were actually more than enough "visa numbers" to accommodate the number of Jews who might wish to immigrate to the United States. The problem, however, was that as of July 30, 1968, America's immigration policy was changing, and those numbers would no longer be open only to Poles wishing to immigrate. Thus, Katzenbach suggested a preemptive loophole that would ensure that even after the immigration policy changed, Jews wishing to immigrate to the United States from Poland would be able to do so. Katzenbach claimed that of the roughly twenty thousand Jews in Poland, likely only three–five thousand would wish to go to the United States in any case, and thus, this would hardly create a refugee crisis. The symbolic power of the decision was far stronger: allowing in the Polish Jews who wished to immigrate to the United States would allay the fears of those American Jewish leaders haunted by the memories of America's shut door during the Nazi period.

Katzenbach urged Johnson to approve the provisions, as well as to sign off on the assurances for the American Jewish leaders that the United States would set aside all numerical limitations. Katzenbach believed that it was important for Johnson to assure the concerned American Jewish leaders that he was aware of the plight of Poland's Jews. Furthermore, Katzenbach noted the need to keep a close eye on the situation in Poland with the understanding that if it worsened, the administration might have to take an even stronger stance, perhaps through a public Presidential statement "listing the steps we have already taken, declaring our willingness to admit all refugees from religious persecution in Poland, and restating in the clearest possible forms our national abhorrence of anti-Semitism."[50] Before getting to that point, however, Katzenbach prioritized the exhaustion of all private channels. Moreover, he urged others to consider that a public statement could have a negative impact on the Jews who were still in Poland.[51]

Generally speaking, those who left Poland were considered stateless, and thus the United States would allow many of them to enter as refugees. Once in America, they could then begin the process of becoming American citizens. Yet this group's immigration was complicated by the fact that many of them were members of the Polish United Workers' Party (PZPR), which technically should have excluded them from immigrating to the United States. Yet, the State Department explained that history was the true motivation behind the granting of refugee status to so many, despite this connection to a communist party. In a telegram from Katzenbach to Ambassador Gronouski, Katzenbach wrote, "having in mind the profoundly serious consequences of refusals to Jews or other applicants who face prospects of religious persecution, I believe we should be very reluctant to question the veracity of such statements by such applicants as to their intentions."[52] The Consular section of the Warsaw Embassy was instructed to "pursue [a] line of questioning which will in most cases reveal Jewish refugees."[53]

Expressing a desire to leave because they were Jewish was key, as there was a difference between those who claimed they were fleeing from religious persecution (in this case as Jews), and those who were simply fleeing. The former would qualify for preferential treatment under US immigration law's section 203(a)(7), which "allowed persons from communist or communist-dominated countries and persons from countries in the general area of the Middle East to be admitted as 'conditional entrants' under the seventh preference category." Those who did not mention that they were fleeing persecution, or in the words of one US consular official, did not reveal his or her "problem," were only able to immigrate under a loophole that allowed them to apply for immigrant visas.[54]

The US government found it difficult to accept those who admitted to being "voluntary" members of a communist party, however. According to the Embassy in Warsaw, "As for those ineligible under 212(a)(28) because of voluntary membership, we have not intended to take special measures to permit them to come to [the] U.S. We understand Israel will accept them."[55] Two exceptions to this particular section of the Immigration and Nationality Act included those who were involuntary members and those who were former members. In determining whether one could qualify for an exception, the memo stated that the consular officers would be responsible for determining one's degree of voluntariness, although according to a telegram from the Embassy sent a few days earlier, it appears that only those who revealed that their membership was for ideological reasons were to be refused refugee status.[56] The Embassy recognized that not allowing these people into the United States could "lead to charges that we are not helping as we should," but they wished to stick to this policy nevertheless.[57]

It is not clear the extent to which Washington agreed with Embassy officials in Warsaw. While the Embassy in Warsaw was reluctant to allow for too many exceptions, a document from Washington, DC sent to Warsaw stated that, "The USG [United States Government] had made arrangements for granting U.S. visas for any Polish Jews who succeeded in leaving Poland."[58] Was this simply a statement made to appease the American Jewish leaders or was this a true commitment on the part of the government to assist *any* Jew who managed to leave? It appears that the government was, in fact, willing to find loopholes even for those Jews who technically should not have been admitted because of their membership in a communist party. The United States Government was aware that many Polish Jews had to join the Party in order to attend university or hold their particular position in Poland, and this was taken into account.[59] The officials based in the United States seemed to be more willing to make exceptions for Polish Jews who were attempting to immigrate than the officials based in Warsaw, perhaps because the US-based officials had direct contact with American Jews, whereas Warsaw had to deal with the local government.

As soon as reports from Poland arrived indicating an outbreak of antisemitism related to the 1968 March events, American Jewish leaders from across the religious and political spectrum mobilized in response to the campaign. Given that Polish Jews were unable to really fight on their own behalf, American Jews—from college students to the heads of major Jewish organizations—engaged in the most vocal response to the Polish campaign. They did not use Zionist rhetoric to fight the anti-Zionist campaign, however. Instead, they linked their concern about the latest developments to previous periods of antisemitism in Poland (especially the Holocaust), as well as to contemporaneous instances of minority (and racial) oppression within the United States, and to Cold War affairs. They immediately understood this to be an antisemitic, *not anti-Zionist*, campaign. They also understood that this was part of a larger political struggle in Poland, in which Jews were viewed and targeted as scapegoats.

While initially they hoped that statements, protests, and petitions condemning the campaign—from Jewish leaders and individuals alike—would be sufficient, the continued attack on Polish Jews forced American Jewish leaders to take a harder stance. This harder stance, which was taken more by the leadership than individuals, pushed for the revocation of Poland's MFN status and ensured that despite restrictions on immigration for those who had been members of communist parties, Polish Jews could indeed immigrate to America. Of course, a lingering question remains: how effective was the collective Jewish attempt to end the campaign? Ultimately it lasted about three years, and because of this relatively short time span and the continued flow of emigrants from Poland, it never developed into a movement of its own, as the Soviet Jewry Movement would later. Yet the response from American Jews had an impact on Polish-American relations during this period. While Poland's MFN status was not revoked, damage had been done. According to documents from the Polish Embassy in Washington, DC, Poland believed that it was facing a major public relations fiasco and worked to counter what it perceived to be a Jewish anti-Polish campaign for the remainder of the communist period. Although American Jews were unable to halt the 1968 campaign and, more generally, to curb antisemitism in the region, they certainly tried, believing that it was their obligation, according to the Talmudic concept "*kol yisrael aravim ze bazeh*" (all of Israel is responsible for one another).

Notes

1. "JDC Head Depicts Jewish Condition," *The Jewish Exponent*, July 31, 1970.

2. While anti-Zionist sentiment was widespread in the region at the time, only Poland experienced a full-fledged attack on the Jewish population that led to their emigration. The Soviet Jewry Movement focused on opening the borders for Jews to leave the USSR and immigrate to Israel, while the Polish anti-Zionist campaign opened the doors for mass emigration, despite the fact that most Jews living in Poland had no desire to emigrate before the regime turned against them. Thus, even within the communist bloc, there were major differences in how each country approached its Jewish population, although in this case the objective was essentially the same: controlling Jewish movement.

3. For detailed analyses of the March events and the anti-Zionist campaign, see Josef Banas, *The Scapegoats: The Exodus of the Remnants of Polish Jewry* (London: Weidenfeld and Nicolson, 1979); Michael Checinski, *Poland, Communism, Nationalism, Anti-Semitism* (New York: Karz-Cohl Publishers, 1982); Jerzy Eisler, *Polski Rok 1968* (Warsaw: Instytut Pamięci Narodowej, 2006); Jerzy Eisler, *Marzec 1968: Geneza, przebieg, konsekwencje* (Warsaw: Państwowe Wydawn. Nauk., 1991); Michał Głowiński, *Marcowe gadanie: komentarze do słów 1966–1971* (Warsaw: Pomost, 1991); Marcin Kula, Peter Osęka, and Marcin Zaremba, eds., *Marzec 1968: trzydzieści lat później*, 2 vols., (Warsaw: Wydawnictwo Naukowe PWN, 1998); Piotr Osęka, *Syjoniści, inspiratorzy, wichrzyciele: obraz wroga w propagandzie marca 1968* (Warsaw: Żydowski Instytut Historyczny, 1999); Anat Plocker, "Zionists to Dayan: The Anti-Zionist Campaign in Poland, 1967–1968 (Doctoral Dissertation, Stanford University, 2009); Konrad Rokicki and Sławomir Stępień, eds., *Oblicza Marca 1968* (Warsaw: Instytut Pamięci Narodowej, 2004); Grzegorz Sołtysiak and Józef Stępień, *Marzec '68: między*

tragedią a podłością (Warsaw: "Profi," 1998); Dariusz Stola, *Kampania antysyjonistyczna w Polsce 1967–1968* (Warsaw: Instytut Studiów Politycznych (Polska Akademia Nauk), 2000); Dariusz Stola, "Anti-Zionism as Multipurpose Policy Instrument: The Anti-Zionist Campaign in Poland, 1967–1968" in *Antisemitism and Anti-Zionism in Historical Perspective: Convergence and Divergence*, ed. Jeffrey Herf (London: Routledge, 2007), 159–85; Dariusz Stola, "Fighting against the Shadows: The Anti-Zionist Campaign of 1968" in *Antisemitism and its Opponents in Modern Poland*, ed. Robert Blobaum (Ithaca: Cornell University Press, 2005), 284–300; Leszek W. Głuchowski and Antony Polonsky eds., *Polin:1968, Forty Years After, Polin: Studies in Polish Jewry* 21 (Oxford: Littman Library of Jewish Civilization, 2009). The term "Pole with Jewish roots" is often used to designate Poles who have Jewish roots, but who do not necessarily identify in any way with these roots.

    4. The figure ranges widely. The Polin Museum of the History of Polish Jews gives the figure 13,000, while scholars like Michael Checinski have suggested that the figure is closer to 15–20,000 (Post-war Gallery, Warsaw, Polin Museum of the History of Polish Jews; Checinski, *Poland, Communism, Nationalism, Anti-Semitism*, 245–246). According to one document that Jerzy Eisler has cited, more than 15,000 emigrated between 1968 and 1972 (Eisler, "Jews, Antisemitism, Emigration," 56).

    5. The Soviet Jewry movement began in the United States in the mid-1960s to fight for Soviet Jews' right to full freedom of religion in the Soviet Union. Activists also pushed for the right of Soviet Jews to leave the Soviet Union in order to live Jewish lives abroad, if they so desired. For more on the Soviet Jewry Movement, see Stuart Altshuler, *From Exodus to Freedom: A History of the Soviet Jewry Movement* (Lanham, MD: Rowman & Littlefield Publishers, 2005); Gal Beckerman, *When They Come For Us, We'll Be Gone: The Epic Struggle to Save Soviet Jewry* (Boston : Houghton Mifflin Harcourt, 2010); Henry L. Feingold, *"Silent No More": Saving the Jews of Russia, the American Jewish Effort, 1967–1989* (Syracuse, N.Y.: Syracuse University Press, 2007); and Murray Friedman and Albert D. Chernin, eds., *A Second Exodus: The American Movement to Free Soviet Jews* (Hanover, NH: Brandeis University Press: Published by University Press of New England, 1999).

    6. As to the question of why the American Jewish response to 1968 has largely been forgotten, the documents provide several hypotheses. The rhetoric comparing what was going on in Poland in 1968 with earlier episodes of widespread antisemitism in history indicates that this could have been seen as just one more example of Polish antisemitism. The inability, or perhaps undesirability, to distinguish between periods of antisemitism and instead to see this as one of many instances of Polish antisemitism constructs a Poland that is unequivocally and continuously antisemitic. Another possible explanation is that by the end of the campaign, the waves of emigration from Poland had ended and the country had a new, more Western-looking government under Edward Gierek. These closer ties with America, and American Jews, by the mid-late 1970s may have overshadowed the earlier events. It may also have been overshadowed by the Soviet Jewry Movement, which occasionally included Poland in its work, but was focused on the Jews living in the Soviet Union. Finally, I believe that the rhetoric that cast the anti-Zionist campaign as being the final chapter of Polish history led many simply to forget about Polish-Jewry until the appearance of articles in the 1990s and 2000s celebrating the "revival" of Polish-Jewish life. Thus, the politics of memory are very much at play here, and perhaps this may explain why the campaign has received so little attention from American Jewish historians.

7. While each of these organizations has its own mission and goals, their work overlaps in terms of working to protect Jewish interests in America and abroad, fighting anti-semitism, and advancing social justice and humanitarianism.

8. Jewish Telegraphic Agency, "News Brief," March 14, 1968, www.jta.org/1968/03/14/archive/the-american-jewish-committee-today-denounced-current-anti-jewish.

9. Ibid.

10. Jewish Telegraphic Agency, "Synagogue Council Condemns 'blatant Anti-semitic' of Polish Regime," March 22, 1968, www.jta.org/1968/03/22/archive/synagogue-council-condemns-blatant-anti-semitic-of-polish-regime.

11. Jewish Telegraphic Agency, "Los Angeles Jewish Community Denounces Polish Anti-semitic Campaign," March 27, 1968, www.jta.org/1968/03/27/archive/los-angeles-jewish-community-denounces-polish-anti-semitic-campaign.

12. Jewish Telegraphic Agency, "U.S. Government is Asked to Protest Polish Anti-Semitism, Admit Jewish Victims," April 16, 1968, www.jta.org/1968/04/16/archive/u-s-government-is-asked-to-protest-polish-anti-semitism-admit-jewish-victims.

13. "Informational News Release-Polish Regime Condemned at Warsaw Ghetto Exhibit," for period ending 5/17/68, B'nai B'rith Collection, Folder 139 Poland I/II, American Jewish Archive (hereafter AJA).

14. Ibid.

15. "Letter to Armand Kaplan in Paris," March 29, 1968, World Jewish Congress Collection, Box B9, folder 19, AJA.

16. Ibid. Most-Favored-Nation (MFN) status gave a country favorable trading rights and tax rates based on an agreement with the United States. Poland and Yugoslavia were the only two communist bloc countries to receive MFN status in the early 1960s. MFN status would later become a major bargaining tool for the Soviet Jewry Movement with the 1974 passing of the Jackson-Vanik Amendment, which denied MFN to countries that denied emigration or violated other human rights. For more on Jackson-Vanik, see J.J. Goldberg, *Jewish Power: Inside the American Jewish Establishment* (Reading, MA: Addison-Wesley, 1996).

17. "Letter to Armand Kaplan in Paris," March 29, 1968, World Jewish Congress Collection, Box B9, folder 19, AJA.

18. Ibid.

19. Jewish Federations, working under the umbrella "Jewish Federations of North America (JFNA)," fund and oversee Jewish life in America. Most major Jewish institutions, including synagogues, schools, summer camps, etc., receive funding through the Federation system. For more on the JFNA, see their webpage: www.jewishfederations.org.

20. Jewish Telegraphic Agency, "Gomulka Reportedly Defied by Party over Dampening Anti-zionist Drive," March 25, 1968, www.jta.org/1968/03/25/archive/gomulka-reportedly-defied-by-party-over-dampening-anti-zionist-drive.

21. "Memo," March 20, 1968, B'nai B'rith Collection, Folder 139 Poland I/II, AJA.

22. "Memo from Rabbi Jay Kaufman to District Secretaries," March 29, 1968, B'nai B'rith Collection, Folder 139 Poland I/II, AJA.

23. "Letter to Pope Paul VI," April 3, 1968, B'nai B'rith Collection, Folder 139 Poland I/II, AJA.

24. Ibid.

25. Jewish Telegraphic Agency, "Synagogue Council Condemns 'blatant Anti-semitic' of Polish Regime," March 22, 1968, http://www.jta.org/1968/03/22/archive/synagogue-council-condemns-blatant-anti-semitic-of-polish-regime.

26. Jewish Telegraphic Agency, "Jewish Labor Committee Urges UN Rights Commission Session on Polish Jews," April 2, 1968, www.jta.org/1968/04/02/archive/jewish-labor-committee-urges-un-rights-commission-session-on-polish-jews.

27. Memo of Conversation—"Anti-Semitic Statements of Polish Government," March 21, 1968, General Records of the Department of State/Central Foreign Policy Files, 1967–1969, Box 3089, SOC POL 14 (4/1/68), National Archives and Records Administration—College Park (hereafter NACP).

28. Jewish Telegraphic Agency, "President's Conference Condemns 'vile Slander' of Zionism by Gomułka," March 21, 1968, www.jta.org/1968/03/21/archive/presidents-conference-condemns-vile-slander-of-zionism-by-gomulka.

29. "Protokoł z Narady Partyjno Zawodowej grupy PZPR przy Ambasadzie PRL w Waszyngtonie," May 16, 1968, Polska Zjednoczona Partia Robotnicza (PZPR) 237/XXII/1618, Archiwum Akt Nowych (hereafter AAN).

30. Jewish Telegraphic Agency, "Jewish Labor Committee Urges UN Rights Commission Session on Polish Jews," April 2, 1968, www.jta.org/1968/04/02/archive/jewish-labor-committee-urges-un-rights-commission-session-on-polish-jews.

31. "Protokoł z odbytego w dniu 26.III.1968 roku odwartego zebrania POP PZPR przy Ambasadzie PRL w Waszyngtonie," March 26, 1968, PZPR 237/XXII/1618, AAN.

32. "Communist Poland's Trade Status with the United States" June 4, 1968, B'nai B'rith Collection, Folder 139 Poland I/II, AJA.

33. Ibid.

34. "Statement of Dr. William A. Wexler of Savannah, GA, President of B'nai B'rith Before the House Ways and Means Committee," June 12, 1968, B'nai B'rith Collection, Folder 139 Poland I/II, AJA; "Statement of Dr. William A. Wexler of Savannah, GA, President of B'nai B'rith Before the Senate Banking and Currency Committee," June 13, 1968, B'nai B'rith Collection, Folder 139 Poland I/II, AJA.

35. Jewish Telegraphic Agency, "Warsaw Anti-semitic Campaign is Denounced from Floor of Congress," March 14, 1968, www.jta.org/1968/03/14/archive/warsaw-anti-semitic-campaign-is-denounced-from-floor-of-congress.

36. "Letter from Thomas J. Dodd to Wexler," July 15, 1968, B'nai B'rith Collection, Folder 139 Poland I/II, AJA.

37. "Letter to the Editor," June 18, 1968, B'nai B'rith Collection, Folder 139 Poland I/II, AJA.

38. "Letter from William B. Macomber," May 13, 1968, Central Foreign Policy Files, 1967–1969 Social—Box 3089, SOC 14 POL 5/1/68 (folder 2), NACP.

39. "Macomber Letter to Eilberg," December 31, 1968, Central Foreign Policy Files, 1967–1969 Social—Box 3089, SOC 14 POL 6/1/68 (folder 2), NACP.

40. "Letter from Akiva Kohane in Geneva," April 2, 1968, Poland—Emigration, 1965–1969—AR 65/14-#325, American Jewish Joint Distribution Agency Archive (hereafter JDCA).

41. "Telegram from U.S. Embassy in Vienna," March 1969, Central Foreign Policy Files, 1967–1969 Social—Box 3089, SOC 14 POL 4/1/68 (folder 2), NACP.

42. Jewish Telegraphic Agency, "Bill in Congress Would Provide 1,000 Pounds for Jewish Immigrants from Poland," April 4, 1968, www.jta.org/1968/04/04/archive/bill-in-congress-would-provide-1000-pounds-for-jewish-immigrants-from-poland.

43. Jewish Telegraphic Agency, "Committee Asks Polish, U.S. Governments to Facilitate Exit of Jews from Poland," April 4, 1968, www.jta.org/1968/04/04/archive/committee-asks-polish-u-s-governments-to-facilitate-exit-of-jews-from-poland.

44. Nicholas deB. Katzenbach memo to Lyndon B. Johnson, "Memorandum for the President: Subject: Jews in Poland," May 15, 1968, Accessed via Declassified Documents Reference System.

45. Ibid.

46. Ibid.

47. Ibid. He noted in the memo that visas would be granted "subject to the normal security check" and that they would be given only to those who were able to get out of Poland.

48. Ibid.

49. Ibid.

50. Ibid.

51. Ibid.

52. "Outgoing telegram from Department of State to Embassy Warsaw," May 24, 1968, Central Foreign Policy Files, 1967–1969 Social—Box 3089, SOC 14 POL 5/1/68 (folder 2), NACP.

53. "Telegram from Embassy Warsaw," May 25, 1968, Central Foreign Policy Files, 1967–1969 Social—Box 3089, SOC 14 POL 5/1/68 (folder 2), NACP.

54. "Memo from Embassy Warsaw," May 28, 1968, Central Foreign Policy Files, 1967–1969 Social—Box 3089, SOC 14 POL 5/1/68 (folder 2), NACP.

55. Ibid.

56. Ibid; "Telegram from Embassy," May 25, 1968, Central Foreign Policy Files, 1967–1969 Social—Box 3089, SOC 14 POL 4/1/68 (folder 2), NACP.

57. "Telegram from Embassy," May 28, 1968, Central Foreign Policy Files, 1967–1969 Social—Box 3089, SOC 14 POL 5/1/68 (folder 2), NACP.

58. "Under Secretary's Discussion of Polish Jews with Members of Conference of Presidents," May 24, 1968, Central Foreign Policy Files, 1967–1969 Social—Box 3089, SOC 14 POL 5/1/68 (folder 2), NACP.

59. "Letter to Mr. Israel Poliner," July 15, 1968, Poland—Emigration, 1965–1969—AR 65/14-#325, JDCA.

Contributors

ELIYANA ADLER is Associate Professor in the Department of History and Jewish Studies Program at Penn State University. Previously she taught at the University of Maryland and held fellowships most recently at the United States Holocaust Memorial Museum and Yad Vashem. She is the author of *In Her Hands: The Education of Jewish Girls in Tsarist Russia* (2011) and co-editor, along with Sheila Jelen, of *Jewish Literature and History: An Interdisciplinary Conversation* (2008). Her articles have appeared in numerous volumes and journals, including *Polin, East European Jewish Affairs, Holocaust and Genocide Studies, Yad Vashem Studies*, and *Nashim*.

SAMANTHA BASKIND is Professor of Art History at Cleveland State University. She is the author of several books, including *Raphael Soyer and the Search for Modern Jewish Art* (2004) and a solely authored encyclopedia, *Encyclopedia of Jewish American Artists* (2007), which was named a *College and Research Libraries* Selected Reference Work from 2006–2007. She is also co-editor, with Ranen Omer-Sherman, of *The Jewish Graphic Novel: Critical Approaches* (2008). More recent publications include *Jewish Art: A Modern History* (2011), co-authored with Larry Silver; *Jewish Artists and the Bible in Twentieth-Century America* (2014); and *The Warsaw Ghetto in American Art and Culture* (2017). She served as editor for US art for the twenty-two-volume revised edition of the *Encyclopaedia Judaica* (2007) and is currently series editor of *Dimyonot: Jews and the Cultural Imagination*, published by the Pennsylvania State University Press.

RACHEL DEBLINGER is the Director of the Digital Scholarship Commons at the UCSC Library and Co-director of the Digital Jewish Studies project through the Center for Jewish Studies at UCSC. Deblinger completed her doctorate in History at UCLA in 2014 and is currently writing a book manuscript titled *Saving Our Survivors: How American Jews Learned about the Holocaust* (under contract with Indiana University Press). This work explores the construction of Holocaust memory in postwar America through efforts of Jewish communal organizations to aid survivors in Europe. To expand the conversation about postwar Holocaust narratives, media technology, and survivor memory, Deblinger has created an online exhibit and blog, "Memories/Motifs," http://memoriesmotifs.com.

HASIA DINER is the Paul S. and Sylvia Steinberg Professor of American Jewish History at New York University, with a joint appointment in the Department of History and the Skirball Department of Hebrew and Judaic Studies. She is also the Director of the Goren Center for American Jewish History. A specialist in immigration and ethnic history, American Jewish history, and the history of American women, she is the author of numerous published books, including *In the Almost Promised Land: American Jews and Blacks, 1915–1935* (1977, reissued, 1995); *A Time for Gathering: The Second Migration, 1820–1880* (1992); *Lower East Side Memories: The Jewish Place in America* (2000); *The Jews of the United States: 1654–2000* (2004); and *We Remember with Reverence and Love: American Jews and the Myth of Silence After the Holocaust, 1945–1962* (2009), published to critical acclaim. It received the National Jewish Book Award in American Jewish studies in 2010 as well as the Saul Veiner Prize for the Outstanding Book in American Jewish History. Most recently, Yale University Press published *Roads Taken: The Great Jewish Migration and the Peddlers Who Led the Way*.

GENNADY ESTRAIKH served as Managing Editor of the Moscow Yiddish monthly *Sovetish Heymland* from 1988–1991. Beginning in 1991 he lived in Oxford, England, where he defended his doctoral dissertation (1996) and worked at the Oxford Institute of Yiddish Studies and the London University's School of Oriental and African Studies. In 2003 he became a Professor at the Skirball Department of Hebrew and Judaic Studies, New York University. His monographs include *Soviet Yiddish: Language Planning and Linguistic Development* (1996), *In Harness: Yiddish Writers' Romance with Communism* (2005), *Yiddish in the Cold War* (2008), and *Yiddish Literary Life in Moscow* (in Russian, 2015). He has co-edited volumes on various aspects of Jewish intellectual history, including, most recently, *1929: Mapping the Jewish World* (2013, National Jewish Book Award); *Uncovering the*

CONTRIBUTORS

Hidden: The Works and Life of Der Nister (2014); and *Soviet Jews in World War II: Fighting, Witnessing, Remembering* (2014).

SHEILA JELEN is an Associate Professor of English, Jewish Studies, and Comparative Literature at the University of Maryland, College Park. She is the author of *Intimations of Difference: Dvora Baron in the Modern Hebrew Renaissance* (2007), and a co-editor, along with Michael Kramer and Scott Lerner, of *Modern Jewish Literatures: Intersections and Boundaries* (2011), among other titles. Jelen is an associate editor at *Prooftexts: Modern Jewish Literary History*, and she is currently working on a monograph entitled *Salvage Poetics: Post-Holocaust Popular Ethnographies in Photography and Literature*. Her articles and reviews have appeared in *Nashim, Journal of Jewish Identities, Religion and Literature, Journal of Hebrew Higher Education, Prooftexts, Tikkun*, and *Shofar*, among others.

DAVID JÜNGER is a research fellow (Wissenschaftlicher Mitarbeiter) at Free University Berlin and the Center for Jewish Studies Berlin-Brandenburg. In 2013, he earned a PhD in history at the Simon Dubnow Institute for Jewish History and Culture at Leipzig University. He has been awarded fellowships by the Hans Böckler Foundation, the Saxon Government, the American Jewish Archives, the Max Weber Foundation, the German Historical Institute, and the United States Holocaust Memorial Museum. He is currently working on his second book, about the life and times of the German-American rabbi Joachim Prinz (1902–1988). His most recent publication is "Jahre der Ungewissheit. Emigrationspläne deutscher Juden 1933–1938" [Uncertain Years. Emigration planning of German Jews, 1933–1938], Schriften des Simon-Dubnow-Instituts, hrsg. v. Dan Diner, Bd. 24 (Göttingen: Vandenhoeck & Ruprecht), 2016.

ELLEN KELLMAN researches and writes about modern Yiddish literature and literary history, specializing in the history of the Yiddish periodical press and publishing industry, with a particular focus on Abraham Cahan's role in shaping the development of American Jewish culture through the press. Among her scholarly publications are "Exile in Warsaw: The Kultur-Lige in Poland, 1921–1924" (2015); "Aiding the Female Immigrant Reader or Entertaining Her?: *The Jewish Daily Forward* and its 'Gallery of

Missing Husbands'" (2014); "Faint Praise: the Early Critical Reception of Joseph Opatoshu's Historical Novel *In poylishe velder*" (2013); "*The Pregnant Bride from Suffolk Street*: Intraethnic Class Conflict in a Yiddish Serial Novel" (2011); and "Uneasy Patronage: Dovid Bergelson's Years at the *Forverts*" (2007). She teaches Yiddish language and literature and modern Jewish literature in the Department of Near Eastern and Judaic Studies at Brandeis University.

ANN KOMAROMI is an Associate Professor in the Centre for Comparative Literature at the University of Toronto. Komaromi edited a version of Yuli Kosharovsky's *We are Jews Again: The Jewish Movement in the Soviet Union*, due out from Syracuse University Press in 2017. Her first book, *Uncensored. Samizdat Novels and the Quest for Autonomy in Soviet Dissidence*, was published by Northwestern University Press in 2015. Her electronic archive, the "Project for the Study of Dissidence and Samizdat," including a Timeline of the Jewish Movement, launched at the University of Toronto Libraries in 2015.

MARKUS KRAH is a lecturer in Jewish Religious and Intellectual History at the School of Jewish Theology, at University of Potsdam, Germany. He received his PhD in Modern Jewish Studies from the Jewish Theological Seminary (JTS) in New York. His book, *American Jewry and the Re-Invention of the East European Jewish Past*, scheduled to be published by de Gruyter in 2017, analyzes how various players within organized American Jewry presented highly divergent lessons, aesthetics, and narratives of the East European Jewish experience to advance their respective agendas for the future of the community. His new project explores how the transnational background of Schocken Books shaped the publishing house's cultural impact in post-1945 America.

ELI LEDERHENDLER is the Vice-Dean for Research in the Humanities at the Hebrew University of Jerusalem, where he holds the Stephen S. Wise Chair in American Jewish History and Institutions. He is the author of numerous studies on American and East European Jewish history, including *The Road to Modern Jewish Politics* (1989); *New York Jews and the Decline* of *Urban Ethnicity* (2001); *Jewish Immigrants and American Capitalism* (2009); and *American Jewry: A New History* (2016).

HOLLI LEVITSKY is the founder and Director of the Jewish Studies Program and a Professor of English at Loyola Marymount University in Los Angeles. Her research on Holocaust representation appears in academic journals and books, as well as periodicals. *Summer Haven: The Catskills, the Holocaust, and the Literary Imagination*, her co-authored book (with sociologist Phil Brown) was published in 2015 and recently released in paperback. Her college textbook, *Literature of Exile and Displacement: American Identity in a Time of Crisis*, was published in 2016. At LMU, she teaches courses on Holocaust Representation, Israeli Literature, and American Jewish Literature. Through an initiative of the Jewish Studies Program, she takes students to either Poland or Israel each summer for engaged learning courses. Dr. Levitsky regularly lectures to the community on these subjects and conducts workshops on Holocaust pedagogy to secondary school and college educators. In addition to organizing the annual Jewish American and Holocaust Literature Symposium, Dr. Levitsky was a Schusterman Fellow at the Summer Institute for Israel Studies and a Fellow at the United States Holocaust Memorial Museum Center for Advanced Holocaust Studies. She held the 2001–2002 Fulbright Distinguished Chair in Poland in American Literature.

GIL RIBAK is currently an Assistant Professor of Judaic Studies at the University of Arizona. A former Fulbright Fellow, he completed in 2007 his PhD degree in history at the University of Wisconsin-Madison. After graduation he taught at Washington University in St. Louis as the Lewin Postdoctoral Fellow, and as the Schusterman Postdoctoral Fellow at the University of Arizona. He also served as the director of the Institute on Israeli-American Jewish Relations at the American Jewish University in Los Angeles. His book, *Gentile New York: The Images of Non-Jews among Jewish Immigrants*, was published by Rutgers University Press in 2012. His articles appeared or will appear in journals such as *American Jewish History* (2008), *Israel Studies Forum* (2010), *Journal of American Ethnic History* (2013), *AJS Review* (2014), *Polin: A Journal of Polish-Jewish Studies* (2016), and

Modern Judaism (2018). Finally, he published book chapters in books such as *Germany and the Americas: Culture, Politics and History* (2005); *War and Peace in Jewish Tradition: From the Ancient World to the Present* (2012); *Wealth and Poverty in Jewish Tradition: Studies in Jewish Civilization* (2015); and will publish chapters in two forthcoming books, *American Jewry: Transcending the European Experience?* (2017); and *Anti-Zionism, Antisemitism, and the Dynamics of Delegitimization* (2017).

RACHEL ROTHSTEIN completed her PhD at the University of Florida in 2015. Her dissertation, "'Small Numbers, Big Presence:' Poland, the U.S., and the Power of Jewishness after 1968," explores how Polish and American politicians and Jewish individuals continued to preserve Polish Jewishness even after the 1968 Polish anti-Zionist campaign. She teaches Jewish history at the Weber School in Atlanta, GA.

DAVID SLUCKI is currently an Assistant Professor in the Yaschik/Arnold Jewish Studies Program at the College of Charleston. Previously, he was an Early Career Development Fellow in 2011–2013 at Monash University, where he received his PhD in 2010. His book, *The International Jewish Labor Bund after 1945: Toward a Global History*, was published by Rutgers University Press in 2012, and looks at the attempts of Bundists to adapt their shattered movement in the wake of the Holocaust. His current research focuses on Holocaust survivors in the postwar United States; humor and Holocaust representation; and generational memories of the Holocaust. He has published articles in a range of journals, including *Jewish Social Studies*, the *Journal of Modern Jewish Studies*, *East European Jewish Affairs*, and *Studies in Contemporary Jewry*.

Index

Note: page locators rendered in *italics* denote images on the page.

Abella, Irving, 296n73
Adamic, Louis, 47
Adler, Eliyana R., 13–14, 15; introduction, 1–17; "Mapping a Lost World," 68–85
African Americans: civil rights movement, 14, 297, 298–99, 304–7, 313; race relations and racism, 301–3, 305, 307, 313
"aftermath studies," 15
Agar, Herbert, 47
Allison, Alida, 184, 185
alte heym. *See* Eastern European Jewish life; nostalgia; *shtetlekh*
Alter, Robert, 139
American Council for Judaism, 266
American Federation of Polish Jews, 44, 46, 47, 48–49, 55, 59, 65n16
American Friends of Polish Jews, 46–48, 49
American ideals and identity, 26, 250, 264–65, 266–67, 298, 305
American Jew as Patriot, Soldier and Citizen, The (Wolf), 219
American Jewish agencies and organizations, 14, 44, 46–49, 65n16, 247, 298, 303–5, 321–22, 324–25, 327
American Jewish Committee, 100, 266, 282–83, 327, 334
American Jewish Congress, 14, 96, 158, 297, 298, 299, 303–5, 307, 313, 314n6

American Jewish Joint Distribution Committee (JDC): *landsmanshaftn* relationships, 65n16; Supplies for Overseas Survivors (SOS), 247–48, 250, 251–54, *252*, 255, 257; work and messaging, 249, 263–64, 319, 321; on Zionism and Polish emigration, 333–34
American Jewish Yearbook, xvii, 65n16
American Jews: American diaspora and Israel, 310–11, 313–14; assimilation, xv, xii, 2, 3, 4, 8, 9–10, 11, 26, 89, 90, 99, 103, 107n14, 113, 114–15, 127–29, 308, 311–12; Catskills life and themes, 204–5, 213; in Civil Rights Movement, 14, 297, 298–99, 301–7, 312–13, 314; cultural background and heritage, 9, 10, 12, 13, 25, 27–28, 72, 75, 80, 84, 93, 98, 102, 103–5; cultural criticism and diversity, 88–89, 90, 102, 301–2, 303; European refugees and immigration, 1–3, 9, 14, 68, 69, 72–73, 85, 264–66, 335; Holocaust responses and humanitarian aid, 247–67; Holocaust witnessing (literature), 199–200, 205–7, 208–13; identity and cultural power, U.S., 93–94, 100; identity and global power, xi–xii, 250; identity and history, 15–16, 17, 25, 40, 59, 72, 89, 91–92, 96, 98, 100–101, 119–20, 129,

INDEX

American Jews (cont.)
152–53, 248; intellectuals, literature creation and influence, 87–88, 89, 92–105; Jewish and American identity, 249–50, 254, 255, 260, 264–65, 266–67; "Jewishness," defining and redefining, 90–92, 93, 96–97, 98–99, 100, 101, 103–5, 123–24, 125–26, 127–29, 238, 248, 255; journalism coverage, 113–15; lack of identity, 273–74; literature utilization and understanding, 14, 15, 17, 25, 28–30, 31–32, 36, 53–54, 59, 76, 87–90, 93, 100–101, 102–3; memorial books and culture, 48, 57–58, 68, 69, 71, 75, 80, 83, 84–85; politics and activism, 10, 12, 14, 16, 30, 46–49, 72, 253, 297, 298–99, 302–5, 306–7, 321–39, 338; population data and locations, xi, xii, xiv, 26, 90, 106n8; postwar American Jewry, 9–17, 24, 91, 96–97; postwar travel/return, 80; women, 250, 251–54, 257–58, 264, 268n7, 268n11

"American Jews" (Lestschinsky), 113–15
American South, 302–3, 305
Amir, Michlean, 74
Androfski, Andrei (literary character), 216, 221, 222–25, 238–39
Anielewicz, Mordecai, 222, 232–33
Ansky, S., 140
anthropological and ethnographic works: ethnography/fiction, 15, 139–40, 142–43, 144, 145, 148–49; *Life Is with People*, 25, 31–32, 88, 100, 139–40, 144, 151n40, 153, 164; salvage ethnography and montage, 140–42, 144, 148–49; *World of Our Fathers* (Howe), 138–39
antisemitism: American attitudes and history, 5–6, 9, 53, 203, 204, 220–21, 305, 311, 313, 336; and American racism, 303, 305, 313; emasculation themes, 220–21; literary portrayals, 178–79, 194; memoirists' accounts, 152, 153, 154–55, 157–58, 159, 163, 165, 166; Poland, and anti-Zionism, 319, 320–39, 339n2, 340n6; prevention, 220, 239, 336, 339; Soviet Union, 279, 280–81, 281–83, 292n27, 293n44; surveys mentioning, 30
anti-Zionism, Poland, 319–39, 339n2, 340n6
Antopol, Belarus, 77, 79, 81–82, 82, 84
Apenszlak, Jacob, 48, 56, 58–60, 67n50
Apostle, The (Asch), 120–21
Arab-Israeli conflicts, 319–20
"architecture of memory," 77–78
archival materials. *See* documentary materials and research
Ari (literary character, *Exodus*), 221, 238–39
art. *See* films; illustrators and illustration; theatre; visual art
Art of Maurice Sendak, The (Lanes), 190, 193
Asch, Sholem, 113, 115, 120–21, 128, 178
Ashkenazi Jews: memorialization methods, 69; works about, 87–88, 102, 160
assimilation. *See under* American Jews
Auschwitz camp, 50, 51, 60, 61, 141
Australian press, 54
Avrich-Skapinker, Mindy, 292n13

Babel, Isaac, 108n25, 165, 274
Baeck, Leo, 300, 306
Bara, Walter, 53
Bar Kochbha revolt (132 CE), 234–35
bar mitzvah, 112, 119, 125, 133n52
Baron, Salo W., 25–26, 29, 36, 50
Bartal, Israel, 39, 76, 163–64
Barthes, Roland, 148, 150–51n39

352

INDEX

Baskind, Samantha, 14, 16, 215–40
Bass, Saul, 217
Battle Cry (Uris), 222, 227
Battle for Survival (film; UJA), 260–61, 262, 271n54
Bauer, Yehuda, 145, 259–60
Ben-Ami, Jacob, 235–36
Ben Canaan, Ari (literary character), 221, 238–39
Ben-Gurion, David, 225, 241n36, 310
Benjamin, Walter, 141, 150n17
Berenbaum, Michael, 267
Berg, Mary, 228, *230*
Berkovits, Eliezer, 98, 109n35
Berlin, Germany, Jewish community, 300–301
Bernini, Gianlorenzo, 227
Bernstein, David, 107n17
Bernstein, Michael André, 148
Bialik, Hayim Nahman, 120
Bible: characters, art and stories, 227, 232–33, 235, 236, 239; characters, service and sacrifice themes, 249, 252, 260, 264, 266, 267, 268n7; Jewish history, 123; sacred texts and learning, 137–38
bibliographies, 32–34
Binimetsky, Yisroel, 165
Birnbaum, Martin, 123
Biuletyn Informacyjny (newspaper), 225
Black Book: the Nazi Crime against the Jewish People, The (1946), 55–56
Black Book of Polish Jewry, The (1943), 13–14, 44–63, 71; audiences, 47–49, 57–58, 59; contents details, 44, 49–52, 58–59, 61–62; as memorial site, 56–62, 62–63; objectivity and tone, 51–53, 55; reviews and legacy, 53–56, 58, 59, 62–63; successors, 55–56, 67n45
Black Book of Russian Jewry (1946), 57, 66n36

blacks, United States. *See* African Americans
Blau, Joseph, 123
B'nai B'rith, 255, 324–26, 328–29, 331
Boaz, Franz, 140
Bokser, Ben-Zion, 97
book jackets, 216–17; *Exodus,* 216–17, *218, 219,* 221–22, *223,* 226, 229, 240; *Mila 18,* 216, 221, 225–27, *226,* 229–30, *231, 232, 233,* 240; *The Wall,* 229; *Warsaw Ghetto,* 230
Borghese Gladiator (sculpture), 227
"Borscht Belt," 204
Botwinik, Berl, 119, 127
Boyarin, Daniel, 242n46
Boyarin, Jonathan, 57, 71, 78, 80
Brandel, Alexander (literary character), 224–25, 239
Brandel, Wolf (literary character), 223
Breines, Paul, 232, 242n46
Breslaw, Joseph, 129
Bronfman, Edgar, 287
Bronfman, Samuel, 262, 285
Bronski, Paul (literary character), 221
Bronski, Rachel (literary character), 223
Buber, Martin, works, 37, 88, 100
Buck, Tim, 279
burial customs, 70, 121
Burkenwald, Israel, 265
Burning Lights (Chagall), 31
Butchkes, Sidney, 217
Byrd, Harry F, Jr., 328

Cahan, Abraham, 111, 113, 115, 122, 129, 203
Caldecott Medal, 180, 187
camps, Zionist, 202
Canada: politics and Soviet Jewry, 274, 275–76, 277–78, 279, 280, 282, 283, 288, 294n46; WWII, 278

INDEX

Canadian Jewish Congress, 284, 285, 288, 294n50
Canadian Jewish News (newspaper), 290
Canadian Jews: activism, 284–85; humanitarian appeals, 262; identity and history, 16, 276–77, 283, 285, 286–87, 291n12; immigration and policy, 284, 285, 289, 290, 291n11, 291n12, 294n48, 294n49, 296n73; literary portrayals, 273–74, 283; memorial books, 75; population, 284, 291n11, 294n48; responses, Soviet Jewry, 274–90
cantors, 126–27, 133n57, 147
Carr, Sam, 277
cartoons and comics, 236, 238
castration, 221
Catholic Church, 326
Catskills: Jewish experiences and literature, 199–200, 203–13; regional history, 201–2, 203
Celler, Emanuel, 323
Central Intelligence Agency (CIA), 292n28
Cesarani, David, 12
Chagall, Bella, 31
Chagall, Marc, 31, 98
Chanukah: Americanization, 128–29; literary portrayals, 187, 189, 192, 193–94
Chelm stories, 180, 189–92, 197n42
children's literature, 16, 173–94; awards, 180, 184, 187, 188; illustrators and illustration, 16, 176, 177–78, 179, 180–83, 187–89, 190–91, 192–93; themes and tone, 176, 178, 179, 194
Chmielnik, Poland, 77, *78*, 82
Christianity and Judaism: antisemitism, 152, 154–57, 165, 166, 178–79; holidays and religious expression, 125, 127, 128–29; Jewish-Gentile relations, 160–62, 163–64, 166–67; Jewish writers' work and criticism, 113, 120–21, 239; Polish Jewish persecution, 326; postwar aid and philanthropy, 260
circumcision, 220–21
Citizens Committee on Displaced Persons, 264, 266
citizenship: Polish emigration, 320–21, 333–34, 336; Soviet Jews, 293n44
civil disobedience, 304
Civil Rights Movement (United States), 14, 297, 298–99, 304–7, 313
Cohen, Elliot, 92, 94, 101–2, 103–4
Cohen, Jocelyn, 162–63
Cohen, Lisbeth, 254
Cohen, Morris Raphael, 157
Cold War: American Jewish populations and, 90, 321, 325, 338; Canada and Soviet Union, 277–78, 279, 284–85, 288, 289; European Jewish populations, 14, 23–24, 25–26, 30, 321–22, 323–24, 325–26, 329; geopolitics, 319–20, 322, 328, 329–30, 331–32; memory of Jewish life, 78; "winning the peace" and American leadership, 249, 254–57, 266
collected goods, humanitarian aid, 247–48, 249–50, 251–54, 255, 256, 257, 269n23
"collected memory," 83–84
collective memory, 83
Colwin, Laurie, 186
commemoration. *See* memorializing and memorials
Commentary (periodical): articles, Jewish society, 123–24; content and mission, 90, 94, 100–104, 105; cultural pluralism, 99, 105; drama criticism, 152–53; fiction, sources,

and criticism, 1–4, 5, 6–9, 88, 100; rabbis' contributions and writings, 87, 88–89; staff, 92–93, 94, 101–2, 103–4
Commonwealth nations, 278, 291n12
communism: Communist Party and Soviet Jewry, 277–78, 279–83, 288, 292n19; Communist Party of Canada, and politicians, 274, 275–76, 277–78, 279, 280, 282, 283, 288, 292n14, 294n46; Communist Party of the Soviet Union, 279, 280, 282, 283, 292n28; Eastern Europe bloc, 319–20, 331–32; religious Judaism and, 275; secularism links, 120; U.S. immigration policy, 337, 338–39
concentration and death camps: accounts, *Black Book of Polish Jewry*, 44, 50, 51, 52, 61; geography, 61; literary portrayals, 223; photography and coverage, 141, 256; scholars' work and family ties, 35
Conference of Presidents of Major Jewish Organizations, 304, 326, 335
Conference on the Future of Jews in Germany (1949), 308
consumerism, 249, 251, 253–54
Cotler, Irwin, 288
"Country Passover, A" (Sholem Aleichem), 178
Croce, Benedetto, 164
Crystal, Leon, 279–80, 281
cultural Judaism. *See* ethnic/cultural vs. religious Judaism; secularism
Czechoslovakia, 328, 329, 332

David and Goliath, 227, 232–33, 235
Davis, Mac, 220
Dawidowicz, Lucy, 25, 37, 38, 145, 150n26, 160
"Dead Town, The" (Peretz), 146–47
Deblinger, Rachel, 14, 16, 247–67
"Decline of European Jewry, The" (Tartakower), 31
Decter, Midge, 152–53
Decter, Moshe, 281, 293n30
Delayed Pilgrims Dinner (radio broadcast), 264–65
de Monti, Christopher (literary character), 225
Der sotn in Goray (Singer, I. B.), 183–84
Derwinski, Edward J., 331
"Devil's Trick, The" (Singer, I. B.), 185, 187, 192, 193–94
Diary of Anne Frank, The, 12, 18n25, 233–34
Didi-Huberman, Georges, 141–42
Dilemma of the Modern Jew, The (Prinz), 312
Diner, Hasia: myth of silence, and Holocaust memory, xiii–xiv, 11–12, 18n22, 67n56, 289; on political associations, 253; postwar American Jewry and the catastrophe, xi–xviii, 91, 175; Soviet Jewry movement, 285, 294n57, 296n74
Displaced Persons Act (1948), 265
displaced persons (DPs). *See* refugees/displaced persons
Displaced (radio play), 260
Dobroszycki, Lucjan, 36
Dobrynin, Anatoly, 287
documentary materials and research: American postwar Jewry, xvi–xviii, 10–11, 72, 249; memorial books' documentary material and function, 44, 45, 46–47, 50–53, 69, 71, 73–84; methodology critiques, 55; published primary sources, xvii; source types compared, 45, 55; Warsaw Ghetto, 50–51, 51–52, 53, 237

INDEX

Dodd, Thomas J., 331
Donatello, 227
"Dreyfus in Kasrilevke" (Sholem Aleichem), 145–46
Duban, James, 7
Dubnow, Simon, 28, 29, 102–3
Dubrowa: A Memorial to a Shetl (memorial book), 75
Duker, Abraham, 36
Dusk in the Catskills (Wallenrod), 199, 200, 205–13, 214n13

Earth Is the Lord's, The (Heschel), 15, 87–88, 102, 139, 144, 148, 153, 160
Eastern European Jewish life: American scholarship, 10, 13, 15, 16, 23–40; American travel and writing, 80; children's literature, 173–94; Cold War era, 23–24, 30, 78; global scholarship, 10, 26–27, 34–35, 36, 39; literature, and American Jewish learning, 14, 15, 17, 25, 28–30, 31–32, 36, 53–54, 59, 76, 87–89, 93, 100–101, 102–3; literature, and American Jewish production, 14, 31–32, 87–90, 95–96, 98, 103–5, 137–49, 152–53, 175–76; mapping illustrations, 76–80, 81–83, 84; memorial books/memorialization efforts, 13–14, 44–63, 68–85; "persistence of Judaism," 38; photographic exhibitions, 87, 153; -pre and post-Holocaust, 10, 15, 23–24, 25, 31, 37, 53, 56–57, 61, 71, 75, 81, 84, 104–5, 138, 140, 143, 144–45, 148–49, 153, 164–65, 166, 258, 309; traditional culture and salvage, 140–42, 144, 148–49; Yiddish children's lit, 174, 175–76, 180–83, 185–94; Yiddish-language memoirs, 15, 152, 154–67
Edelsberg, Herman, 329–30

educational attainment: American Jews, 9–10, 89, 123; literature study, 179–80, 196n21; Yiddish, 112, 177–78, 185
Ehrenburg, Ilya, 56
Eichmann, Adolf, xvi
Eilberg, Joshua, 333
Einsatzgruppen, 44, 47, 50, 61
Einstein, Albert, 50
"Eli, the Fanatic" (Roth), 1–4, 5, 6–9, 88
Elijah the Prophet, xiv, 179, 181, 182, 183
emigration. *See also* immigration and immigrants: American relief and programs, 250, 264–66, 335; Poland, and U.S. resettlement, 333–39; Poland, forced, 320–21, 339n2
"empathic unsettlement" (LaCapra term), 4–5
Enemies: A Love Story (Singer, I. B.), 201
Engländ-Wasserstrom, Isaac, 156
English language: American bias, 26; Holocaust scholarship and language gaps, 13, 24; limitations, 3; memoirs, 156–57; -press, and Jewish identity, 14; rates of publication, 23, 29, 34; scholarship, Eastern European Jewish life, 13, 23, 24–40; translation and translations, 24, 27, 29, 37–38, 50, 113, 173–74, 179–80, 184, 185, 193, 194, 206–7, 209, 210–11, 214n13
Entin, Joel, 111–12
epi- and paratext, 216
espionage, 277–78, 288
Es shtarbt a shtetl: megiles Skalat (memorial book; 1948), 71
Esther, 249, 252, 257, 264, 266, 267, 268n7
Estraikh, Gennady, 14, 16, 111–30

INDEX

Eternal Light, The (radio program), 265
ethnic/cultural vs. religious Judaism: anti-secularism opinions, 97–98; Communism, 275; lectures and debates, 119–20; as literary topic, 93, 98–99, 104; postwar American Jewry, 90–92, 93, 97–99, 100–102, 103–4, 106n8, 128; Yiddish-language newspapers, 111–16, 119–20, 121–30
ethnographic works. *See* anthropological and ethnographic works
exile: literary themes and examples, 161, 207, 212, 213; religious leaders, 301
Exodus Revisited (photo essay; Uris), 234–35, 236
Exodus (Uris), 215, 222; characters, 221, 238–39; cover, 216–17, *218, 219,* 221–22, *223,* 226, 229, 240; reader responses, 239; Zionism, 88, 237
Eynhorn, David, 127–28

Fackenheim, Emil, 289, 296n75
Falenica, Warsaw, *74,* 81
Farbstein, Leonard, 331
"Fast, The" (Peretz), 178
Fefer, Itsik, 286
Fein, Richard, 99
Feingold, Henry, 294–95n57
Felman, Shoshana, 4–5
feminization and stereotyping, 220–21
Fiddler on the Roof (play): criticism, 100, 148, 153, 167n3; reception and perceptions, 12, 15, 88, 105, 153
Fiedler, Leslie, 100
Fighting Jew, The (Nunberg), 220
films: European Jewish life portrayals, 12, 27, 31, 76, 152, 167n3; *Exodus* (1960), 217, 222; *Fiddler on the Roof* (1971), 12, 167n3; *Four Seasons Lodge* (2008), 199; philanthropic projects (*Battle for Survival* (1946), and *The Future Can Be Theirs* (1948), 248, 260–61, 262, 263–64, 271n54; *The Pianist* (2002), 238
Finder, Gabriel, 70–71
Fink, Steven, 8–9
Finkelstein, Louis, 29–31, 32
"First Shlemiel, The" (Singer, I. B.), 189–90
Fishman, Joshua A., 36
Fleming, Michael, 51
folklore: children's literature adaptations, 173–74, 176, 177–78, 179, 180–83, 185–87, 189–94; international tropes and tales, 190–91, 192, 197n47; Jewish-Gentile relations, themes, 160–61; research, 25, 140
Folks-shtimme (newspaper), 280, 293n30
Fools of Chelm and Their History (Singer, I. B.), 180, 191–92
Forverts (newspaper): fiction, 185, 191–92, 198n48; foreign reporting, 279–80, 281; letters to the editor, 111, 121–22, 124, 125; passages, 112, 116–17, 125; politics, 111, 112–13, 119; religion and Jewish authenticity, 111–30; secularism, 111–12, 119–20, 121, 124–25
Four Seasons Lodge (Jacobs), 199
Frank, Anne, 233–34
Fredman, John, 232
freethinkers, 103, 111, 112, 121, 124, 128, 129–30
Freud, Sigmund, 220–21
Friedenstempel Synagogue (Berlin, Germany), 300
Friedman, Mark, 36
Frontiers of Hope (Kallen), 28
Future Can Be Theirs, The (1948), 263–64

INDEX

generation gap: American Jews and religiosity, 115, 120, 125, 129, 130; intergenerational literary collaboration, 16, 181; literary portrayals, 209, 211

Genette, Gérard, 216

Gentile-Jewish relations: Catskills literature, 203, 204; Jewish writers' works and influence, 239; language use, 165; memoirs content, 152, 154–57, 160–62, 163–64; Polish Jewish persecution and appeals, 326; postwar aid and philanthropy, 260

"geography of memory": mapping, 77–78, 79–80, 81, 84; modes of return, 69, 80–83; nomenclature, 79

German Jews, 297–98, 299, 300–301, 303, 308–9, 314. *See also* Holocaust

Gershman, Joshua, 291n8

ghettoization, 47, 50, 51, 302

Ghetto Lane of Vilna, The (Vorobeichic), 148–49

Gilman, Blanche, 252, 257

Gilman, Sander, 220–21

"Gimpel the Fool" (Singer, I. B.), 88, 95

Ginsburg, Isidor, 128

Ginzberg, Louis, 28

Gitelman, Zvi, 36, 293n44

Gitis, D., 121–22, 124

Gittleman, Sol, 7

Glatstein, Jacob, 47, 137–38

Glenn, Susan A., 107n14

Glicksman, William, 75

Goldberg, Itche, 123, 173, 174, 176–80, 196n21

"golden era" of American Jewry, 91, 106n8

Golden Tradition, The (Dawidowicz), 25, 145

Goldfaden, Abraham, 127

Goldmann, Nahum, 304

Goldovsky, Morris, 155–56

Goldstein, Israel, 305, 307

Gomulka, Wladyslaw, 320

Goodbye Columbus (Roth), 5

Goodhart, Arthur, 28

Goodman, Henry G., 285–86

Goodman, Saul, 102–3

Gordis, Robert, 96–97, 98, 99, 105

Gordon, Albert I., 124

Gordon, Yehuda Leib, 287

Gorelik, Mordecai, 161

Goren, Arthur, 91, 106n8

Gotesfeld, Khone, 158–59

Gouzenko, Igor, and Gouzenko Affair (1945), 277–78

"Grandmother's Tale" (Singer, I. B.), 187, 192–93

graves and gravestones, 70

Greenbaum, Alfred, 36, 42n26

Greenberg, Eliezer: anthologies, 88, 137, 138, 139, 140, 142–44, 145; literary construction, sites of memory, 14

Greenberg, Louis, 29, 31, 36, 41n13

Grine Felder literary colony, 201–2

Gronouski, John, 335, 337

Gross, Naftali, 125

Grossman, Vassily, 56

guilt and shame: American Jews during Holocaust, 210, 213; American Jews' giving and philanthropy, 259–60, 261, 270n43

Hadassah, 253, 268n11

Halper, Leo (literary character), 205–6, 207–10, 211–12, 213

Halperin, Israel, 30

Halpern, Leyvick (H. Leivick), 235–36

Halpern, Seymour, 331

Hans Christian Andersen Medal, 188

Harkavy, Alexander, 161
Harper and Row, 184, 187
Hart-Celler Act (1965), 335, 337
"Hasidic Tales" (Buber), 100
Hasidim: literary treatments, 100, 139; Lubavitch Rebbe's USA visit, 115–17
Haskalah Movement in Russia, The (Raisin), 28
Hayes, Saul, 284
Haynt (newspaper), 114
Hebraist writers, 206
Hebrew language: font design, 217; as living language, 206, 207; memorial books, 57, 73, 74, 75, 77, 78, 156; novels, 206–7, 210–11; revival, 129; scholarship publishing and translations, 27, 37–38
Hecht, Ben, 54
Heidelberg Conference (1949), 308
Hersey, John, 227–28, *229*
Hersh, Jake (literary character), 273–74
"Hershele" (Mendele the Bookseller), 177
Hertzberg, Arthur, 87, 89, 100, 102, 306
Herzog, Elizabeth, 15, 25, 31–32, 88, 139–40, 144, 153, 164
Herzog, Marvin, 36
Heschel, Abraham Joshua: civil rights, 306; criticisms, 89; lectures, 159–60; works, 15, 87–88, 102, 139, 144, 148, 153, 160
Himmelfarb, Milton, 304
Hirsch, Marianne, 175, 188–89, 194
Historical Society of Israel, 27
History of Jewish Literature, A (Waxman), 28
History of the Jews in Russia and Poland (Dubnow), 28, 29
History of Yiddish Literature in the 19th Century, A (Weiner), 28

Hofman, Ben Zion, 119, 122, 124
Holocaust. *See also* Eastern European Jewish life; refugees/displaced persons; silence, and Holocaust memory; survivors; Warsaw Ghetto and uprising: American Jews' witnessing, literature, 199–200, 205–7, 208–13; American Jews' witnessing, positioning, and memorials, xi–xvi, xvii–xviii, 9, 10–12, 16, 24, 210–11, 212–13; archives, xvi–xvii; civil rights movement response, 299, 307, 313–14; geographic effects, 79–80; information and testimony transmission, 4–5, 10–11, 35, 47, 48, 50–52, 56, 66n34, 68, 141, 158; Jewish life pre- and post-Holocaust, 10, 15, 23–24, 25, 31, 37, 53, 56–57, 61, 71, 75, 81, 84, 104–5, 138, 140, 143, 144–45, 148–49, 153, 164–65, 166, 258, 309; literary and artistic portrayals, 1, 3–4, 10, 176, 187–88, 195n7, 215–40; localized vs. broader foci, 45–46, 55, 57–58, 59–62; memorializing and memorials, xiv, xv–xvi, xvii–xviii, 10–12, 44–63, 68–85; photography, 141, 256; Polish Jewry protection response, 319, 321, 322, 329, 330, 334–36, 338; precursors, 158, 163, 164–65, 166–67, 330, 331; religiosity following, 120, 122; Soviet Jewry movement response, 274–75, 278–81, 283–84, 285, 288–89, 296n72; survivor communication, xv, 3, 10–11, 50, 68; survivor memoirs, 56, 68, 158, 159; terminology and language, 3, 11–12; timelines, xvi–xvii, 15, 47–48, 49, 50, 52–53
Holocaust memoirs. *See* memoirs
Horetz, Shmuel, 127
Horowitz, Louis, 319, 321

Horowitz, Rosemary, 57
hotels, Catskills, 199, 201, 202, 203, 205, 206, 207, 208–9, 213
Howe, Irving: anthologies, 88, 137, 138, 139, 140, 142–44, 145; biography, 93, 145; literary construction, sites of memory, 14; literary criticism, 153, 167n3; *World of Our Fathers*, 93, 137, 138–39
humanitarian aid: fundraising goals and totals, 258, 259–60, 270n37; marketing and messaging, 251, 252, *252*, 254–57, 258, 260–61; "winning the peace", Cold War, 249, 256–57
Hundert, Gershon D., 38, 145
Hungarian Jews, 44, 55, 59
Hungarian Revolution (1956), 283
Hurvitz, Haim Abraham, 118, 126–27
Hyman, Paula, 220

"If Not Still Higher" (Peretz), 179
illustrators and illustration: cartoons and comics, 236, 238; children's literature, 16, 176, 180–83, 187–89, 190–91, 192–93; Eastern European heritage works, 16, 31; memorial book maps, 76–78, *77*, 82; WWII/Warsaw Ghetto, 236
Images in Spite of All (Didi-Huberman), 141
immigration and immigrants. *See also* American Jews: American Jews' religiosity, 111, 112, 115, 117–18, 123, 125, 126, 129; American laws and policy, 72, 250, 264–66, 267, 334–39; American rates, and cultural change, 9–10, 24, 28; American themes, 26; Canadian Jews, 276, 284, 285, 289, 290, 291n11, 291n12, 294n48, 294n49, 296n73; Canadian policy, 289; first-person accounts, 68; immigrant literature, 175–76, 180, 184, 201–2, 205–6, 228, 236, 290; immigrant scholarship leadership, 24, 29, 34–35, 36, 37, 38; literary portrayals, 4, 9, 93, 138–39, 205–6, 207–8
Immigration and Nationality Act (1965), 335, 337
Ink and Blood: A Book of Drawings (Szyk), 236
intellectuals: American, literature creation and influence, 87–88, 89, 92–105; Jewish, in Soviet Union, 279, 286, 295n59; Jewish refugees and knowledge transfer, 23, 34–35, 37
interdisciplinary scholarship, 16–17
International Ladies' Garment Workers' Union, 124, 129–30, 154, 158, 169n16
"In Those Days" (Steinberg), 178
Intrator, Genia, 288
ironwork, 217, *219*
Isaac Bashevis Singer: Children's Stories and Childhood Memoirs (Allison), 184, 185
Israel: conflicts, and Jewish politics, 10, 319–20; consulate protests, 128; creation, and American civil rights, 307; creation, and Jewish identity, 128–29, 239, 309–10, 313–14; creation, and literature, 7, 91, 216, 217, 225; creation, and Zionist philanthropy, 263, 271n58, 310; Law of Return, 115; memorial book publication, 74, 80–81; Polish immigration, 333–34; scholarship and publishing, Eastern European Jewish life, 24–25, 26–27, 36, 37–38, 39–40, 57

Jabotinsky, Vladimir, 202
Jacobs, Andrew, 199

INDEX

Janowa, Poland, 76–77, 81
Janowsky, Oscar, 28–29
JDC. *See* American Jewish Joint Distribution Committee (JDC)
Jelen, Sheila E., 14, 15, 16, 76; introduction, 1–17; "A Treasury of Yiddish Stories," 137–49
Jeremiah (prophet), 206, 207
"Jew as a Soldier, The" (Twain), 218–19
Jew in Battle, The (Learsi), 220
Jewish Anti-Fascist Committee, 278, 280, 282, 286, 292n27
Jewish armed resistance: artistic depictions, *218, 219, 226, 231,* 236–37; memorialization and memorial books, 45, 51–52, 53, 56; novels' portrayals, 215–40
Jewish Black Book Committee, 55–56, 66n40
Jewish Book Annual, xvii
Jewish businesses and products, 253–54
Jewish communal organizations, 249
Jewish Currents (periodical), 212
Jewish Enlightenment, 140
Jewish Federations (and local chapters), 322–23, 324, 341n19
Jewish holidays and rituals. *See also* specific holidays: Americanization and commercialization, 125, 127–29; Hasidim and authentic traditions, 117–18; literary portrayals, 147–48; secular and religious identities, 111–12, 119, 123, 124, 125, 128, 133n52; symbolism, postwar philanthropy and aid, 249, 252, 263–64, 271n58
Jewish Labor Committee, 237, 326, 327
Jewish Nationalist writers, 206
"Jewishness." *See also* "muscular Judaism": American organizations, identity, 298; defining/redefining, American Jewry, 90–92, 93, 96–97,
98–99, 100, 101, 103–5, 123–24, 125–26, 127–29, 238, 248, 255; European debate and works, 300, 301; false, and nostalgia, 152–53; literary journals' differing modes, 94–105; as literary topic, 93, 95–96, 238–40; postwar philanthropy and Jewish identity, 248, 250, 255, 260, 263, 266; *Yiddishkayt,* 98–99, 104, 119, 122, 125–26
Jewish Peoples' Fraternal Order, 177
Jewish populations. *See also* American Jews: American history and shifts, xii–xiii, 26, 90, 309, 313–14; Canadian history, 284, 289, 291n11, 291n12, 294n48, 296n73; future, 247, 250, 251, 257–58, 260–61, 308–9; history and sacred texts, 137–38; Israeli history, 309; Jewish diaspora, 307, 309, 310–11, 313–14, 321; postwar shifts (global), xi, 309, 313–14; scholarly sources and surveys, 29–31, 38
Jewish Publication Society, 28
Jewish Renaissance in the Russian Revolution (Moss), 38–39
Jewish secularism. *See* secularism
Jewish studies (academic field), 35–36
Jewish Telegraphic Agency, 47, 236, 326
Jews, Their History, Culture, and Religion, The (Finkelstein), 29–31, 32
Jews Fight, Too! (Davis), 220
Jews in Soviet Russia, The (Schapiro), 26
Johnson, Lyndon B., 326, 328, 331, 334–35, 336
Joseph, Samuel, 28
Joshua, Then and Now (Richler), 283
journalism. *See Forverts* (newspaper); publishing and publications

361

INDEX

Judaism as a Civilization (Kaplan), 312–13
Judaism (periodical): content and mission, 90, 96–99, 100, 104, 105; staff, 96–97, 99, 105
Jüdische Geschichte (Prinz), 300
Jüdische Rundschau (newspaper), 300
Jünger, David, 14, 16, 297–314

Kaiser, Henry, 269n23, 270n27
Kallen, Horace, 28, 109n41
Kantoroff, Samuel, 116
Kapel, Aleksander, 159
Kapiszewski, Andrzej, 48–49, 65n16
Kaplan, Mordecai, 312–13, 318n68
Kassow, Samuel, 35
Katzenbach, Nicholas, 327, 334–37
Kaufman, Jay, 325
Kayser, Stephen, 98
Kellman, Ellen, 14, 16, 173–94
Kelner, Shaul, 294n52, 295n65
Keys to a Magic Door: Isaac Leib Peretz (Rothchild), 173
Khruschev, Nikita, 279, 280, 282–83, 292n28
Khurbn Otvotsk, Falenits, Kartshev (memorial book; 1948), 71
King, Martin Luther, Jr., 293n30, 297, 298–99, 304, 305
King, Willis Jefferson, 302–3
Kirshenblatt-Gimblett, Barbara, 37, 139–40, 144, 151n40, 153, 164, 238
Kliger, Hannah, 72
Komaromi, Ann, 14, 15–16, 273–90
Korczak, Janusz, 223
Kornbluth, William, 68
Kosygin, Alexei, 284
Krah, Markus, 14, 15, 87–105
Krakowitz, Harlan, 217, 225
Kristol, Irving, 102
Kubert, Joe, 238
kuchalayns, 201

Kugelmass, Jack, 57, 71, 78, 80
Kuperman, Shifra, 127–28
Kurzweil, Baruch, 97, 98
Kushner, Meyer, 155, 158
Kvitko, Leib, 286

Labour-Progressive Party (LPP; Canada), 277, 279, 280, 292n15, 293n32
LaCapra, Dominick, 4–5, 6
La Guardia, Fiorello, 50
landsmanshaftn: conference reports, 64n8; first-person accounts, 68; kinship and mutual aid functions, 70, 72; memorialization functions, 48–49, 57, 68, 69, 70–71, 72–75, 83; organization ties, 48–49, 65n16; publications, 57, 69, 72–75, 84; studies, 72–73
Lanes, Selma G., 190, 193
language. *See also* English language; Hebrew language; Polish language; Yiddish language and literature: American Jews, Yiddish, 114, 118, 128, 129, 154, 166–67, 174, 177, 187, 201; Canadian Jews, Yiddish, 281, 285, 286–87, 290; Holocaust, terms and scope, 3, 11–12; shifts, 13, 77; textbooks and exercises, 125–26; town names, 79; Yiddish terms and literature translation, 165, 173–74, 179–80, 193
Lazaroff-Shaver, Emma, 236
Learsi, Rufus, 220
Lederhendler, Eli, 13, 15, 23–40, 129
Leff, Mark, 262
Leivick, H., 235–36
Leningrad Hijacking Trial (1970), 284–85, 294n53
Lestchinsky, Jacob, 29, 36, 113–15, 117, 128
Levin, Shmaryahu, 165

Levinson, Stanley, 304
Levitats, Isaac, 31, 36
Levitsky, Holli, 14, 199–213
Levy, Adele, 257–58, 259, 261, 262
Lieberman, Chaim, 113, 121, 122, 124
Life Is with People (Zborowski and Herzog), 15, 25, 31–32, 88, 100, 139–40, 144, 151n40, 153, 164
Linville, James, 76
literary colonies, 201–2
literature and literary criticism. *See also* publishing and publications; specific authors and works: American-Jewish intellectual journals, 14, 32, 87–105; anthologies, 15, 28, 29–31, 32, 88, 137–38, 142, 176; Catskills literary activity, 199–213; children's lit, 16, 173–94; cultural continuity, 173–75, 178, 194; genres, publication trends, 12, 23, 31–32, 57, 62, 71, 73–75, 83; intergenerational collaboration, 16, 181; Jewish fiction aspects, 15, 76, 95, 147, 190; literary construction, sites of memory, 14, 15, 56–62, 62–63, 69–70, 71, 72, 77–78, 80–81, 200, 211–13; select bibliographies, 32–34; Yiddish literature, 137–49; Yiddish memoirs, 15, 152–67
Litin, Ruth, 251–52
"Little Hanukah Lamp, The" (Peretz), 179
Los Angeles, California, 322–23
"Lost Young Intellectual: A Marginal Man, Twice Alienated, The" (Howe), 93
Lubavitch Rebbe, 115–17
Lubetkin, Zivia, 234, 235
Lustiger, Arno, 62

MacLaod, A. A., 292n15
Macomber, William B., Jr., 332–33

"Magician, The" (Peretz), 175, 179, 180, 181–82
Magician, The (Shulevitz), 175, 180–83
Magician and Other Stories from the Yiddish, The (Goldberg), 173, 177, 178–79
Mahler, Raphael, 36, 55, 56, 58, 59
Maier, Kurt, 260
Mailer, Norman, 100
Mann, Thomas, 47
maps: mapping and "geography of memory," 77–78, 79–80, 81, 84; in memorial books, 50, 51, 69, 71, 74, 75–80, *77, 78, 79*, 81–83, 84
March on Washington for Jobs and Freedom (1963), 297, 298, 301, 305, 306, 313
Mark, Yudel, 29
Markish, Peretz, 286
martyrdom accounts and themes, 45, 47, 58–59, 67n47, 67n48, 237
Martyrs and Heroes of the Ghettos (art exhibition; 1945), 237
Marx, Karl, 115
Masada siege (73–74 CE), 232, 234–35
Massey, Raymond, 264
material goods collection (humanitarian aid), 247–48, 249–50, 251–54, 255, 256, 257, 269n23
Maurer, Herrymon, 8
Mayn heymshtetl strykov (Unger), 154
Mead, Margaret, 25, 139, 151n40
Medem, Vladimir, 100, 102
memoirs: holocaust survivors and refugees, 56, 68, 158, 159; literature and publishing, 12, 15; narrative timeframes, 10–11; writing contests, 162–63; Yiddish-language, 15, 50, 56, 152, 154–67
memorial books, 13–14, 57–58, 156; *The Black Book of Polish Jewry*, 44–63; "collected memory," 83–85; family

memorial books (cont.)
connections, 75; funding and financing, 69, 74, 75, 83, 85; history, 67n44, 69; international interaction and collaboration, 84–85; literary construction, sites of memory, 56–62, 62–63, 80–81; literary genre and details, 57, 71, 72, 73–75, 83–84; map inclusion, 50, 51, 69, 71, *74*, 75–80, *77, 78, 79*, 81–83, 84; professional production, 73–74; (re)creating the past, postwar, 68–85

memorializing and memorials. *See also* "geography of memory"; memorial books: American Jews, Holocaust memory, xiv, xv–xvi, xvii–xviii, 10–12, 14, 59, 68, 83, 84–85, 212–13; human behavior and culture, xvi, xvii, 63, 68, 69, 70, 212–13; illustrations, children's literature, 187–88; *landsmanshaftn* functions, 48–49, 57, 68, 69, 70–71, 72–75, 83; literary construction, sites of memory, 14, 56–62, 62–63, 69–70, 71, 72, 77–78, 80–81, 200, 211–13; physical memorial creation efforts, 80–81; towns, 70–71, 73, 76–78, 80, 81–83, 84

memory. *See* "collected memory"; collective memory; "geography of memory"; personal memory; "postmemory"; silence, and Holocaust memory

Mendele Mokher Sforim (Mendele the Bookseller), works, 138, 140, 143, 163, 177

Mendelevich, Yosef, 287

Mendelsohn, Ezra, 36

Menes, Abraham, 29, 31, 125

Michalowski, Jerzy, 327, 334

Michelangelo, 227, 232–33

Middle East conflict, 319–20

Mila 18 (Uris), 215–16, 221, 222–34, 237–40; covers, 216, 221, 225–27, *226*, 229–30, *231*, 232, 233, 240; editions and printings, 228–29, *231*; reviews and fan responses, 228, 231–32, 239

military participation: Jewish stereotypes, 215–16, 217–20, 235, 237; Jews, Israel's wars, 222, 232; Jews, WWII, 220, 222; women, 128

Milwaukee, Wisconsin, xv–xvi

Minkoff, Isaiah, 307

Mintz, Alan, 11, 13

Miracle of the Warsaw Ghetto, The (Leivick), 235–36

Miron, Dan, 163

"Mixed-Up Feet and the Silly Bridegroom, The" (Singer, I. B.), 185, 189–90, 190–91, 198n48

Molotov-Ribbentrop pact (1939–1941), 278

montage, 140–42, 148–49

Montreal, Quebec, 280, 284, 291n11

Morgen, Der (periodical), 302

Morgenthau, Henry, 28–29, 263

Moses, 123, 249, 264, 266, 267

Moskowitz, Bessie, 163

Moss, Kenneth, 38–39

most favored nation status (trade), 327–33, 338–39, 341n16

"Motke Won't Suckle a Rag" (Asch), 178

Motl, the Cantor's Son (Sholem Aleichem), 178

Mukdoyni, A., 159

Muni, Paul, 260

"muscular Judaism," 215–18, *218*, 221–27, 232–33, 234–35, 237–39

mutual aid societies, 70, 72

"My Day" (column; E. Roosevelt), 53–54

Nagy, Al, 225
names: changes, writers and intellectuals, 93; writers' pseudonyms, 120, 122, 123, 159, 191–92, 198n48
National Association for the Advancement of Colored People (NAACP), 306
National Council of Jewish Women, 253, 255, 264, 268n11
National Federation of Temple Sisterhoods, 251–52, 257
nationalism movements: *Forverts*, 129; "Jewish Nationalists," 206; Nazis, 158; Poland, 320, 322; Ukraine, 164–65
Nativ bureau (Israel), 281, 286
Nazarene, The (Asch), 113, 121
"Neilah in Gehennah" (Peretz), 147
Neusner, Jacob, 138–39
New Fraternal Jewish Organization, 283
New Jewish Folk Theatre, 235–36
New Leader (periodical), 281
newspapers. *See Biuletyn Informacyjny; Canadian Jewish News; Folks-shtimme; Forverts; Haynt; New York Times; Palestine Post; Sydney Morning Herald*
New York City: Jewish assimilation, 114–15; Jewish immigration, 26; race relations, 302; yeshivas, 118; Yiddish language and press, 111, 113–21
New York Times (newspaper), 47, 53, 292n28, 331–32
Niborski, Itzhok, 79, 80
Niger, Shmuel, 98–99, 101, 184
Norich, Anita, 35
North American Jewish Youth Council, 326
nostalgia, 72, 80–81, 117, 130; Catskills, 204; literature, 138, 145, 152–53; memoirs' attempts to counter, 166–67; WWII and wars, 271n51
Novick, Peter, 11
Nunberg, Ralph, 215–16, 220
Nuremburg Tribunals (1945–1946), 56

objective and scientific reporting, Holocaust, 51–53, 55
O'Dwyer, William, 264
"On Account of a Hat" (Sholem Aleichem), 2
On Destiny: An Epistle to the Christians (Asch), 121
Ontario, Canada, 275–76, 277, 290, 295n61
Organization for Relief through Training (ORT), 253
orphans, 257–58
Orthodox Jews (Canada), 291n12
Orthodox Jews (Israel), 310
Orthodox Jews (United States). *See also* Hasidim; religious piety and activity: dress customs and appearance, 2, 4, 5, 6, 118; literary portrayals, 1–9, 100; organizations and philanthropy, 258, 268n11; synagogues and cantors, 126–27, 133n57

Pale of Settlement, 164–65
Palestine, 309
Palestine Post (newspaper), 54
para- and epitext, 216
Partisan Review (periodical), 92; content and mission, 89–90, 94–96, 100, 104, 105; cultural pluralism, 99; staff, 92–93, 95
Parzen, Herbert, 88–89, 97
Passover: literary portrayals, 181–83; old and new country traditions, 117–18, 123, 125, 127, 128; rituals and remembrance, xiii–xiv, 123, 263–64;

Passover: literary portrayals (cont.) symbolism, postwar philanthropy and aid, 249, 263–64, 271n58
passports, 293n44
Paul (apostle), 120–21
Paul VI (Pope), 326
peace: American postwar leadership and philanthropy, 249–50, 254–55, 256, 257, 259, 266, 270n27; Jewish communities, 146, 154, 156; Jewish values, 268n7, 313; postwar politics and conferences, 49, 279, 288
Peck, Eli (literary character), 1–4, 5, 6
Peretz, I. L.: children's literature, 179, 196n21; literary criticism, 95; work adaptations/collaborations, 16, 175, 180–83; works, 14, 31, 120, 138, 143, 146–47, 163, 175, 177, 179, 181–82
Peretz, Pauline, 294n51, 296n72
Perlzweig, Morris, 322, 323–24
personal choice: generosity and aid, postwar, 260–61; Jews' self-preservation, 233–34; societies, 26
personal memory: Holocaust's effects on, 79–80, 158, 166, 175; literary examples, 200, 205–6, 208–9, 212, 213; nature of, 165–66; scholars' and writers' self-reflection, xv–xvi, 213
Petrovsky-Shtern, Yohanan, 145
philanthropy. *See* humanitarian aid
Phillips, William, 92–93
photographs and photographic evidence: exhibitions and criticism, 87, 153, 199; Holocaust images, 141, 256; Jewish revolts, 234–35; memorial books, 51, 70, 71, 74–75, 83; "salvage montage," 141, 142, 148–49; souvenir journals, mutual aid societies, 72
Pianist, The (Szpilman), 238
Pioneer Women, 253, 271n58
Podell, Bertram, 334
Podhoretz, Norman, 93, 94, 100, 139
"Poetic Rebirth of the Jewish Religion, The" (Zhitlovsky), 112
poets, 127, 155, 286
pogroms: American responses, 330; historical references and analogies, 331; history and fears, 155, 156, 158, 159, 163, 166; memoirs' content, 164–65, 166–67
Poland and the Minority Races (Goodhart), 28
Poland–US relations, 323–25, 326–39
Polanski, Roman, 238
Poliak, Moshe, 79, 84
Polier, Shad, 304, 307, 313
Polish anti-Zionism, 319–39, 339n2, 340n6
Polish Jews. *See also* Warsaw Ghetto and uprising: American organizations, 44, 46–49, 55, 59, 65n16; antisemitism and anti-Zionism, 1967–1968, 319–39, 339n2, 340n6; historical works: memorial books, 13–14, 44–63, 71, 80–81; historical works: surveys and population histories, 28–29, 30–31, 34, 38; Holocaust and aftermath, 13–14, 15–16, 44–63, 278–79; literary portrayals, 95, 205–6, 208, 223–25, 231–32, 234, 237–40; local focus and Holocaust geography, 45–46, 49–50, 55, 57–58, 59–62; photographs, 153; yeshivas, 118–19; Yiddish language use, 114
Polish language: Holocaust eyewitness accounts, 50; memorial books, 81
Polish United Workers' Party, 320, 336
political cartoons, 236
"politics of consensus," 91, 107n12
Polland, Annie, 112
Ponomarev, Boris, 282

INDEX

"Poor Community, The" (Reisen), 147–48
Pope Paul VI, 326
Popular Culture and the Shaping of Holocaust Memory in America (Mintz), 11
population data. *See* Jewish populations
Porter, Stephen Ross, 256
Portnoy's Complaint (Roth), 5–6
"postmemory," 175–76, 188
"Pot, The" (Sholem Aleichem), 142
Prell, Riv-Ellen, 91, 123
Prince of the Ghetto (Samuel), 95
Prinz, Joachim: biography, 300, 314, 314n7; on German Jewry, 308–9, 316n20; Jewish postwar America, and civil rights, 14, 297–99, 301–7, 312–13, 314, 322; rabbinical work, 300–301, 303–4, 305, 306; works, 300, 301, 307–8, 312, 314n7; Zionism, 301, 309–13, 322
Prisoners of Zion, and releases, 287–88
"Problem of European Jewry, 1939–1945, The" (Tartakower), 29, 31
psychoanalysis, Freudian, 220–21
publishing and publications. *See also* literature and literary criticism; memorial books: American press, 47, 53–54, 279–80; English-language scholarship, 13, 23, 24–40; genre trends, 12, 23, 31–32, 57, 62, 71, 73–75, 83; Jewish populations, and political activism, 46–49, 53; Jewish populations, primary sources, xvii; Jewish populations, surveys, 29–31, 38; periodicals/journals, 14, 32, 87–105; Polish papers, 48; Yiddish-language newspapers, 111–30, 279–80, 293n34; Yiddish-language press, 34, 88
Purim, 249, 252

race and racism, United States, 301–3, 305, 307, 313
radio plays and programs, 234, 260, 264–65, 270n44
Rahv, Philip, 93, 95
"Raisala" (Reisen), 178
Raisin, Jacob, 28
Rapaport, Aleksander, 156
Rapoport, Nathan, 232
Reconstructionist Judaism, 312–13, 318n68
Red Cross, 259
Reform Judaism, 128
refugee/displaced persons camps: donations and aid, 247, 251, 256, 267; memorial events and books, 70, 84; survivors and scholarship, 35
refugees/displaced persons: aid organizations, 14, 46, 70, 247, 250, 253, 255, 264; American immigration policy, 264–66, 335; American Jews' responses and aid, 9, 10, 14, 17, 63, 247–67; historical symbolism, 249; Jewish intelligentsia and knowledge transfer, 23, 34–35, 37; literary and film portrayals, 1–9, 260–61; memoirs and testimonies, 68, 80; photographs, 10; scholarship, 15, 23, 34–35, 41–42n24
Reisen, Avrom, 137–38, 147–48, 178
religion and society. *See also* religious piety and activity; secularism: American Jewry, and civil rights movement, 297–98, 301–7, 313; American Jewry, and Jewish survival, 311–13; American Jewry, defining/redefining Jewishness, 90–92, 93, 96–97, 98–99, 100, 101, 103–5, 123–24, 125–26, 127–29, 238,

religion and society (cont.)
    248, 255; American Jewry, retaining traditions, 97–98, 128–29; Jewish journals, 94–105; Zionist ideals and Israel, 309–10
religious piety and activity. *See also* ethnic/cultural vs. religious Judaism; Hasidim; Jewish holidays and rituals; Orthodox Jews (United States); Reform Judaism: American Jews, behavior, 115, 117–18, 119–20, 121–22, 123–25, 126, 128–29; American Jews, secular opinions, 112, 129–30; generational differences, 115, 120, 125, 129, 130; Rabbi Joachim Prinz, 301, 318n68
reparations, 62
Reswick, William, 116–17
Ribak, Gil, 14, 15, 76, 152–67
Richler, Mordecai, 273–74, 283, 290, 291n4
Rischin, Moses, 26
"Rising of the Warsaw Ghetto, The" (Uris), 234
Robeson, Paul, 202, 203
Rockwell, George Lincoln, 284, 294n50
Rogoff, Hillel, 129–30
Rolnik, Yaysef, 155, 162
Romania, 328, 329, 332
Roosevelt, Eleanor, 50, 53–54
Roosevelt, Franklin D., and administration, 46, 54, 64n9
Rose, Fred, 277, 292n15
Rose, Kenneth, 271n51
Rosenberg, Elmer, 202–3
Rosenfeld, Isaac, 95
Rosenwald, Julius, 257–58
Rosh Hashanah: celebrations, 125; literary portrayals, 147–48
Roskies, David G., 36
Ross, Yakov, 122, 124

Roth, Philip, 1–9, 17, 88
Rothberg, Michael, 296n77
Rothchild, Sylvia, 173, 174
Rothstein, Rachel, 14, 15–16, 319–39
Rudin, Jacob Philip, 322, 327
Russian Jews. *See* Soviet and Russian Jews

Sabbath, American Jews, 119, 126, 127
sacred texts, 137–38
sacrifice and salvation: calls for American sacrifice, 257–58, 259–64, 266, 267; symbolism, 16, 250, 267; war effort, WWII, 261–62, 271n51
Sadowski, David, 288
Safran, Gabriella, 142
Salant, B., 117
Salsberg, J.B.: activism leadership, 285–87; biography, 274, 275; journalism, 281, 288, 290, 293n34; political career, 274–78, 280–81, 282, 283, 292n16; postwar travel and reporting, 278–79, 281–83, 286; responses, Soviet Jewry, 274–90
Saltzman, Roberta, 191
salvage ethnography and montage, 140–42, 144, 148–49
salvage poetics, 142
Samo, Eva, 300
Samson, 235, 236
Samuel, Maurice: memorial books, 47; works, 15, 31, 87, 95, 139, 144, 145, 152–53
Sarna, Jonathan, 265
Schachter, Herschel, 327
Schaechter, Mordkhe, 36, 37
Schapiro, Leonard, 26
Schechter, Solomon, 28
Schmitt, Maurice, 98
Schneersohn, Yosef Yitzchok, 115–16
Scholem, Gershom, 150n17
sculpture, 227, 232

secularism: Communism and Judaism, 275; intellectual communities and influence, 37, 90, 92, 97, 99, 102–3, 105, 111–12; literary portrayals, 2, 7; newspapers' policy and messages, 111–13, 115, 119–20, 121–22; religious thinkers on, 97, 119–20

seder rituals, xiv, 263–64

Sefer Yanovah, 77

segregation: Jews' separateness, 113, 156–57, 204–5, 303; United States history, 305, 307

self-reflection: American Jews and Holocaust witnessing, 62, 208–10, 211–12; American Jews and "Jewishness," 89–90, 103, 125–26

Sendak, Maurice, 16, 175–76, 187–89, 190–91, 192–93

separatism and separateness, Jewish, 113, 156–57, 204–5, 303

Serge, Victor, 54

"Seven Years of Plenty" (Peretz), 179

shame and guilt: American Jews during Holocaust, 210, 213; American Jews' giving and philanthropy, 259–60, 261, 270n43

Shandler, Jeffrey, 77, 80, 81, 84, 145, 167n3, 174, 253–54

Shapiro, Edward, 270n43

Sharansky, Natan, 288

Shatzky, Jacob, 36

Shefner, Borekh, 124–25

Shmeruk, Chone, 184–85, 191, 196n27

Shmulevitsh, Yitshak, 124

Shoah Foundation, archives, 11

Sholem Aleichem: influence, 139; work adaptations, 180; works, 2, 31, 88, 98, 100, 120, 138, 142, 145–46, 152–53, 163, 177, 178

shtadlanut, 276–77

shtetlekh: American immigrant perceptions, 80, 116–17, 145, 167;

anthropological works, 88, 148, 151n40, 153, 164; literary treatments, 15, 76, 88, 137–39, 143, 144–49, 152–67, 180–83, 188; mapping and memorializing, 76–78, 81

Shub, David, 126

Shub, Elizabeth, 175, 183, 184, 185, 187, 188, 192, 193

Shulevitz, Uri, 16, 175, 180–83, 192

Shurin, Aaron Ben-Zion, 122

silence, and Holocaust memory: individual consideration and culpability, 281; individual consideration and research, xiii–xvi; as myth, and addressing, xiii–xvi, 9, 10–11, 11–12, 18n22, 67n56, 212, 237, 289, 296n77; refuting via postwar aid/activism, 248; theories/scholarship supporting, 11

"Simchas Torah Flag, The" (Sholem Aleichem), 178

Simon, Elliott, 7

Singer, Isaac Bashevis, 16; biography, 183, 201–2; children's literature, 173, 174, 175, 183–94, 196n27; contributions, *Forverts*, 120–21, 184, 185, 191–92, 198n48; illustrated works, 180, 183, 187; works, 88, 95, 173, 175, 183–84, 191–92, 201

Singer, Israel Joshua, 161–62, 184

Six Day War (1967): Israeli militancy, 222; political and geopolitical effects, 10, 319–20; political effects, 305

Sklar, Yakov, 125

Slave, The (Singer, I. B.), 95

slavery, 297, 305

Slucki, David, 13–14, 15, 44–63, 71

Smolar, Boris, 119–20, 127

"Snow in Chelm, The" (Singer, I. B.), 187, 189–90

Social-Cultural Organization of Polish Jews, 320
socialism: Catskills groups and activities, 202–3; movements pre-WWII, 158; newspapers' editorial policy, 111, 119, 129–30; organizations, 129–30; theory, 115
Soloveitchik, Joseph Dov, 119–20
Sonderkommando, 141, 149n14
Songs from the Ghetto (Weiner), 28
Sontag, Susan, 95
Soviet and Russian Jews: citizenship rights, 293n44; historical works, 28, 29, 31, 38–39; Holocaust and aftermath, 15–16, 23–24, 25–26, 57, 66n36, 279; lack of coverage, Holocaust reporting, 55; Pale of Settlement and WWI, 164–65; population data, xi; Soviet Jewry movement, and Canadian responses, 274–90; Soviet Jewry movement, U.S., 281, 282–83, 285, 321, 333, 339, 340n5
Soviet Union: Cold War era, 14, 23–24, 25–26, 277–78, 279–80, 283, 319–20, 328, 329–30, 331–32; Communist Party, 279, 280, 282, 283, 292n28; press and reporting on, 279–80, 281, 282–83; Stalinism and purges, 23–24, 26, 279, 280–81, 282, 286, 322; WWII, 278
Soyer, Daniel, 72–73, 162–63
Spektor, Mordkhe, 165
Spicehandler, Ezra, 102
Spielberg, Steven, 11
spies, 277–78
St. Urbain's Horseman (Richler), 273–74, 291n3, 291n4
Stalin, Joseph, 26, 278, 279, 281, 282, 322
Staub, Michael, 107n14
Steinberg, Yehudah, 178
Stern, Barbara, 288
Stories for Children (Singer, I. B.), 183, 185–86, 191
student protest, 287–88, 320, 326, 331
Students, Scholars, and Saints (Ginzberg), 28
Studies in Judaism (Schechter), 28
Sunset (Babel), 274, 291n3, 291n4
Superman: The Man of Steel #82 (1998), 238
Supplies for Overseas Survivors project (SOS), 247–48, 250, 251–54, 252, 255, 257
surveys: Jewish scholarship, 29–31; traditional Jewish life, 140
survivors. *See also* American Jews; Holocaust; immigration and immigrants; refugees/displaced persons: Catskills populations and writings, 199, 203–13; children of, 175–76, 188; diversity and stratification, 46, 60–62, 63; eyewitness experiences, 50, 56, 260, 270n44; Holocaust's effects on memory, 79–80, 158, 166, 175; interviews, 11; media portrayals, 260, 265; memoirs, 56, 68, 158, 159; memorial books' content creation, 73, 80, 83–85; memorial culture and questions, 63, 68, 212–13; philanthropic givers and recipients, postwar, 248, 249, 250, 251, 254, 255–56, 257–58, 259–61, 262–63, 264, 265; postwar return, 80, 81
Suslov, Mikhail, 282
Sydney Morning Herald (newspaper), 54
symbolism: American survivor narratives, and sacrifice, 16, 249–50, 251–52; memorial books, 70; visual media, 217, 221, 227
synagogues: American Jews' choices and authenticity, 117, 122, 123–24,

125, 126–27, 127–28, 133n52; Berlin, Germany, 300; cantors, 126–27
Szajkowski, Zosa, 36
Szpilman, Wladyslaw, 238
Szyk, Arthur, 47, 236

Taft, William Howard, 330
Tartakower, Arieh, 29, 31, 36, 53
Tcherikower, Eliyahu, 36
Tchernichowsky, Saul, 120
television films, 31
Tel Hai, Battle of (1920), 241n36
Tenenbaum, Joseph, 47
Thanksgiving and themes, 249, 250, 264–66
theatre: *Fiddler on the Roof* (play), 12, 15, 88, 100, 105, 148, 153, 167n3; New Jewish Folk Theatre, 235–36
Time (periodical), 256
Toldot kehilat Pinsk Karlin (1970s), 75
Toronto, Ontario, 275, 277, 281, 290, 291n11, 295n61
totalitarian states: Soviet Union, 26
trade relations: U.S.–Poland, 327–33, 338–39, 341n16; U.S.–Russia, 330
translation processes, 174, 185, 194. *See also* language
"traumatizing identification," 4–5
travel writing, 80
Treasury of Yiddish Stories, A (Howe and Greenberg), 137–38, 139, 142–44, 145
Treblinka death camp, 44, 49–50, 51, 52, 61
Troper, Harold, 296n73
Trudeau, Pierre, 284
Truman, Harry, 254–55, 257, 259, 270n27
Trunk, Isaiah, 36
Tsivion, 119, 122, 124
Tsukerman, Borekh, 152, 154, 158, 165, 167n1

Tulchinsky, Gerald, 291n6, 291n12, 292n16
Tuwim, Julian, 47
Twain, Mark, 218–19
Tygel, Zelig, 46–47, 48
typography, 217, 225–27, *226*, 229
Tzuref, Leo (literary character), 1–3, 7

UJA. *See* United Jewish Appeal (UJA)
Ukraine, 164–65
Unger, Avrum Pinkhes, 154
United Jewish Appeal (UJA): appeal figures and themes, 249, 250, 257–58, 261, 262–63; fundraising size and scope, 258–59, 270n37; "Year of Survival" and "Year of Sacrifice" campaigns (1946, 1947), 250, 259–64
United Jewish People's Order, 285
United Jewish Relief Agencies of Canada, 262
United Jewish Welfare Fund, 285–86
United Nations Clothing Collection (UNCC), 249–50, 255–57, 269n23
United Nations Human Rights Commission, 326
United Nations Relief and Rehabilitation Administration (UNNRA), 255
United Service for New Americans (USNA), 264–66
United States. *See* American ideals and identity; American Jews; Cold War; specific presidents
Unknown Soldier, The (Kubert), 238
Uris, Leon, 14, *223*; biographic details, 221, 222, 242n42; *Exodus*, 88, 215, 216–17, 218, *219*, 221–22, *223*, 226, 229; *Mila 18*, 215–16, 221, 222–34, *226*, *231*, 237–40; works' themes and purpose, 215–17, 221–25, 232–33, 237–40

Ury, Scott, 37
U.S. Congress, 265, 323, 327–33, 334
U.S. Department of State, 48, 113, 323, 327, 334–38

Vaad Hatzala, 258
Venuti, Lawrence, 174, 176, 194
Victory Clothing Collection (UNCC; 1946), 255–56, 270n27
Vilna massacre (1941–1944), 47
Vishniac, Roman, 87, 153
visionary societies, 202
visual art. *See also* illustrators and illustration: commercial: book and film advertising, 217, 225–27; drawings and comics, WWII/Warsaw Ghetto, 236, 238; Eastern European, 98; exhibitions, 237; sculpture, 227, 232
"Visual Arts in American Jewish Life" (Kayser), 98
Vladeck, Baruch Charney, 129
Vochenblatt (newspaper), 281, 291n8
volunteerism, 249, 250, 251–54, 256
Vorobeichic, Moshe, 148

Wall, The (Hersey), 227–28, *229*
Wall, Wendy, 107n12, 256
Wallace, Henry, 203
Wallenrod, Reuben, 14, 199, 200, 205–13, 214n13
Warburg, Frieda Schiff, 254
war crimes evidence collection and transmission, 49, 50–53, 55–56
War Refugee Board, 46, 264
Warsaw Ghetto and uprising: anniversaries and political action, 237, 323, 331; Berg's diary, 228, *230*; comics and cartoons, 236, 238; documentation and exhibitions, 50–51, 51–52, 53, 237; drama productions, 235–36; figures and events, 52, 222, 232–33, 234, 235; Hersey's *The Wall*, 227–28; maps, *74*, *81*; news reporting, 225; Szyk's *Ink and Blood* (drawings), 236; Uris' *Mila 18*, 215–16, 222–40
Waxman, Myer, 28
Weimar Republic, J. Prinz experiences, 297–98, 299, 300–301, 303
Weiner, Leo, 28
Weinreich, Max, 34, 36, 115–16, 119, 123, 124
Weinreich, Uriel, 36, 37, 125–26
Weinryb, Bernard, 30–31, 36
Weisbord, Merrily, 277–78, 280, 293n33, 294n46
Weissmandl, Michael Dov, 8
Welles, Orson, 261
Weltsch, Robert, 300
We Remember with Reverence and Love: American Jews and the Myth of Silence after the Holocaust (Diner), xiii–xviii, 11–12, 67n56
Werner, Alfred, 53
Westchester County, New York, 8
Wexler, William A., 324–26, 329–32
"What the Moon Told" (Peretz), 178
Whitaker, Francis, 217, *219*
Whitfield, Stephen, 95, 306
Wierviorka, Annette, 79, 80
Wiesel, Elie, 288–89
Wildstein, Julius, 306
Wilkins, Roy, 306
Wir Juden (Prinz), 300, 301, 307–8
Wirth-Nesher, Hana, 7–8
Wise, Stephen, 47–48, 303–4, 307
Wise Polier, Justine, 304–5, 307, 313
Wisse, Ruth, 36
Wolf, Simon, 219
Wolf of Masada, The (Fredman), 232
Woodridge, New York, 203
Workmen's Circle, 121, 130, 154, 177, 203

INDEX

World Jewish Congress, 48, 53, 236, 287, 304, 322, 323
World of Our Fathers (Howe), 93, 137, 138–39
World of Sholem Aleichem, The (Samuel), 15, 31, 87, 139, 144, 145, 148, 152–53
World War I: immigration laws following, 72; memoirs' content, 158, 159, 164–65; memorial literature, 71; Poland, 159
World War II. *See also* Cold War; Holocaust: American Jewish activism, 46–49; American war effort and nostalgia, 261–62, 271n51; "German-Jewish symbiosis," 308–9; information transmission, 44, 47, 48, 49, 50–52; Jewish military, 220, 222; memorial literature, Eastern European Jews, 44–63, 76, 158; survey literature, Eastern European Jews, 29; war crimes evidence, 49, 50–53, 55–56
"Writing About Jews" (Roth), 6
Writing History, Writing Trauma (LaCapra), 4–5, 6
Wyden, Peter, 300

Yafe, Shneyer, 155
"Yearning Heifer, The" (Singer, I. B.), 201
"Year of Survival" and "Year of Sacrifice" campaigns (UJA; 1946, 1947), 250, 259–64
yeshivas: American, 8, 118–19; literary portrayals, 1–9
Yiddish language and literature: academic fields, 35, 36–37; American/Canadian use, 114, 118, 128, 129, 154, 166–67, 174, 177, 187, 201, 285, 290; children's lit, 173–94; fiction anthologies and treasuries, 15, 88, 93, 137–38, 139, 142–43, 145, 176–80; folklore, 160–61, 173–74, 177–78, 179, 180–83, 185–87, 189–94; memoirs and memoirists, 15, 50, 56, 152–67; memorial books, 57, 73, 77, 78, 81, 156; newspapers, 111–30, 279–80, 293n34; -press, and Jewish identity, 14, 27–28, 111–30; scholarship function and reach, 12, 24, 27, 34, 35–36; textbooks and exercises, 125–26, 177
Yiddish Stories for Young People (Goldberg), 177–78
Yitzchok, Yosef, 115
YIVO Annual of Jewish Social Science, 32
YIVO Institute: autobiography contests, 162–63; Eastern European Jewish life, presentations, 87–88; leadership and events, 34, 119–20, 323; lectures, 160
yizker-bikher. *See* memorial books
"Y. L. Peretz and the Jewish Child" (Goldberg), 179
Yom Kippur, 111, 126, 128, 147
Young, James, 70, 83
Yugoslavia, 328, 341n16
Yunge Poalei Zion (political party), 275
Yungvarg (journal), 123

Zausner, Philip, 156–57
Zborowski, Mark, 15, 31–32, 88, 139–40, 144, 151n40, 153, 164
Zemel, Carol, 148
Zhitlovsky, Chaim, 112, 161, 169n13
Zikhroynes (Tsukerman), 152, 154, 158, 165, 167n1
Zionism opposition, Poland, 319–39, 339n2, 340n6

373

Zionist groups: Canada, 284, 294n49; Catskills community, 202; philanthropy, 253, 258, 263, 310; political parties, 275; Prisoners of Zion, releases, 287–88; United States, per Prinz, 301, 302–3, 310

Zionist ideals, 309–10

Zionist literature: American Jewish writers, 91; fiction, 7, 88, 216–18, 225, 229, 236, 237; newspapers, 300; nonfiction, 300, 301, 307–8

Zionist rabbis. *See* Prinz, Joachim; Wise, Stephen

Zipperstein, Steven, 40n1, 40n9, 151n40

Zlateh the Goat and Other Stories (Singer, I. B.), 173, 175, 183, 184, 185, 186–94

"Zlateh the Goat" (Singer, I. B.), 189

Zuckerman, Antek, 234, 235